Advance Praise for *Fixed Stars Govern a Life: Decoding*

"With clarity and erudition, Ms. Gordon-Bramer illureflects a clear and intentional alignment with the Tarot and the Qabalah's Tree of Life. With each poem, and the collection as a whole, Gordon-Bramer weaves the esoteric mysteries with historical interpretation in a fascinating scholarly analysis that is original, provocative, magical. *Fixed Stars Govern a Life* is an incantation of great resonance and power, and its publication will be a sensation."
—Susan L. Woods, Ph.D., Emeritus Professor of Women's Studies, Eastern Illinois University

"Like her beloved Yeats, Sylvia Plath was drawn to numerous and often contradictory systems of belief and ways of knowing, including mystical and magical systems. Julia Gordon-Bramer, in her dazzling and meticulously researched book, shows us how Sylvia Plath may have drawn upon the images of the tarot to fuse and merge the many ways of knowing she was so profoundly inspired by—myth, science, current events, folklore, alchemy, literature, motherhood, art and other sources to create the poems in *Ariel,* one of the great literary achievements of the 20th century. In doing so, Julia Gordon-Bramer illuminates, expands on, and asks profound questions about the very nature of making and creating poems."
– Catherine Bowman, winner of the Peregrine Smith Poetry Prize, the Kate Tufts Discovery Award for Poetry, the Dobie Paisano Fellowship, a New York Foundation for the Arts Fellowship in Poetry, and author of *The Plath Cabinet* and other collections

"A wonderful exploration of Plath's *Ariel* poems in relation to myth, symbol, and the creative process."
– Kathleen Connors, author of *Eye Rhymes: Sylvia Plath's Art of the Visual*

"Lucid and intriguing… what is valuable about *Fixed Stars Govern a Life* is that it is such a great source study with commentary on what Plath read, what was happening at the time of the poem, and more."
– Carl Rollyson, author of *American Isis: the Life and Art of Sylvia Plath*

"An intriguing book that prompts the reader to look at Plath with fresh eyes. *Fixed Stars Govern a Life* aims to explore the poet's hidden side and as such it is a refreshingly welcome addition to Plath studies."
– Andrew Wilson, author of *Mad Girl's Love Song*

Fixed Stars Govern a Life: Decoding Sylvia Plath

Volume I: The Major Arcana and the First 22 Poems of Plath's *Ariel*

Julia Gordon-Bramer

Stephen F. Austin State University Press
Nacogdoches, Texas

For information address:
Stephen F. Austin State University Press,
1936 North Street, LAN 203
Nacogdoches, TX 75962

sfapress@sfasu.edu

Distributed by Texas A&M University Press Consortium
www.tamupress.com

LIBRARY OF CONGRESS CATALOG-IN-PUBLICATION-DATA

Gordon-Bramer, Julia
Fixed Stars Govern a Life: Decoding Sylvia Plath
p.cm.
ISBN: 978-1-62288-064-5

I. Title

Acknowledgements

Thanks to: Sylvia Plath and Ted Hughes for leaving it all in plain sight; Tom Bramer for his severely tested patience, his enduring love, and amazing support; Sam and Ross Gordon, just because; Professor Steven Schreiner at UM-St. Louis for pushing me toward the greatest work of my life; Tom Reynolds for his conception of the narrative that became *The Magician's Girl* (forthcoming), a biography focusing on Plath's and Hughes' occult endeavors, and his unceasing encouragement in this project from Day One; my friend and mentor, Zulfikar A Ghose; Christine Butterworth-McDermott for the foot in the door; Russell K. Allen for the hard work on the layout; Mom, for reading Plath's *Journals*, poetry, and biography to understand my obsession; Kristina Morgan for the laughs, the tears, the tarot cards, and the faith in me as "The Oracle"; Beth Mead at the Lindenwood University Graduate Creative Writing Program for giving me an opportunity to teach a course in this subject; Melanie Smith for her early reading, her generous gifts, and her friendship; Judy Ryan and Typewriter Tim Jordan for the faith and friendship; Catherine Rankovic and BookEval for the eagle-eye and friendship in Plath, tarot, and poetry; Catherine Bowman for her poetic and culinary talent, Bloomington hospitality and friendship, her blurb, and her unfailing belief in my work; Ellen Herget for throwing down some tarot cards and brightening my days; Ian Didriksen for the book trailer; Kim Dziurman for some early reading and online friendship; Peter K. Steinberg, William Buckley, and *Plath Profiles* for publishing excerpts from this book and *FSGL Vol. Two*; Kathleen Connors for her charm and grace at the 2012 Sylvia Plath Symposium, the blurb, and especially for the irreplaceable gift; Alexander Balogh and his thoughtful, careful edits and comments on an early version of the narrative; Julio Javier Hernández for the 1961 issue of *American Poetry Now*; Kyle Hendrickson for some sleuthing and a wild fast pitch to the U.S. Poet Laureate; Carl Rollyson for his friendship, support, and close reading; The staff at the Sylvia Plath archives in the Lilly Library, Indiana University-Bloomington; Karen V. Kukil, Barbara Blumenthal, and assistants with the Sylvia Plath archives in the Mortimer Rare Book Room at William Neilson Library, Smith College; Rabbi James Stone Goodman for his Kabbalah wisdom; Dr. Sophia Wellbeloved at the Cambridge Centre for the Study of Western Esotericism for her good advice; and finally, Mary K. Greer, Dr. Ann Skea, and Peter K. Steinberg for asking the tough questions and challenging everything. It was the adversity that taught me to truly separate from ego and not be deterred from what I know to be true. The critics and doubters made this even better than if I had had an easy road. Buddha teaches that there is a gift in everything. I see that now.

An excerpt of the interpretation for "The Rabbit Catcher" was presented at the Racial Formation/Racial Blindness Graduate Conference at the University of Wisconsin-Milwaukee, February 2014.

An excerpt of the interpretation for "A Secret" was presented at the Lawrence Durrell Centenary at Goodenough College, June 2012 in London, England.

An excerpt of the interpretation for "The Detective" was presented at the Sherlock Holmes Conference, June 2013, at the University of London, Senate House, London, England.

An excerpt of the interpretation for "Ariel" was presented at the Sylvia Plath Symposium at Indiana University -Bloomington, October 2012.

An excerpt of the interpretation for "Death & Co.," as well as some of the Introduction was first published in *Plath Profiles 3*, an Interdisciplinary Journal for Sylvia Plath studies.

An excerpt of the interpretation for "The Courage of Shutting-Up" was presented at the Popular Culture Conference, March 2013, in Washington, D.C.

What Set Me Going:

While working toward my Master of Fine Arts in Creative Writing degree, my professor, Dr. Steven Schreiner, assigned me to come up with an end-of-semester project for my Poetry Form and Theory class at the University of Missouri-St. Louis. I had no idea what to do.

He suggested, "Why don't you follow up on that tarot symbolism you told me you kept seeing in Plath?"

Dr. Schreiner knew that I had been reading tarot cards since I was sixteen years old. My professor had brought me and my thirty-plus years of experience into some of his classes and parties as a special guest to explore poetry and occult connections. For those not familiar with the tarot, it first began as a medieval card game. The pack of 78 cards evolved to be used for divination, as they contain a bounty of universal archetypes and symbolism delving into the subconscious much in the way that dream interpretation does. The idea is that, as the tarot card reader, I reflect what the questioner already knows on a higher level. Blessings are hoped for, and trouble can sometimes be averted.

Like a regular deck of playing cards, a tarot deck contains ten ranks and four suits, as well as court cards. The tarot's four court cards (Page, Knight, Queen, and King) compare to a playing card deck's three (Jack, Queen, King). In addition, the tarot contains twenty-two major arcana cards, which are considered the most powerful cards in the tarot. These begin with number zero, The Fool card (which is sometimes compared to the joker), and end at number twenty-one, The World. If one has ever seen tarot cards, the major arcana are probably the most familiar. They include the infamous Death card, The Hanged Man, The Lovers, and others. The word *arcana* comes from the Latin *arcanus*, the same root as our English word *arcane*, meaning secret or mysterious, and understood by only a few people. The tarot's major and minor arcana are indeed arcane to the everyday reader of poetry, explaining why Plath's tarot symbolism has gone unnoticed for so long.

I have always loved Sylvia Plath, having read *The Bell Jar* in high school. Back then, I knew only her poetic Greatest Hits: "Mad Girl's Love Song" (printed in the back of my 1971 edition of *The Bell Jar*), and those unforgettable poems such as "Lady Lazarus," "Daddy," "Ariel," and "Cut." I was not sure that I could put a finger on what her poetry actually meant, but there was something about the *feel* of it. I knew that Plath's work had a kind of magic. It was musical, like an incantation or dark nursery rhyme. Images haunted me: the lopped off thumb-tip, unpeel-ing skin, the Panzer-man, and eating of men "like air". Who *eats* air, I asked myself. Does this make sense? Not literally, it doesn't. And yet it resonates with a sort of familiarity. Plath's poetry spoke to me, yet I could not re-ally put words on it as to *why* or *how*. Not then, anyway. All I knew was the overwhelming feeling that her work triggered in me, as when someone says something that causes an inexplicable well of emotion. Sylvia Plath reached down into that dark core of my soul and pressed on the tingling, raw nerve. oThat was power.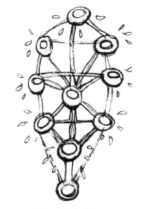

In graduate school I had come across a lot of tarot symbolism in Sylvia Plath's work. As I weighed the frequency and meanings, I knew it could not have been accidental. Her words from "Daddy" pushed me towards making sense of it: "And my Taroc pack and my Taroc pack"—surely she *had* to be addressing my beloved tarot[1]. The first edition of Sylvia Plath's poetry collection, *Ariel*, was arranged by Ted Hughes, Plath's husband, after

The Qabalah
Tree of Life

1 She was. *Taroc* is derived from the Italian Renaissance card game *Tarocci*, from whence the first tarot cards originated. Plath's letters and calendars at the Lilly Library at Indiana University in Bloomington, Indiana are also full of references to playing this game, which she calls "Taroc."

her death and published in 1965 by Faber and Faber. Hughes had rejected some of Plath's poems and inserted others into the collection which she had not intended to include. Plath and Hughes' daughter, Frieda Hughes, published *Ariel: The Restored Edition* in 2004. This was the collection Plath had originally intended. In 2007, I opened *Ariel: The Restored Edition* and began my semester project. It is important to note that if Frieda Hughes had not published her mother's book with the poems in their originally intended order in 2004, I might not have picked up on the correspondences. This is probably why full interpretations of the poems have been undiscovered for almost fifty years.

Initially, I identified a perfect lining up of the first twenty-two poems in the restored edition of *Ariel* with the tarot's major arcana. This is what you see here, in Volume One of *Fixed Stars Govern a Life*. I had long been aware that Ted Hughes pursued many forms of mysticism and the occult throughout his life, before, with, and after his time with Plath. I knew that Hughes had written to Sylvia Plath's mother stating that the ordering of the *Ariel* poems were important in their "unity." In that same letter Hughes denied that Plath was a "confessional" poet and instead insisted that she was a mystical poet "of the very highest tradition" (*LTH*, 258). Indeed, in addition to her many occult-themed poems, and in addition to personal testimonials from family and friends, in her own journals and letters Plath has written of her witchy bonfires, Ouija, crystal-ball gazing, astrology, tarot and more.

Throughout my tarot-based study of *Ariel*, it puzzled me that a perfectionist such as Sylvia Plath would order twenty-two poems so intentionally, but then throw in an extra eighteen poems to follow with no higher structure.

She did not. As I pored over the poems in *Ariel: The Restored Edition*, it became immediately evident to me their clear alignment with the tarot—not just with the major arcana, but all the way through. [2]

There is one poem for each of the minor arcana ranks following (the one's, two's, etc.), and then the court cards (Pages, Knights, Queens and Kings), and finally, the four suits (Pentacles, Cups, Swords and Wands). I suppose that one had to be both a Plath scholar and a tarot scholar, like me, to make the initial connection. There cannot be too many of us around.

Soon after I completed my graduate project, it dawned on me that the abundant chemical language of Plath's poetry was referencing alchemy, which made sense as both she and Hughes were devotees of Carl Jung and his Jungian alchemy. I compiled an obscene amount of research, next looking for astrological terms, as Hughes was also well-known to indulge in astrology. That was present in the poems too, as was mythology, a subject that Plath knew inside and out, and which has already been explored by some scholars such as Judith Kroll. I tore through volumes of books, webpages, drawings and text from medieval grimoires, examining each poetic fragment as it might apply to the Qabalah. I found everything I was looking for; each line, sometimes each word, extended to a minimum of six different-yet-related meanings, all working like individual stars as part of a greater constellation. Meanwhile, I discovered historical correlations and artistic reflections within Plath's work. Everything led back to Qabalah, an ancient system that unifies these varied occult subjects (the word *occult* meaning simply, *hidden*) and is said to be the framework of the modern tarot deck.

The Hermetic Order of the Golden Dawn's modern Rider-Waite Tarot deck was in fact the result of an adaptation of earlier tarot decks. The Golden Dawn was a Victorian-age occult group building upon ancient magic and tradition with members as distinguished as William Butler Yeats and T.S. Eliot, both poets highly revered by Plath and Hughes. One of the Golden Dawn's achievements was to more completely reconcile the tarot deck with the Qabalah's Tree of Life. As they saw

---

2 The minor arcana poems of *Ariel* will be explored in *Fixed Stars Govern a Live: Decoding Sylvia Plath,* volume two.

and others see it, the Tree of Life is a kind of divine road map for how the universe works, encompassing all occult practices of tarot, alchemy, astrology, etc.

My work seemed, and still seems at times, never-ending. "I guess you could say I've a call" (Plath's "Lady Lazarus"). At times I have wept with joy over new discoveries. Other times I have felt lost and quite alone, knowing that until I published a lot of explanatory material, no one in the world really knew what I was even talking about. Yet every time I felt stuck or was ready to give up, I had a dream that either gave me an answer directly, or else I had an experience lead me there.

Once when working on the title poem, "Ariel," I actually became frightened. I had uncovered language that to my un-indoctrinated mind felt as if it referenced Satan. Tarot or no tarot, my religious upbringing had been thoroughly Christian, and this scared me enough that I almost gave up the entire project. "Could my literary hero have been a satanist?" I feared.

It seemed ridiculous. Awful. Preposterous. I didn't *want* to know something like that. That night, I went to bed distraught, and in my dreams I heard Sylvia Plath speak to me, so loudly and clearly that it woke me up: "Move through," she insisted. It was a direct and forceful voice, yet in the perfect New England diction of all her recordings. I will never forget it.

In the light of the following day, this directive made perfect sense: the next card after the card for the "Ariel" poem is The Devil. The Devil is a necessary phase before the collapse of The Tower card of that superficial material life and its shaky foundation. *Move through* I did, to her poem for the Devil card, "Death & Co."

I titled my book Fixed Stars Govern A Life, after Plath's final lines in the poem "Words," the last piece in the first publication of Ariel that Hughes edited and rearranged. Plath had not intended to include "Words" in Ariel, but Hughes was evidently struck hard enough with the resonance and heft of that concluding phrase to close out her collection with them.

For over seven years, I have been slowly moving through these interpretations of Sylvia Plath's work, primarily the qabalistic structure of the poems in Ariel, but also in her other writings. Diehard qabalists have challenged me on the minutiae, but it has never been my intention to explain how or why this works, nor do I seek to teach Qabalah and tarot in this book. There are plenty of other publications out there already doing that. An astrophysicist does not attempt to explain or prove God, but rather just to focus on the wonder of what is. This is also my goal. It is the reader's choice as to how to explain it, as it relates to Plath and to all of us. In Fixed Stars Govern a Life, I seek only to reveal that something intentional and ordered is going on beneath the surface of each Ariel poem: something appearing to be bigger than we are and beyond scientific explanation.

I have published some scholarly articles and excerpts of Fixed Stars Govern a Life in several editions of Indiana University's Plath Profiles, and presented my explications of Plath's work in London, England; St. Louis, Missouri; and Washington, D.C.; among other locations. I am also in the midst of writing a biography, The Magician's Girl, exploring Plath's history of family, friends, and how events of the times and her endeavors into mysticism consciously shaped her work. *Fixed Stars Govern a Life, Volume Two* will decode the minor arcana poems, from "Nick and the Candlestick" through to "Wintering." It has all been happening at once; it is overwhelming and wonderful, exhausting and exciting.

The facts have almost all been out there on Sylvia Plath, but until now no one had thought to view them seriously and collectively. From the time she was a young girl, there is evidence of interest in mysticism and even specifically in Hermeticism.[3] Plath's mother Aurelia had done her master's thesis on Paracelsus, the great alchemist, and she and her teenage daughter shared nearly every one

---

3 Plath family friend Richard Larschan owns a Hermetic caduceus that Sylvia Plath carved in high school. Additionally, Plath drew pictures of Greek goddesses, read all the mystic writers, and wrote a great deal of juvenilia poetry with occult titles and themes.

of Aurelia's school books. With the publication of *The Unabridged Journals of Sylvia Plath* and some recent biographies, the world has learned that this fiercely disciplined and even rigid young woman, while amassing impressive publications any adult writer would envy, also had a wild sexual side. In our more sexually permissive times, most Plath fans are able to comfortably accept that. Yet Plath's interest in the occult has not been examined with any seriousness. What kind of statement is this about our own time? No one has seemed to realize that when one claims to be an atheist, which Plath did on a number of occasions, this does not mean a denial of a spiritual life; it is just the denial of a deity in charge and accepting the related dogma. Sylvia Plath in fact embraced the Unitarian church, known for its mysticism and transcendentalism, and declared herself a Unitarian almost right until the end of her life. Taken collectively, the seemingly circumstantial evidence of occult practice mentioned in their peripheral and casual way across the many Plath biographies, journals, and letters point to Plath being very much invested and even somewhat obsessed with mysticism.[4]

It is quite probable that Plath was reluctant to let the world know she dabbled in the occult. After all, she had a history of mental illness that if known would have left her feeling ostracized and labeled as crazy; she was building her reputation in the then-conservative world of academia; and she was the mother of two small children whom she wanted to protect from gossip and harm. In addition there was a great social stigma attached to witchcraft, which had only been taken off the books as a crime in England in 1951. Finally, there are her fans and scholars who, perhaps out of love and respect to honor Plath as they would like to see her, and perhaps also out of their own personal disdain for weirdness and things outside the norm, have decided to ignore the facts right in front of them and look the other way.

It is a curious thing that the work of Sylvia Plath, one of literature's most famous suicides, would one day build the case for proving a meaning and order to life, but I think readers here will soon learn that this is what she has done. Through the poetry collection *Ariel*, Plath presents a beautiful connectedness and mirroring of patterns, complementary relationships, and a definitive, spiritual structure for the universe in line with Qabalah, to which the modern tarot conforms. Did she do this consciously, or was she just a natural mystic? It seems unlikely that coincidence such as this would happen at least six times within each poem, and forty times across the forty *Ariel* poems, and all in perfect order.[5] A Harvard graduate in Statistics explained it for me this way in a formula:

For those of us less familiar with mathematics, the factorial of six to the fortieth power means there is essentially *no chance*, one in a googol,[6] that Plath's Qabalah-mirroring structure was a random

$$\frac{1}{(6!)^{40}}=0$$

occurrence. The number becomes even less possible when taking into account that the forty poems are within their own exact ordering as well.

I am aware that some readers might feel tempted to skip the tarot/Qabalah, alchemy, myth and astrological/astronomical mirrors that might be initially confusing and unfamiliar, to read only the two of the easier-to-grasp mirrors that I present: History and the World, and the Arts and Humanities. I did entertain the idea of keeping the more esoteric mirrors to myself; I could have pretended that the brilliance was simply my own, and had a comfortably shorter book, to boot. Readers who do skip the mysticism and head straight to those more comfortable, traditional interpretations will be surprised that these obvious cultural and artistic influences were missed. The truth is that I would not have found these historical and artistic associations without the other mirrors to point me in the right direction.

---

4 My forthcoming book, *The Magician's Girl*, explores Plath's biography with a focus on her mysticism, before and with Ted Hughes.

5 Additionally, I have found this structure in Plath's fiction, her prose, and other work since her time with Ted Hughes. But that is for another book.

6 A googol is the digit 1 followed by 100 zeroes.

It would have felt like a lie if I were to pretend that it was just my own dumb luck or keen associations.

Readers will soon understand Qabalah as a kind of metaphor game: Every word or image is worked for all it can do. Qabalistic theories of emanation are also theories of language, according to Rabbi Gershom Scholem, founder of modern Qabalah. Scholem claimed, "The God who manifests himself is the God who expresses Himself" (Bloom, 9). Harold Bloom states that Qabalah ("Kabbalah," in his writing) is primarily complex language figurations, "tropes or turns of language that substitute for God." Bloom goes on to say that some qabalists subscribe to "the rather dangerous formula that God and language are one in the same" (Bloom, 10).[7]

Bloom believes that poets since Wordsworth have identified the system, even if they weren't educated in it. Other poets, he admits, knew exactly what they were doing and yet chose to hide it in an attempt to appear more professional: "Poets from the Renaissance through today have sought occult authority in Kabbalah, but I suspect that this seeking concealed and conceals a more professional and technical concern. However 'unconsciously,' poets seem to have known that the revisionary patterns of their work followed the Kabbalistic model" (Bloom, 47).

"…there are crucial patterns of interplay between literal and figurative meanings, in post-Miltonic poems, and these patterns, though very varied, are to a surprising degree quite definite and even over-determined."

— Harold Bloom,
Kabbalah and Criticism

How did Plath work Qabalah into *Ariel*? Well, a corresponding tarot card, for instance, relates to a Greek myth. That myth's protagonist may also correspond to the name of a planet, which relates to an alchemical metal, and is also echoed in actual history and great works of art. As one tours through *Fixed Stars Govern a Life: Decoding Sylvia Plath* and picks apart each work, the connections are astounding: Plath's deceptively simple lines reflect and reference so many different meanings without needing so much as a change in register or tone. Line by line, each one of Plath's *Ariel* poems opens to six completely different stories, all supporting the greater qabalistic/tarot theme in line with it. It is no wonder Sylvia Plath is the star of contemporary American female writers. Everyone has known instinctively that she deserved it; now we can precisely explain *why*.

The fact is this: Sylvia Plath's work still resonates powerfully today because it touches the reader's subconscious mind through embedded layers of myth, symbolism, nods to great art, to historic events of the ages, and to the flora and fauna of our world. Its touch is inescapable; these works appear to have been crafted, structured, and ordered to work upon the human mind and heart. Plath's *Ariel* is a poetic spell of the grandest sort.

Sylvia Plath killed herself on February 11, 1963, soon after completing *Ariel*. Perhaps she assumed no one beyond her estranged husband, Ted Hughes, truly understood the full magnitude of her work. Plath's poems no doubt were initiated by and also reflect some of her sad autobiography, but it is truly a shame for readers to limit her work to merely that. Even Hughes seems to have missed some of her genius to have rearranged the poems for *Ariel*'s first publication. Perhaps at that time of her death, her physical and emotional isolation was the final straw. Plath was privy to the knowledge and patterns of a higher power, however she might have conceived it to be, yet she could

---

7 It is curious that Harold Bloom, who wrote *Kabbalah and Criticism* [Continuum, 1975], and called Plath's work "Hysterical insanity" in his Introduction to *Bloom's Modern Critical Views: Sylvia Plath* [Infobase Publishing, 2007], did not identify Plath's qabalistic structure himself.

not freely speak of it. Prior to her death, Plath dealt with romantic betrayal, single parenting, depression, the flu, and England's coldest and most brutal winter in a hundred years. She was becoming increasingly famous for her work, yet it seemed that her readers missed the point, as they took and continue to take her poems' meanings only on their face value. And then, the final insult: For the next fifty years, Plath would instead be held to a narrow-minded view that her poetry and prose are merely the musings of a desperate, suicidal woman. She would be relegated to the category of her suicidal friend Anne Sexton and labeled a "confessional poet."

Am I making impossible claims regarding the power of Sylvia Plath's work? That is for readers to decide. *Fixed Stars Govern a Life* attempts to present all the pieces, clearly and in one place, enabling all to make their own connections without any preaching. No faith is required. One needs only the time to read and observe the correspondences. More than fifty years later, perhaps it is time for us to understand the real genius of Sylvia Plath. Perhaps, through her written work and its miracles, we might also understand ourselves.

Julia Gordon-Bramer, 2014

Author's Notes on How to Read these Interpretations:

Fixed Stars Govern a Life was not written with the intention of teaching or converting readers to Qabalah or any other kind of mysticism, nor does it teach art, literature, or world history in any great depth. Likewise, this is not a new edition of Sylvia Plath's *Ariel*, and it is highly recommended that readers have their own copy of *Ariel: The Restored Edition* in order to compare and experience the poems in their complete forms. One does not have to know or learn Qabalah or tarot to make sense of this book. In *Fixed Stars Govern a Life: Decoding Sylvia Plath*, each one of Sylvia Plath's *Ariel* poems is held up separately *and* as a part of the entire collection against the framework of the Qabalah Tree of Life. While readers may want to skip around to read the analyses of their favorite *Ariel* poems, I recommend reading this book straight through in the order Plath intended here for maximum clarity and understanding.

> *"All religions, arts, and sciences are branches of the same tree."*
>
> — Albert Einstein

After seeing how a few of Plath's poems interrelate and mirror the same symbols, the reader will begin to understand the Tree of Life as a kind of divine roadmap: a system that explains the creation and order of the universe. This Tree's roots, branches and fruit are said to contain the knowledge of God. The Tree of Life symbol has appeared in Celtic, Norse, Native American, and other mythologies through the ages and around the globe. The Tree of Life/Knowledge makes an appearance in the Bible's Book of Genesis, as it bore the fruit of temptation to obtain the knowledge to "be as gods" in the Garden of Eden. A thousand years earlier, The Tree of Life appeared in the Hindu Rig Veda, and in the Sumerian tablets' epic of *Gilgamesh* around that same time. In the arts, it has been celebrated by John Milton, William Blake, Chaucer, Shakespeare, Dante, and others. It is easy to see the appeal of Qabalah for Sylvia Plath, with her love for these poets, as well as for history and mythology. Add Plath's husband, Ted Hughes, to the mix, with his background in anthropology and a passion for mysticism, and the environment is fertile for poetic experimentation.

The Tree of Life design is hexagonal, meaning it has six sides. There are many six-sided symbols and images in Qabalah: the Cube of Space, which represents all four directions in addition to up and down; the snowflake, which represents the knowledge of God drifting down to earth; the Jewish Star of David (Qabalah began as "Kabbalah," a form of ancient Jewish mysticism), and the shape of the hexagon itself. This book makes no claim that the hexagon, or the cube, or the snowflake, or the Jewish star *is* the Tree of Life, nor does it attempt in any way to teach the complex and varied practices of Qabalah, alchemy, or other occult arts. The six mirrors I present here for each poem are my own system of organization for ease of explanation for the reader. You will see that, as the Qabalah's Tree of Life splits off into its various paths and sephiroth (sephiroth are divine emanations of God, by which all reality is structured. They are the ten stations on the Tree, usually pictured as circular points), so too do some of these mirrors. Within the Arts and Humanities mirror for instance, one might find that Plath has layered a work of sculpture with a work of related literature with a corresponding painting—one set of words addressing three different artistic works as a single reflection. Each mirror relates to the others, working in conjunction to reflect the principal ideas and imagery of the corresponding tarot card, which reflects a qabalistic station on the Tree of Life. Occasionally, the correspondences seem to go on infinitely, just like Qabalah. In fact, in revisions to this work, some of the more tangential correspondences have been cut for space.

Qabalah has long been associated with spiritual secrets, and even the name itself holds some mystery.[8] Its many layers and correlative meanings can be quite confusing. Much of its complexity

---

8 The word *Qabalah* has a number of spellings: It is *Cabala*, or some variation if you're using the Christian version, while it is *Kabbalah*, or a variation, if you're partial to the ancient Jewish brand. This book spells it with a Q, in the Hermetic style, as evidence suggests Plath and Hughes were steeped in Hermeticism.

has been intentional to keep it relatively secret over the ages. In the late 1800s, the Hermetic Order of the Golden Dawn identified the amazing correlations between the Qabalah Tree of Life and tarot, astrology, mythology, alchemy, and more. The Qabalah is the umbrella that shelters the family of related occult sciences, all doing the same thing, yet in their uniquely different ways. Throughout this book, readers will get an overview of these correlations as they work within Sylvia Plath's *Ariel*. One must keep in mind the overriding theme, which can be most easily understood through the representative pictures and personalities of the tarot; the tarot is a perfect mirror of the Tree of Life with its ten stations and twenty-two paths. The basic Tree of Life with corresponding tarot cards looks like this:

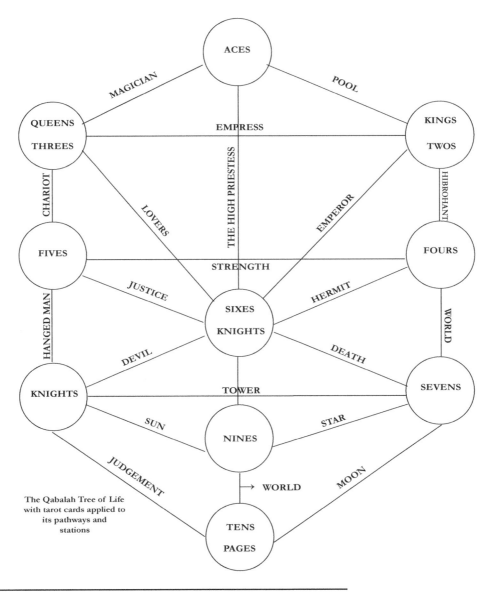

The Qabalah Tree of Life with tarot cards applied to its pathways and stations

The purpose of this book is to reveal that there are, correspondingly, six multi-form aspects or mirrors (related themes) to each Plath poem: *Tarot/Qabalah; Alchemy; Mythology; History and the World; Astrology and Astronomy; Arts and Humanities*. Qabalists see these mirrors as God viewing Himself from different angles, "an immutable knowledge of a final reality that stands behind our world of appearances," and "neither *things* nor *acts*, but rather [they] are *relational events*" (Bloom, 11). Another qabalistic metaphor explains these mirrors as working like a prism, breaking apart divine light into its separate colors of the same being. Since the thirteenth century, qabalists believed that these mirrors reflected "themselves within themselves, so that each 'contained' all the others" (Bloom, 15). They are "supernatural channels of influence (or rhetorically speaking divine poems, each a text in itself" (Bloom, 16).

To follow is a diagram of the Qabalah Tree of Life, with both major and minor arcana tarot cards laid over their corresponding paths, widely known to qabalists. I have matched Plath's *Ariel* poems as they fit upon this structure:

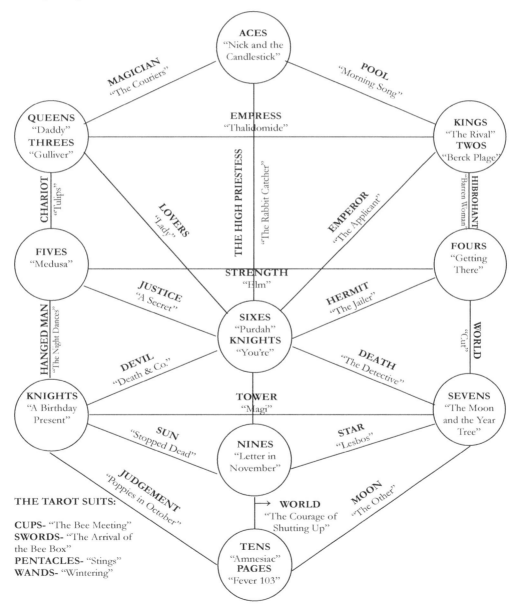

By adhering to this qabalistic structure, Plath might have known that her poetry would resonate at multiple levels in her readers' subconscious, creating a lasting body of work that would endure through generations. When Hughes called Plath a mystic poet "of the very highest tradition," he wasn't kidding.

Held against the structure of the Tree of Life, Plath's *Ariel* is a beautiful match. One's own adoption of mysticism is not essential to realizing the power of the mystic structure of these poems. As readers look at the poems' multi-dimensions and mirrored meanings throughout this book, they will see how one image does sixfold work corresponding across these mirrors. Mystic or not, Sylvia Plath conjured the perfect formula to do this again and again and again. Was she conscious of this? As I have shown previously, the mathematics say, *yes*. Is this a holy pattern? A magical Pythagorean equation? Uncanny random chance? Are we all personally able to incorporate Qabalah in our lives, artistic or otherwise? Or perhaps Qabalah has always been there, the *deus ex machina*? Only you can decide what this means for you.

Just as a crystal's facets reflect each other, qabalistic mirrors complement and relate. Think of the sides of the Tree of Life as the points of a star: each one is important and equal to the structure of the whole. For the greatest understanding and appreciation of the correspondences and interplay of images and relationships, it is important to read all six mirrors of each poem, and the worlds within each mirror.

Understanding the Mirrors

In **The First Mirror: Tarot/Qabalah**, the major symbolism and meanings of the corresponding tarot card and Qabalah station are laid out in an examination of the pictures, values, and correspondences on the face of each tarot card, and how these relate to their correlating *Ariel* poem. The first mirror includes an examination of where this poem sits upon the Tree of Life; Hebrew correspondences; numerology; Hermetic Order of the Golden Dawn ceremony, ritual, scripture, or prayer; and even Enochian Chess, a spiritual chess game. Enochian Chess was designed based on secrets of the apocryphal and apocalyptic Book of Enoch, from which Qabalah descends (Bloom, 7). In Hebrew, there are acrostics, anagrams, Gematria, and meanings of the letters themselves, stretching the possibilities for the written word even further. Hebrew includes pictures, letters, and numbers. Sylvia Plath and Ted Hughes were avid and not even all that secretive regarding their pursuits of tarot, astrology, the Ouija board, crystal ball gazing, and more. Two of their most revered writers and mentors, W.B. Yeats and T.S. Eliot, were members of the Hermetic Order of the Golden Dawn, so their interest and pursuit makes sense.

In Plath's own book on the tarot, *The Painted Caravan: A Penetration into the Secrets of the Tarot Cards*, which Ted Hughes bought her with a pack of tarot cards for her birthday in 1956, author Basil Ivan Rákóczi wrote:

> "Did they want an Egyptian rite? The Tarot provided it. The Kabalistic lore of the Jews, methods of alchemical transmutation, the direction of one's life according to the stars, Scottish rites, Hindu rites, those of the Aztecs,—why a Gypsy could produce any of them. Incredible as it may be, out of his Tarot wisdom, he could draw the whole gamut of occult lore and ceremonial magic" (Rákóczi, 18).

In 1954, Plath's mother, Aurelia Plath, gave Sylvia the book, *The Golden Bough: A Study in Magic and Religion* by Sir James George Frazer. This book studies the culture and belief systems of people across the world, with myth, legend, and ritual, especially of Indians and primitive peoples inside and outside of western civilization. It shows the progress of magic and religion, alchemy, astrology, and more as it has all formed modern science and thought. Frazer's book was important to Plath, which she mentioned in her letters home (*LH*, 145).

For Christmas in 1957, Aurelia Plath bought Sylvia and Ted a copy of Virginia Moore's *The Unicorn: William Butler Yeats' Search for Reality*.[9] This book is a study on Yeats' personal philosophy-religion, loaded with Hermeticism, Qabalah, Rosicrucianism, Irish rituals, lore and Druidism, and other forms of esotericism. Additionally, there are tales and discussions about Madame Blavatsky and Theosophy, Aleister Crowley, William Blake, Rudolf Steiner, Carl Jung, Enochian systems, and more. It is also a detailed study of Yeats' doctrinal sources for his spiritualism: a virtual *how-to* handbook. Lest readers think the findings here in *Fixed Stars Govern a Life* are too esoteric for Plath to have known of them, rest assured, they are in *The Unicorn*.

---

9   The book is inscribed in Aurelia Plath's handwriting: "Merry Christmas to Sylvia and Ted 1957." Plath's copy is located in the Sylvia Plath archives of the Lilly Library, Indiana University-Bloomington.

The Second Mirror: Alchemy explores this practice in its simplest definition, the process of turning lead, or base metal, to gold. There are three forms: practical alchemy, which is actual chemistry performed in a laboratory; psychological alchemy, which is the process of self-actualization; and spiritual alchemy, which is becoming one with God. It is believed that the true alchemist must be a practitioner of all three forms at once to achieve complete self-actualization. Alchemy is a complicated, ancient tradition with a jargon full of mystery and oftentimes, sexual metaphor. The psychologist Carl G. Jung recognized the value of the alchemical metaphor in his work, and out of it he developed Jungian Alchemy, with a goal of *Individuation*—advancement on the psychological aspect of alchemy. Plath and Hughes read a great deal of Jung's work, along with that of his mentor, Sigmund Freud, and Hughes' work on alchemical correspondences has been studied and written about.

This leads to **The Third Mirror: Mythology,** which examines not only Greek and Roman myths, but also culls myths of the Hindus, Buddhists, Celts, the Norse, Meso-American and North American Indians, and other cultures with which Plath and Hughes were familiar. Mythology was once religion to many peoples, and a fine line differentiates the two. Some religious traditions and scripture still practiced today (Christian, Jewish, Buddhist, Hindu, etc.) are also included in this mirror. It is the author's intention to respect all religious faiths and practices, and by no means does grouping religion with myth mean to suggest otherwise. Ted Hughes' university major was anthropology, and primitive cultures and religion held a special fascination for him. Sylvia Plath, meanwhile, was well-schooled on the ancient Greeks, Romans, Celts, and her own heritage of Norse myth. Two favorite books addressing myth, for both Plath and Hughes, were Robert Graves' *The White Goddess: A Historical Grammar of Poetic Myth*, and Sir James George Frazer's *The Golden Bough*, mentioned previously. Her pocket calendar of May 12, 1956, also noted her awareness of the Buddhism within Ted Hughes' poems.

In Plath's personal copy of *The Portable James Joyce*, she underlined: "William James termed 'the stream of consciousness' to what Jung terms 'the rational unconscious,' beyond individual dream to collective myth" (Joyce, 14). Plath also underlined the editor's statement, "Joyce has managed, by invoking an ancient myth, to conjure up a modern one"[10] (Joyce, 3). It is clear that Plath consciously chose to do this in *Ariel*.

The Fourth Mirror: History and the World— This mirror includes not only actual historical events, but close examinations of species, lifestyles and the peculiarities that set them apart as the exact right fit for the corresponding *Ariel* poem. By the time the reader has reached the fourth mirror, there should be a strong sense of how the preceding three facets relate to and support the History and the World facet. Sylvia Plath considered herself an avid history buff and very political. She wrote newspaper and magazine editorials and letters to the editor about the subjects she was passionate about, such as ending the nuclear arms race. In Plath's personal copy of *The Portable James Joyce*, she underlined and starred this comment from the editorial introduction on Joyce: "he evoked the past to illuminate the present" (Joyce, 14).

---

10 Plath's personal annotated copy of *The Portable James Joyce* is held at the Lilly Library, at Indiana University-Bloomington.

Hughes had suggested that Plath "read not novels or poems only, but books on folklore, fiddler crabs, and meteorites" (*LH*, 342). Plath wrote of researching spiders, crabs, and owls in the college library; of wanting books on wildflowers, birds, and animals of North America; and of reading *Man & the Vertebrates*, *The Personality of Animals*, and *The Sea Around Us*. Hughes meanwhile was reading Carson's *The Sea Wind*. Plath said, "The animal world to me seems more & more intriguing" (*UJ*, 398). Every bit of information, every detail she might learn, was a potential metaphor, simile or image to be transformed in some way into her deceptively personal words and phrases. Every line sculpted in Plath's poetry would eventually carry the weight of these and many other mirroring references.

The Fifth Mirror: Astrology and Astronomy— While astrology and astronomy are two very different things, in ancient times they were one and the same. This mirror explores ancient Babylonian astronomy, astronomy and astrology of the West, and occasionally Native American and Chinese astrology and astronomy. Much of western astrology is based upon Greek myth especially, so the reader will usually note a strong correlation between the third and fifth mirrors of each poem. Plath's journal entries and letters have appreciated the stars and stargazing since she was in the sixth grade.[11] Ted Hughes was a serious practitioner of astrology; he calculated every auspicious date for mailing out poems to be published, and credited the stars for every event in his life, including his meeting and marrying Plath.

Hughes' friend Lucas Myers believes Hughes saw astrology not as a science, "but as an instrument for intuitive insights" and claims that Hughes had written him from America during his time with Plath, stating that vision, the controlled dreaming awake, was common in the Middle Ages. It was Hughes' goal to awaken this sleeping gift (Myers, 9).

In his article, "Ted's Spell," Hughes' friend Ben Sonnenberg wrote, "At times Ted's belief in astrology seemed almost mediæval to me. At other times it seemed of a piece with his scholarly interest in spirits, witches, magic, alchemy: elements of understanding the Elizabethian [sic] world picture" (Sonnenberg).

Finally comes **The Sixth Mirror: Arts and the Humanities**— It is no secret that Sylvia Plath was well-read and well-educated, and she used references to other great works of art in literature, music, sculpture, and more to complement images and ideas behind her work. As both a writer and a visual artist herself, Plath's sense of description, color, texture and the importance of art are used to support the preceding five mirrors within each of her poems.

From the dates on the drafts of Sylvia Plath's poems, she did not write the *Ariel* poems chronologically, in the numerical order of the tarot. Rather, it seems that she chose her inspiration in the moment and chose a tarot card to match it. There is no evidence Plath acted this out as a creative version of the initiatory journey, as has been questioned by some scholars challenging my work. Plath was instead giving her poems power to take the reader on his or her own journey. It is my belief that most modern readers are not well-versed enough in the classics of literature to understand most of Plath's meanings. This book attempts to summarize stories, plot

11 The first notation, "Mother & I went out and stargazed for a few minutes," is recorded on August 11, 1944, in Plath's childhood journal. This journal is held at the Sylvia Plath Archives in the Lilly Library, Indiana University-Bloomington.

lines, and key themes of major artistic works as they match with Plath's lines and symbolism, to aid in reader understanding. As readers go through *Fixed Stars Govern a Life*, they will understand that each poem appears to be carefully positioned in the manuscript for reasons higher than poetic aesthetic.

One last important note: The poems by Sylvia Plath that are analyzed and reinterpreted in *Fixed Stars Govern a Life: Decoding Sylvia Plath* are not able to be quoted in their entirety and must be largely paraphrased due to copyright permissions and restrictions. Readers will benefit by having a copy of *Ariel: the Restored Edition* to which to refer. Likewise, references to unpublished early drafts of poems are not permitted to be quoted at all. I have made attempts to paraphrase this imagery when it is relevant.

The Major Arcana

Chapter One: A Brave New World
Card #0   The Fool   Corresponding Poem: "Morning Song"

Plath wrote that she wanted to start her *Ariel* collection with the word "Love" and end it with the word "spring"[12] With this enforced mythic narrative, Plath defied the dark circumstances of her failing marriage with positivity and light. It was quite different from the first published arrangement of *Ariel* by her husband, Ted Hughes, although both arrangements begin with this poem. "Morning Song" is widely considered to be Sylvia Plath's "definitive statement on Motherhood," about her infant daughter, Frieda (Alexander, 256). While a beautiful poem in the context of motherhood alone, skimming through the mirrors soon makes clear the stifling limitations of holding Plath solely to her biography.

First Mirror: The Tarot/Qabalah

The tarot's major arcana begins with The Fool card, the sacred child, and here is where the first correlation between poem and Tarot/Qabalah begin as well. Since The Fool is a child, the child is the dominating theme of Plath's introductory poem, "Morning Song." The Fool is a traveler; his first journey is into the world. He is a bridge of purity between the old and new life. This card is about beginnings and thought becoming form. He is found walking on the first path of the Qabalah Tree of Life, that unending circle of being, which stems from the highest point, Kether the Crown, being and nothingness. New life, innocence and naïveté are his qualities as he begins the journey.

The word "Fool" stems from the Latin *Follies*, meaning "a bag of wind," the first life-breath at birth. In numerology, the number 0 is believed to contain air, or breath. It is a limitless, never-ending ring and shaped like an egg, another symbol for birth and occult initiation. The Golden Dawn attributes to the Hebrew letter for The Fool card, *Aleph*, meaning "the unspoken letter in the Mind of God." God is considered unknowing and unknowable in Qabalah. When He created the world out of nothing, as is written in Genesis, He created the world out of Himself.

The Qabalah's color for The Fool card is yellow, which dominates this Rider-Waite design, pictured above. Yellow, combined with the roundness of the number zero, encompasses Plath's "Morning Song" poetic images of "fat" and "gold."

"I'm no more your mother" is one of Plath's genius lines with three possible meanings: as an introductory phrase to the next line; that the baby is a wholly separate and complete being; or this might be a spiritual statement that she is ultimately not the great creator.

The mirror, omnipresent in Plath's work, is a symbol of the ego, the subconscious and the double. The tarot is said to "mirror" the subconscious, effectively distilling meaning through the images, as Plath's cloud reflects itself in the third stanza. Plath's use of the word "effacement" alludes to both cerical effacement in childbirth, and to spiritual purification: opening and peeling

---

away the face (ego). Tarot is a divination tool to reflect the path one is on, yet this Fool has no plans, and travels, as they say, "whichever way the wind blows." The element of wind (Air) represents his force and energy for creation.

The idea of "moth breath" is another nod to Air, but also refers to the new, perfect butterfly hatching from its chrysalis.[13] In Rákóczi's *The Painted Caravan*, Plath's guide to the tarot from her personal library, the illustration of The Fool features a variation of the classic Tarot de Marseilles design, with a butterfly flying beside The Fool's mouth: *moth-breath*. The word *moth* contains the letters of *mouth* (another metaphor for the womb), and if one entertains the concept of connective association (as Freud and Jung did, of whom Plath and Hughes read), *mouth* is *moth* plus a *u* (you), and *moth* is also the first four letters of *mother*. Plath played with this association, writing "the mother of mouths" in her 1959 poem, "Maenad" (*CP*, 133). Metaphorically, the moth calls to mind a creature of the darkness that seeks light or the open flame. In this way of flying about in the dark, the moth may be likened to the bat imagery of other Plath poems. The moth and butterfly both are symbols of transformation, but the moth, with its dark side, was the best fit for Plath.

Plath's "cow-heavy" points to the Hebrew letter *Aleph*, associated by Qabalists with the Fool tarot card, and also the ox. Plath's description connotes the sacred cow of the Hindus, representing the earthly mother with her abundance of milk. The "floral" refers to the pattern design in The Fool's garment.

The square image ending the second-to-last stanza is a qabalistically important symbol of the four elements. Plath's last stanza idea of whiteness refers to the Kether, the qabalistic Crown, pure consciousness, and power of God. To approach it, one must be purified.

Enochian Chess is important to Qabalists and Rosicrucians, the latter being another philosophical secret society with occult practices, and popular in Plath's time, regularly advertising in major magazines she read such as *The Atlantic Monthly*. Both claim the game of chess corresponds with the tarot and Qabalah. Enochian Chess is a four-handed variant of the standard chess of today. The Golden Dawn considers Enochian Chess to be the most powerful form of elemental magic. Chess, like Qabalah and tarot, has fuzzy beginnings, with its exact origin unknown. Both tarot and Enochian Chess began as games before being used as tools for mysticism.

Like tarot and Qabalah, chess is believed to mirror the struggles and stages of life, and "Morning Song" introduces us to the Pawns, the children, of Enochian Chess.

Plath's first line with its watch symbol means the game has begun and the timer has started. The "footsoles" and baldness mark the foot soldiers pawns play in battle. When set on the board, they take their position among the other elements in the game. As there are eight pawns, their arrival is magnified, in accord with Plath's second stanza. This is a "drafty" marbled board—draft paper bearing grid lines as a chessboard's squares, and museums being often built of marble. Both nakedness and shadowing for safety are roles of the pawn, exposed and protecting the more valuable pieces. Plath speaks for the other pieces when she claims that they stand around blankly. The game of chess is "slow" and as it progresses both sides are effaced.

In chess, the white player moves first. The most powerful character, the Queen, sits on her color in her star-crown, reflecting the final stanza's first line. The Queen appears to be wearing a Victorian-style gown as does Plath's speaker, and the Queen is the largest, heaviest piece on the chess board—the cow reference again. When the white pawn takes its opponent's piece, the window-like squares clear out and half turn white. Pieces are removed like "dull stars." The pawn may move one square or two, and can capture at diagonals, its "handful of notes" compared with the other pieces limited moves.

---

13 For a larger and more comprehensive treatment of this moth/butterfly metaphor, see *Fixed Stars Govern a Life*'s interpretation of "The Detective" for the Death card (vol. one), and "Gulliver" (vol. two) for the rank of the Threes.

Early versions of the tarot deck, such as the Tarot Marseille de Jean Noblet and the Dodal Tarot de Marseille, have a cat chasing at The Fool's ankles, as Plath mentions in the fifth stanza. This cat is said to represent the Ancient Egyptian's Bast, cat goddess of motherhood, and said to create the desire to be born into form from the disembodied world.

At least since their stay at Yaddo, Plath and Hughes were familiar with and practicing Eastern mysticism and Kundalini yoga. In both practices, Chakras, or energy centers of the human body, are important. Plath's image of baldness in the second line corresponds with the Crown chakra and the Fool card's elemental property of air.

The only vowel that is "clear" is the written letter O, the balloon-like letter in the English language with no edges or serifs obstructing it. O, of course, mirrors the number zero, the Fool card's position in the tarot's major arcana and on the Qabalah's Tree of Life. There are 55 O's in Plath's "Morning Song," and the number 55 is a master number in Qabalah, designated to the element of Air. Zero equals "love" in the game of tennis, reflecting the first line of the poem, and zero is used as a placeholder, reflecting Plath's third line in "Morning Song." The number zero is round and blank in shape, apposite to the last line of the second stanza. Continuing on to the Alchemy mirror of this poem, the reader will understand yet another aspect of creation and children.

Second Mirror: Alchemy

Not to conflict with the previous Tarot/Qabalah interpretation, but rather to enhance and complement it, is the alchemical reading for "Morning Song." In addition to addressing motherhood, "Morning Song" is a perfect correlation with alchemy, considered to be The Great Work of the Hermetic arts. As the reader journeys through each mirror of "Morning Song" and all of Plath's *Ariel* poems as they are presented here, each poem's line may be interpreted at least six different ways, yet every reading supports the greater idea of the poem's corresponding tarot card. Plath's husband Ted Hughes' work has been closely examined and written about with regard to alchemy.[14] "Morning Song" is most certainly a poem focusing on alchemical creation, mirroring that Fool card again. In alchemy, the goal of chemical, physical, psychological, and spiritual transmutation is love. This is represented by the gold Plath names in the first line, the most precious and pure of metals. It is known by several names: the *magnum opus*, the perfect work, philosopher's stone, or alchemical child. In alchemy, the tarot's Fool is the alchemist beginning his work; it is the point before the journey to the philosopher's stone. Composed of the mysterious "fifth element," the stone possesses the qualities of all things. It is believed by alchemists to cure any illness, to be the fountain of youth, to turn lead into gold, and to turn an ordinary person into an enlightened sage. Alchemists use practical laboratory work in conjunction with mental and spiritual work, believing a simultaneous pursuit of all three aspects is essential. Laboratory references are throughout the *Ariel* collection. The chemical procedures of practical alchemy—the lab work—is timed, hence Plath's clock is running. The alchemist is on watch. A midwife is another expression used in alchemy for an alchemist in this poem; she assists to bring forth feeling and life in the work, bringing the golden child into the world.

Plath's reference to the elements reflects both chemistry's Periodic Table of elements, and the Hermetic Sciences of Qabalah, astrology, and alchemy. These sciences share four elements. Alchemy embraces earth, air, fire and water; tarot respectively owns pentacles, swords, wands and cups; and Jungian alchemy corresponds with the psychological elements of sensation, thinking, feeling, and intuition.

---

14 See works by Dr. Ann Skea, Ekbert Faas, and Keith Sagar.

Plath's image of magnifying is metaphorical and literal; the alchemist must magnify for close examination. The alchemist's lab must be cool and well-ventilated as a museum. Using the museum image, Plath may have also intended a double meaning here of written "drafts," either of formulas or poems.

Alchemists correlate *shadow* with the night that begins and ends each day, defining light and dark. Famous alchemist Michael Maier stated, "The Sun and its shadow complete the work" (Maier, 278). Alchemist or not, the reader understands Plath's shadowing safety hints at her awareness of her own mortality. This new life in the world, like the night, both reinforces her existence and her imminent end—the ultimate meaning of The Fool card.

To be standing around as blank as a wall represents wonder over a new life, the chemical effect, and the roundness of the Qabalah's Tree of Life that reflects the circular work of the elements, alchemy's *opus circulatorium*. This blankness of meditation is necessary to open mind and spirit to love and individualization, the true philosopher's stone. "[R]ound" also implies standing in a circle. In Hermeticism and pagan faiths, a circle of individuals is defense against unwanted influences and spirits.

The distilling cloud of the third stanza uses multiple alchemical meanings: The Hermetic Sciences of astrology, tarot/Qabalah, and alchemy, "echo," "mirror" and clarify, or "distil", each other. Also, distillation is the first, The Fool's, chemical process within alchemy. Whether psychological, spiritual, or chemical, the process is always "slow." In alchemy, "cloud" is the name for the volatile vapor or spirit rising to the top of the vessel during distillation. Plath's use of the word "distils" is no coincidence. Roses reference the Rosicrucians, a.k.a. the Brotherhood of the Rosy Cross, who were mystics known for great interest in alchemy (Lindgren). Roses symbolize spiritual unfolding, and are a central emblem for many famous mystics.[15] The rose was originally a symbol of the Egyptian god Horus, whom the Greeks and Romans later regarded as the god of silence. This clarifies why Plath wakes to listen. She describes the darkness ahead of her as a distant sea whose exploration is necessary for transformation. The sea is also representative of the great mother in alchemy, circling back to the tale of Jonah and the Leviathan, addressed in the Mythology mirror of this interpretation.[16] The newborn state feels far away to Plath as an adult.

"By George!" cried the inspector. "How ever did you see that?"

"Because I looked for it."

— from the Sherlock Holmes story, *"The Adventure of the Dancing Men,"* by Sir Arthur Conan Doyle

Plath's "bed" from which she stumbles is the alchemical term for the vessel where male-designated properties of sulfur and female-designated properties of mercury are united, and where the philosopher's stone is conceived and born. Plath knew all about sulfur; her mother Aurelia, an expert on alchemy herself, used sulfur as a home remedy for sore throats.[17]

The floral image is another nod to Rosicrucian roses. Alchemists consider "flowers" to be the powdery form of the first part of the distillation process. Red and white roses are the most significant alchemical symbols with their unfolding. The nightgown image in the fifth stanza, mirroring the Fool's garment in the previous mirror, now shifts to reference the alchemist's smock. Although

15 W.B. Yeats' poetry collection, *The Rose*, begins with a summary poem, "To the Rose Upon the Rood of Time," encompassing meanings for the 22 stations of the Qabalah. His following 22 poems mirror each individual station of the Qabalah, upon which the tarot deck's major arcana is based.

16 For more on the Sea, see *Fixed Stars Govern a Life*'s interpretation (vol. 2) of Plath's poem for the rank of fives, "Medusa."

17 Plath's sixth grade journal on August 9, 1944, reads Aurelia Plath "blew sulphur" down her daughter's sore throat. This journal is kept in the Sylvia Plath Archives at the Lilly Library, Indiana University-Bloomington.

alchemy has been practiced for thousands of years, its heyday in Western civilization was during Victorian times.

When Plath writes of the cat, it is a nod to alchemy's green lion, the earliest stage of the philosopher's stone, as well as the red lion, or *elixir:* a devouring sulfur to create the *magnum opus.* Plath's "window square" reflects the square as a symbol of matter and the four elements of creation. It is a qabalistically-relevant geometric figure corresponding to the Swastika, or squared circle.

The Fool's purification returns in alchemical whitening. Alchemy's white phase takes place during distillation, seen in the third stanza. As Plath performed her alchemical experiment, she swallowed minerals; literally, figuratively, or both.

As seen previously, alchemy is the triple work of the laboratory, the mind, and the spirit, and so Plath's "notes" in the second to last line may reference psychological and spiritual effort toward growth based on interior revelations, as well as actual note-taking.

The clear and rising vowels relate to the Enochian language, developed and used by mystics and alchemists for centuries. Believed to be an angelic language with a corresponding system of magic, Enochian was created in the seventeenth century for alchemical secrecy. The language was adopted in the late 1800s by the Hermetic Order of the Golden Dawn.[18]

Plath's rising balloons are the globed alembic glassware, a critical part of any practical alchemical operation. A two- or three-liter bubble of glass holds condensed liquids during the distillation process (Aniane). In the tarot card picture, The Fool's pack, tied to the end of the pole carried over his shoulder, was drawn to intentionally mirror this apparatus. And so as the Fool card's pure child is present as both a physical and an alchemical child, he also is presented as the mythological fool Dionysus, explored in the next mirror.

Third Mirror: Mythology

The tarot cards have mythological stories behind their meanings, as Greek myth was one of the first forms of psychology and human archetypal systems. Plath loved Greek myths and "Morning Song" is a reflection of this too, as Ancient Greece's playful god Dionysus is portrayed on the Fool card. Born as a baby from the cave-womb of the underworld, Dionysus leaps into the void of the unknown, representing the alchemist and the alchemical child of the last mirror. He represents the Hermetic idea that all enter life as individuals, learning their parts in universality as each goes about his own journey. This is why "Morning Song" is full of hopefulness for the future and joy for the pure new baby. It is not sentimental or forced; Plath's poem is the story of human and spiritual creation of self and one's place in the universe.

The cat reference in "Morning Song" represents The Fool's animal instinct over reason. Old Norse myth held that the cat pulls the chariot of the fertility goddess; cats were considered a blessing on newborns and a good family omen. With her extensive knowledge of myth, Plath layered meanings, strengthening images to resonate deep within the reader's subconscious as true, even if not easily explained. Psychologist Carl Jung, whom Plath read and admired, claimed that primal cultural archetypes reach the subconscious. Perhaps this is the real magic behind Plath's haunting, often strange, yet authentically truthful poetry and prose: Through her brilliance and skill, she knew which psychological buttons to push.

Plath's word "bald" is an important detail in alchemy's myth of rebirth which begins with a night

18 Plath and Hughes' friend and contemporary T.S. Eliot was a member of the Golden Dawn, as well as some of their other literary idols such as Yeats. Further interpretations of Plath's work suggest she was well-familiar with the Golden Dawn, their scripture and teachings.

journey below the sea where a Jonah-like hero is swallowed by a monster. As explained in *Alchemy: the Cosmological Yoga* by Maurice Aniane:

> "the belly of Leviathan becomes a matrix: an egg forms around the imprisoned man; it is so extremely hot there that the hero loses all his hair; ejected by the monster he springs forth from the primordial sea, bald as a newborn babe" (Aniane).

Plath uses this bald image, as well as its homophone, "balled," in several other poems.[19] In her April 1958 journals, she wrote of rereading Melville's *Moby-Dick* (UJ, 370).

According to mythologist Robert Graves, mentor to Plath and Hughes, the whale was the first living thing birthed by Jehovah (God), and the royal "fish" of Britain. Graves claims the whale symbolizes the end-of-the-year monster, "re-born as a New Year fish," and the Babylonian she-monster, Tiamat (Graves, 480). Tiamat was the mother of harlots, and later in Orphic art she symbolized The Fool's ritual of initiation. The initiate is swallowed by this sea-monster, the universal mother, and reborn as the Sun-God. Jewish prophets knew Tiamat as *Rahab*, the goddess of the moon and sea, rejecting her as mistress of fleshly corruptions. In Hebrew text, the faithful are promised "no more sea," an echo of Plath's third-stanza line rejecting the mother.

The next mirror, History and the World, explores how mushrooms play a role in "Morning Song." Connecting mushrooms to the Mythology mirror, interpretations suggest that *A. muscaria*, or "magic mushrooms" were ingested by Adam and Eve, Moses, Elijah and Elisha, Isaiah, Ezekiel, Jonah, Jesus and his disciples, and others (Heinrich, 64-134). Plath likely learned this reading Robert Graves' feature, "Mushrooms, Food of the Gods" in the August 1957 *Atlantic Monthly*.

Fourth Mirror: History and the World

Plath was not only looking backward to the ancient mythmakers, qabalists and alchemists for power in her work. She looked also at her own times to build in further resonance and meaning. Valentine's Day, February 14, 1961, a day for love, was four days before Plath wrote "Morning Song." It also happened to be the day that the new element 103, Lawrencium, was born. Using the cyclotron (a "fat gold watch"), scientists determined 103 was indeed an element to be placed upon their square chart. Its electron configuration may be said to resemble either a flattened rose or an open mouth.

Plath's ticking watch and the act of waking both fit the early Indo-Iranian ritual drink, soma, mentioned in 120 different Vedic Sanskrit hymns praising its energizing qualities. In 1959, Plath worked in Harvard's Department of Sanskrit and Indian studies, a likely place for her to learn this, if not from Hughes. The drug soma ruled over the gods, and its name, derived from the Proto-Indo-European *suhnu-*, means *pressed out*, or *newly born*. Soma was used to inspire poets, to commune with the gods, and for immortality and sexual potency (Cashford, 90). Some believed it could be found on water, a tie-in with Plath's sea from the previous mirror. The soma plant was harvested and flattened like Plath's roses, the Rosicrucian alchemist's roses, and the roses on the Fool card. In the Vedas, the juice is mixed with cow's milk, her metaphor for a nursing mother's heaviness. Knowledge of the original ingredients for soma, as well as the actual plant, has been lost over time. In Sanskrit epics, soma first appears in the story, "The Churning of the Ocean of Milk," when gods and demons stopped fighting to churn milk together. They create a potion for immortality arising as clarified butter, Plath's "fat gold." The Vedas equate soma with the moon god and fertility, and there is much of the moon's time-keeping in Plath's poem: its round and bald appearance, and its movement of the tides.

19 In "Barren Woman," Plath writes of "*bald-eyed Apollos*"; in "Berck-Plage," she writes "*bald surfaces*"; "Death & Co." has eyes "*balled like Blake's*"; and "The Moon and the Yew Tree" contains "*She is bald and wild*." An early meaning of "bald" was "white-headed."

A candidate for the original soma is *Amanita muscaria*, known as *fly agaric* or *fly Amanita*, a psychoactive mushroom used in shamanic ritual. Plath's husband, Ted Hughes, read extensively on shamanism. For many years, this mushroom was both sprinkled in milk and also used as an insecticide, returning to Plath's moth image. A medieval belief that flying insects could enter a person's head and cause mental illness links with this mushroom's regional names meaning either "mad" or "fool," echoing the associated tarot card for this poem.

Mushrooms are as bald as Plath's cry, and first appear as white eggs. The northeastern variety of *guessowii*, found in Plath's home state of Massachusetts and throughout the northeastern United States, is round and bright gold, like the watch in Plath's first line. The mushrooms often grow in rings, called "fairy rings," and therefore "stand round." The Koryak of eastern Siberia tell the tale of the fly agaric mushroom enabling the Big Raven to carry a whale to its sea far away (Heinrich).

These first four mirrors neatly reflect and complement each other in Plath's expressions of creation, forms of soma, and various leviathans. The next mirrors continue to expand upon and reflect these same images of the Fool card.

Fifth Mirror: Astrology and Astronomy

The constellation Cetus is also known as "the Whale" or the "Sea Monster." Just as The Fool card is number zero, a part of neither arcana in the tarot deck, but the gate from the end to its beginning, so too Cetus is not considered part of the zodiac. Cetus represented the gates to the underworld in early Greek legends for this same reason. Cetus' most notable star is Mira, the first variable star to be discovered, with changing intensities of light that serve as a good metaphor for The Fool's changeability. In ancient Mesopotamia, Cetus was identified as the sea-monster Tiamat, representing the primordial cosmic female principle.

The Greeks believed that Andromeda was sacrificed to the sea monster Cetus before Perseus saved her; the Arabs also saw a giant leviathan creature in Cetus (Allen).

"[S]wallows its dull stars" recognizes that this self-actualization process is greater than all the power of the zodiac. Despite its size as the fourth-largest constellation, Cetus has been noted for having rather dull stars (Ridpath). Cetus echoes the mythological leviathan from the third mirror of "Morning Song," and in this astronomical way, it is as unique as The Fool card is to the tarot deck.

Sixth Mirror: Humanities and the Arts

The Humanities and the Arts mirror may be one of the most satisfying with regard to interpreting Plath's work, for the reader can see not only Plath's inspiration in keeping in line with the tarot and Qabalah, but how these systems, consciously or unconsciously, influenced other great artists. The Fool's vision of the future is naïve and optimistic, one might even say utopian—despite the illustration on his tarot card showing him being about to step off of a cliff.

Aldous Huxley's *Brave New World* [20] illustrates The Fool's traits, with a special emphasis on motherhood and a government-provided drug, soma, seen in the fourth mirror of this poem. Huxley's soma provides the people with The Fool's kind of mindless happiness. Plath read the book first at seventeen years old, and it was part of her personal library (Wilson, 96). The characters of this novel happily swallow their dull white pills, like little stars in their hands. Too much soma causes respiratory paralysis, leading to Plath's poetic expressions of slowness and effacement.

In *The White Goddess*, author Robert Graves wrote that the paternalistic and scientific turns of

20 See *Fixed Stars Govern a Life*'s interpretation of Sylvia Plath's poem, "Thalidomide" for more on Aldous Huxley's *Brave New World*.

society have hurt both the goddess and man. Graves uses Huxley's example of *Brave New World* as an extreme, and offers Huxley's *The Perennial Philosophy* in its place: a study of the golden thread of truth common throughout all religion, philosophy, and spirituality (Graves, 483). *The Perennial Philosophy* holds that this truth "is expressed most succinctly in the Sanskrit formula […] and the last end of every human being, is to discover the fact for himself, to find out who he really is." This is The Fool's journey.

The Fool sometimes represents sexual liberation, another key theme of Huxley's *Brave New World*. While sex is plentiful in the book, it is a loveless society. Like The Fool, the fictional genetically-designed citizens are shallow, promiscuous, and oftentimes stupid. Sounding like Plath's second stanza of "Morning Song," the government shadows everyone, supposedly for safety. Citizens blankly stand around. A Huxley scholar claims "the price of universal happiness will be the sacrifice of the most hallowed shibboleths of our culture: 'motherhood', 'home', 'family', 'freedom', even 'love'" (Pearce). Huxley's fictional character John Savage fights for a right to his unhappiness and refuses to use soma, attempting to secure permission to leave for the Other Place, reminiscent of Shakespeare's famous Miranda in *The Tempest*. Savage's name even reflects the barbarian nature of The Fool who has not yet been schooled, and the baseness of alchemy's lead before it is processed. Savage's mother denies her biological role out of shame, and in a pivotal scene in *Brave New World*'s chapter eight she hollers at him, "I'm not your mother. I won't be your mother," sounding like the first line of Plath's third stanza of "Morning Song." Like The Fool, Miranda and Savage both are innocent, initially optimistic, and naïve children. Huxley's character Savage paraphrases her words: "O brave new world that has such people in't." *The Tempest*, it should be noted, also has fairy rings of mushrooms in Act V, Scene I. Aurelia Plath has written that *The Tempest* was Plath's first Shakespearean play, and was a significant event in Sylvia Plath's literary maturity.

In addition to having Melville's *Moby Dick* in her personal library, Plath owned a copy of Thomas Hobbes' *Leviathan*. [21] Written during the English Civil War, the 1651 book concerns the structure of society and legitimate government, arguing for a strong social contract and rule. Hobbes believed strong central government would protect the people from the wrongs and discord of war. In *Leviathan*, Hobbes postulates what life would be like with no government authority, presenting a kind of dystopian anarchy hell, and war against all. It is a curious meld of government and monster.

William Blake, another favorite artist and writer of Plath's and Hughes', painted "Oberon, Titania and Puck with Fairies Dancing." This painting was inspired by another of Shakespeare's plays to include mushrooms in fairy rings, *A Midsummer Night's Dream*. In this Shakespeare play, our Fool is Nick Bottom, the overconfident weaver who is completely ignorant of his own ridiculousness. He is stupid, self-important, and unaware that the mischievous fairy, Puck, has changed his head into that of an ass. Fairies in art and literature are almost always depicted as tiny naked people, echoing Plath's naked image. Fairies also are often portrayed as having wings and coming out at night like moths.

Irish poet and dramatist, William Butler Yeats, a member of the Hermetic Order of the Golden Dawn and one of Plath and Hughes' most revered writers, wrote of fairy rings in his 1903 play, "The Land of Heart's Desire," when a fairy child entices a newlywed to a fool's life of laughter, dancing and mindless joy instead of reality. It is a brave new world!

---

21 Her college notes on Hobbes' *Leviathan*, dated November 8, 1956, are held at the Lilly Library, Indiana University -Bloomington. Plath's heavily annotated copy of Hobbes' *Leviathan* is held at Washington University Library's Department of Special Collections, St. Louis, Missouri.

Chapter Two: Smoke and Mirrors
Card #1   The Magician   Corresponding Poem: "The Couriers"

Most readers interpret the deceit in "The Couriers" as belonging to Plath's autobiography: Her husband was known for his infidelity and lies during their marriage. "The Couriers" is often considered to be one of Plath's more difficult poems. This is not a surprise; readers must rely upon the Magician component to open this poem up for a full understanding.

First Mirror: The Tarot/Qabalah

When the Magician tarot card is read in reverse (its upside-down meaning) as Plath seems to have intended for "The Couriers," it denotes a trickster or con-artist. He is a man with all the tools (the elements on his table) for trouble. The Magician is considered to be a gypsy, like the Hungarian *Czigany*: a nomad, tinker, and thief (Borrow). Today, gypsies are known as the Roma people. According-ing to Plath's tarot book, *The Painted Caravan*, by Basil Ivan Rákóczi (1954), the Hungarian gypsies were the couriers of ancient mystical knowledge throughout Europe.[22] Europeans assumed the dark-skinned Roma people were Egyptian, and thus gave them their name, *Gypsy*.

The Golden Dawn attributes the Hebrew letter *Bet* to the Magician card. *Bet* is "the letter with which the creative act can take place." Alche-mists believe we all begin as The Magician, a cocky and overconfident youth learning to manipulate the elements. Each element (fire, earth, water, and air) has properties represented by the tarot's suits of Wands, Pentacles, Cups, and Swords, pictured on The Magician's table. The Magician holds an arm up to the heavens, indicating he draws his power from above and not within. Plath's refrain of lack of ownership in "The Couriers" echoes this.

Qabalists profess, "What is outwardly solar is inwardly corrosive": a false front shone to the world destroys the soul. The initiate is instructed to put energy on the inner self. This explains much about mirror symbols across Plath's work: What is reflected outward goes on within. The word *solar* also fits Plath's reference to the sun, opening the third stanza.

Plath's golden ring is the traditional symbol of a wedding ring. In Hebrew, the letters RING refer to the pupil or iris in *the eye of God*, connected with the Sun. The sun-centered ring is a fine de-scription for the Pentacle on The Magician's table too. Gold and Sun are important symbols for the Golden Dawn, Freemasons, and Rosicrucians, representing truth and the power of God; gold is the symbol for the Sun and the purified state, the philosopher's stone.

Plath's lies and grief echo feelings about her cheating husband and abandoned promises. It is ascertained that her ring of gold is a lie. The first precept of Hermeticism, correlating with The Magician's number of one, is: "True, without falsehood, certain, most certain." This means Hermeti-cism is universally true at all levels.

To receive The Magician card reversed in a tarot reading is a warning, and to be warned against accepting something not genuine refers to these gypsy couriers, with their bleak news, propensity for thievery, and bad gifts.

22 Many tarot scholars dispute this today.

Plath's leaf-frost symbolizes change in seasons. The formerly innocent Fool is born "immaculate," only to become hardened into The Magician by the cold world. The Magician stands erect, looking straight ahead, explaining an earlier draft of this poem's idea of standing straight. The man gestures toward manna from heaven, a sweet dew like Plath's frost.

Emotion is represented by the tarot's Cups suit, sometimes called "cauldrons." Here, Plath's cauldron talks and crackles alone with abandonment.

The "nine black Alps" refers to the nine cards of the major arcana featuring the symbolic Rosicrucian mountaintops in the Rider-Waite tarot deck scenery: The Fool, The Lovers, The Hermit, Death, The Tower, Temperance, The Star, Moon, and Judgment. Looking at the storyline these nine cards present in their numeric order, it is Plath's own tale as she might have cast it: innocence, union with a lover, knowledge of the truth, the end of a past life, complete destruction of her relationship, evaluating and recreating her life, dreaming, mysticism and the inner world, and redemption.

In Hermeticism, The Magician card represents the second step of man's journey. After The Fool begins his self-actualization, The Magician begins his initiation. He is on a quest to obtain the knowledge and art of making perfect that which nature left imperfect, or man degraded by the misuse of his free will. This poem is about the latter. The Magician applies his power to benefit himself first, and then his fellow men; he recognizes man's first duty to the self, empowering him to do greater work for all. The proceeding alchemical mirror will also reflect this idea.

Second Mirror: Alchemy

Alchemists consider The Magician to be mythology's Hermes, the god who delivers the secrets of alchemy to man. Hermes' gestures, "as above, so below," indicates the design of heaven upon earth. Hermes is both light and dark, deceitful and ambiguous, and therefore a trickster. He begins his work as an alchemist does, separating the elements and experiencing each on all levels, so he might truly know them.

A snail's word can only be slime. This slime is the *litharge* of alchemy, leftover waste from a metallic operation. Plath's plate now is read as a plate in a laboratory.

In alchemy, the basest man is like elemental lead—the barbarous Magician. The alchemical initiate's first goal is to leave behind barbarity and walk toward the light. In other words, base man, the con artist and trickster of "The Couriers," is lost or fallen. To achieve transcendence, he must return to his first, perfect, true nature.

Plath's acetic acid is the alchemical element that gives vinegar its sour taste and pungent smell. Vinegar was sometimes mixed with mineral acids by fraudulent dealers (the trickster in action again), an effort to make the vinegar appear stronger. Acetic acid is the second stage of alchemy, when fermentation takes place. Plath wrote of having to know the difference between alcoholic and acetic acid fermentation for chemistry classes at Smith College (*UJ*, 33).

In alchemy, Plath's "sealed" means "hermetically sealed," the airtight closing of a vessel. In ceremonial magic, this may be a seal, or *sigil*: a design, initial, or device traced in the air during invocations. Medieval alchemists and magicians believed each spirit had a corresponding seal or hand movement as a signature.

Acetic acid is corrosive, and the "sealed tin" also refers to the Old Testament *Book of Amos*, Chapter 7, verses 7-8:

Now the Lord was standing by a wall of tin and tin was in His hand.
YHWY said to me, "What do you see, Amos?" and I said, "Tin."
And the Lord said, "I am going to put tin within my people Israel.
I shall never again forgive them."

In the context of this scripture, "tin" represents a hardening. Tin is one of the seven metals of the alchemists, associated with the operation of Dissolution, an important metaphor for Plath's marriage. Tin is the flimsiest of metals, not to be relied upon. In Hebrew, its name is a homonym with the word *grief*.[23] Plath acknowledges these feelings over her husband. She wants to rise above them, to a higher spiritual place, and refuses to accept them.

In alchemy, tin is associated with the planet Jupiter, and matched with the tarot's Magician. Jupiter shares its symbol with that for the material form of tin.

A handwritten draft of "The Couriers" reveals Plath tried out ideas of a vinegar tin, and wine. These are important, as alchemists seek the "Elixir of Life," a cure-all made from gold. Renaissance alchemists claimed that to make potable gold, vinegar and tin ash were required in the mix (Cavendish, 189-95).

Finally, "Tin" is the Hebrew name for Raphael, an angel in human disguise in the *Book of Tobit*. He behaves like The Magician with his trickery and fast-talk.[24] Other fast-talking angels and gods are seen in the next mirror.

Third Mirror: Mythology

Hermes, messenger of the gods and figurehead of Hermeticism, was said to have one day come upon an empty shell on the beach, supporting the mythological interpretation of Plath's snail reference. From the shell, Hermes fashioned a small harp-like instrument, the lyre. The lyre is a nice echo of the word "liar," suggesting the lies in Plath's sixth line of "The Couriers." In the right hands, the instrument produced the most beautiful music ever heard. Hermes gave this instrument to the sun god, Apollo: Plath's sun imagery. Later, Apollo presented the lyre to his son, Orpheus. Upon hearing Orpheus play, Pluto, the Lord of the Underworld, wept tears of iron, matching Plath's disturbance of mirrors and the grey, shattered sea of the sixth stanza. Ultimately, Orpheus was killed by the Maenads: mad, uncontrollable women who tore men apart. After Orpheus' death, Zeus sent an eagle to retrieve the lyre, and placed both the eagle and the lyre permanently in the sky.

The fourth stanza's frost and cauldron parallel the Germanic pagan tale of Buri. Buri, the *first* Norse god (correlating with card number one of the tarot), was born when his mother licked the salted frost from Ymir, the great creator ("immaculate"). Ymir himself was said to have sprung from a seething cauldron out of which flowed twelve streams into the great void.[25] An early draft of this poem coupled a reference to the Alps with the idea of a "tremor"; a possible reference to Ymir's volcanic appearance and the nervous flinch of a liar.

---

23 [Translation from the Net Bible, www.netbible.com] tn The Hebrew word אֲנָךְ,('anakh, "tin") occurs only in this passage (twice in this Bible verse and twice in the following Bible verse). The tin wall of the vision, if it symbolizes Israel, may suggest weakness and vulnerability to judgment. The term אֲנָךְ,in v. 8b may be a homonym meaning "grief" (this term is attested in post-biblical Hebrew). In this case, there is wordplay, as אֲנָךְ,("tin") of the vision suggests the אֲנָךְ,("grief") that judgment will bring upon the land. For more on this, see *The Journal of Hebrew Scriptures*, "The Structure and Meaning in the Third Vision of Amos (7:7-17)" by Martha Campos, http://www.jhsonline.org/Articles/article_150.pdf

24 See the *Fixed Stars Govern A Life* interpretation of Plath's "Elm" for more about tin.

25 This tale shows up again in the poem for The Emperor card, "The Applicant."

Plath may also have enjoyed connecting the Alps to her own heritage, suggesting the dark Norse mythologies full of wizards, sorcerers and tricksters from Germany, Austria, and their Alps. Plath was a lover of all mythology, and also had toured the Tyrolean Alps region by train in April 1956.

Hungarian myth embraces a Tree of Life, as does the Qabalah. Roma folklore tells that the sky was thought to be a big tent, full of holes, which were the stars. Plath used this same image in her poem, "Insomniac."

Finally, mythology from across the world uses the mirror as a symbol of death and a trapped soul. Plath wants to rise above it all and to choose Love as her element, her eternal, never-dying season. This matches the lemniscate symbol of infinity over The Magician's head. The earlier draft of this poem masculinized Love (because The Magician is male), proclaiming the season a man.

Fourth Mirror: History and the World

Plath's "nine black Alps" are a fine fit for the mountainous province of Montenegro, meaning "Black Mountain," in the Gypsy homeland of Hungary or occupied by Austria-Hungary at different times. Aluminum ("tin") makes up most of Montenegro's industrial production. Alfred, Lord Tennyson, celebrated Montenegro with his poem "Black Mountain."

The flower edelweiss grows in Montenegro's black Alps. Edelweiss is also Austria's national flower, the country of Aurelia Plath's heritage.[26] The outside petals of edelweiss are pure white; its center is a ring with a sun-shape inside. It grows in cold, high altitudes and its name means "noble purity," like Plath's immaculate leafy frost. Edelweiss was supposed to cure all forms of ailments, ward off evil, and be the ultimate love charm, the alchemist's elixir. Of course, a gypsy-like charm arouses suspicion and distrust; Plath suggests rejection. Dozens of men were said to perish each season attempting to collect the flower from hard-to-access ledges and crags to win the hearts of their lady friends. It is a dangerous season for love.

The influence of Hungary was all around Plath and Hughes, beyond the lore of her tarot book. In 1956, Hungary had risen up in revolution and Soviet troops had overrun the country. This was the leading news story throughout that winter; *Time* magazine had made the Hungarian freedom fighter its Man of the Year. Hughes and his sister Olwyn had extensive interest in Hungarian poetry. In a letter dated November 8, 1956, Hughes was asked to join the guerillas and become a Hungarian freedom fighter. Plath was shocked by this invitation, which Hughes did not accept.

The *Magyars*, echoing the word *Magi*, are ethnic Hungarians. Plath wrote of reading Magyar folk tales in the university library in 1956.[27] The earliest Magyars practiced shamanistic forms of worship, a subject in which Hughes had great interest. Like both Jewish and Roma minorities in Hungary, since the Middle Ages shamans have been viewed as nomads and travelers. The Magyars were led by poet-healers and ritual singers who passed myth and legend, incantations, curses, and blessings down through generations. Occultist Alan Moore claims magic was first called "The Art." It was considered a science of manipulation using symbols to change consciousness, making an artist or writer the closest thing to a modern-day shaman (TTBOOK).

The practice of climbing the toroo tree is a shaman ritual to ecstasy. By ascending alone up a representation of the Tree of Life, the shaman, "All to itself on the top of each," leaves this world and enters the world of spirit. The toroo tree has nine steps, "nine black Alps." As the shaman climbs

---

26 In an unpublished excerpt of a letter dated October 28, 1960, Sylvia Plath asked her mother, "What time do the Alpine flowers bloom?" with regard to planning a trip to Innsbruck, Austria.

27 In an unpublished excerpt of a letter to her mother, Sylvia Plath wrote of reading Magyar folk tales and Siberian fairy tales on May 10, 1956. The letter may be found in the Sylvia Plath Archives of the Lilly Library at Indiana University-Bloomington.

higher and higher, he sings. Eurasian shamans speak of passing nine landmarks (*olohs*) during a journey. One of the most important tools of a shaman is the *toil*, a metallic, circular mirror. It is placed over the chest to deflect spirit attack: another example of "The Couriers'" mirror disturbance.

Lake Balaton, Central Europe's largest freshwater lake at the base of the Black Forest Alps, is also known as "the Hungarian Sea." Lake Balaton is known to reflect sunlight to neighboring vineyards like a mirror. An earlier draft of this poem had an additional line claiming that the sea mimicked; this is Plath's awareness of the smoke-and-mirrors trick, and the mystic's need to recognize that what is wrong outside is also wrong within. Plath would surmount her troubles with love. Or so she believed.

Perhaps the most famous magician of all time was Harry Houdini, born Erich Weiss, almost an anagram for *Edelweiss*. Houdini was born in Hungary and raised as a Jew in Wisconsin. Houdini spent a great deal of his adult career battling spiritualists and mediums to expose them as frauds.[28] The master showman Houdini was an escape artist of great notoriety, known especially for being sealed in a tin, an act called "The Milk Can Escape." Houdini believed that psychics, spiritualists, and mediums preyed on grief. He toured the world, educating the masses about fakery and encouraging them not to believe, as Plath's poem advises.

In 1904, in one of the greatest publicity stunts ever, Houdini had London's *The Daily Mirror*[29] newspaper commission a special set of handcuffs from which he would escape. Houdini made a huge production of the effort, with bloody knees and teary red eyes in over an hour's struggle before the more than four thousand watching in London's Hippodrome Theatre. In his famous escape, Houdini adjourned alone to his secret chamber to remove the custom-designed manacles with nine circular tumblers.

The Daily Mirror was an untrustworthy tabloid known for its lies and famous grief column. The paper's masthead included a ring with the three-letter abbreviation of the day of the week—the SUN-day paper being the most popular edition. The only known capture of Houdini's voice is a crackling recording made on wax cylinders in 1914, Plath's eighth line.

The celebrated author of the *Sherlock Holmes* stories, Sir Arthur Conan Doyle, had been friends with Houdini. Doyle believed Houdini to be a spiritualist of great power. Houdini broke off their friendship, declaring Doyle was going senile, suggesting the eighth and ninth lines of "The Couriers." Doyle wrote of the relationship in his 1931 book, *The Edge of the Unknown*.[30]

Houdini, meanwhile, published a famous debunking book, *A Magician Among Spirits* (1924), and seven other books using ghost writers such as author, H.P. Lovecraft. Lovecraft was said to have realized that Houdini's adventures for the book *Imprisoned with the Pharaohs* were largely fictional, not accepting them as genuine, to use Plath's language in "The Couriers."

Harry Houdini died on Halloween night, 1926, of peritonitis from a ruptured appendix, like acid bursting from a tin. He had promised his wife that if there was life on the other side, he would say to her, "Rosabelle, believe." Houdini's wife held séances for ten years after her husband's death; it is a topic of dispute as to whether or not she reached him.

Slightly less famous than Houdini, but the most important Hungarian in the 20th century and one of the most important men of modern times, was Nikola Tesla, developer of the alternating current electrical system, among other great inventions. A Serbian, his people were gypsies on the

---

28 In 1953, the year of Plath's first suicide attempt, a movie was made of Houdini's life starring the famous Hollywood actors Tony Curtis and Janet Leigh. In February 1960, Ted Hughes' story, "The Rain Horse" was published alongside friend Robert Graves' magician story, "You Win, Houdini!" in the *London Magazine*.

29 See *Fixed Stars Govern a Life*'s interpretation of Plath's poem, "The Courage of Shutting-Up" for more about *The Daily Mirror*.

30 See *Fixed Stars Govern a Life*'s interpretation of Plath's poem, "The Detective" for more about Sir Arthur Conan Doyle.

move (Carlson, 13).Tesla truly embodied The Magician card with the real-life magic he created: the alternating current is a fine match to The Magician's ambiguous and variable nature. Tesla was a master showman and performer when demonstrating his inventions to the public, and called "a magician of the first order," as well as "a prophet" (Carlson, 152-153); the famous Tesla induction motor looked like "a ring of gold with the sun in it," and the Tesla Coil resonant transformer looked like "The Couriers'" crackling cauldron. The idea came to him in a vision as he recited a poem from Goethe's *Faust*. Additionally, the coil's applications could also be used for sound, likening it to words from a snail.

Plath would certainly have had a soft spot for Tesla. He was handsome, brilliant, fragile in his youth, suffered from depression and a nervous breakdown, and treated himself with shock therapy (Carlson, 217). Eccentric and celibate ("immaculate"), many considered Tesla to be mad. He was taken advantage of and publicly attacked, suffering the lies and grief of the poem's sixth line. His greatest adversary was Thomas Edison, who fought for his direct-current electrical system against Tesla's alternating current. The modern battery, which is essentially Plath's acetic acid once again sealed in a tin package, operates on a direct-current system. Many inventors made their names from inventions and patents that Tesla first conceived but had not gotten credit for. One of these was Marconi, who won the 1909 Nobel Prize in Physics for the radio. If one goes by the "The Couriers," it seems that Plath believed Marconi should not have accepted the award.

Tesla's closest friends were artists and poets, his Serbian Orthodox background shared a great deal with Qabalah, and he became fascinated by Hinduism (Carlson, 10, 31). Tesla's ideas came to him in shamanic dreams and flashes of insight, with visions of perfectly formed machines in detail and blinding light. Tesla spent a good deal of his time attempting communication with life on other planets, and wrote, "I base my faith on the feeble planetary electrical *disturbances*[31] which I discovered in the summer of 1899, and which, according to my investigations, could not have originated from the sun, the moon, or Venus." Tesla used the word *disturbances* often when explaining electricity (Carlson, 266, 338). Tesla attempted sending signals with mirrors, and believed Earth's atmosphere was his chief obstacle to contacting Mars. Tesla wrote that "locating our observatories one mite above sea level" significantly reduced his ability for communication (New York Times). Plath's metaphorical sea shatters once again.

"The invention of the wheel was perhaps rather obvious; but the invention of an invisible wheel, made of nothing but a magnetic field, was far from obvious, and that is what we owe to Nikola Tesla."

—Reginald Kapp (1956)

Tesla had an obsessive love for animals, and took injured birds into his room to care for them. A pacifist like Plath and also an altruist, Tesla wanted all peoples of the earth to benefit from his gift of electrical power, living from principles of peace and love that ends "The Couriers." Greed had other ideas: Tesla's electrical generator, Wardenclyffe Tower, was quashed by investor J.P. Morgan, because it could not be metered and make a profit.

Nikola Tesla died alone and penniless in room 3327 at The New Yorker Hotel, close to Penn Station, Macy's, and the parts of New York City that Plath would have known from her *Mademoiselle* Summer internship. The New Yorker Hotel's Art Deco style is designed in such a way as to have nine peaks in its set-back, black brick pyramid-style tower that once again feels like the tenth line of "The Couriers."

---

31 Italics mine.

Fifth Mirror: Astrology and Astronomy

*"The brightest he, but sign to mortal man
Of evil augury."*

-Homer, on the star called Sirius

The brightest star in the sky is Sirius, also known as the Dog-Star. It has been given the traits of being "Restless, Impetuous and Blazing," and known for marked scintillation, light and color changes. This also sounds like The Magician of the tarot. Chinese astrologers believed that when Sirius, which they called "the Heavenly Wolf," was unusually bright, it portended attack from thieves. Egyptians and Hebrews also claimed it devilish and akin to a "he goat" (Allen, 117-131)

Lyra is the constellation for Hermes, The Magician. Its brightest star was also called Lyra by Ptolemy. A lyre is a harp created by Hermes in myth. However, the Sumerians and Babylonians, and later the Arabs, saw the constellation of Lyra not as the musical instrument of mythology, but as a vulture. Early writings claim the constellation is a harp being carried by a vulture, although the Greeks considered it to be an eagle. Instead of being the Harp star, Lyra is therefore sometimes called "The Vulture Star," a character of ill repute.

The Lyra constellation contains the Ring Nebula, which holds a central condensation of light, like a star, in its center. It is another mirror of Plath's sixth line; The idea of lies in the seventh line is now a play on the word *lyre*. Lyra is known for its double stars, and even "the Double Double," a quadruple star. Also in the Lyra constellation, Beta Lyrae, is a celebrated variable star (changing in degrees of luminosity). Both the doubling and the variability lend support to the theme of lies in "The Couriers" poem.

Sixth Mirror: Humanities and the Arts

In her November 1, 1958, journal entry, Plath noted seeing Ingmar Bergman's film, *The Magician*, which she called "fine, magnificently entertaining." In this film, a 19th-century traveling gypsy mesmerist and peddler of potions has his magic put to the test (Criterion). The scientific-minded disbelievers try to expose the gypsies as charlatans, but the magician and his crew prove too clever for them. A man is driven mad, seeing the "disturbance in mirrors" of a face not his own. The mirror is eventually shattered. In 1959, this movie was given the "Best Film" prize at the British Academy Awards, the "Best Foreign Film" prize at the New York Film Critics Awards, and two prizes at the Venice Film Festival. Critic Pauline Kael wrote that the theme of the film is one of "magic versus rationalism or, if one prefers, faith versus skepticism, or art versus science, or illusion versus reality" (Bergman).

In literature, Sylvia Plath and Ted Hughes learned from the best. When William Shakespeare wrote *As You Like It*, his character Jaques delivers the famous speech that begins, "All the world's a stage."[32] Starting with the twenty-first tarot card, the World, Shakespeare circles back through the Major Arcana to card #0, The Fool, as an infant, and then moves into The Magician card with these lines: "And then the whining school-boy, with his satchel / And shining morning face, creeping like

---

32 The major arcana runs through lines 143-170 in *As You Like It*, Act II, Scene VII, ending with The Tower card for the words "sans everything." It resumes with a change of speaker, Duke Senior, covering The Star card in lines 171-174; Adam, for The Moon card, in lines 175-176; Duke Senior for The Sun card, lines 177-179, Amiens (the song) for Judgement, lines 180-196; and Duke Senior returning to The World card for lines 197-207. See my essay in Plath Profiles 5, "As *We* Like It: *Ariel's* Forewords: Plath, and Hughes Pay a Mystic Debt to the Bard" for more.

snail / Unwillingly to school." Shakespeare's inspiration for The Magician appears to be the source of Plath's snail image for "The Couriers."

Perhaps one of the most famous gypsies in literature is *Wuthering Heights'* dark, brooding, passionate Heathcliff, to whom Hughes was compared in both looks and character. In a 1956 letter, Plath compared her relationship to a "happy Heathcliff and Cathy."[33] Plath fondly mentioned the book and movie often in her journals and letters, and she has a 1961 poem by the same name. In Emily Brontë's novel, many of Plath's "Couriers" images are present. *Wuthering Heights* opens with the narrator saying, "I shrunk icily into myself, like a snail," the area is "full of snail-shells and pebbles," and Heathcliff jokes about a lame horse being reared on "snails and sour milk."

The question of paternity, character, and ownership is throughout *Wuthering Heights*. Memorable lines are "They are not mine," and "my father's character is not mine." It also seems that accepting invitations gets one into trouble at Wuthering Heights, and there are three instances where one is forced to accept an invitation, reminiscent of the second lines of Plath's first two couplets.

Heathcliff is said to be "sealed in an expression of unspeakable sadness," and his vinegar-sour personality is congruent with Plath's symbol of acetic acid. In another scene, the servant Joseph is called "Vinegar-faced," suggesting acetic acid, a main component of vinegar. In Chapter XXI, Heathcliff pronounces, "Don't you think Hindley would be proud of his son, if he could see him? almost as proud as I am of mine. But there's this difference; one is gold put to use of paving-stones, and the other is tin polished to ape a service of silver. *Mine* has nothing valuable about it." This quote has Plath's denial of ownership in the second line, as well as her tin and the gold of the third and fifth lines.

Heathcliff's great love, Catherine, has long golden ringlets and he watches the sun on her hair. In another scene, his wife, Isabella, takes off her gold ring and throws it on the floor. The book contains many instances of message carriers (couriers) and a continual waiting for messages.

The story of *Wuthering Heights* is full of lies and grief, with lines like "Your bliss lies," "She lies with a sweet smile," and "now you believe the lies your father tells." In the settings, the English country air is often frosty, and the coals in the fire crackle like Plath's cauldron.

The nine principle characters in *Wuthering Heights* are all alone in their way, tormented and depressed like Plath's fifth couplet states. Additionally, *Wuthering Heights* is in the hilly Yorkshire moors, with mountainous stony black "Alps," perhaps not comparable to the Austrian Alps, but mountains all the same. There is talk of "the serious disturbance of Catherine" as well as other disturbances. Catherine stares at her reflection in a mirror, terrified of faces in mirrors not her own. Images of the sea are also in *Wuthering Heights*, where "the whole hill-back was one billowy, white ocean," and in Catherine, "the sea could be as readily contained in that horse-trough as her whole affection be monopolised by him."

In one memorable scene, Heathcliff stands outside a window, watching Catherine inside the Linton's home. He later tells Nelly, "I intended shattering their great glass panes to a million fragments," sounding like Plath's last full couplet of "The Couriers."

Finally, in *Wuthering Heights* it is a "season of deliverance," and a season of "cold reflection," like Plath's season and mirror images. Heathcliff the gypsy is also said to be an "unseasonable visitor."

It should be noted that in 1960, an art film by director Pierre Kast called *The Season of Love* was released. It is the story of a playboy novelist named Sylvain, who meets his true love Genevieve.

<hr>

33 An unpublished excerpt of a letter dated September 2, 1956 from Sylvia Plath to Aurelia Plath. The letter may be found in the Sylvia Plath archives at the Lilly Library, Indiana University -Bloomington.

They decide they must move to the country, where he can settle down with her with less temptation from other women and write. The marriage crumbles. This irony could not have been lost on Plath, who loved artistic foreign films and saw as many as possible.

"The Couriers" therefore faces this darker, base side of man and the higher desire for self-mastery. Both the poem and The Magician card are in accordance with the second Emerald Tablet scripture: "What is above is like what is below, and what is below, like that which is above. To make the miracle of the one thing."

While Plath saw lies in her trickster husband's behavior, she also knew it was a reflection, a mirror of her inner self, as *Wuthering Heights'* Catherine exclaimed, "I *am* Heathcliff!" Sylvia Plath was not yet whole and united with the alchemists' *Infinite Continuum*: the sea had shattered its grey "one." Finally, this poem is a fine tribute to Hungary, redeeming the idea of the gypsy/magician, as we can identify and learn from him, good and bad, on our separate journeys toward spiritual growth.

18

Chapter Three: Human Rights and Folkloristics
Card #2   The High Priestess   Corresponding Poem: "The Rabbit Catcher"

When Plath wrote "The Rabbit Catcher," she was newly aware of the beginnings of her husband's affair. Hughes has written that on a day trip to the seaside, Plath became upset by rabbit traps and began ripping them out of the ground. Plath's marriage felt like a trap she could not escape, and this remains the popular interpretation.

First Mirror: The Tarot/Qabalah

The High Priestess tarot card represents an independent, intuitive, silent, and secretive woman. She holds the sixth sense and embodies female mystery. Her throne stands for equilibrium and sexual restraint. The pillars on this card are said to symbolize labial lips, concealing the "Holy of Holies," a qabalistic metaphor for the womb. They are also the deep pegs of which Plath writes.

In a man's tarot card reading, the High Priestess can symbolize the sometimes frightening female aspects of himself. Interestingly, "The Rabbit Catcher" was left out by Hughes when he edited the first-published edition of *Ariel*.

The High Priestess is Ancient Egypt's Isis, a goddess Hughes identified with Plath, and to whom Plath felt kin. Isis is seductive, mysterious and beautiful, but not young. Many times she represents a spinster or one who is sterile. Isis manages on her own, by her own power. She complements Plath's theme of yearning for independence and escape from constriction in "The Rabbit Catcher."

The Golden Dawn writes that the Hebrew letter for the High Priestess card, *Gimel*, is the camel, the ship of the desert that crosses vast distances with no water available or required. The two first stanzas of this poem take the reader to both sea and the gorse flower's desert.

Plath's fifth stanza "Ringing" calls to mind the Torah's RING, meaning, "the eye of God."[34] The High Priestess holds the china-white Torah upon her lap. *Tarot* is a derivation of both *Torah* and *Rota*, the root of the word 'rotate,' and a reference to the ring, or circle, of life.

In The High Priestess' picture, the bottom of her gown appears to turn into water. The palms and pomegranates on her veil represent the oppositions of male and female. In a literal interpretation, they mirror Plath opposing rabbit traps, an event of which Hughes wrote. The palm-pomegranate design also represents the equal truths of Christianity, represented by the palm, and the ancient mysteries, represented by the pomegranates. In medieval times, Isis was often renamed the Virgin Mary to unite pagans and Christians. Pomegranates, full of seeds, are symbols of fertility, as are rabbits. Note the rabbit-like ears of The High Priestess' headpiece.

Images of snares and effacement suggest a female trap and female reproductive organs, followed by contractions of childbirth. However, this poem and card correlation suggests a woman closing up her sexuality. The High Priestess has no need of men, and when this card is laid down in reverse, she despises them. Plath's "absence of shrieks" is the consequent lack of a child from sexual restraint.[35] Plath's shutting zeros image visually describes the pomegranates behind the priestess, the disc of her crown, and the rings of the fifth and last stanza.

34 For more on the Torah's RING, see *Fixed Stars Govern a Life*'s interpretation of the Plath poem, "The Couriers."
35 This poem is not likely to be a statement about Assia Wevill's pregnancy by Hughes, Wevill's lack of children, or her later abortion. "The Rabbit Catcher" was written May 21, 1962, in the first days of Hughes' and Wevill's affair.

The moon orbits on a twenty-eight day cycle like the female menses. The crescent moon is set at The Priestess' foot like a trap; thus, a woman is trapped in and by her own sexuality. It is an explanation for Plath's connection to the moon as a frequent symbol, and our association with Plath as a literary feminist.

Earlier drafts of "The Rabbit Catcher" are filled with lines appropriate to The High Priestess, including alchemical words and terms, and descriptions of The High Priestess' quiet and cool temperament.[36]

Returning to Enochian chess, The High Priestess corresponds with the knight. As the knight pieces move in their L-pattern, they spread like Plath's oil. White pieces taken and set aside might be compared to the dead. In the poem's second stanza, a player has suffered the black spiked rook's power and unction. Chess is a game of beauty and efficiency, yet Plath's second stanza explains that losing feels torturous.

The third stanza identifies the "one place to get to": checkmate. Paths to the opponent's king diminish and "efface themselves" as pieces are taken. The opponent then begins Plath's idea of closing in on the nothing of an emptying board. Reflecting the fourth stanza, the pieces in chess are first set down close to each other. It is a quiet game, with "shrieks" generally absent. When a player takes a piece from the other, they may be said to make "a hole," leaving the space vacant. The fifth stanza illustrates that playing chess is a way to keep busy, full of intention. Plath plays the black side, positioning her pieces in a captor's ring around the white. Most probably Hughes, the opponent, believes he has the upper hand and is excited to beat Plath's narrator. He views each taken piece as a little death, awaiting his next move. The expression "little death" is English for *la petite mort*, the French metaphor for female orgasm, and the ideas of sweethearts and excitement take the poem back to female sexual imagery and conquest.

In the last stanza, the lines on the chess board look like wires strung tight.[37] The chess pieces resemble the pegs of the last stanza, and the deep, historical roots of the game. Finally, the game of chess requires intelligence, and according to Benjamin Franklin in "The Morals of Chess," requires The High Priestess' skills of foresight, circumspection, and caution, as seen in third and fourth lines of Plath's last stanza.

Second Mirror: Alchemy

Water, associated with The High Priestess and represented by her flowing robes, is one of the four elements of alchemy, representing cleansing and purification. Water is associated with the second operation in alchemical transformation, Dissolution. It is represented by the metal tin, as seen in "The Couriers," the preceding *Ariel* poem. Dissolution is the process of dissolving a solid in liquid, or the reduction of dry matter in water. It is also represented by the astrological sign for the constellation of Cancer.

"The Rabbit Catcher" is full of alchemical elements and laboratory terms. Air, wind, and force are considered to be one and the same in view of the elements. Alchemically, Plath's first stanza is a reaction from an inhalation experiment, actual or metaphorical, or even a small explosion. Alchemists often refer to the mercurial vapor during the process of *sublimation* as "wind." The word "blown" is also key as the alchemist must blow the bellows to keep ("force") the fire going, or the magnum opus will be ruined. Likewise, hair is considered to be an alchemical code word (Villanova).

---

36 Copyright law forbids unpublished drafts to be quoted.

37 Hughes used this language to describe Plath in April of 1958 (Feinstein, 82-83).

Plath's first stanza image of tearing off her voice refers to the abandonment of the ego, which speaks for her. In practical alchemy, the spreading oil is the separation of the oily Sulfur element from mineral or vegetable form. In Jungian alchemy, it is the mystical quest of separation of the spirit from body. Yet, Plath is also "unreeling" in this light containing the lives of the dead; she is coming apart as a weaker, base self and facing the alchemists' infinite continuum, the place of universal oneness represented by the sea. "Unreeling" is an image similar to the spiritual "unpeel"-ing seen later in the poem "Ariel," and the "unloose" in her poem "Purdah." It is metaphor for loosening and shedding layers of self, the "old whore petticoats" of her poem "Fever 103°", the old whore being another face of Isis, High Priestess.

Throughout "The Rabbit Catcher," Plath wrestles with her suppression of the physical self, and maybe also the urge to speak of alchemical or mystical secrets. Plath's lines about her long hair, a traditional symbol of femininity, gagging her mouth and tearing off her voice in the first stanza reveal these frustrations. She alludes to an inability to behave as the quiet and powerful High Priestess. As one of the first literary feminists, Plath wrote as a victim of her time, and she felt blinded by the light of the lives of the dead feminists before her.

Plath's "place of force" also well fits Isaac Newton's 1680 translation of The Emerald Tablet (Newton, lines 7, 10):

> "Its force or power is entire if it be converted into earth," and "Its force is above all force for it vanquishes every subtile [sic] thing & penetrates every solid thing."

Newton's preceding lines speak of the sun, the moon, the wind and the earth, images all very present in "The Rabbit Catcher." The sun becomes a hot hole in the day's sky; and the moon is white china.

In alchemy, the single destination starting Plath's third stanza is birthing the Great Work, the philosopher's stone. As it cooks in the laboratory, actual or metaphoric, it is both "simmering" and "perfumed."

In addition to the word "unction" meaning "to soothe or comfort," unction is the act of anointing,

"I had discovered, early in my researches, that their doctrine was no mere chemical fantasy, but a philosophy they applied to the world, to the elements, and to man himself."

— William Butler Yeats,
Rosa Alchemia

especially in medicine, religion, and alchemy. Therefore, Plath's "yellow candle-flowers" may also be the blossoms of tincture over a flame. Alchemy's Yellow Phase is a term used by Alexandrian alchemists to describe changes during the fermentation operation. Flowers, seen in the first *Ariel* poem, "Morning Song," designate the powdery substances said to bloom during the alchemical process of sublimation. Ultimately, Plath's "The Rabbit Catcher" lines about efficiency, beauty, simmering, and perfume are apt to both flowers and to the High Priestess' temperament. The Druids knew the gorse plant as a "light seekers." More on gorse can be found in the History and the World mirror of this poem.

Looking at the Gorse plant through alchemy's view of personification (alchemists believe that spirit is in all things), alchemists and Druids alike observed the seeds flinging off parent plants on bright warm days, distancing themselves as far as possible to start new colonies in the sun. The Druids believed this was a spiritual message to secure independence when one feels he or she is being overshadowed by others. The gorse, an aspect of mother goddess energy (Isis), reminds us to independently seek the higher road, the path of light. Pictured on this tarot card are Plath's yellow candle-like flowers, resembling gorse. It is a favorite herb of alchemists, best known for its associations with the sun.

Plath's glass and light of the fourth stanza is the laboratory equipment again, "glass" being the common name for the alchemical vessel, test tubes, and beakers. In the fifth stanza there is more about laboratory work and equipment. Alchemists sometimes called the vessel a "glass prison" or "house of glass," reinforcing the poem's trap of snares.

The still in this poem, an apparatus used for distillation, is busy; it is important that Plath put those two words together in her fifth stanza. It is contradictory for a person to be both still and busy, but a still, as a noun, can certainly be busy.

The idea of connection and being a part of the infinite continuum is reflected in the last stanza's mention of relationship and tight wires. The deeply-rooted pegs refer to the practice of alchemy itself. Persecuted for hundreds of years, the practice of alchemy has almost always existed and will continue; it cannot be uprooted. Alchemists believe in what Carl Jung would come to call the collective unconscious, so the "mind like a ring" is the joining of all alchemical minds, united as one, through spirit and time.

The constriction killing the narrator mirrors death of the old form, necessary for renewal or regeneration. Known as the "Black Phase," it is a time when all impurities burn and peel away. From the psychological perspective of Jungian Alchemy, this phase is emotionally painful.

The Emerald Tablet teaches, "And as all things were made from the contemplation of one, so all things were born from one by adaptation" (Sacred, 12th C.). As one creates by contemplation and meditation, these things must then "birth" what they desire by a similar process. It is a worldly adaptation of God's process and a fine echo of The High Priestess' contemplative wisdom. These ideas are shared by many ancient and primitive cultures and throughout Hermeticism. The African Yoruba religion, mentioned shortly, hold that human thought has power to interact with all other living things and achieve transcendence. Thoughts are "pegs too deep to uproot."

Third Mirror: Mythology

In Greek myth, The High Priestess is Persephone, who was abducted by Hades, lord of the underworld. From this event, she carries the secrets of the dead. She was held in Hades by the snare of River Styx, which encircled the realm.

Remembering the sea and desert of The High Priestess' Hebrew letter *Gimel*, "The Rabbit Catcher" nods to Jörmungandr, a female sea serpent from Norse mythology. The serpent devouring itself is called *Ouroboros*, seen on The Magician's belt. This serpent-goddess has hold of her own tail, physically becoming a ring. The serpent's body is half-black, symbolizing earth and darkness, and half-white, representing heaven and light and echoing The High Priestess' temple columns. This goddess used a snare of binding magic to render enemies physically or psychically helpless.

Plath's snares also draw from the Tibetan *Book of the Dead*, which Hughes studied during his time with Plath at the Yaddo artists' colony. In the book, a traveler must pass by boat through the Field of Reeds in the Elysian Fields. The traveler's greatest dangers are those who "lay snares, and who work the nets, and who are fishers," for "the god who hath gained the mastery over his heart" would capture him (Tour). This tale of head-over-heart and mystical knowledge is in the province of The High Priestess, and Plath may have been giving herself a cautionary tale too late.

Late Medieval and Renaissance tarot practitioners considered the Egyptian goddess Isis equivalent to Artemis, the huntress. The two share much governance over the living, but Isis is also goddess of rebirth and reincarnation, and protector of the dead. By the late Egyptian period, Isis became the most important and most powerful deity of the pantheon because of her magical skills. Isis' many names are throughout "The Rabbit Catcher": her *Star of the Sea* and *Moon Shining Over the Sea*, illuminate the first stanza in which Plath paints a perfect portrait of moonlight on the sea.

Plath's symbol of the sea in the third line is the sea behind Isis' veil in Solomon's temple. The High Priestess' tarot card pictures Solomon's temple as described in *1 Kings* 7:15-22 and *2 Chronicles* 3:14-17, with the B and J on the pillars, meaning *Boaz* and *Joachin*. Boaz and Joachin represent Severity and Mercy, the twin principles on which all creation rests, and a dominating theme of "The Rabbit Catcher."

The North American Algonquin Indians have many rabbit and hare myths, starring a trickster shape-shifter who is one of the creators of the world. The Great Hare is regarded as the supreme deity among tribes in eastern Canada. In folklore from cultures of Africa, the Cherokee Native American Indians, and in the last hundred and fifty years the Uncle Remus stories of the Southern United States, a trickster rabbit just like the tarot's preceding crafty Magician succeeds through wits over brawn. He provokes authority and breaks social proprieties as he pleases. Hughes wrote of the modern world's lack of appreciation of primitive literature and folklore, and of its great power over Plath's work. He cited the "explosive transformation Radin's African collection worked on the poetry of Sylvia Plath" (*WP*, 78).

To read Plath's "The Rabbit Catcher" with folklore in mind, her black and spiky gorse represents the briar patch. Now, the hair of the first stanza can be read as a homophone for the rabbit-cousin *hare*, found in Radin's tales.

In the famous "Br'er Rabbit and the Tar Baby" story, which has at least 267 versions across cultures worldwide (Espinosa, 31-37), the rabbit takes offense when a sticky doll made of tar will not speak to him. He punches it with the force of Plath's first line. He is trapped in the muck, "Unreeling in it, spreading like oil." A Buddhist myth shares a similar set-up, with the future Buddha encountering an ogre called "Sticky Hair" in a forest. Most of the stories share the rabbit pleading for his life to be thrown into the thorny thicket to die, like the torture Plath mentions in the quiet thicket in her fourth stanza.

Fourth Mirror: History and the World

Four days before Plath wrote "The Rabbit Catcher," news was broadcast that British soldiers had erected a ring of barbed wire along Hong Kong's border with the People's Republic of China. These are another kind of tight and separating wires of which Plath would have been aware, and the china cup symbol may now be read as white Hong Kong. The British government attempted to block four thousand-plus starving refugees trying to escape at any given time, and they imposed penalties on Hong Kong residents who aided a refugee's escape. These refugees running for their lives were treated no better than pesky rodents raiding a garden. Plath was a humanitarian and a pacifist who kept up on news and politics, and this event would likely have upset her.

In "The Rabbit Catcher," Plath equates tasting the gorse with evil. While gorse is toxic to most animals, rabbits are known to eat it. Traditional Jews do not eat hare as it is a non-kosher food, contributing to the meaning of Plath's "malignity." The hare was considered taboo to eat in ancient Britain, too; it was the royal animal the female warrior Boadicea took into battle. Author Robert Graves wrote that the Kerry peasants said that to eat hare meat was to eat one's grandmother

(Graves, 293). Emotionally, the evil Plath tasted was facing her husband's infidelity with Assia Wevill, who had once been her friend.

Gorse is a yellow, weedy, toxic flower with spikes of black thorns that grows in poor, desert soil. It has large, bright yellow candles of flowers, even in late winter. At the tune if of Plath's writing "The Rabbit Catcher," she had just begun to suspect an attraction between Assia Wevill and Hughes." Assia Wevill had grown up for part of her life in both desert countries of Palestine and Tel Aviv, Egypt, and Plath saw the gorse plant as an excellent metaphor for this toxic, beautiful woman.

Plath may have known that the American Cottontail rabbit, the most common in North America, is of the *Sylvilagus* species—a close anagram to her own first name. The rabbit is known for its enthusiastic breeding, and sexuality is throughout "The Rabbit Catcher." Poets, philosophers, astronomers and alchemists have all noted the hares' remarkable fertility and ability to breed in all seasons, "spreading like oil." The expression "Mad as a March hare" came from witnessing unreceptive females (a High Priestess trait) using their forelegs to repel overenthusiastic males during the long British breeding season (Gardner, 66).

"The rabbit died" has been a common western euphemism since the late 1920s, meaning a pregnancy test is positive. In May of 1959, Plath wrote of dreaming about catching a tiny white rabbit, and she contemplated if it meant something about menstruation, so she knew the expression (*UJ*, 486). With this in mind, the fourth stanza's hole in the heat of a yellowy day becomes a ring in yellow urine, held in a glass test tube to the light. The goal in the poem is pregnancy, in which the speaker feels intentionally busy even in her stillness, reflecting the first line of the fifth stanza. Closing that fifth stanza, her husband meanwhile enjoys the attempts at trying for pregnancy with her and others, anticipating the little deaths and excitement of his sweethearts.

The Uncle Remus stories, compiled and published in book form in 1881 by fiction writer and folklorist, Joel Chandler Harris, were American slave stories told in America's Deep South slave dialect. Much of "The Rabbit Catcher," echoes the painfully efficient idea of slavery seen in the second stanza, complete with its torture and a desire to escape over all else. Slaves in America and the West Indies were sometimes forced to chew dieffenbachia or "dumb cane," a toxic plant that swelled their tongues, irritated their vocal chords and rendered them speechless, resonating with Plath's mouth gagging and voice-torn images, the poisonous gorse, and the idea of escape (Living). The fourth stanza now becomes the hot day's work on the plantation, and the subservient, strained relationship of slave to master as it has been through history, best shown in last stanza of "The Rabbit Catcher."

Fifth Mirror: Astrology and Astronomy

Plath's first stanza's dead lights refer to the stars we see from earth, most already expired. The second brightest star, in line with the High Priestess' card number Two and her Hebrew letter *Gimel*, is Canopus, found in the constellation of Argo Navis, known as the Ship Argo. Ancient Egyptians said this ship bore Isis. Canopus, in the southern hemisphere, never rises above 37°N latitude. Set just above the horizon in the view from North America, it shows "only a few of its unimportant stars," wrote astronomer/astrologer Richard Hinckley Allen. And so, like the High Priestess, Canopus stays mostly hidden. Isis' ancient star was said to pierce into the heart of the wild man, rendering him speechless. In southern Egypt, Canopus was associated with water and navigation (Allen, 64-75), both themes within "The Rabbit Catcher."

The constellation Lepus, "The Hare," is located at the feet of Orion the hunter, and held sacred in Pelasgian Greece. It is said: "According to Ptolemy, [Lepus] gives a quick wit, timidity, circumspection, fecundity, and defiance," all traits of the rabbit in myth, and The High Priestess (Robson). Lepus is also said to magically guard against deceit and madness.

Orion's dog, Canis Major, chases this starry rabbit in relentless pursuit. The ancient Greek poet Aratus wrote of Lepus: "Close behind he rises and as he sets he eyes the setting hare." The dog zeroes in on the rabbit in pursuit of its unattainable goal of nothing, like Plath's zeroes again.

In the famous astrological text, the *Atlas Coelestis of John Flamsteed* (1729), the skies are charted with lines drawn like Plath's tightly-pulled wires. In Chinese astrology, four stars within Lepus form a ring as in Plath's imagery called *Junjing*, meaning, a well of drinking water. For the Chinese, Lepus also holds *Ping*, a privacy screen for a toilet that slides as shut as Plath's snare in the last stanza (Ridpath). Might Plath have been having a little fun with her last line, with the killing constriction applying also to constipation?

According to astrologers, the constellation of Cancer the Crab and The High Priestess are both believed to be ruled by the power of the moon. In astrology, Cancerians are very safety and security-minded, sometimes never leaving their home shells as self-imposed prisoners. Varied cultures claim a hare can be seen in the pattern of dark patches in the moon, similar to the western "man in the moon" myth.

There are also suggestions of The High Priestess' planet Jupiter in this poem. The paths of round snares are set as close as Jupiter's moons, and its great stormy red spot is like a hole in a hot day of revolution.

Sixth Mirror: Humanities and the Arts

Plath's husband, Ted Hughes, responded to "The Rabbit Catcher" decades later through a poem of his own by the same title. Hughes' poem recounts Plath's vehement reaction to her discovery of a hunter's rabbit traps. She sounds like The High Priestess herself, staring "with iron in [her] face," and Hughes describes her: "Germanic scowl, edged like a helmet / Would not translate itself," and, "I saw sacred / Ancient custom" (*BL*, 144-146). A larger theme of Hughes' poem is his inability to understand Plath. It is no coincidence that in Hughes' collection, *Birthday Letters*, this poem sits in chronological correspondence with The High Priestess card.[38]

Thomas Hardy's *Tess of the D'Urbervilles: A Pure Woman Faithfully Presented,* is also a story very much in line with "The Rabbit Catcher." Plath had this book in her personal library. Hardy used "petite mort" ("those little deaths!") to describe the pain the character Tess feels upon meeting with her own rapist: "She felt the *petite mort* at this unexpectedly gruesome information, and left the solitary man behind her" (Hardy, XLV). This behavior fits the tarot's High Priestess, who is pure and wants nothing to do with men. Like the relationship in Plath's poem, Tess knew her rapist. Things between them were tense as Plath's tight wires. In shame and secrecy, those quiet Plathian thickets, Tess gives birth to a sickly male child who dies within a few weeks, another kind of little death. Tess puts a white china marmalade jar full of flowers on his grave. Ultimately, Tess kills her rapist. In the end, after visiting Stonehenge, she is hanged for her crime, with its killing constriction.

---

38 Hughes designed *Birthday Letters* to begin at The Fool card poem, "Fulbright Scholars," run its course through the Major Arcana to "55 Eltisley," and repeat through "Portraits." Then, it reverses direction, a favorite Hughes game, to "Setebos," for The Hanged Man. From there, it moves forward again, with "A Short Film" for the Death card through to the end of "Dream Life" for The World. The Fool appears again with "Perfect Light." Sometimes, Hughes' poems contain more than one tarot card image, sometimes several images, but always appearing to be in an intentional qabalistic order.

A 1926 black-and-white silent film, *The Conjure Woman* (another High Priestess), was based on a short story collection about race by African-American writer Charles W. Chesnutt (1858 – 1932), an author heavily influenced by Uncle Remus. *The Conjure Woman* (1899) was a collection of short stories told in southern black dialect. Its front cover features three rectangular panels. The center panel is a caricature of an African-American man, and on either side are caricatures of identical white rabbits, continuing the rabbit theme (Chesnutt). Chesnutt wrote of complex issues focusing on racial identity, social place, and repression of those with African ancestry. In the book, *The Conjure Woman*, Uncle Julius, a freed slave, tells supernatural allegorical tales of haunting and transfigurations to a white couple from the North. His stories are coded with commentary on discrimination and slavery.

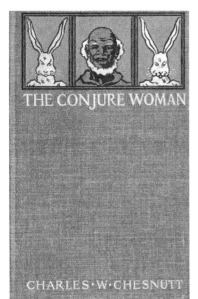

Cover of
The Conjure Woman
by Charles Chesnutt

Other Chesnutt books address issues such as a man who discovers his wife's racial background with repugnance. Again, it is Plath's deep pegs unable to be uprooted. The last stanza of "The Rabbit Catcher" eerily fits an American-style southern lynching.

In Plath's last years in the early 1960s, there was a revival of critical discussion and re-evaluation around Chesnutt's work, crediting him for breaking new ground in race-relations literature, use of African-American speech and folklore, and challenging the Jim Crow logic of the day (Chesnutt Digital). Plath also had a close African-American friend at Cambridge, Nathaniel LaMar. Given her pacifism, humanitarianism, and interest in politics, as well as interpretations of early poems such as "Hardcastle Crags" being in part about the Little Rock Nine,[39] it is not a stretch to believe that Plath cared for the plight of minorities.

The film, *The Conjure Woman*, was directed by Oscar Micheaux, known as the father of Afro-American cinema and the most prolific African-American filmmaker of the silent era. The first stanza of "The Rabbit Catcher," with the gagged mouth, the torn-off voice, and the blinding lights showing the dead alive and unreeling all paint a great picture of what were known as race movies of the silent era. *The Conjure Woman* movie has been lost to history, and perhaps Plath was referring to that too, as the end of the third and all of the fourth stanza might well portray a film burning up on a hot projector lens, effacing itself, each close-set frame shutting in on nothing. There is no sound of shrieking and the heat burns a hole through the film, leaving the vacancy of glass, light, and quiet.

Of the same era was author Louis Tracy (1863-1928), a prolific British novelist and journalist who grew up in Yorkshire, England, as did Hughes. Some of Tracy's novels went to the screen during the silent film era. Tracy had a penchant for writing about High Priestess-like subjects such as mesmerism, ghosts, mystery, and India. He gave his work titles that fit this tarot card, such as *The Strange Disappearance of Lady Delia* (1901), *The Wooing of Esther Gray* (1902), *A Matter of Initials* (1903),[40] *The Man with the Sixth Sense* (1927), *The Silent Barrier* (1909), *The House of Silence* (1911), *A Mysterious Disappearance* (1913), *Sylvia's Suitors* (1914), *Diana of the Moors* (1914), *Flower of the Gorse* (1915) and *His Unknown Wife* (1915) (Bookman, 22-28).

39 See my paper, "Sylvia Plath's Hidden Civil Rights Messages," addressing the Little Rock Nine meanings of "Hardcastle Crags," as well as other hidden civil rights messages in other works by Plath. The paper was presented at the University of Wisconsin-Milwaukee's *Racial Formation, Racial Blindness* conference in February 2014.
40 The word "Initials" references the *J* and *B* on the columns of The High Priestess' temple.

Despite her own and Hughes' poems of the same name, the facts are that Plath was not against killing rabbits. An accomplished cook on a tight budget, she made and ate rabbit stews to feed her family (*UJ*, 246, 256, 258, 259). Early in their marriage, Hughes complimented her of how well she cooked rabbit and how his own didn't compare (*LTH*, 61-62). In another of Hughes' *Birthday Letters* poems, "The Afterbirth," he wrote of putting baby Nick's placenta in a bowl he had recently jugged a hare in, a process of stewing meat by marinating an animal in wine and its own blood (*BL*, 130-131;144-146).

In a 1960 letter by Hughes to Plath's mother and brother, Hughes told a tale of a man who shoots a hare, only to turn into one himself. "It's a moral fable," he wrote, "you see: when you hurt something or somebody else, there is also a spirit in you which receives the hurt" (*LTH*, 173).

In Plath's "The Rabbit Catcher," Sylvia Plath faced her independence after suffering hurt from her trickster husband's antics. In the spirit of the High Priestess' and the freed slaves' fierce independence, "The Rabbit Catcher" is about breaking free from subservience, or alchemical sublimation. It is Newton's Emerald Tablet translation again, when he wrote: "It ascends from ye earth to ye heaven & again it desends [sic] to ye earth and receives ye force of things superior & inferior" (Newton). Moreover, in "The Rabbit Catcher," Plath took her anger and her isolation, her oneness, and tried to view it from a position of power and wisdom as she transformed and grew through the pain into a new life of ultimate freedom—as the High Priestess would.

Chapter Four: The Great Mother's Doors of Perception
Card #3   The Empress   Corresponding Poem: "Thalidomide"

Sylvia Plath had written in her journals about her dark "dreams of deformity and death," most likely originating from childhood memories of her father losing his leg to diabetes shortly before his death. When Plath wrote "Thalidomide," she had just miscarried a child and was having dreams of infertility (*UJ*, 500). On the day "Thalidomide" was composed, the *London Observer* ran an article called "The Thalidomide Babies," featuring graphic photographs of an armless Afro-Caribbean Thalidomide baby. This article surely influenced the poem. As Plath considered her pregnancy difficulties, she was grateful to have been protected from bearing a disfigured child. Readers tend to assume the poem is about Plath's grieving, and the Thalidomide infant tragedies of the era which no doubt horrified her. "Thalidomide," however also addresses the power of the dark subconscious and twisted distortions of perception and hallucination.

First Mirror: The Tarot/Qabalah

The Empress tarot card is linked to the feminine, fertility, creativity, motherhood, and Mother Nature. She stands for both sides of motherhood: joyful and sorrowful, as creation of new and separate life is sometimes bittersweet. Reversed, she represents sexual difficulty, infertility, miscarriage, or abortion.

The Golden Dawn associates the Empress with the Hebrew letter *Daleth*, meaning: "the door through which the divine plan can engrave itself on the vast emptiness of space."

The word "Thalidomide" feels kin to *Thaumiel*, the dark side of Kether, the qabalistic crown on the Qabalah's Tree of Life. As Kether represents unity with God, Thaumiel is its opposite, shadowy forces. Thaumiel is symbolic of the human struggle, represented by two giant heads with bat wings, explaining Plath's bat symbolism in "Thalidomide": the leatheriness; creatures with knuckles at the shoulder-blades; a caul (call) for blood; two eyes, and screeching; and revolving and falling "dark fruits." An early version of this poem contains a reference to abortion, contributing to the Empress' reversed meaning. Plath's image of buds corresponds to the Empress' beginnings unseen suggesting the onset of puberty, conception, birth and other fruitfulness. This card's picture is full of buds.

In Enochian chess, The Empress' Qabalah station corresponds with the Bishop piece. Plath's opponent, assumed to be Hughes, plays the black side: He is "Negro." His amputated dark pieces crawl across the board and appall her. Plath ponders what she has done correctly to be protected from his shadowy presence. The pieces appear as "indelible buds," and as the players move, their finger knuckles at the shoulders of the pieces. The pieces have faces the players shove along into existence, dragging them across and off the board as Plath's eighth stanza suggests. Chess players are always concerned with the absence of pieces, and Plath spends the evening strategizing how to protect her king in the ninth and tenth stanzas. The eleventh stanza describes the nearby knight, with eyes, sound, and spit of a horse. As the pieces move around the board, she closes the poem comparing them to fruit circling and dropping.

In the year 1527 C.E., Vida, the bishop of Albay, published a poem about a chess game between Apollo and Mercury. Aside from its alchemical meanings to be discussed shortly, Plath's last line in "Thalidomide" might also be taken to mean that Mercury lost the game.

Second Mirror: Alchemy

Alchemists refer to The Empress as the White Queen, representative of Earth, attraction, fertility and the feminine. Alchemically, as the sun represents the father, the moon represents the mother. A child is half of each, Plath's half-moon image. In alchemy, the moon, *Luna*, is considered the female seed of metals, or Philosophical Silver, and the previous interpretation of "The Rabbit Catcher" aligned the moon's 28-day cycle with the feminine menses. *The Booke of Secrets* claims philosophical silver is more refined than "vulgar" silver: "Luna is made of a pure fine Mercury, and a pure white Sulphur by the influence of the Moon" (Linden, 126).

"Thalidomide" is full of alchemical terms: amputations, dismemberment, and beheadings all signify the dissolution, putrefaction, and division of the body during the Black Phase, known as *Nigredo*. Nigredo becomes "Negro" for Plath, a term that was socially accepted in the early 1960s. Nigredo is integral to the shamanic dismemberment experience: a similar symbolic transformation from the slain, fragmented self to one who is whole and powerful. Plath's adding of the white mask image refers to Artephius' famous alchemical text: "Now as to colours, that which does not make black cannot make white, because blackness is the beginning of whiteness and a sign of putrefaction and alteration, and that the body is now penetrated and mortified" (Artephius, 36).

The half-moon and brain of "Thalidomide" refer to the menstrual cycle controlled by the moon, and feeling half-crazy over it. *Menstruum* is an alchemical term for a solvent or alkahest with power to dissolve and coagulate at the same time, based upon the belief that the ovum takes its life and form from the menses. Menstruum is referred to as the Mercury of the Philosophers. In late 1977 or early 1978, Ted Hughes had written a chapter for Peter Redgrove's 1978 book, *The Wise Wound*, called "The Menstrous Traveller," which looked at Plath's menstrual imagery. The chapter, however, was never included or published (*LTH*, 392).

Toxic mercury, called "quicksilver" by the ancients, plays an important role in "Thalidomide." Mercury is a liquid metal sometimes found dripping from rocky cracks or accumulating in small mountain grotto pools. It was also obtained by roasting cinnabar (mercury sulfide), recalling the last line of "Thalidomide." The shiny metal seeped from the rocks and ran down into the ashes, where it was collected.

Aside from the image of buds meaning Thalidomide's terrible birth defect of unformed limbs, buds may refer to these drips of quicksilver, and to the potential flowers of *sublimation* ahead. The dark substance of sulfur is masked within alchemy's white phase, as the poem's first full couplet suggests. In the third stanza, Plath cuts away, or amputates, her laboratory stone in the fire as it expands in a scary, crawling way. It has become spider-like and is a volatile "unsafe" substance. The alchemist wears leather gloves, recognizing their spirit in her personified thinking of the fourth and fifth stanzas. It is just as Plath once wrote in her journals, "A god in breathes himself in everything. Practice: Be a chair, a toothbrush, a jar of coffee from the inside out: know by feeling in" (*UJ*, 307).

The word "faces" in the seventh couplet plays on alchemy's *faeces*, a variant of "feces," meaning the impure parts to be separated from the pure matter of the stone. Faeces are dead, useless matter.

Early alchemists made red mercuric oxide by heating quicksilver in a solution of nitric acid. The acid, called *aqua fortis*, was made by pouring sulfuric acid over saltpeter. The reaction of quicksilver in nitric acid is impressive: A thick red vapor, a "Blood-caul,"[441] hovers over the surface, and bright red crystals precipitate to the bottom. This striking effect demonstrated the simultaneous separation of mercury into the above and the below.

Mercury's all-encompassing properties were exhibited in other compounds too. If heated, mercury oxidizes into poisonous white mercuric oxide, a white substance resembling saliva, and red crystals (red mercuric oxide). Plath's "spit" image of course can also mean to cook something over open flame.

When mixed with other metals, liquid mercury tends to unite with them and form hardened amalgams. These and other properties convinced alchemists that mercury transcended both solid and liquid states, earth and heaven, and life and death. It symbolized Hermes himself, the guide to the above and below.

In addition to illustrating bats, the twelfth stanza's revolving fruits represent the cycle of the great Mother Nature, The Empress.[442] Fruits are traditional symbols of fertility and an expression of alchemical harvest. The Latin word *Mater*, meaning "Mother," is equated with matter in alchemy. The work of the alchemist lies in the rotation (Plath's revolving) of the elements (Roob, 15).

The second to last stanza may reference the Bible's *Revelation* 12:15, when a woman crowned with twelve stars (as on the Empress tarot card) gives birth to a son, and the serpent tries to destroy them both. It is the glass tube or beaker cracking in the alchemical experiment, dropping Plath's mercury.

In addition to its quicksilver image, mercury serves as its own triple metaphor for this Empress card bearing the number three: Pregnant women have been known to experience spontaneous abortion due to exposure to mercury from dropped fever thermometers; like mercury, doctors were first unaware of the drug Thalidomide's health risks; and Mercury was once liberally used to improve health by ancient Greeks, Romans, Egyptians, and Chinese, with sometimes disastrous effects. In a similar way, Plath's own personal alchemical experiment, her pregnancy, did not work and was naturally aborted.

The Emerald Tablet, considered the greatest alchemical text, states of the philosophical child or perfect work:

"Its Father is the Sun, Its Mother is the Moon; The Wind carried it in its Womb, the Earth breast-fed it; It is the Father of all works of the wonder of the world."

The belief is that the existence of one implies the existence of the other half, the opposite polarity. It is also the Taoist's Yin-Yang concept. This is why Plath began her poem with half-moons and half-brains, the dark and the light. This part of the Emerald Tablet, like the Empress card in the tarot, is about Creation, the downward movement of Force into Form, reflected in the eighth and twelfth couplets of "Thalidomide."

Hermetic text relating to this principle states of the human monsters* that result from loss of control:

"Within man there are two constantly active fires. One is his creative energy, while the other is his Divine Principle. All men are familiar with their creative energy, how it governs and controls their every action. Because of lack of control, all the crimes in the catalog are committed daily. It makes a monster out of a weakling, a demon out of a physical wreck. Under control, it is the impetus of the imaginative faculty, and men become inventors, artists, scientist, musicians, authors, physicians, masters of scientists, musicians, authors, physicians, masters of science, but still no more than men."
* The author does not suggest in any way that thalidomide babies or any other disfigured individuals are "monsters." Hermetic text was written well over a hundred years ago in less politically-correct times.

---

41 See paragraph on the mystic symbolism of the placenta ("blood caul") in the interpretation of the poem "Medusa" for the rank of the Fives.
42 For more on bats, see the *Fixed Stars Govern a Life* interpretation of "Elm."

Third Mirror: Mythology

The Empress of the tarot is the Greek goddess Demeter, earth mother and ruler of nature. She represents the physical processes of mothering: gestation, birth and nurturing, and their psychological aspects. Because of the wheat surrounding her, Arthur E. Waite, creator of the Rider-Waite Tarot deck, connected this card with the Roman goddess Ceres, goddess of agriculture and mother love. Demeter ripens the grain; therefore she shoves them "into being." As Mother Nature, she bears the fruit of Plath's twelfth stanza. She governs orderly cycles as they revolve like Plath's ripened fruits. The shield, cushion and gown on the Empress card's picture bear the sign of Venus, the Roman goddess of love and sexual healing.

"…everything actually was all-meaningful, that every symbol and combination of symbols led not hither and yon, not to single examples, experiments, and proofs, but into the center, the mystery and innermost heart of the world, into primal knowledge. Every transition from major to minor in a sonata, every transformation of a myth or a religious cult, every classical or artistic formulation was, I realized in that flashing moment, if seen with a meditative mind, nothing but a direct route into the interior of the cosmic mystery, where in the alternation between inhaling and exhaling, between heaven and earth, between Yin and Yang, holiness is forever being created."

-Hermann Hesse
(from *The Glass Bead Game*)

In myth, Demeter is also the mourning mother who cannot relinquish her children. One day while her daughter Persephone went out for a walk, Hades, the lord of the underworld, took her for his own and Persephone vanished without a trace.

In a correlating tale, Corvus the crow was sacred to the god Apollo. Mythologists ascribe Corvus to have been a cormorant, "the raven of the sea." Apollo directed Corvus to watch over his pregnant love, Coronis. When the bird reported back on Coronis' infidelity, Apollo turned his feathers black, corresponding with Plath's first line of the second couplet. In anger, Apollo took away Corvus' ability to speak, his love of a screech. In another version of the story, Apollo sent the raven to fetch water. The bird procrastinated, waiting instead for figs to ripen, Plath's "dark fruits" again. He was punished by becoming eternally thirsty, illustrated by the white saliva in Thalidomide's eleventh stanza.

In Norse myth, Odin had a pair of ravens, representing mind and memory. They sat on each of his shoulders like Plath's knuckle image. All raven connotations fit the eyes and screeching sound in the eleventh stanza.

Fourth Mirror: History and the World

Abortion has always been a controversial subject. In Plath's era of Thalidomide use, panicked mothers-to-be were sometimes demonized for not wanting to birth deformed babies. The drug was developed by a German pharmaceutical company, and in Plath's post-war era there were connections to the disastrous efficiency of Nazi medical experiments. In the Nazi mindset, the crippled and disabled were dispensable as defectives. Two months prior to Plath's writing "Thalidomide," Sherri Finkbine, the host of the children's television program *Romper Room* and mother of four, was publicly blasted for going to Sweden to obtain a legal abortion after learning she had taken the drug in the first few weeks of her pregnancy. The Arizona State Supreme Court denied her right to an abortion, and Finkbine was vilified by anti-abortionists across the United States. This very public scandal made the BBC News.

Surprisingly, much of Plath's "Thalidomide" addresses Native American Indian peyote ritual. Peyote grows on a little knotted cactus, Plath's knuckles upon shoulders metaphor. The cactus bears Plath's buds before it flowers, and produces fruit that may be "lopped" off. The plant has a "Spidery" cotton web in its center. The Kiowa Indians included peyote ritual in fertility rites, and for treating syphilis and women's menstrual cramps the tarot's Empress once again. Plath's journals and letters reveal that she was no stranger to menstrual cramps, and it makes sense she might have read of holistic and even mystical remedies, in addition to reading on Native American Indians.[43]

A nickname for peyote is "Moon," returning to the feminine and silver images again. Peyote first hit the streets of America as a recreational drug in the 1950s. It was perceived as a safe alternative to LSD by those fearing chromosomal damage affecting future children, like the damage caused by Thalidomide.

Peyote cacti flower in the summer. The ovules are fertilized and mature into seeds a year later. The cylindrical fruit grows to look like amputations, slowly arising as Plath's crawling image, from the center before it matures. The cacti's walls are dry and thin, and seeds drop (Cronquist, 177-80). In *The Peyote Ritual, Visions and Descriptions of Monroe Tsa Toke*, a Kiowa Indian says "He prays to the great light to understand the light within himself" (Denman, 9). This is yet another corresponding meaning for that treasure space of Plath's tenth stanza.

The Kiowa people's name derives from an Indian myth of a tribe coming out of a hollow log until a pregnant woman got stuck. In Kiowa art, the cormorant holds great symbolic importance. The raven of the sea holds the symbol of the peyote plant on its shoulders, returning to that knuckle-shoulder union. Kiowa Indians describe the movement of bird wings as: "Birds are two yellow hammers, male and female." This explains Plath's carpentry metaphor of the ninth stanza. The cormorants Plath would have been familiar with in Europe and North America are black-bodied, with white patches on their cheeks and chests, sounding like her second stanza's "Negro, masked like a white." They are known to circle high in the sky and dive great depths into the water, as do Plath's dark fruits. Cormorants have "leatheriness" in their webbed feet, build large nests, and feed screeching young through regurgitation of spit.

Cormorants are close relatives to pelicans, an alchemical symbol of the mother Empress. The name "Pelican," derived from the Greek *pelekys*, means "axe," another contribution to Plath's images of lopping something off, and also to carpentry. The pelican is common in heraldry and medieval ornamentation, believed to be an example of the selfless mother piercing her breast with her beak to feed her children her own blood. The pelican also has come to represent the passion of Jesus and the Eucharist.

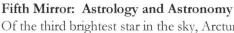

Fifth Mirror: Astrology and Astronomy
Of the third brightest star in the sky, Arcturus, Chaucer wrote, "ye sterres of Arc-tour." Arcturus is part of the constellation Bootes, rising and coinciding with the autumnal equinox, the great harvest of the Empress. These stars were considered slow-moving and sluggish by early astronomers, qualities given to the Empress' character, as she is heavy with child.

The Pelican Nebula is contained in the constellation Cygnus, "The Swan". It is a large mass of white stars, like Plath's bud image against "Negro" blackness. In photographs, it often appears as a blood-red mass in outer space, Plath's ninth stanza, as well as the space image in the tenth. Its two brightest stars appear as two glittering "wet eyes." Because this nebula consists of gases, it is ever-changing, crawling, amputating, and as spider-like as Plath's words. Four of its stars are in "the Throne of the Unarmed One," referring to the star Spica (Allen). This throne is described much like a Thalidomide deformity. Spica, in Virgo, marked the 12th Arabic Moon Mansion, and in early astrology was a sign of barrenness and trouble producing offspring.

---

43 See *Fixed Stars Govern a Life*'s interpretation of "Elm" for more on Native American Indians.

Sixth Mirror: Humanities and the Arts

In Milton's *Paradise Lost*, the cormorant symbolizes deception and greed. He sits upon the Tree of Life, a dark Satan masked as something pure, to enter into paradise and tempt Eve. The corresponding Hebrew word for the Empress, *Daleth*, means "door," steering us toward Aldous Huxley's famous 1954 work, *The Doors of Perception*. *The Doors of Perception* is an essay collection on Huxley's experiences with peyote, and the brain's response in differing forms of consciousness.

Like Plath, Aldous Huxley was a humanist and a pacifist, interested in parapsychology and philosophical mysticism. Huxley was friends with one of Plath's most revered writers, D.H. Lawrence, and Huxley once dined with Golden Dawn's former leader, Aleister Crowley. Huxley read a wide number of works on mysticism and alchemy, including William Blake, Jacob Boehme, William Law, and *The Tibetan Book of the Dead*.

Huxley wrote of the terror of schizophrenia; the dark Satan subconscious. Dr. William Sargent reviewed *The Doors of Perception* in *The British Medical Journal*, saying, "The book brought to life the mental suffering of schizophrenics" (Sargent, 1024).

In his book, Huxley was inspired by William Blake's metaphor of a cavern, from Blake's *The Marriage of Heaven and Hell*. In "Thalidomide," Plath attached her peyote cormorants and alchemical pelicans to these caverns. Hence, the bat symbolism.

"If the doors of perception were cleansed everything would appear to man as it is, infinite. For man has closed himself up, till he sees all things through narrow chinks of his cavern," said Huxley, quoting William Blake (Blake, 14). Plath owned Blake's *Marriage of Heaven and Hell*, Huxley's *Brave New World* and his philosophical essay on Blake's work, *Heaven and Hell*, three other Huxley novels, and even the Hindu Bhagavad Gita with an introduction by Huxley. She most likely read the popular *The Doors of Perception*, too. In Plath's copy of Huxley's *Heaven & Hell*, she underlined passages on personal consciousness, mescaline and lysergic acid, and hypnosis.[44]

Huxley wrote, "The shadow world inhabited by some schizophrenics and neurotics closely represents the world of the dead" (*Doors*, 180). Plath recognized her own dark side, and moments she might have been close to madness herself. Her fourth and fifth couplets of "Thalidomide" become her question.

Huxley biographer Sybille Bedford wrote that *The Doors of Perception*, "reflects the heart and mind open to meet the given, ready, even longing to accept the wonderful" (Bedford, 155). Here is yet another meaning for the ninth couplet's love and space.

Huxley's most famous work, the fictional dystopia, *Brave New World*,[45] fits both the Empress card's fertility message and peyote themes, a novel of themes and ideas Plath played upon in her first poem, "Morning Song." *Brave New World* engineers human children in decanting bottles, designing varying intelligences for different social castes. The population is kept under control through steady consumption of soma, a peyote-like hallucinogen.

"Thalidomide" had been the dark alchemical experiment put into words, and the empty, clear glass test tubes were to portray the *Daleth*, that "vast emptiness of space" on paper, in the womb, and in the Pelican Nebula of our universe. It is a bat in its cave, and a Cormorant in her nest, the Kiowa peyote ritual; and the hypnagogic, dark works of Aldous Huxley. It is the height of the Empress' creative powers, and Sylvia Plath created it divinely.

---

44 From Plath's personal library, held at the Lilly Library, Indiana University -Bloomington. Cover inscribed: "Sylvia Plath Cambridge 1956."

45 *Brave New World* is explored in *Fixed Stars Govern a Life*'s interpretation of Plath's "Morning Song."

Chapter Five: Necessity's sharp pinch![46]
Card #4   The Emperor   Corresponding Poem: "The Applicant"

Readers interpret "The Applicant" as Plath feeling easily replaced in her role as a housewife role—that almost anyone might do just as well. She is assessed to be sure that she meets the physical requirements and will fulfill her wifely duties. She is treated like a working, talking doll with has no mind of its own, and the repetition of the word "it" in the final line further dehumanizes. Plath wrote "The Applicant" when she knew she was leaving Hughes and separating entirely from The Emperor's domain: her material interests, her ego, and from the form she knew in that world.

First Mirror: The Tarot/Qabalah

The Emperor is a masculine card of power, force, control, ambition and achievement. When read in reverse, he is an unbending tyrant. He represents Zeus, the king of the gods, who sat atop Mount Olympus and established a hi-erarchy of gods who obeyed his law. He is an unemotional father, boss, or leader. Matters of worldly status, accomplishment and gain are most important to him, and he cares little about feelings. His ruling planet is Mars; his tree is oak, the hardest wood; and his color is red. The Golden Dawn attributes the Hebrew letter for the Emperor as *Heh*, meaning, "the window through which the inner (microcosmic Adam) may perceive the plan of the greater (macrocosmic Divine)." The Emperor is card number four in the tarot deck, the fifth card starting at zero. Plath wrote "The Appli-cant" in unrhymed quintets.

In the tarot, there are four sorts of persons, depending upon the suit: Swords, Wands, Cups, and Pentacles. The *sort*ing of the tarot cards determines which personality comes up. The Emperor's "sort" would be the Swords with an intelligent, strong, and cold personality. Plath's readers have long puzzled over where Plath might have gotten her images for "The Applicant" of glass eyes, false teeth, crutches, braces, and hooks. Certainly Plath, or any women known to have been with Hughes, had none of these attributes. One need only to take a close look at the tarot: The Emperor himself looks to have a glass eye, as his left eye looks straight ahead and his other drifts to his right. Across the 78 tarot cards, there are naked, rubbery bodies; crutches are pictured; and Knights' stirrups look like leg braces, and spurs appear as hooks. In "The Applicant," The Emperor asks, "Are you one of us?" If you are not on the tarot's path of personal growth, he is not interested.

Close-up of the Emperor's eyes

The tarot's commanding Emperor speaks in strings of impera-tives: There will be no crying, the hand must be open. He judges that the head is empty. Emotion does not get in The Emperor's way; he is all business and selects a mate who best fits his needs. Despite a lack of emotion, it is important for The Emperor to be married. When the spouse is dead, the eyes are thumbed shut.

---

46 From *King Lear*, 2.4.231 by William Shakespeare.

The "Black and stiff" tarot "suit" is the Swords, a match to the spades in a deck of standard playing cards. In some deck designs, The Emperor holds a sword as a rationalist: a thinker and not a feeler. He is one who always needs "proof." There is an attraction in The Emperor's security and emotional rigidity that Plath seems aware she had been drawn toward.

When the Emperor is read in reverse, he is not interested in problems, only solutions to meet his end. The last stanza of "The Applicant" reflects his quick problem-solving. Plath's "poultice" and the "image" are fast solutions to match the hole and eye to their roles. Plath implies: *here is a job to fill your nothingness,* and *here is something to look at.* What the applicant needs emotionally or might be interested in is inconsequential. This is The Emperor's cold, efficient force in action, to be addressed in the alchemy mirror of this poem. Additionally, practitioners of mysticism and religions such as Buddhism believe that all problems are gifts. To be emptied is purification; to see the self, the ego, the *I,* is mere illusion, or Plath's "image."

When Plath's narrator addresses the applicant as "My boy," this reinforces male gender and all the masculinity The Emperor represents. The Emperor is the father figure, an important character in Plath's personal drama as she lost her own autocratic father, Otto Plath, at a young age. The Emperor embodies the spiritual ideals, ethics, intelligence and independence needed to survive. He has foresight and ambition, and the discipline to accomplish his goals. He leaves the nurturing and unconditional love to the mother. These were all characteristics of Otto Plath, and of Zeus. They shared a dark side too, of rigidity, stubborn self-righteousness, and arrogance. Finally, Plath's idea of a "last resort" may be interpreted as re-*sort*: sorting the tarot cards again for a final reading.

In Enochian chess, the "sort" of person depends upon the color of the pieces: black or white. A player commits to one color or the other, a marriage to their side. The poem, "The Applicant" and The Emperor are therefore aligned with the king piece on the chess board. The long game of chess promises to close all eyes when over. At that time, nothing is lost. The pieces are put away until the next game, as Plath writes of new stock made. The king offers his color as a fit for the player.

Chess is a thinking-person's game, and the king/Emperor addresses empty-headedness with a command to think. The character pieces on the chess board perform like living dolls; if there is an open space, a piece may be a "poultice" for that hole. Lastly, when a king is in check it is his "last resort." Hermetic text professes the greatest of all victories is the victory over the carnal self. This is The Emperor's ultimate meaning: victory.

Second Mirror: Alchemy

Alchemically, the title, "The Applicant," can refer to the medieval definition of "applicant," meaning "one who applies"; it is not someone who applies for a job, but who applies a solution or substance to matter.

"The Applicant" begins with the Emperor-alchemist's order of work: the word, "First," points to the original, pure substance from which alchemists believe the universe is made and will return. Aristotle said this *prima materia,* the beginning materials for creation, is "receptive," like the applicant's personality in this poem. Just as a subservient wife behaves, the first material barely exists as its own element. It is "imprinted by an essential determinant" (Abraham 153).

The emptiness of the second stanza is important. The philosopher's stone cannot be made without first being dissolved to *prima materia.* The Emerald Tablet claims:

"Its power is complete if turned towards Earth. It will separate Earth from fire, the subtle from the gross."

This tarot Emperor of Earth causes an opposite action from the Empress of Creation. He is separation of force *from* form; the image from the eye in Plath's final stanza. Metaphorically speaking, and almost all alchemy is metaphor, this phase separates base self from higher self, the alchemical processes of *putrefaction* and *fermentation*.

In the *prima materia* stage, the fire of mercury acts upon the whole, shedding the clothing of matter from the stone. It is "Black and stiff," stripped of form through *putrefaction*, a process of burning and stagnation, and moving into the black phase. Plath's fifth stanza burial refers to the blackened earth, stripped of its impure properties. It is Plath's image of nakedness.

Emptiness is preferred, and this is a condition throughout this poem. Things are missing; what can be given is unknown, and heads and hands are empty.

Separating the higher self from the base self is the same alchemical process seen in the earlier *Ariel* poems, but now viewed from above as The Emperor sits on his throne. First, the earth is removed from the fire, implying an ascent of conscious awareness. One burns off worldly hindrances and becomes aware of his or her fire. This fire acts upon itself, separating its essence from bodily aspects. It is a process of the father/fire self-consciously releasing from form, a reversal of The Empress' creative process.

The alchemist's task is to unite opposing substances of 'male' sulfur and 'female' quicksilver in the *chemical wedding*, explaining Plath's suggestions of marriage. The fourth stanza reference to salt is one of three minerals that Paracelsus defined: sulfur for the soul, mercury for the intellect, and salt for the human body. Salt is the final manifestation of the perfected stone after the influence of sulfur and mercury. Salt represents action of thought and spirit on matter; it is the universal mind acting on the wholeness of the universe, or in a physical sense, the alchemist meditating in his laboratory.

The fourth stanza suggests cooking soup. Alchemists called The Emperor's putrefaction and fermentation processes "cooking," "boiling," or, in their paternalistic, old-world mindset, "women's work" (Abraham 29). Sewing, in the seventh stanza of "The Applicant," also fits.

"[P]roof" has several meanings: in addition to proof as "evidence," it may mean standard strength, as in alcohol content. *Proof* can be a trial image, as in photography, or a check for errors, as in proofreading. In Scots Law, a proof is a trial by a judge with no jury. In alchemy, to proof something is to make it indestructible. Plath's proofs are brilliant because they hit upon each of these meanings.

The empty head of the sixth stanza is the alembic glass vessel, called "the head," where distillation, separation, and putrefaction occur. The alembic represents the human head in Shakespeare's *Macbeth,* and in a great deal of Renaissance writing. As a verb, "alembic" was defined "to rack the brain," implying emptiness again (Abraham 96).

The pet name "sweetie" refers to the sweet smell in the burning process. Because The Emperor is so harsh, "He deserves not sweets," claims the medieval *Fasciculus chemicus* text. Yet he gets them anyway, at least in the form of fragrance (Dee).

Plath's repetitive question of marriage challenges the initiate to question if this physical, psychological, and spiritual process is worth it for ultimate unity with the *Infinite Continuum.* Alchemy's lead is said to ripen first to silver, Plath's twenty-five year silver anniversary, and then to gold for the golden fiftieth. Gold is believed to be nothing but mature quicksilver (Dobbs, 276).

Plath's "living doll" is alchemy's homunculus.[47] For centuries, man has attempted procreation in the laboratory without female participation, reflecting The Emperor's male power as a god on earth. Medieval Kabbalists[48] attempted to form *simulacrums,* or *golems,* striving to bring them to life through the correct

---

47 The homunculus image surfaces again, by name, in Plath's poem, "Cut," and also in "A Secret."
48 The Hermetic form of Qabalah had not yet begun.

magical ritual. Paracelsus, studied by Plath's mother Aurelia for her master's degree, is considered the first and greatest alchemist. He sought the correct chemical ingredients to do the same.

Plath chose the alchemical word, "poultice" not just for sound, but for the idea of the moist, adhesive mass or clay representing the female body in alchemy. The Emperor-alchemist recognizes opportunity in everything for growth. A problem, Plath's "hole," is really an opportunity to heal. An eye, the homophone for the pronoun *I*, is the image of the ego, and not real at all. The idiom "last resort," first used in the 1600s, refers to a court of law with no appeal, appropriate for The Emperor's Blackening stage (Ammer).

Third Mirror: Mythology

The Emperor on this corresponding tarot card is Zeus, the ancient Greeks' ruler of gods. Zeus is the penultimate judge, employer and interrogator, as shown in "The Applicant." High atop Mount Olympus, Zeus is elevated over all the other gods and man, who defer to his mental and spiritual heights. Like the predatory and often aggressive eagle, one of his emblems, Zeus' will rises above all limitations. His symbols of power are thunder and a lightning bolt, in accordance with Plath's fifth stanza's theatrics. These powerful crashes represent power, inspiration, truth, and sudden creative vision. Zeus was the problem-solver; his solutions were accepted whether or not man or gods liked them. It is the attitude of the speaker in "The Applicant."

In Greek myth, Zeus' father was Cronos. It was prophesied that one of Cronos' sons would overthrow him. To prevent this, every time Cronos' wife Rhea gave birth, he snatched the baby away and swallowed it whole. Rhea gave birth to her sixth child, Zeus, secretly in a cave. She then wrapped a large stone in blankets and presented it to Cronos as his son, which he promptly ate without looking. Zeus grew to manhood elsewhere, and returned to his father in disguise, implied by Plath's glass eye, false teeth, and rubbery appendages. Zeus prepared a potion that made his father violently ill, as Plath's catering hand brings a teacup in "The Applicant."

Disguises were popular with Zeus, who took many of his lovers in the forms of an animal or an object, such as a shower of gold. Zeus had three known wives, matching the final line of "The Applicant" with its three repeating questions of marriage.

In the manner of his father, Zeus ate his children when it was foretold they would be bringers of bad news. Plath's headache image is the terrible pain Zeus suffered before Hephaestus split his skull open. No one ever spoke against Zeus or ignored a command without suffering his wrath. Zeus could be compassionate when he saw mistreatment or wrongdoing, and angry and vindictive when his laws were broken. Everyone did as Zeus commanded, as in the third stanza of "The Applicant."

The pet name "sweetie" might be used by Zeus for any of his many women. His wife, Hera, was the goddess of marriage and childbirth, addressing "The Applicant" question of marrying.

Zeus is syncretized with the Roman god Jupiter, as well as Perun, the ruling Slavic god, and Amun, the Egyptian king of the gods. The Germanic counterpart of Zeus and Taranis was Thunor, brought to England by the Anglo-Saxons. Zeus' oracle at Dodona consisted of a single, holy oak tree. The oak tree was sacred to those who worshipped Thunor, Perun, and Zeus, who share this emblem along with mighty thunder. The Druids danced between twin sacrificial fires to the oak king on Midsummer Eve. Taranis, meaning "thunder" was the Celtic version of Zeus and considered also to be the wheel-god, Plath's rolling away in the third stanza.

The Viking name for Thunor was Thor. He too had Zeus' characteristics, hard temperament, and thunderbolts. Thor rode across the sky in an oak chariot, pulled by two goats. His weapon was a magic oak hammer, and Thor was worshipped in sacred oak groves and oak temples (Icons).

Since Ancient Greece, a famous theme of tragedy has been that suffering produces wisdom or greater self-understanding. In Aeschylus' *Agamemnon*, the chorus sings, "Zeus, whose will has marked for man the sole way where wisdom lies, ordered one eternal plan: man must suffer to be wise" (Aeschylus).

In Robert Graves' *The White Goddess*, many pages are devoted to Zeus' oak in myth, and more still to certain species of oak. This becomes important in the next mirror of this poem. Graves translates an early Celtic work of antiquity known as Câd Goddeu, or "The Battle of the Trees," by Gwion, about a magic wand that transforms trees into fighting men (Graves, 37). He ascribes the mighty oak as "the tree of Zeus, Juppiter,[49] Hercules, The Dagda (the chief of the elder Irish gods), Thor, and all the other Thundergods, Jehovah in so far as he was 'El', and Allah" (Graves, 176). "The Oak is a tree of Druids and the king of trees," wrote Graves, "and the Wren, *Drui-én*, is the bird of the Druids and the King of all birds. And the Wren is the soul of the Oak. Black is the colour of the Oak when the lightning blasts is, and black the faces of those who leap between the Midsummer fires" (Graves, 298).

Fourth Mirror: History and the World

The mighty oak of the Thundergods dominated the myth mirror of "The Applicant." As the largest tree in Europe, it is most often hit by lightning. The oak is therefore a good match for these gods, and makes itself known in Plath's poem. As Zeus fathered children among countless goddesses and mortal women, the oak reproduces with other species of trees, constantly evolving the species. Like the Emperor tarot card, Zeus, and his equivalents, this tree's wood is known for hardness and great strength, as well as resistance to (fungal) attack. Waterproof and virtually shatterproof, oak wood has been used for the construction of Naval war ships prior to the 19th century. Oak was also used for European timber-framed buildings because it was good in the fire and attack of Plath's fifth stanza. Oak tree acorns form in a cup-like structure called a cupule, reflecting Plath's teacup image. These rounded acorns roll as the applicant will roll headaches away.

The Celts called the oak tree "the tree of doors," believing it served as a portal or gateway between the worlds. Oak is a popular wood for caskets, apposite with this poem's comment on burial (Michigan). Tannin, found in oak bark, is used in the tanning process to "proof" animal hides. The English word "tanning" is derived from Oak's Latin name, *tannāre*. Oak barrels are sometimes charred "Black and stiff" for liquor and wine. A symbol of strength and endurance, the oak is the national tree of many countries important to Plath and Hughes; their ancestral nations of the United States, England, Germany and Poland all embrace the oak in heraldry, and these countries make appearances in other *Ariel* poems.

> *"Newly acquired insights are at first only half understood by the one who begets them, and appear as complete nonsense to all others... Any new idea which does not appear very strange at the outset, does not have a chance of being a vital discovery."*
>
> — Niels Bohr

---

49 Graves' spelling.

King Leir, a legendary ancient king and direct descendant of Brutus[50] for whom Britain was named, also figures in "The Applicant" as yet another example of the Emperor. The story of Leir was told by Geoffrey of Monmouth, but is best known as Shakespeare's tragedy, *King Lear.* Plath read *King Lear* on November 6, 1955, per her calendar.[51] Neither the king of real history, nor the king of the drama, had a male heir to the throne. Both had three daughters to marry off, the second stanza's offer of a hand, and the triple-marriage question of Plath's last line. Leir, and the fictional Lear, sought royal unions for their daughters, which would have resulted in hard questioning, as in Plath's poem. In both stories the older daughters, Goneril and Regan,[52] flattered their father for the kingdom, and were married off to dukes. The youngest daughter, Cordelia, insisted on being truthful, while the elder sisters told their father what he wanted to hear and were awarded half the kingdom each. Cordelia was left with nothing. When Cordelia became betrothed to Aganippus, the king of the Franks, her dowry was refused. This sounds like the second stanza of "The Applicant." Leir/Lear grew old and strained after mistreatment from his two oldest daughters. He began to lose a hold of his mental faculties, becoming empty-headed as in Plath's sixth stanza. It was Cordelia who stayed with Leir/Lear in the end, happily in Monmouth's telling, and tragically in Shakespeare's play.

Zeus' bird, the eagle,[53] is known for its excellent eyesight. Like telescope glass, the eagle eye is another interpretation for "A glass eye." In the military, the Emperor's world, to assume "a brace" is a stiff, rigid posture as the perched eagle maintains. The eagle has a hooked beak like the hook in "The Applicant." At least twenty-eight nations have the eagle on their national coat of arms and historically, the bird has been the symbol for many great empires. The eagle has been worshipped since ancient times in civilizations such as the Peruvian Incas, the Native American Indians, and India's Hindus. What better representation for the tarot's Emperor?

Bald eagles are committed and faithful mates, but if one of the pair dies, the other will "make new stock." The Bald Eagle, with his white head and spindly yellow legs, appears to wear a stiff suit. Eagle feathers are water-repellant and the head, with no crest or ornate plumage, might be called "empty" and white. Newborn eagle chicks are "Naked as paper to start." A Bald eagle lives twenty-five to fifty years, fitting silver and gold anniversaries. Navajo Indians of Northern America use a poultice from the plant Gilia Beardtongue, like that bearded Emperor, to treat eagle bites (Michigan).

Fifth Mirror: Astrology and Astronomy
The fourth brightest star, corresponding with the Emperor, is Alpha Centauri. It is part of one of the largest constellations, Centaurus, the centaur. Alpha Centauri is the nearest visible star to our solar system and believed by astrologers to have a beneficial influence. However, like the Emperor, Alpha Centauri can show emotional disturbance or dissatisfaction, and it can also strain relationships.

In Celtic Tree astrology, those born under the sign of the Oak, June 10th – July 7th, are born leaders, speak the truth, are often vain, and formidable opponents; all echo the tarot's Emperor, Zeus, and equivalent mythologies and literary heroes (Irish).

---

50 For more on Brutus, see *Fixed Stars Govern a Life*, volume two's interpretation of Sylvia Plath's poem, "Daddy."
51 This calendar is held in the Sylvia Plath Archives of the Lilly Library, at Indiana University-Bloomington.
52 Shakespeare used the same names as Leir's daughters for his play.
53 For more on the eagle, see *Fixed Stars Govern a Life*'s interpretation of Plath's poem, "Death & Co.", first published in Indiana University's *Plath Profiles 3.*

Zeus' constellation is Aquila the Eagle, the god-king's emblem because of its majesty and ability to soar at great heights. It was said about this northern constellation that Aquila was Jupiter (Zeus) himself carrying the abducted Ganymedes to heaven. Emperor Julius Caesar claimed Aquila represented the eagle of military Rome. Those born under the influence of Aquila bear the Emperor's indomitable will, a dominating character, keen intelligence and strong passions.

Sixth Mirror: Humanities and the Arts

William Shakespeare's work is full of examples of the Emperor which Plath wove into "The Applicant." When Shakespeare wrote *King Lear* in 1606, he seems to have been obsessed with sight; what it means to see, and the ways that eyes deceive and reveal, all corresponding to Plath's third line of the first stanza. The King says to the Earl of Gloucester in Act IV, Scene 6: "Get three glass eyes; / And, like a scurvy politician, seem / To see the things thou dost not."

After the betrayal of his two eldest, smiling daughters ("false teeth" and "rubber breasts" with no maternal/familial sort of love), Shakespeare's King Lear wound up as a blind, exiled beggar, suggesting Plath's images of the crutch, brace, and hook. Shakespeare wrote that Lear lost the "vile jellies" of his face with the new awareness of his crime against his only loving child.

"How sharper than a serpent's tooth it is to have a thankless child!" Lear says in Act I, Scene IV, another meaning for "false teeth." Once full of confidence and power, in Act 4, Scene 6, he says, "They told me I was everything. 'Tis a lie, I am not ague-proof."

Here is Plath's "proof," as well as proof of the Emperor's great ego. In addition, Lear speaks of "oak-cleaving thunderbolts," a connection to Zeus (*King Lear*, Act III, Scene II).

King Lear's personality reflects other Shakespearean kings and lords, suffering tragedies of character and morals due to ego, ruthless ambition, and a desire for battle. Shakespeare's Macbeth and Marc Antony both fight and kill for a throne. In Shakespeare's Renaissance Europe, the belief of the "Divine Right of Kings" within the "Great Chain of Being," an alchemical-ish order of hierarchy from the lowest to the highest forms of life on the planet, was widely practiced. In *King Lear*, Shakespeare states that everyone has something to hide, Plath's sixth stanza imperative to stop hiding in a closet. Shakespeare takes the metaphysical point of view that none are guilty, as we exist as pure souls outside of the stories of our lives ("Well, what do you think of that? / Naked as paper to start // But in twenty-five years she'll be silver, / In fifty, gold").

Like Shakespeare's *Romeo and Juliet*, "The Applicant" shows an arranged marriage. The narrator, a Zeus-like Emperor, questions and instructs a young man ("My boy"). Plath's narrator pulls a girl out of the closet for him; any one will do. In Act 1, Scene 1 of *Romeo and Juliet*, Lady Capulet yells: "A crutch, a crutch!" to Old Capulet when he attempts a sword fight. She mockingly suggests a crutch would be more useful at her husband's age than a sword. And in Shakespeare's *Richard III*, King Richard seduces Lady Ann, a very Zeus-like move. But first, he removes the metal brace he wears on his crippled leg.

In the last week of her trimester term at Cambridge, Sylvia Plath got a splinter in her eye. The discomfort could not be subdued and it had to be removed surgically. She wrote to her mother that as the doctor operated, she recounted "how Oedipus and Gloucester in King Lear got new vision through losing eyes, but I would just as soon keep my sight and get new vision, too" (*LH*, 229).

The world we see, according to Shakespeare, alchemists, Hermeticists and mystics, is merely an image of the ego. For them, there are no real problems; nothing is wrong with anything as the world is illusion. The Emperor and Shakespeare's kings knew that problems contain their own solution; the *hole* becomes the poultice. The self is created in the mind, and so the eye is an *I* …only an image.

Chapter Six: Falling Stars and Diving Dolphins
Card #5   The Hierophant   Corresponding Poem: "Barren Woman"

About a year and a half before Sylvia Plath wrote "Barren Woman," she fretted about her own potential barrenness in her journals. No doubt the pressure was upon her: Hughes had just written "Lupercalia," the title poem to his second book, which included a fertility ceremony to make a barren woman fertile, and they were both writing children's books at the time (*UJ*, 500). Plath may have likened herself to Hera, jealous of her rival for Zeus, as she was jealous over Hughes' love. She did later refer to Hughes' mistress, Assia Wevill, as the "barren woman," due to Wevill's disinterest in motherhood and her many abortions (Koren, 109). The poem "Barren Woman" however, was written on February 21, 1961, over one year *before* Wevill was any sort of threat to Plath and Hughes' marriage. Early drafts reveal that the poem had two previous titles: "Night Thoughts," and "Small Hours." Dido Merwin has also been cited as the subject of "Barren Woman," as Plath later wrote of her and Assia Wevill as "a set of barren women." However, to look at this poem through tarot and the Qabalah is to see there are bigger stories than mere autobiography at work:

First Mirror: Tarot/Qabalah:
The Hierophant card represents learning, religion, orthodoxy, solemn rituals, dogma, order and structure. The Golden Dawn attributes the Hebrew letter *Vav* to The Hierophant, meaning: "the hook or pin on or through which one's faith expands - in other words, we do not function in a vacuum, but pin our thoughts and beliefs on the structural framework brought to us by our social milieu" (Plath's "great public").

THE HIEROPHANT

"Barren Woman" is written in five-line stanzas, corresponding with this card's number five. The Hierophant illustration informs much of "Barren Woman": A Pope is in a museum with pillars, but no statues. Lilies adorn the coat of the supplicant to the right, and pillars bear lily-like crowns. The other supplicant's coat bears roses, the most important emblem of the Rosicrucians. Older tarot decks called The Hierophant "Popess" or "Pope Joan," after a 13th century female who led the Church disguised as a man.

The Hierophant's picture and meaning well-fit the first lines of Plath's second stanza about fame and reputation. In the illustration, the Pope's expression is neutral. His hand is held up as if he might lay it upon a member of his congregation, in the way Plath's moon lays a hand on her forehead. The moon is the symbol of Isis, mother-creator. Plath works the double-meaning for "mum," meaning both *quiet* and *mother*.

Plath's water falling into a pool in the third line of "Barren Woman" represents positive and negative potencies of life force in the tarot.

In Enochian chess, The Hierophant corresponds to the strongest piece on the chessboard, the queen. She corresponds to The Hierophant card's number five as fifth in the row of pieces from left to right. The queen responds to the smallest "footfall" on her marble museum board. In "Barren Woman," the pawns become pillars and the rooks, rotundas. The Golden Dawn says the Enochian chess queen "is ascribed unto the Great Goddess Isis, who is the Cherisher of Life" (Regardie, 691). The queen piece is firm and commanding, always doing what her side needs. She has a nun's pure heart and blindness to the outside, seen in the first stanza. Her crown looks like a marble lily. The queen is more powerful with her pawns surrounding her, her public image. "Barren Woman" is thus the voice of the white queen; some might associate her with Robert Graves' "White Goddess," who is the mother of Nike. Plath's "bald-eyed Apollos" are the pawns.

When "the dead injure" the speaker with attention, as in Plath's second stanza, a captured queen stands off the board, surrounded by other dead pieces. Nothing *does* happen as Plath's "nothing can," unless she is traded back into the game. The game player is a blank moon face overhead, moving the queen by her forehead. And in the last line of "Barren Woman," both queen and player show no expression, trying not to give anything away to the opponent.

Second Mirror: Alchemy

In alchemy, lilies represent lunar and feminine qualities (Abraham, 117). Alchemical references to the Greek god Apollo signify the Sun as spirit or solar consciousness. Water is a universal symbol for life, and in the tarot, Qabalah, and alchemy, it represents stream of consciousness. In "Barren Woman," water becomes menstruation; Plath writes of a woman's empty womb as a courtyard with her watery cycles leaping and sinking back again. The moon, with its 28-day cycle like the menses, has laid a hand on her.

Through the alchemical lens, Plath's museum becomes the laboratory. *Womb* or *bed* are terms for the alchemical vessel where the chemical wedding of Sol and Luna, form and matter, take place. It is sometimes called *impregnation* when the white matter, the purified body, is planted with the growing seed/soul of the philosopher's stone, also known as a "child" (Abraham, 81, 219). The speaker of "Barren Woman" resounds with the quiet knowledge of self-awareness through her descent into form, and subsequent ascent back to a form-less state.

Looking at the first stanza of "Barren Woman," the fountain image is a flame or solution rising and falling; it refers to mercurial water. To have a heart like a nun is to be pure, or striving to be so. The mystic's goal is to ignore the world, to be blind to its illusion. The Initiate has gone through the first stage of alchemy; *separating the subtle from the gross*, as in the Bible's separation of wheat from chaff, the valuable from the worthless. The whiteness of lilies is released like perfume mist; the alchemist strives to release the essence from the form.

In the second stanza of the poem, Plath weighs her spiritual knowledge against worldly talent and accomplishments, but she has slipped into the trap of ego and imagining fame. Plath often wrote in journals of her awareness of ego as her downfall; she knew she sought the wrong attention, injurious and stifling to the spirit. Her freedom would arrive when she detached from the world and paid attention to what was truly important.

The mother image is alchemy's impregnated matter. Apollos connect with the philosopher's stone as Apollo's symbol is an alchemical symbol for the red tincture of Sol, or gold (Abraham, 8). Plath was a great reader of Plato and her mention of injury proclaims Plato's truth in the Allegory of the Cave: it is painful to become enlightened and turn away from the world. Until she does, she is her own obstacle to achieving the Great Work and "nothing can happen."

Third Mirror: Mythology

Apollo was the Greeks' god of the Sun and fine arts. His chariot drove the sun across the sky each day, making Apollo one of the most beloved gods. Apollo was said to have first appeared in the guise of a dolphin, associating him with dolphins and as dolphin-god.

The importance of the dolphin in myth and legend throughout the world is dizzying: The ancient Minoans and later, the Greeks, identified the dolphin with virile, strong and lusty gods and men. There are many, many Greek myths about dolphins. In some, gods such as Poseidon are wooing pure, nun-like virgins such as Amphitrite. In another, the mortal queen Ino bore an illegitimate son, Dionysus, to Zeus. In despair over Zeus' wife, Hera's wrath and her abandonment, Ino threw herself into the ocean. Zeus took pity on Ino, and turned her into Leucothea, the white goddess of the sea, who is also commonly represented as a dolphin.

South American folklore has the Amazon River dolphin shape-shifting into a handsome young man at night, and seducing and impregnating young women. In *The White Goddess*, Robert Graves tells the story of *Silvia*, a Vestal Virgin raped by a god in the form of a werewolf during a total eclipse of the sun, when the moon might be said to be laying a hand on the sun's forehead. Silvia was sentenced to death by drowning after twins were born. The true form of her rapist-god proved to be a dolphin. There is also mention of the ancient Roman Guild of Lupercal's priests sending the werewolf to her—reminiscent of Hughes' second book of poems, *Lupercal*. In an imagined dialogue with Theophilus over the changing fashion in religion, Graves explained that the ancients once celebrated eroticism and sexual symbols such as the dolphin. Now, religion seeks Vestal Virgins offering up prayers to chaste gods. Graves wrote:

"I see them devoutly circling the fish-pool which the sacred fish also mystically circles the cool, pale-faced fish, as chaste as they—"
Theophilus interrupted: 'Who was dark-faced and hot in Silvia's day,'
'And in his pool drowns each unspoken wish" (Graves, 359-363).

The cool, pale-face is pictured on the priest in the tarot's Hierophant card, also representing the heart of the nun, the lilies of marble, and the scent of the incense. The church and organized religion, the subject of Graves' fictional discussion, embodies The Hierophant card. Continually, the imagery in "Barren Woman" points to mythology of lusty men and virginal women.

After slaying a great python on Mount Parnassus, Apollo established the Oracle of Delphi, named after his cult title, "Delphinios," meaning dolphin or porpoise. The Greek god Zeus had deemed Delphi the center of the Earth. There, Apollo selected a sibyl, or prophetess, to speak for him. The sibyl was a spinster, a "Barren Woman," called Pythia after the slain python. Fumes from the decomposing python's body intoxicated the sibyl as Plath's exhaled pallor. The sibyl fell into trances and spoke in riddles priests interpreted (Leadbetter).

The mother of Nike, in the second stanza, is Styx, goddess of the underworld river. Nike's father was Pallas, which in Greek meant "lusty young man." Homer wrote that Pallas was the moon's father, identifying Nike as the most likely candidate to be the moon, and circling back to Isis (Graves, 360).[54] The name "Pallas" is a homonym for "palace," complementing the scene Plath sets in the first stanza. The old Mother Goddess was said to have been served by daughters of Pallas,

---

54 See *Fixed Stars Govern a Life*'s interpretation of Plath's poem, "The Other," in which she also identifies Nike as the moon.

near the headwaters of the River Styx. These daughters, her priestesses, ate dolphin meat in sacrificial feasts. Pallas, then, is a multi-personality: son, lover, victim of the Mother Goddess, and dolphin (Graves, 353). Mother Styx personified the spirit of hatred. She is connected to the darkness of the night and the wrath of the earth. Like the queen and the Hierophant, public acclaim rules. Styx offered the service of her children for war against the Titans: Nike (Victory), and the Apollo-like siblings Kratos (Strength), Zelos (Rivalry), and Bia (Force). To hand her children over, one might say Styx was left "barren."

In Hesiod's Greek epic, *Theogony*, the first stanza of Plath's "Barren Woman" is portrayed in this passage about Nike's mother, Styx:

> "And there [in Hades] is housed a goddess loathed even by the immortals: dreaded Styx, eldest daughter of Okeanos, who flows back on himself, and apart from the gods she lives in her famous palace which is overroofed with towering rocks, and the whole circuit is undergirded with silver columns, and pushes heaven; and seldom does…."(Hesiod)

Similarly, in *Metamorphoses*, Ovid wrote:

> "There is a dropping path in twilight gloom of deadly yews; it leads through silent slopes down to the Infernae (Underworld), where sluggish Styx exhales her misty vapours. By that path new Umbrae (Ghosts), the duly buried dead, descend."

With Hesiod's description of the water which "flows back on himself," along with the elaborate palace architecture and status as Nike's mother, and Ovid's "misty vapours" like Plath's exhaled pallor, there is little doubt Styx dominates the "Barren Woman."

Fourth Mirror: History and the World

On the date Plath wrote the poem, "Barren Woman," the Hollywood goddess Marilyn Monroe was in a very public decline. In her earlier journal entries, Plath had documented dreams of Monroe, and had been delighted about her marriage to playwright Arthur Miller. By the time of "Barren Woman," Monroe had had a series of abortions, no children, and just divorced Miller.

Monroe then checked herself into a psychiatric clinic, probably pushing some emotional buttons with Plath regarding her own past. At this time, the evidence shows that Plath did not yet harbor negative feelings toward Assia Wevill or Dido Merwin. Plath's first line of "Barren Woman" displays Monroe's grand show without substance and her need to perform for the least bit of attention. The poem illustrates the grandeur of Hollywood and also its emptiness. Often dressed in white and with platinum blonde hair, the marble and white in "Barren Woman" also fit Marilyn Monroe well.[55] This idea of public attention directly corresponds with The Hierophant tarot card.

Plath's mention of Apollo in the second stanza directs the reader to the site of Apollo's most famous temple, the Oracle at Delphi. "Delphi" means *dolphin* in Greek. To look at the ruins of the Oracle at Delphi, it is Plath's poetic museum in all its description. There are no statues left, and it has grand pillars, porticoes, and rotundas. The Castalia Spring was a place for purification before one entered the sanctuary, and was later replaced with a Roman fountain, as in the third line of the poem. The Delphic Oracle was internation-

"I knew I belonged to the public and to the world, not because I was talented or even beautiful, but because I had never belonged to anything or anyone else."

— Marilyn Monroe

55 See *Fixed Stars Govern a Life*'s interpretation of Sylvia Plath's poem, "Lesbos" for more on Plath and her interest in Marilyn Monroe. Author Carl Rollyson's book, *American Isis: The Life and Art of Sylvia Plath*, © 2013 St. Martin's Press suggests more of a Plath-Monroe connection.

ally renowned; Greeks consulted its pure and wise virgin, a "Barren Woman" named Pythia, before their every endeavor. The building was made of marble, and its amphitheater above the Temple of Apollo could seat 5,000 people, echoing The Hierophant and Plath's public image. Apollo was a very popular god to Greeks and Romans for several centuries; one might say the "movie star" of the ancient pantheon (Morden).

The poet Lord Byron wrote of Rosicrucianism, and a great deal about Greek myth. Byron was strongly moved by the Oracle at Delphi. He wrote in his journals, "On the day before, I composed the lines to Parnassus [in Childe Harold], and, on beholding the birds, had a hope that Apollo had accepted my homage. I have at least had the name and fame of a poet during the poetical part of life (from twenty to thirty);—whether it will last is another matter." Byron famously autographed the oracle (Moore, 11). This public "name and fame" is The Hierophant's domain.

The etymology of the word *dolphin* comes from the Greek *delphus*, meaning "womb" and circling back to our other meanings for "Barren Woman." The dolphin communicates through echolocation, as in Plath's first line. Its blowhole for breathing is like a fountain that is leaping and sinking. Its underwater ocean habitat has its own pillars, porticoes, and rotundas in the form of coral, rock formations, etc. Because dolphins are mostly underwater, they are "blind" to life on land.

Dolphins are beloved for their intelligence and playfulness and, like Zeus, known for breeding outside of its genus species; these hybrids are usually fertile. Dolphins do not have any body hair, and have bright, round eyes, like the Apollos in Plath's second stanza.

There is another potential History and the World mirror in "Barren Woman": Dauphin Island, a barrier island off Alabama's Gulf Coast, was named not after the dolphins often seen there, but for France's King Louis XIV's *Dauphin* (meaning "heir"). Louis XIV was known as "the Sun King," like the god Apollo, linking to The Hierophant's status symbols once again.

As history and anthropology buffs, Plath and Hughes may have learned that Welsh navigator and prince, Madoc Gwynedd, landed upon the island's white beaches in 1170 (Hearin). Legend tells of Welsh Indians who were descendants of Madoc's settlers, evidenced by burial mounds and Indian artifacts with Welsh markings.[56]

King Louis' French explorers found Dauphin Island to be "burning heat, barren soil, and sand so white as to injure the eye" (Carmer, 246-251). Understanding Plath's "pallor" as this sandy whiteness lifting with the heat, "Barren Woman" fits this description. The French first called it "Massacre Island," due to the large number of human skeletons found there; it is another way that the dead might injure, to echo Plath's language. In 1704, France sent a ship of women trained as ideal wives and mothers to marry the settlers in the new colony at Dauphin Island. One woman, Marie-Francoise de Boisrenaud, famously would not marry; she chose instead to be a "Barren Woman," acting as the island schoolteacher. Boisrenaude went on to make history as a powerful female leader. A thriving colony in the 1700s, Dauphin Island was eventually wiped out by a storm, reflecting the emptiness and abandonment of entire first stanza of "Barren Woman."

---

56 In the 1961 issue of *American Poetry Now*, edited by Sylvia Plath, William Stafford's poem "In the Oregon Country" features *Modoc* Indians. Some believe Madoc Gwynedd's voyagers are related. This particular issue of *American Poetry Now* has themes of American history, westward expansion, and the injustices to the Native American Indians, Jews, and African slaves. These themes are prevalent through Plath's work, as interpreted in *Fixed Stars Govern a Life*. Also, in October 1956, Ted Hughes studied Welsh connections to native people in North America and in Europe. This is in an unpublished letter from Ted Hughes to Sylvia Plath, dated October 17, 1956. This letter may be read in the Sylvia Plath archives of the Lilly Library, Indiana University-Bloomington.

Huge mounds of oyster shells were found at Dauphin Island too. Oysters and other pearl-making mollusks fit the fourth line's purity and blindness, as well as marble qualities. Pearls are iridescent like the moon, apposite to Plath's last two lines of the poem. The oyster in its shell fits Plath's "Barren Woman" poem from beginning to end, as the mother-of-pearl inner shell produces, or does not produce, pearls. Plath's second line of the second stanza reflects this image.

Fifth Mirror: Astrology and Astronomy

The sixth brightest star in the night skies, in correlation with the sixth Hierophant card (beginning with zero, The Fool), is Rigel, in the constellation of Orion. Astrologers believe Rigel affects inventiveness, honor, leadership and responsibility, all characteristics of The Hierophant. Visible from every part of the globe, Orion therefore promotes fame. Arabian astronomers considered Orion's belt to represent a string of pearls, apposite to the oysters in the History and the World mirror of this poem. Orion portended fleeting public honors bestowed to those born under its influence. Early astronomers ascribed the star Rigel with marine characteristics, possibly because it is found at the foot of what astrologers call a "river of stars."

Also relating is Delphinus, a small constellation on the edge of the Milky Way, just west of Pegasus. It is in the portion of the sky called "The Water." Delphinus, the dolphin, was discovered by Ptolemy. Its four main stars are known as "Job's Coffin," returning to Plath's second stanza image of the dead. Two of its stars, Sualocin and Rotanev, are purported to be two astronomers' names backwards (contributing to fame), but are in fact Arabic words meaning "swift flow of water" and "swiftly running water" (as in a trough); it is another version of Plath's leaping and sinking fountain.

Delphinus was an emblem of philanthropy, The Hierophant's public good. Pliny described the *Simon* dolphin as Delphinus, a flat-nosed porpoise with a blank face, as in the last line of "Barren Woman." The 13th century astronomer Kazwini wrote that Arabs called it "The Pearls or Precious Stones adorning Al Salīb," recalling pearls of the last mirror.

The Alfonsine Tables (1545) provided information to compute the position of the sun, moon and planets related to fixed stars. They state Delphinus' stars are cognizant of human births and influential over character. Ptolemy echoed this in his *Four Books*, and certainly, a "Barren Woman" might have concern over how Delphinus affected her stars (Allen, 198-201). Ptolemy believed the influence of Delphinus recognized a fondness for ecclesiastical matters, also very much in line with The Hierophant card (Robson, 42).

Pearls are found in the night sky, too. Corona the Crown, a.k.a. Corona Borealis, the Northern Crown, is a lustrous ring the Greeks sometimes called a wreath. It represents the diadem Ariadne wore at her wedding to Dionysus, and its shape might be compared to Plath's museum in "Barren Woman." This constellation twinkles with varying luminosity, and its circle is dominated by a single pearlescent star, Alphecca, "The Pearl." Alphecca may honor Apollo, or his twin sister, Artemis, represented by the moon. Corona the Crown is in close proximity to Delphinus. The crown is said to shine in memory of Ariadne, after Theseus deserted her and in accord with the first line of "Barren Woman." The 17th century work, *the Astronomicon of Manilius*, wrote of these stars:

> "Births influence'd then shall raise fine Beds of Flowers, / And twine their creeping Jasmine round their Bowers; / The Lillies, Violets in Banks dispose."

Plath's image of childbirth and lilies, pictured on The Hierophant card, are also mentioned in "Barren Woman." The *Astronomicon of Manilius* regards this crown as "The Monument of the forsaken Maid." This forsaken maid is the perfect "Barren Woman."

Plath has paid playful tribute to famous alchemists and mystics in other poems,[57] and "Barren Woman" is no exception. One of Plath's favorite repeating images are lilies, and when the flower symbol is applied to this poem, it nods to 17th century William Lilly, known as "the English Merlin." Astrologer Lilly was said to have predicted the plague and the Great Fire of London. Lilly was regarded as one of the principle authorities on astrology, a prophet, and practitioner of talismanic magic, crystal gazing, invocation of spirits and other forms of occultism that Plath and Hughes practiced together. Lilly is credited for working alongside the famous alchemist, Elias Ashmole. Together, the two recovered and translated the writings of the mystic, John Dee, a Welsh occultist and consultant to Queen Elizabeth I. Lilly devoted much of his life to alchemy, divination and Hermetic philosophy, and sometimes put his prophecies in code, either in picture or writing (McCann). Obfuscating occultism has been common practice among practitioners up to Plath and Hughes' time and beyond. Suiting The Hierophant tarot card's element of fame, Lilly was a best-selling author and wrote a long treatise on the theory of Great Conjunctions in 1644, illustrated with astrological charts of famous people. William Lilly wrote *Starry Messenger* in 1645, "an Interpretation of that strange Apparition of three Suns seene in London" on the King's birthday; it is Plath's great white sun accompanied by small Apollos. In 1652, Lilly published *Annus Tenebrosus or the Dark Year*, with a "short Method to Judge the Effects of Eclipses." Here is Plath's moon again. Lilly died of paralysis, Plath's last line of "Barren Woman" (Plant).

Sixth Mirror: Humanities and the Arts

Apollo has always been a favorite subject in the arts. In literature, he first appears in Homer's epic poem *Iliad;* Raphael painted his famous "Parnassus Apollo" in 1511; an ancient marble statue of Apollo exists in the Citadel Museum in Jordan; and Apollo's likeness appears on much ancient pottery. Before numerous episodes of pillaging and raids, the Oracle at Delphi once housed many statues. As was tradition with Greek and Roman sculpture, the eyes are bald, blind, and blank, as described in Plath's poem.

Geoffrey Chaucer, a favorite author of Plath and Hughes', wrote the 1380 poem, "House of Fame," addressing the Delphinus constellation, and corresponding with the theme of Plath's public.[58] The poem is a dream of the poet awakening in a glass temple, illustrated in Plath's first stanza of "Barren Woman." Chaucer's "House of Fame" echoes of the works of Ovid, Virgil's *Aeneid*, and Dante's *Divine Comedy*. "House of Fame" references reputation, weddings, and other social institutions of The Hierophant.

Alexander Pope, one of Lord Byron's chief influences, adapted Chaucer's work as *The Temple of Fame*. Pope's poetry and translations of Greek epics such as *Iliad* brought him success and fame. In 1719 he created the now-famous grotto and gardens at his home in Twickenham, London, decorated with alabaster, marbles, valuable mineral ore, crystals, precious diamonds, and semi-precious stones. One of Pope's famous poems is called "Know Thyself," the same words carved over the temple doorway at the Oracle at Delphi.

---

57 See *Fixed Stars Govern a Life*'s interpretation of Sylvia Plath's poem, "The Jailor."
58 Many consider medieval poets Chaucer, Dante, and Shakespeare to be Christian mystics who infused their writing with alchemy, cosmology, and other forms of occultism.

Aphrodite, a.k.a. Venus, goddess of love, has been depicted in art as risen from the sea, and birthed from an oyster shell.[59] Because Aphrodite was born as an adult, her virginity was said to be perpetually renewed ("Nun-hearted"). A Pompeian mural of Venus is the oldest painting of this subject still in existence. There are many others, including Botticelli's 1486 painting, and Bouguereau's 1879 painting, both entitled, "The Birth of Venus." In classical antiquity, the sea shell represents the female womb.

The "Barren Woman" of Plath's poem is pregnant with meaning, if not a living child. She is Apollo's Sybil; the raped Silvia; the old mother goddess; the goddess Venus; and the angry, disenchanted River Styx. Sometimes, she is the sexy dolphin, but in almost every case, she lives among or has been charmed by a dolphin or a rogue. She is the crown of stars, and the oyster with her pearl. She suffers for her reputation, and is left abandoned in the society which The Hierophant represents.

---

59 For more on Aphrodite, see the *Fixed Stars Govern a Life* interpretation of Sylvia Plath's poem, "Lady Lazarus."

Chapter Seven: Freedom's Feminine Fire
Card #6   The Lovers   Corresponding Poem: "Lady Lazarus"

"Lady Lazarus" is an *Ariel* poem most often read as literal autobiography. The narrator tells of weathering three suicide attempts. Readers therefore perceive Sylvia Plath as the survivor in this poem, rising like Lazarus to ultimately devour the male species. The idea of feminine power is inescapable in "Lady Lazarus," literally and qabalistically. One might say that being a woman in man's society is a survival test itself. That is one of Plath's points for this feminist poem featuring, among other themes, the Statue of Liberty, resurrecting sharks, and the goddess and planet Venus.

First Mirror: The Tarot/Qabalah
In the book Plath used to learn to read tarot cards, *The Painted Caravan*, by Basil Ivan Rákóczi, the definition of the Lovers card is one who passes "through all manner of tests and trials, both of his physical and mental strength […] parallels the Temptations of Christ in the wilderness, and those of Buddha by Mara, the Lord of Evil."

The Golden Dawn attributes the Hebrew letter for The Lovers card as *Zain*, meaning: "the sword of discrimination and the sword wielded by the hand of the faithful and zealous." The Hebrew language has a numeric correlation to its letters and words. The numeric equivalent to the Lovers and its corresponding verb meaning "to slaughter, kill, sacrifice" is 17 (ZaBaCH), meaning ego must undergo total death before resurrection.

In the tarot, the Lovers is a card of choice, complementary forces, and a battle between the sacred and profane. It holds the same thrill or charge of excitement Plath gives the reader in the nineteenth stanza of "Lady Lazarus." Read right-side up, The Lovers card is union; reversed, it is a split. The three figures represent the conscious mind (male), the unconscious mind (female), and the higher self (the angel, or Cupid, in some decks). Some consider the couple to be Adam and Eve in the Garden of Eden. Therefore, this is also a card of opposites and attraction: active to passive, light to dark, conscious to unconscious, and positive to negative.

"Lady Lazarus" and The Lovers card both embody a battle and a choice between wanting to live or die. This is occult initiation into new life, and the art of killing the old one. The choice to be made is conflicting, and so the Lovers card also represents loss, because to choose one thing is to give up another, as we see in the nineteenth stanza.

When Plath marks one of every ten years,

Two Versions of the Lovers card in early Tarot de Marseilles decks

this references the number ten's milestone as completion of a cycle within the tarot and Qabalah (Gray, 188). Thus, the first lines of "Lady Lazarus" are the repetition of this cycle of tens.

The raising of Lazarus is important in the Bible. The Pharisees, as representatives of the Old Mysteries, considered Lazarus' raising a betrayal and violation of ancient tradition. What had been secret was now public, just as Plath poetically revealed the skeletons in her own closet. Cupid, pictured in another deck used in Plath's time, the Tarot de Marseilles, was a mischievous, winged child who taunted humans, firing his gold-tipped arrows of desire. Cupid is a pictorial representation of a "pure gold baby."

Qabalists believe female energy was separated from the attributes of God by man's sin and exiled to the Qliphoth, the dark side of the Tree of Life. Hermeticists believe the Qliphoth holds "The Seven Infernal Habitations," or seven hells, strengthening this

"Nations, races and individual men are unified by an image, or bundle of images, symbolical or evocative of the state of mind, which is of all states of mind not impossible."

— William Butler Yeats,
"Four Years" Part XXII

seventh poem with this seventh tarot card as we start from zero. Translated, Qliphoth means "peel" or "shells." It is new understanding of the napkin Plath peels off in the fourth stanza, and the shells of the peanut-crunchers in her ninth stanza. The feminine fire is said to be imprisoned within the Qliphoth hells. One of the hells is called *Golachab*. Personified as a woman, she destroys the wicked and fights evil and injustice, maintaining equilibrium with her positive side of lovingkindness. Golachab destroys with fire, sometimes burning everything including what should not be burned.

Qabalists believe that only through love can the feminine energy be freed to spiritually transform the Earth. Pure ego, a masculine trait, will recombine at a higher level to reactivate *the Sophia*, the female mythological personification of wisdom and the feminine expression of God. Plath knew that in earlier times, Qabalah was forbidden to women and non-Jews, and it was said no one under the age of forty might delve into its secrets without risking insanity. As a non-Jewish woman declaring her age of thirty,[60] Plath defiantly peeled off the napkin/veil hiding her fiery feminine power.

Some relevant lines and ideas were excised from earlier drafts of this poem also supporting this card's relation to "Lady Lazarus": referring to lovers; involvement; choice; sex; virginity; to the green common pictured on the card, and of Liberty Island, on which the Statue of Liberty stands. This statue will be addressed in more detail in the following mirrors.

The precept of the Hermetic Emerald Tablet that correlates with this poem is: "Thus you will receive the glory of the distinctiveness (light of Lights) of the world. All obscurity (darkness) will flee from you."

Second Mirror: Alchemy

The alchemical initiate seeks to separate from the world and develop his or her senses of perception to great heights. The world and the physical body mean nothing, merely encasing the spirit. Plath alludes to this with her Nazi-like perception of the human body: flesh which can be used to make household objects in her second and third stanzas. The first four stanzas in "Lady Lazarus" present a Josef Mengele-ish alchemical madman ("Herr Doktor"), transmuting the human body not to higher spirit, but to the mundane: lampshades, paperweights, and linens.

Plath's "paperweight" might be an important alchemical text called the "Stockholm Papyrus" that discusses terms such as "laundering" in the transmutation of metals. "Linen" is a term for the White Stage in alchemy, when impurities are cleansed and matter is regenerated and transformed.

---

60 Plath acknowledges being underage for this practice again in the following poem, "Tulips."

The biblical Lazarus' face was bound with a napkin that Jesus commanded to be removed (John 11:44). Plath commands her enemy to do the same, to reveal the truth of her.

The features of the face in the fifth stanza are also aspects of the alchemical process. Part of the alembic glassware is called a "nose." The eyes reference "fishes' eyes," when the stone has reached the state of whitening and takes on an undeniable iridescence compared to pearls or "teeth" (Abraham, 77). Plath's image of bad breath in this same stanza is the foul smell during putrefaction, the Black Phase. The "grave cave" of "Lady Lazarus" is the alchemist's alembic vessel during the Black Phase, known as *the grave*. All impure matter burns and disintegrates there.

Plath's cat simile in the seventh stanza corresponds with the red and green lion symbols of alchemy, and that all four elements must be killed nine times to get to the tenth new cycle.

The idea of trash refers to the waste, or *dross*, of alchemical work. "A million filaments"[61] are the repeated burnings during this process. The old ways no longer work in a new, changed form as Plath annihilates past decades in her eighth stanza.

Physical decomposition is an important stage in complete alchemical union. Plath claimed to have been near to death three times in her life: in an accident as a ten-year-old child[62]; from intentionally taking too many sleeping pills at twenty; and, as A. Alvarez wrote in *Sylvia Plath: A Memoir*:

> "…about her recent incident with the car. It had been no accident; she had gone off the road deliberately, seriously, wanting to die. But she hadn't, and all that was now in the past. For this reason, I am convinced that at this time she was not contemplating suicide. On the contrary, she was able to write about the act so freely because it was already behind her. The car crash was a death she had survived, the death she sardonically felt herself fated to undergo once every decade" (Alexander, 196).

In a literal interpretation of "Lady Lazarus," the reader sees Plath step away from emotion to witness the horrors of death as an impersonal circus sideshow or exhibit, with voyeurs of peanut-eating spectators. However, through the alchemical view these lines represent the *dross*, or earthy alchemical remains at the bottom of the vessel. They are useless and dry, like crunched peanuts after the valuable part has been separated and lifted out.

In the process of unwrapping, the speaker discards the outside layers of unclean matter. Called *Ablution*, this is a precursor to the White Phase of rebirth.

The Lovers tarot card pictures a naked couple before an audience, reflecting the tenth and eleventh stanzas of the poem. An earlier draft and the recorded version of this poem also referenced the Japanese. In World War II, the Japanese went through six months of fire bombing, followed by the atom bombs of Hiroshima and Nagasaki: Japan is the ultimate alchemical metaphor for the Black phase of fire before rebirth.[63]

The idea of rebirth correlates with "Nevertheless, I am the same, identical woman." Plath seemed to like the word "nevertheless," also using it twice in her poem "Medusa." "Nevertheless" is more than a conjunctive adverb in these poems. It echoes that idea of a being equivalent to, or greater than she, expanding the feminist elements featured in other mirrors of this poem. Also, note the comma after "same." Plath has not changed who she is, and yet she looks at a mirror image. "[S]ame" and "identical" is no careless redundancy. It is the alchemy of ascending from earthly form ("Nevertheless") to spiritual formlessness ("same"), and then descending back into the original form as a forever-changed being ("identical woman").

---

61 See the discussion of "million" in the *Fixed Stars Govern a Life* interpretation of Sylvia Plath's poem, "Cut."
62 While Plath claims near-death at age ten in the poem "Lady Lazarus," this has never been verified.
63 See *Fixed Stars Govern a Life*'s interpretation of "Ariel" for more about Japan and the bombings of Hiroshima and Nagasaki.

When Plath "rocked" shut in stanza 13, this is the closed Black phase of the philosopher's stone. The poem's seashell image is from the Mother Sea, the mercurial waters or prima material from which Venus rises and everything is made. "[W]orms" are synonymous in alchemy with the serpent and the dragon symbols, devouring the old, corrupt body, while simultaneously giving life to the infant stone. When the stone reaches the White phase, its "teeth" take on the glittering opalescence of "pearls."

Plath's art of dying in the fifteenth stanza sums up alchemical transmutation; the old form must be killed for the *opus magnum* to be born. The cells of the seventeenth stanza are the cells of matter as much as a prison; "prison" is also a term for the alchemical vessel during the Black phase of *putrefaction* and *nigredo*. To "stay put," then, is to be stuck in putrefaction, when the stone is "killed" (Abraham, 31).

Alchemy and theater were closely associated in the 16th century. Shakespeare had countless alchemical references in his plays. Alchemical treatises were often entitled "theatres," as books to give "a view" or "conspectus" on a subject, another take on Plath's "theatrical / Comeback" (Abraham, 199). Alchemists also regarded the alembic vessel as the theater in which a miniature creation imitated the creation of the greater world.

In addition to cost, the word "charge" means duty and responsibility. It is work the alchemist takes on willingly. Famous alchemist George Ripley wrote of experimenting with hair and blood, among other substances (Abraham, 84). Words, touch, blood, hair, and clothes are examples of physical matter left behind, and are full of Nazi allusions.

Plath's reference to an "opus," corresponds with the Latin *magnum opus*, or "Great Work"; it is success transmuting base matter into gold, creation of the Philosopher's stone, and metaphor for spiritual transformation. In Rosicrucianism, it is the "Chemical Wedding," also apt for the Lovers' card. The famous alchemist Benjamin Lock wrote that the chemical wedding paradoxically takes place through strife, difficulty and opposing forces (Abraham, 141). A sacred marriage of male and female aspects is the goal; its initiation ritual is a procession of tests, purifications, death, resurrection, and ascension. After the 15th century, alchemists considered that there were three stages in this initiation, correlating with Plath's eighth stanza. This third and last stage is *Rubedo*, meaning a reddening, like the hair in the last stanza of "Lady Lazarus." Plath's red hair echoes the red *Herr*, meaning the unification of man or woman with God.

Qabalists consider that Jesus was acting as a Hierophant raising Lazarus in the New Testament. In "Lady Lazarus," Plath is her own Hierophant, her own Initiator, in the alchemical process of creating a higher self. This happens through fire. It is a purification of the gold stone baby of the twenty-third stanza.

In the Biblical legend of Adam and Eve, pictured on the Lovers card, Eve is tempted by fruits from the Tree of Knowledge. When she sins and eats of the forbidden fruit, she has turned away from God and into the burning, as in Plath's twenty-fourth stanza. Eve becomes godlike in the ability to create life, yet with this choice is physical death. Like Adam and Eve, Plath sees contained within death the possibility of spiritual immortality.

In the twenty-fifth and twenty-sixth stanzas of "Lady Lazarus," Plath muses upon being physically reduced to nothing but ash and bits of bone, the waxy soap of fat, and metal. Her spirit, once of the Earth, unites with God. Ash remains after the alchemical phase of Calcination, a conversion of base metal to a fine white powder from heat. Ash can no longer be set on fire. Seen through the psychological metaphor of Jungian alchemy, it is free of passion. This makes ash synonymous with the White phase. Additionally, the "wedding ring" correlates to the chemical wedding, the "gold filling" to filling oneself with or becoming gold.

The word *Herr* is German for Lord; the female counterpart of a Lord is a *Lady*. A "Lord" identifies a prince, a feudal superior, a god or deity. The Hebrew name *YHWH* is rendered LORD. It is Hebrew practice not to speak or write God's true name. Plath united the idea of a healing "Herr Doktor" with his polar opposite destroyer, "Herr Enemy," in the twenty-second stanza of "Lady Lazarus." This correlates with alchemy's uniting of opposites: male and female, good and evil, all represented by this Lovers card. Likewise, in her twenty-seventh stanza, she unites "Herr God" with "Herr Lucifer." Plath as a "Lady" rising from the dead equates with her polar opposite Lord. She becomes the phoenix reborn, the philosopher's stone, a higher, more powerful creature than any mortal.

When Plath calls her hair red, she makes another common alchemical reference. *Red head* is a symbol of the consummation of the opus; red is a property of copper and the goddess Venus, examined in other mirrors of this poem; and it is the color of the *rubedo* phase leading to pure gold (Abraham, 96). Finally, a famous alchemical drawing is of the Green Lion, said to be female. This female lion devours the male sun. Remembering that copper turns green from oxidation, this element shares a symbol for the planet Venus, with the goddess Venus, and with the female sex in biology. It is clarification for this poem's dynamic last line, "And I eat men like air."[64]

Third Mirror: Mythology

The Lovers tarot card is thought by many to be inspired by the mythological tale of the Judgment of Paris, first written of in Homer's *Iliad*. It is a warning of passions run wild, resulting in disastrous consequences. It is a card of powerful, attractive forces that cannot be ignored in the church-mocking line: "I guess you could say, I've a call."[65] Paris was asked to choose between three goddesses: Hera, who held the riches of the world in her hand; Athene, who held power and victory in her sword; or Aphrodite, who offered the cup of love, with its pleasures of sex and sensuality, the feeling expressed in Plath's sixteenth stanza. Author and mythologist Robert Graves wrote in *The White Goddess* that these three women were not jealous rivals, but all aspects of the Triple Goddess, a complete expression of femininity as youth, mother, and crone (Graves, 257).[66] Known as Venus to the Romans, Aphrodite corresponds with the planet Venus, the morning star, equating her with Lucifer, the brightest angel. Lucifer is often confused with Satan, suggesting Plath's references to Hell.[67] Venus, most famously rising from an oyster shell in the Botticelli painting, is associated with the pearls in the fourteenth stanza of "Lady Lazarus." Paris, a weak young man controlled by his libido, chose Aphrodite's pleasures over riches or power, and ultimately lost his kingdom of Troy.

The mythological founder of the Rosicrucians, Christian Rosenkreutz, legendarily wed the goddess Venus in the 15th century work, *The Chymical Wedding of Christian Rosenkreutz*. In the story, Rosenkreutz, born in the 13th century, was said to have died and been reborn in 1378. Rosenkreutz gave the world the watchwords "Liberty, Equality, Fraternity" as goals to live by; ideas encompassing the Statue of Liberty, women's rights, and Freemasonry, all discussed in depth in the following mirrors of this poem. In "The Fifth Day" chapter of the Rosicrucian story, it is written, "Here lies buried Lady Venus, the fair woman who hath undone many a great man," echoing the last line of "Lady Lazarus" (Rosicrucian).

The Egyptian goddess Isis is also identified with the planet Venus, and the Romans and Greeks

---

64 See footnote on eating oxygen in the *Fixed Stars Govern a Life* interpretation for Plath's poem, "Tulips."

65 See footnote on Carl G. Jung's "call" in the *Fixed Stars Govern a Life* interpretation of the poem, "The Jailor."

66 This concept is well illustrated in Plath's verse play, "Three Women."

67 An angel is said to be genderless and have free will, but not freedom of choice. Lucifer is said to be a great and powerful angel, as beautiful and bright as a star. Lucifer's downfall came when it wanted equality with God. In contrast, Satan is portrayed as the ultimate evil and was created to tempt mankind. As this tempter, Satan provides opportunity for man to overcome hardships through faith.

both embraced Isis as their own. One of Isis' symbols was the ankh, the Egyptian cross representing resurrection. In the Egyptian Book of the Dead, Isis' titles read like crib notes for Emma Lazarus' poem, "The New Colossus," which is displayed at the base of the Statue of Liberty. Some of Isis' titles include *she who knows the orphan; she who seeks justice for the poor people; she who seeks shelter for the weak people; she who seeks the righteousness in her people.* Plath related herself to Isis in letters as early as 1956, and Hughes compared Plath to Isis many times. A poster picture of the goddess hung over their fireplace in their Chalcot Square apartment. Of the Statue of Liberty, Plath wrote in her 1957 notebook: "irony: statue of own imprisonment in self, locks shut. 'It's not so much'" (*UJ*, 615).

The Egyptian cat goddess, Eye of Ra, had the body of a woman and the head of a lioness. Cats were associated with Bastet, a solar deity and instrument of the sun god's vengeance. Centuries later, her head evolved to that of a domestic cat's, and like Isis/Venus she became associated with motherhood and fertility. Norse myth posited that there were nine worlds as a cat has nine lives, and these worlds also appear to correspond with the first nine stations of the Qabalah. Welsh legend tells of the Cath Palug, a massive predatory cat that killed and ate "nine score warriors," again like Plath's nine lives in the seventh stanza.

The day of Friday is named after Frige, Norse goddess of romantic love, for her association with the planet Venus. Frige is sometimes equated with Freya, another love goddess, depicted in a chariot drawn by cats. Both goddesses were said to have been married to Odin, and to have shamanistic skills and rituals of symbolic death, dismemberment, and resurrection.

In *The White Goddess*, author Robert Graves tells the story of The Son, Lucifer, a.k.a. Phosphorus, meaning, "bringer of light." Lucifer was the evening star, the planet Venus, born to the Goddess every year, to grow up, destroy the Serpent and then win the Goddess' love. It is Plath's "Comeback in broad day." The Goddess would then destroy him, and from his ashes another Serpent was born that laid a red egg. The Goddess ate the red egg, and her Son (the Sun) would be reborn to her again. Her absolute power was celebrated as "Lady of the Wild Things" and societies worshiping her burned their totem beasts alive. The ash, the red, the consuming of men, and the burning of "Lady Lazarus" are there yet again.

Quetzalcoatl, central Mexico's equivalent to the goddess Venus, is identified with the god GI, who is sometimes understood to have characteristics of a shark. GI's Mayan calendar birthday on "9 Ik with 9 Wind" allows yet another interpretation for Plath's nine in the seventh stanza (Milbrath, 205). See the History and the World mirror of this poem for more on how "Lady Lazarus" relates to the shark.

Finally, Lilith, who is found in Jewish mythology and the Babylonian Talmud, was the first woman created for Adam in the Garden of Eden. Adam and Lilith immediately began to fight. She said, "I will not lie below." Adam told Lilith he would not lie beneath her, as he was superior. Lilith responded that as they were both created from the earth, they were equals. Adam would not listen and Lilith blasphemed God's name, rose into the air, and abandoned Adam.

Fourth Mirror: History and the World

Hitler's Nazi party, an obvious presence in "Lady Lazarus," based their idealism in part in German Neopaganism and Norse mythology, which Plath touched upon in the last mirrors. Rooted in mysticism and the occult, Neopagans ascribe that even inanimate objects have "a charge," their term for soul, corresponding with Plath's nineteenth stanza. German Neopagans believed in fatalism and destiny, attributes of the Lovers tarot card.

German Neopaganism incorporated practices such as runes, astrology, ritual magic, and the idea of a pure Aryan blood line, reworking Nordic traditions to better serve the state. The Thule Society was created to preserve German antiquity, and members believed Hitler was the redeemer of Germany. Prominent members of the Nazi party were a part of this society that proposed the ancient wheel of life, the swastika, be used to represent the Nazis. Heinrich Himmler, leader of the SS, held great interest in mysticism and emulated the structure of St. Ignatius Loyola's Jesuit Order.

It has been observed that the strongest earthquakes, volcano eruptions, storms and tsunamis, droughts and pandemics seem to take place about once every ten years, as in Plath's first stanza. This is also the frequency of the population census for the United States and the United Kingdom, a "walking" count of citizens that first began around the time of the Black Death. More significantly is that once a decade the famous Passion Play is performed in Oberammergau, Germany. This play was important to Plath, as her high school class led took a trip to Europe to attend it. Plath did not have the money to join them (Wilson, 83).

The Passion Play began during the 30 Years' War, the age Plath gives in the seventh stanza of "Lady Lazarus." This was in the 17th century, and the village swore to God to perform "The Play of Suffering, Death and Resurrection of our Lord Jesus Christ" in order to hold back the Black Death that had decimated its people. During this time, Jews were blamed for poisoning wells, and were sometimes burned alive. Over two hundred Jewish communities were attacked across Europe, and over 350 massacres took place.

Cats too were considered in allegiance with the Devil and witches at this time, and killed in great numbers. Plath's details of the corpse and death shroud, of dying, and the burning of bodies to prevent contamination is throughout "Lady Lazarus." With almost half the population of Europe killed from the Plague, it took "A miracle!" to knock it out.

Jumping ahead to the twentieth century, Adolf Hitler and the Nazi party were extremely taken with the Passion Play. Exploiting the 1934 jubilee season, the Ministry of Public Enlightenment and Propaganda pushed its anti-Semitic themes and encouraged the public to see it. Their posters read, "Germany is calling you!" and fit the calling of Plath's fourteenth stanza.

The dark triangular mountain pictured in the background between the lovers on the Lovers tarot card closely resembles a shark fin. Much of "Lady Lazarus" fits the predatory tiger shark with its cat-like name, and the Great White Shark, both known to be man-eaters as in Plath's last line. Why wouldn't the perfect killing machine consider dying an "art"? From its "featureless" face, a prominent nose, blank eye "pits," and a "full set of teeth," the shark is well described. The largest sharks are female and always "smiling." The shark might certainly ask, "O my enemy. / Do I terrify?" Great White Sharks are known to live thirty years and longer. Sharks are known to eat a lot of trash, often revealed when the belly is slit before crowds of people who shove in to look at the beast hanging from its tail. It was not unusual to witness "a million" camera flashes on these occasions. Nine species of shark inhabit Atlantic waters, like Plath's cat's nine lives.

Cousin of the tiger shark, the Lazarus shark of the Great Barrier Reef walks on its fins along the coral   Plath's miraculous walking in the second stanza. When the tide washes out, the fish is often stranded on dry land. Yet it survives for hours without oxygen in a coma-like state. Like Lazarus' resurrection, this shark returns to life when the tide washes it back to sea. Lazarus sharks eat worms and mollusks   Plath's fourteenth stanza. Also fitting this poem is that the Lucifer shark, with its luminescent belly, is lit like the Nazi skin lampshade of the second stanza. All sharks have keen electroceptor sensing organs ("a million filaments") to detect the charge of electric fields in water, corresponding to Lucifer's/Venus' light and Plath's nineteenth stanza charge.

Called "the most wonderful plants in the world" by Charles Darwin (Darwin, 231), the carnivorous Venus flytrap shares the name Venus, along with shark-like characteristics, including those smiling teeth known as cilia that close around insect prey. With its Luciferian correspondence, the plant tolerates fire well, and needs regular burnings of its land to keep competition from taking it over. The Venus flytrap may live up to thirty years old.

When America was asked to foot the bill for the Statue of Liberty's pedestal in an economic depression, *The New York Times* wrote, "no true patriot can countenance any such expenditures for bronze females in the present state of our finances" (Khan, 160).

When the Statue of Liberty was complete, outside of the designers' wives, women were not allowed to attend the ceremony. Suffragists appreciated the irony of forbidding women to witness the unveiling of a female statue, and they took the opportunity to make speeches about equality from boats in Lady Liberty's surrounding water.[68]

Plath shared much in common with American journalist, author, poet, literary critic and Unitarian transcendentalist, Margaret Fuller (1810-1850), who was born in Cambridge, Massachusetts. Fuller wrote what is considered to be the first feminist work, *Woman in the 19th Century*. Originally entitled *The Great Lawsuit: Man versus Woman*, this 1845 work made Fuller one of the most important figures in the women's rights movement, and her rebelliousness and independence inspired Nathaniel Hawthorne for his character Hester Prynne in *The Scarlet Letter*. Fuller was hired as the first female editor for Ralph Waldo Emerson's *The Dial*, and became good friends with Emerson, as would the poet Emma Lazarus, mentioned in the Arts and Humanities mirror of this poem. Fuller, Lazarus, and Plath all shared an obsession with their fathers. Fuller wrote, "My father's image follows me constantly" (Blanchard, 93). Fuller died in a shipwreck off of Fire Island, fire being another shared image in the "Lady Lazarus" poem. Even more fascinating, Fuller had written of an omen of her early death (Slater, 2-3).

In that same era, the African-American Sojourner Truth grew up in slavery. She fled to Plath's Northampton, Massachusetts area to live in a mixed-race utopian community and fight for abolitionists and suffragists. Sojourner Truth gave her famous "Ain't I A Woman" speech, referencing the Bible story of Lazarus, and the importance of sisters Mary and Martha coming to Jesus to raise their brother as a case for women's rights.

Meanwhile, on the other side of the world, Plath was aware that women in Japan fought for their rights as well. Before her death, Plath made a recording of "Lady Lazarus" with additional lines that editor A Alvarez encouraged her to cut. One of those lines referenced being Japanese. The suffrage movement in Japan occurred at the same time as in the United States, and with forced prostitution and polygamy, Japanese women had even harder lives. By seeing herself as "identical" in her womanhood, Plath wrote in kinship with these women who would become America's enemies in World War II. It seems Plath examined women's rights all over the world, throughout the ages. Even women in the seemingly enlightened society of Ancient Greece, the era from which Lady Liberty is modeled, had no citizenship and no right to vote. Female repression and feminism had become a worldwide, timeless shared experience.

Interweaving Greek myth, astronomy and the world, the Ancient Greeks named the evening star, or Venus, "Hesperus." Hesperus was believed to be the son of the dawn goddess, Eos. The short phrase, "Hesperus is Phosphorus" is known as Frege's Puzzle (a homophone to the Nordic goddess "Frige"). A famous philosophy of language, its principle is that if one knows the meanings

---

68 See reference to Julia Ward Howe in *Fixed Stars Govern a Life*'s interpretation of Plath's poem, "The Courage of Shutting-Up," and the interpretation of "A Secret" for a reference to both Mary Wollstonecraft and Elizabeth Cady Stanton.

of the words, he cannot rationally accept that one is more powerful than the other. It is a semantic statement on equality.

One of Frege's[69] best and most famous students was the German Jewish professor, Gershom Scholem, considered to be the founder of modern Kabbalah studies and the first professor of Jewish mysticism at the Hebrew University of Jerusalem. Ironically, Frege was a Nazi sympathizer who tended to make exceptions.[70] It is no accident Plath used "So, so" in her twenty-third stanza, as "so-and-so" is originally a Jewish expression.[71]

The title, "Herr Doktor" was a common address for the German-born Scholem, who fled to Palestine during wartime. In addition to Kabbalah, Scholem is known for his writings on Jacob Frank and Frankism--yet another perfect historical fit for "Lady Lazarus." Frank created Frankism, a mystic religion in 18th century Poland combining elements of Christianity and Judaism. Known for Rasputin-like behaviors of both asceticism and sensuality,[72] Frankists practiced self-flagellation as religious penance, but ignored all prohibitions and restrictions of Jewish law, including incest. Frankists rejected the Talmud, recognizing only the Kabbalah and Zohar as sacred texts. The rabbinical court accused Frank of breaking fundamental Jewish laws of morality and modesty, and in 1756, rabbis demanded Frankists be burned at the stake as heretics. Frank's daughter, Eva Frank, was the only woman to have been declared a Jewish messiah, as well as the incarnation of the female aspect of God, Shekhinah, and the reincarnation of the Virgin Mary. In the Kabbalah's sacred text, *The Zohar*, Shekhinah is "a beautiful maiden who has no eyes," reminiscent of the fifth stanza of "Lady Lazarus." Upon Jacob Frank's death in 1791, Eva became the Frankist "holy mistress" and leader of the cult (Jewish).

Fifth Mirror: Astrology and Astronomy

Venus, a.k.a. "Lucifer," the bringer of light, is the only planet named after a female in the Solar System. Named for the goddess of love, Venus is closer to the Sun than Earth and has been labeled an "inferior planet" in the ancient cosmology of Ptolemy. Venus symbolizes both feminine power and inequality, and is sometimes considered a sister planet to the earth because of similar size, gravity, and bulk composition. We know Plath could identify it due to her pocket calendar notes on May 26, 1956, "Venus in clear bluegreen sky."[73]

Venus rotates clockwise, the opposite direction from other planets on her walk around our Solar System. Brighter than any star and can be seen even in the day, she is the "Evening Star" that becomes the "Morning Star" as it overtakes the Earth in its orbit of the Sun. Despite the time of day or night, she is the "same, identical" planet.

When Plath wrote "Lady Lazarus," the spacecraft Mariner 2, launched August 1962, was in Venus' orbit. Mariner 2 faced continuous setbacks, losing power and overheating, yet persevering. Until Mariner 2, Venus was considered to be a disc without features, hidden under a veil of linen-like clouds, corresponding to the third and fourth stanzas of "Lady Lazarus." The spacecraft revealed a pitted surface, Plath's eye image, and the most active volcanoes of any planet. Venus is believed to periodically undergo entire planetary resurfacing; one might compare it to resurrection. Its "flesh" is self-consumed; the grave is her home surface. Nothing can live on Venus, apposite to Plath's dying theme.

Plath's filaments image is not limited to the inside of a light bulb; a solar filament is a prominence extending from the Sun, viewed as something dark against its bright background. This is true

---

69 For more on Gottlob Frege and "Hesperus is Phosphorus," see the *Fixed Stars Govern a Life* interpretation of Sylvia Plath's poem, "The Detective."
70 Frege shows up again in the *Fixed Stars Govern a Life* interpretation of Plath's "The Detective."
71 See the *Fixed Stars Govern a Life*, vol. II interpretation of "Wintering" for more on "so-and-so."
72 See *Fixed Stars Govern a Life*'s interpretation of Plath's poem, "Tulips" for more on Rasputin.
73 Plath's pocket calendar is kept in the Sylvia Plath Archives at the Lilly Library, Indiana University-Bloomington.

when Venus transits the sun, an astrologically important time for women on Earth.[74] Venus has a slow rotation, Plath's turning and burning. One Venus day is equivalent to about ten Earth days. A mystery of Venus is its "ashen light" on its dark side, Plath's ash image. The Mayan calendar is based, in part, on the motions of Venus. The calendar ends in 2012, at the beginning of the Age of Aquarius, when feminine power is said to reign.

Crossing astronomy and world mirrors are the Pawnee Indians of North America, devout cosmologists, who believed the Morning Star and Evening Star (the planet Venus) mated to create the first human: a girl. The Pawnee were very female-centered, and designed their lodges to correspond to the universe and the womb. A young girl was ritually sacrificed to the Morning Star each spring.

Sixth Mirror: Humanities and the Arts

Germany has touched "Lady Lazarus"/Lady Liberty in numerous ways: in myth rooted in the Statue of Liberty; by German saboteurs; with the Freemasons who built her; the Passion Play; Nazi Neopaganism; and Norse mythological influences. "Lady Lazarus" is also the first *Ariel* poem where Plath uses actual German words and specifically references Nazis. The German language is especially relevant in this poem, as the pronoun for female is the English equivalent of "it." In the amusing 1880 essay, "The Awful German Language," Mark Twain explains:

"Every [German] noun has a gender, and there is no sense or system in the distribution; so the gender of each must be learned separately and by heart. There is no other way. To do this one has to have a memory like a memorandum-book. In German, a young lady has no sex, while a turnip has. Think what overwrought reverence that shows for the turnip, and what callous disrespect for the girl. See how it looks in print—I translate this from a conversation in one of the best of the German Sunday-school books:

Gretchen. Wilhelm, where is the turnip?

Wilhelm. She has gone to the kitchen.

Gretchen. Where is the accomplished and beautiful English maiden?

Wilhelm. It has gone to the opera" (Twain).

Mark Twain was a freemason, belonging to the Polar Star Lodge No. 79 A.F.& A.M., in St. Louis. Interested in parapsychology, he was also close friends with Nikola Tesla and spent a great deal of time in Tesla's laboratory[75]. Along with his wife, Twain became involved and supportive of abolitionists and those fighting for women's rights and social equality. Twain was not a religious man, and wrote of Christianity as "a terrible religion." He did however believe in God, and stated Qabalah-like acceptance that "the universe is governed by strict and immutable laws" (Baender, 56). In 1883, Twain was asked to contribute work to raise funds to build the pedestal to hold the Statue of Liberty. Twain sent a check and a letter to *The New York Times*, December 4, 1883, that included these words:

"…suppose your statue represented her[:] old, bent, clothed in rags, downcast, shame-faced, with the insults and humiliation of 6,000 years, imploring a crust and an hour's rest for God's sake at our back door?—come, now you're shouting! That's the aspect of her which we need to be reminded of, lest we forget it" (Fatout, 135-136).

In 1909, Twain said, "I came in with Halley's Comet in 1835. It is coming again next year, and I expect to go out with it. It will be the greatest disappointment of my life if I don't go out with Halley's Comet. The Almighty has said, no doubt: 'Now here are these two unaccountable freaks;

74 Historical events coinciding with Venus in Transit are throughout the *Fixed Stars Govern a Life's* interpretation of Plath's poem, "A Secret."
75 See *Fixed Stars Govern a Life's* interpretation of "The Couriers" for more on Nikola Tesla.

they came in together, they must go out together'." It is another fine connection with the fiery end of Plath's "Lady Lazarus," and Twain did indeed go out with Halley's Comet.

Americans tend to think German's *Herr* is equivalent to *Mister*. This is not so. The word *Herr* means *Lord*, implying the man is a master over something or someone. The word *Lady* holds no such power. In old days, *Herren* (plural of *Herr*) were nobles, knights, masters, lords, rulers, bosses and gentlemen. *Herr* even accompanies titles for God (*Gott, der Herr*, meaning, *The Lord God*).

Plath's repetition of *so* in "Lady Lazarus" means *that way* or *true* in both English and German. But "So-so," in addition to its Jewish origin explained earlier, has a different connotation: In English, the hyphenated "so-so" means mediocre or not good enough. Was Plath critical of *Herr Doktor*?

The Colossus of Rhodes, one of the seven wonders of the ancient world, was a giant statue of the Greek sun god Helios, erected between 292 and 280 B.C. Destroyed in an earthquake, it inspired the title poem for Plath's first book, *The Colossus and Other Poems*. In the 19th century, America's Statue of Liberty became "The New Colossus." In 1883, a poem of the same name was inscribed upon a plaque at its base:

> "Not like the brazen giant of Greek fame,
> With conquering limbs astride from land to land;
> Here at our sea-washed, sunset gates shall stand
> A mighty woman with a torch, whose flame
> Is the imprisoned lightning, and her name
> Mother of Exiles. From her beacon-hand
> Glows world-wide welcome; her mild eyes command
> The air-bridged harbor that twin cities frame.
> 'Keep, ancient lands, your storied pomp!' cries she
> With silent lips. 'Give me your tired, your poor,
> Your huddled masses yearning to breathe free,
> The wretched refuse of your teeming shore.
> Send these, the homeless, tempest-tost to me,
> I lift my lamp beside the golden door!"

"The New Colossus" poem was written by American-Jewish poet Emma Lazarus soon after a trip to Europe, where she witnessed the persecution of Russian-Jewish immigrants and others firsthand. Lazarus also wrote the poems "Venus," and "Venus of the Louvre," the latter about the Jewish-German poet, Heinrich Heine (another *Herr*), mourning at the feet of Venus de Milo his inability to love. Lazarus dedicated her first book of poems to her father, who had educated her--and to whom it seems no other man could compare. She never married, kept social company with great writers such as Emerson and Browning, and worked tirelessly for Jewish immigrant and abolitionist concerns.

"The New Colossus" was renamed "Give Me Your Tired, Your Poor" for a song in the 1949 Irving Berlin musical, *Miss Liberty*. Aside from the name Berlin hearkening to Germany, the play coincidentally had a cast of characters known as "the Sharks."

The Statue of Liberty's actual name is "Liberty Enlightening the World." While she is said to represent Libertas, the Roman goddess of freedom, her designer Bertholdi admitted she was a composite of goddesses: Hera, wife of Zeus, with her similar face, clothing, sandals and torch; and of Venus, sometimes called Lucifer, or Isis (Claerr). Her original design had been submitted to be built in Egypt at the Suez Canal, but they were not interested. Bertholdi modified his drawings and presented "the same, identical woman" to the French as a gift of goodwill toward the United States.

Plath's "Lady Lazarus" tells the story of the Statue of Liberty. In the beginning, financial problems struck every ten years. To ascend the Lady's spiral staircase to the crown might be considered a miracle of walking. Her skin was made of bright copper sheets. Her right foot stands on a plaque like a great weight.

As the statue was first assembled, her head and arm with its torch were exhibited separately, corresponding with Plath's body parts in the eleventh stanza. In 1875, it was proposed America should jointly fund the project by paying for its pedestal. This presented a problem and almost halted its construction. It was the first trial at ten years old, reflected in the twelfth stanza. After another decade, in 1885, it looked as if the statue project might "die" completely, reflected in Plath's thirteenth stanza. A Pulitzer fundraising campaign solicited funds, most donations under $1 by calling upon common citizens. It is the persistent requests in the fourteenth stanza.

Completion of the statue marked New York City's first ticker tape parade, with its filaments and its crowd shoving in to see. A book from Plath's library on Yeats' spiritism,[76] *The Unicorn*, tells the story that in 1915, occultist Aleister Crowley paddled up the Hudson in a canoe, climbed the Statue of Liberty, and proclaimed an Irish Republic (Moore, 241). At the unveiling, the French flag was draped across her face. Over forty years later, in 1956, Hungarian nationalists hijacked the statue and put their flag across her. These drapes are the napkin image Plath commands to be removed. The statue's enormity was like none seen before, corresponding with Plath's question of terrifying. The Statue of Liberty bears the classic Roman nose, the blank eyes, and a crown with 25 windows resembling teeth, as seen in the fifth stanza. Her critics and their "sour breath" were soon silenced.

By 1900, the statue's copper skin had taken on a green patina. There was fear of corrosion, the grave upon her. At this time, Lady Liberty was about thirty years old from the time construction had begun. In 1916, German saboteurs set off an explosion nearby, corresponding to the words "Nazi" and "Herr" throughout the poem. The statue sustained minor damage and was closed to the public as Plath's narrator closed shut in "Lady Lazarus." There were also problems with lighting, addressing the filaments image. A new generation of Pulitzers raised funds for exterior illumination.

In 1937, the National Park Service took over the Statue of Liberty's management. They transformed her stand on Bedloe's Island into a park and restored the statue. Old buildings were demolished, the land was re-graded and reseeded, and new granite steps were built at the public entrance for her great comeback, described in the eighteenth stanza of "Lady Lazarus." Her lights were put out for wartime blackouts, but lit briefly on victorious occasions, including D-Day, when she flashed the Morse code for victory. A miracle knocked her out.

Visitors to the statue must pay the cost, Plath's "charge," for the ferry across the water to Liberty Island. And of course, the ferry "really goes."

The flame of the torch on the statue is gold-plated like Plath's baby image. While her copper has turned green, she still reflects the colors of sunrise, turning and burning. The broken shackles at the base of Lady Liberty's feet represent freedom from oppression.

The Statue of Liberty has been called a "shrine to the number seven" (Decoded), and the Lovers tarot card is the seventh card when counting from zero. The seventh station on the Qabalah, Netzach, meaning "victory," is assigned to Venus. The Statue of Liberty has seven rays emanating from her crown, and many numerical games are built into her dimensions. Lady Liberty's height and measurements have the curious addition of one inch added to even feet, totaling 1813 inches, evenly divisible by seven 259 times. Adding 259 into itself (2+5+9) equals 16. This is no numerological accident. There are various instances of the number 16 (1+6) and the number 25 (2+5) which, when added together, also equal seven. Plath's "hand and foot" are units of measurement. The hand, with beginnings in Ancient Egypt and the Bible, is the traditional unit of measurement in Britain. Designed and built by Freemasons, the Statue of Liberty's number sevens represent the seven Masonic liberal arts and sciences: grammar, rhetoric, dialectic, arithmetic, geometry, music and

76 Spiritism is based on the five books of the Spiritist Codification by French writer Allan Kardec that document séances in which phenomena was observed that was attributed to incorporeal intelligence (spirits). Kardec sought to differentiate spiritualism and Spiritism. Spiritualism is common to various religions and is defined as the opposite of materialism. Kardec's work popularized talking (Ouija) boards, mesmerism, and other occult activities in the 1900's.

astronomy. Seven is a sacred number permeating aspects of every major religion, representing the seven seas, seven continents, the notes of the musical scale, the colors of the rainbow, days of the week, virtues and sins, sacraments and more.

Conspiracy theorists believe the statue is a symbol of the Illuminati, a new world order secret society working through the masons in past centuries. Formed in Bavaria, a German state in 1776, the Illuminati sought to abolish all monarchies, religion, private properties and nation states, replacing it with a utopia. Known as "the enlightened ones," they were the "hidden hand" in freemasonry, exemplified in portraits by hiding a hand inside a jacket. The most obvious Illuminati correlation is in Lady Liberty's original name, "Liberty Enlightening the World," and her radiant crown that represent enlightenment. The torch is held in the right hand, an Illuminati representation equalizing her with Prometheus and Lucifer. The Statue of Liberty is therefore actually a symbol of Lucifer, the 'one who bears light.' She is the planet Venus, the morning star, and Lucifer is regularly misinterpreted as a name for Satan (Decoded).

In an amusing yet relevant aside, Great Britain's legendary glow-worms are found in Devon, where Plath and Hughes lived at the time she wrote "Lady Lazarus," correlating with the worms of the fourteenth stanza. The glow-worms' numbers began to decline in the 1950s and 1960s. They are literary stars of the insect world, found in the works of writers such as Dryden, Hardy, and Tennyson. Shakespeare wrote that they evoked "ineffectual Fire" in *Hamlet*. Wordsworth called them "earth-born stars." Only female glow-worms glow. Roald Dahl's 1961 story, *James and the Giant Peach* features a six-legged (corresponding to that Lovers' card number) female glow-worm, providing light and ultimately saving the city of New York from an enormous electric bill by illuminating the Statue of Liberty's torch (Independent).

Sylvia Plath spent the summer of 1953 in New York City, a time upon which her novel, *The Bell Jar*, is based. She and Ted Hughes made several trips to New York while living in the States. The Statue of Liberty would have been the first thing Plath saw greeting her to her homeland on her ocean liner trips from abroad. In 1957, Hughes commented on the "Statue of Lib" in a letter.

Elements of the mythic Helen of Troy also cannot be ignored in "Lady Lazarus." The half-mortal love child of Zeus, Helen's white-hot sexuality and beauty "launch'd a thousand ships" in the same way the Statue of Liberty does today. Helen confronts Aphrodite in *Iliad*, accusing her of sexual envy. In H.D.'s poem, "Helen," the color white represents the icy-hatred and envy Greece had for this beautiful woman. The same hands, knees, foot and ash imagery Plath uses is there.

Plath greatly admired feminist forerunner, Virginia Woolf, praising her many times in journals and letters. Woolf's *Mrs. Dalloway*, which came out in 1925 at the height of the Women's Movement, also contains references to the bones, teeth, ash, and other elements in Plath's poem (Connors, 121-122).

In Plath's December 1958 *Journals*, she wrote notes after a particularly powerful session with her therapist, Dr. Ruth Beuscher, about her mother. This would not be relevant to "Lady Lazarus," save for the similar language and images in these six or so pages. She wrote that her father "heiled Hitler" at home (*UJ*, 430). Of her selfless, doormat mother, she said, "I have ulcers, see how I bleed" (*UJ*, 430) sharing the same rhythm and feeling of "These are my hands / My knees." "Life was hell" (*UJ*, 430) conjures "I do it so it feels like hell." Plath's mother Aurelia has become her own Lazarus after her father's death. "My mother killed the only man who'd love me steady through life" (*UJ*, 431) became the man-eater of the last stanza. "I hated men because they didn't have to suffer like a woman did" (*UJ*, 431) echoes women's rights. Additionally, there are references to New York, and to Jews (*UJ*, 432); to the "sticky white filth of desire" (*UJ*, 432) suggesting Plath's poetic pearls; to "Put her in a cell" (*UJ*, 432); and to stinking breath (*UJ*, 434). Meanwhile, Plath expresses the pain of being expected to be perfect (*UJ*, 432). Perhaps Aurelia Plath, the anti-role model, as a downtrodden, subservient woman at the hands of Sylvia Plath's authoritarian German father, has more to do with "Lady Lazarus" than ever guessed before.

Chapter Eight: Holy Devils and Forbidden Fruit
Card #7   The Chariot   Corresponding Poem: "Tulips"

Sylvia Plath wrote "Tulips" in March 1961 as a patient in the hospital. She had just her appendix removed, following a miscarriage the month before. Most readers see this poem as a meditation on convalescence, life, and death. Some have taken "Tulips" to be a woman's renunciation of individuality in order to put the family first, and death to be the sole escape. Plath read this poem at the "Poetry at the Mermaid" festival, sponsored by the Arts Council of Great Britain, in London in July 1961. In "Tulips," we understand that Plath makes do with the numbness of an anesthetized peace. An entire book could be written just on the mystical underpinnings of Plath's "Tulips," as it deftly tours the reader through the wonder of the number seven and the tarot's major arcana. Buckle your seatbelts: This Chariot is going for a furious ride through winter journeys, Russian history, religious and national fanaticism, Plato's *Symposium* and Salinger's seclusion, revealing what these excitable tulips really are, and where they come from.

First Mirror: The Tarot/Qabalah:
The Chariot tarot card foretells excitement, speed, rushing, travel, and triumph over adversity. The sphinxes in the foreground represent the senses; the invisible reins are the mind that drives them; the car is the human body, our vehicle to travel in this world. Plath's "Tulips" is full of The Chariot

card's traveling: passing, coming and going, far-away countries, engines, trolleys, boats, and baggage. "Tulips" is also a mystical masterpiece, doing many different things with tarot, Qabalah, alchemy and the number seven. It is not too surprising then that Plath capitalized on this number with two of her strongest poems, the previous "Lady Lazarus," and her celebrated "Tulips." The Chariot card bears the numeral seven, which the Pythagoras called the perfect number. To Pythagoreans, seven was 3 and 4, the triangle and the square, perfect figures.

Symbolism pictured on The Chariot card and used within the poem includes: the nurses' caps resembling the Charioteer's crown; black and white sphinxes, which echo the black ("pillbox") and white (the room, the uniforms); the tulip-shaped shield affixed to the front of The Chariot looks much like a Greek caduceus, adopted as the emblem for medicine

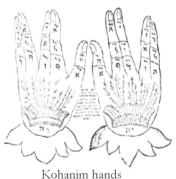

Kohanim hands

("far away as health"); Jewish priests and Qabalists give the priestly blessing, *Kohanim*, with their two hands forming an empty tulip-shaped space representing the three attributes of God: Mercy, Courage and Glory.

When the rabbi blesses the congregation, another hand signal is made, reflecting the sixth line of the second stanza.[77] Historic illustrations of this hand sign show the Kohanim hands from the back, looking like tulips.[78] As mentioned earlier, seven is the numeral on The Chariot card and a holy number. But the Hebrew letter corresponding with The Chariot card is *Chet*, representing the number eight; The Chariot is the eighth card counting

77 American pop culture would compare this hand gesture to the *Star Trek* Vulcan sign.
78 For another picture of Kohanim hands, see: http://en.wikipedia.org/wiki/File:Shefa_Tal.png

62

SEVEN AS A HOLY NUMBER:

The Goths and Romans both had 7 deities. There are 7 steps in Qabalah initiation, 7 chakras, and 7 rungs on Jacob's Ladder (the route to heaven in the Book of Genesis). *Mackey's Encyclopedia of Freemasonry* aligns 7 rites of initiation with the 7 planets of antiquity: Sun, Moon, Mars, Jupiter, Venus, Mercury, and Saturn. Hence, almost all religious systems profess 7 heavens. The Sun was considered the greatest planet of the ancient 7. Next in splendor was the Moon, which changes every 7th day. The Arabians had 7 Holy Temples, and in the Persian mysteries are 7 spacious caverns through which aspirants must pass. There are also 7 alchemical stages & 7 metals of alchemy. The 7 steps to heaven represent Justice, Equality, Kindness, Good Faith, Labor, Patience, and Intelligence. 7 is a prime number, (as 7 is created by adding its two previous Lucas numbers, 3+4); and a Mersenne prime number, as the power of two minus one. There are 7 days of the week, 7 deadly sins, 7 levels in Dante's hell, and 7 ages of man in Shakespeare. The Egyptians had 7 original and higher gods. The Phoenicians 7 kabiris; the Persians, 7 sacred horses of Mithra; the Parsees 7 angels opposed by seven demons, and 7 celestial abodes paralleled by 7 lower regions, often represented as one 7-headed deity. The Hindu religion has a solar deity who rides a chariot pulled by 7 horses, representing the 7 chakras. The 21 major arcana numbers in the tarot are divided by their three stages of life , to equal seven once again. Is it a surprise that Plath's "Tulips" has seven lines in each stanza?

from zero. Eight therefore has importance in Plath's "Tulips" poem, too: Its hieroglyph represents an enclosure, and the action of victorious destruction. The Hebrew word for *chariot* is *Merkaba* (also spelled *Merkabah*). It associates with Ezekiel's vision in the opening of the Bible's Book of Ezekiel. This vision is considered the most mystical of passages in the Hebrew Bible. There was once a prohibition against its study, and scholars of Ezekiel's vision had to be men with proven good judgment, often heading schools, and of *a certain age*. As Plath breaks these rules, she calls herself the "Stupid pupil" who cannot help that she "has to take everything in."

Merkaba, the chariot, is said to be a vehicular tetrahedron of light with a four-fold symmetry, like a tulip's structure. The former anthropology student, Ted Hughes, as well as Plath, with her adoration of Radin's *African Folktales*, might have known that *Merkaba* is also coincidentally the Zulu word for a space/time/dimensional vehicle. The Zulus believed this chariot was how their tribe arrived on Earth. Ancient Egyptians also used the word *Merkaba* with a three-fold meaning: *Mer*, meaning light rotating within itself; *Ka*, meaning spirit; and *Ba*, meaning the human body.

Qabalists believe their Merkaba is counter-rotating electromagnetic energy spirals, based on sacred geometry. To reach Merkaba, one must practice a meditation technique called spherical breathing. It is well known that Hughes gave Plath meditation and breathing exercises, first documented in their time at Yaddo artists' colony. The first stage is to visualize a brilliant white light surrounding the practitioner, and Plath's first stanza of "Tulips" is a fine fit.

In the more specific reading for the Chariot card, the meditating narrator's head and body are "propped" up in the second stanza. The breathing continues as busy thoughts come and go through the mind. The meditator repositions his or her fingers, touching a different fingertip to the thumb at various intervals, more curious hand movements of Plath's second stanza. The eighth stanza is a study of the meditative breath.

Plath refers to herself as a "cargo boat" in the fourth stanza, a vehicle or vessel like the Chariot. One might also tie in the nearby word "slip," as a slip is where one docks a boat.

In "Tulips," Plath wrestles with a reluctant acceptance of the tulips and the life they represent. The strong, brutal, fast force of life moves toward the light and opens to her, like her red wound. It conquers her slow wish for death and, like the Chariot, it wins.

The Chariot's correspondence on the Qabalah's Tree of Life opens "Tulips" up to a radical new interpretation: The Golden Dawn performs a rite for this station called "The Eucharist of Babylon"; "Eucharist" meaning "Holy Communion," as in Plath's fifth stanza. The Book of Ezekiel, from whence the Chariot reference originated, is one of the more sexually explicit books of the Bible, especially chapters 16 and 23, which inspire this Eucharist.

The Eucharist of Babylon was designed to tap into the supernatural erotic power of sexual submission and domination; its sexual sacrament invokes the energies of the archetypal Scarlet Woman and her war-shriek of lust and wrath. "Tulips," in this context, means the two labial lips; Plath is writing about denying the sex drive. This is excitement she wishes to ignore by lying quietly alone. The restraint toward peace, against physical pleasure and orgasmic explosion, are all in the first stanza.

Around 70 C.E., the Hekhalot erotic theology proposed long periods of ritual purification, self-mortification, "sudden tongues" of ecstatic prayer, and meditation, in an effort to journey through the seven stages of mystical ascent. The journey is dangerous and fraught with obstacles in the way that Plath's air in the eighth stanza "snags and eddies."

Qabalistic qualities for the Chariot are Victory, Triumph, and Firmness. The four pillars in this card's illustration represent the conditions in which energy survives: fire, the fiery red of Plath's tulips; air, seen in the breathing and oxygen in the poem; earth, as the image of the body as a pebble; water, which is throughout the poem; electricity, throughout this poem with the suggestion of ECT after a suicide attempt, and in the fourth stanza's swabbing of associations; and finally, Plath covers forms of gas in the first stanza's anesthesia.

Plath's tarot guide, *The Painted Caravan,* includes in its summary of the Chariot card the story of the Egyptian god Ra. Ra suffered the loss of the youthful, beloved half of himself. He followed the chariot into Hades, the land of the dead, to search for and reunite with it. With memories of her father's death, her own hospitalization after her suicide attempt and the resulting electro-shock therapy, Plath detested hospitals. Between the loss of a baby, followed by appendectomy, she must certainly have felt that half of herself had been removed.

As stated earlier, the Hebrew letter for the Chariot card is *Chet* (different from *Merkaba*, the *word* for Chariot), meaning, "the enclosure which allows us to focus our will to the Divine realm." This enclosure is also a metaphor for the female labia, the "closed gate" of the Ezekiel scripture believed to signify the Virgin Mary. On the Chariot card, it is the armor protecting the rider, the body of the car, and the walls of the city beyond. There are many examples of enclosure within the poem, from references to being snowed in, to walls and lids, as well as the actions of closing and shutting, and also reinforced by near-homophones such as "clothes."

Returning to the Eucharistic ritual, the following Golden Dawn incantation is full of similar images to Plath's poem (Crowley, 115). Lines of the incantation are italicized, with tarot and Plath's "Tulips" correspondences explained after each in parenthesis:

> *I kindle a flame like a torrent to rush from star to star;*
> (To *rush* is a Chariot card meaning; the canopy over the charioteer's head is covered with stars; Plath writes of being excited.)
> *Your hair a comet's horrent, Ye shall see things as they are!*
> (Corresponds to Plath's third line in the fourth stanza regarding clarity.)
> *I lift the mask of matter; I open the heart of man;*

(Plath's fourth line of the ninth stanza, with its opening heart.)

For I am of force to shatter the cast that hideth ~~ Pan!

(Pan is the mythological Greek god famous for his sexual powers, from which the word "panic" is derived.[79])

Your loves shall lap up slaughter, and dabbled with roses of blood

(Plath's sixth stanza's redness and wounds, and also including the Golden Dawn term, "corresponds." Roses of blood might also easily replace tulips.)

Each desperate darling daughter shall swim in the fervid blood.

(Plath's image of floating red sinkers in the sixth stanza.)

I bring ye laughter and tears, the kisses that foam and bleed,

(Plath's description of tulips with snow/foam and red blood.)

The joys of a million years, the flowers that bear no seed.

My life is bitter and sterile, its flame is a wandering star.

(Plath's fourth stanza ideas of being a nun and pure, the fifth stanza's not wanting flowers, and the seventh stanza's being faceless. Tulips also are bulb flowers, not grown from seed.)

Ye shall pass in pleasure and peril across the mystical bar

That is set for wrath and weeping against the children of earth;

But ye in singing and sleeping shall pass in measure and mirth!

I lift my wand and wave you through hill to hill of delight

My rosy rivers lave you in innermost lustral light.

(Plath's "snags and eddies" fit the "pleasure and peril" of the Eucharist. These obstacles are also around a river in Plath's poem. The delight of the Eucharist corresponds to Plath's play and rest.)

I lead you, lord of the maze, in the darkness free of the Sun;

(In the seventh stanza, Plath's light widens and thins. She is between the sun and the tulips, suggesting the labial entrance to the woman's body. In this context, the widening and thinning, along with the word "efface," suggest childbirth. The maze corresponds to Plath's walls, now seen as vaginal and possessing the Eucharist's "darkness free of the Sun." The lord of the maze would be either a man to enter it, or God the creator. Both are represented by the sun in alchemy and myth.)

To prepare for this ceremony, the Initiate is directed to contemplate as many forms of self-destruction as possible while bathing in salt water on the eve of the new moon. The last two lines in "Tulips" fit perfectly.

Second Mirror: Alchemy

Ted Hughes was well-known for weaving alchemical themes into his own work. When Plath was hospitalized in March 1961, he brought her the flowers that inspired "Tulips," a poem that also may be read as a trip through alchemy. Tarot cards also mirror the twelve alchemical processes, and so Plath takes the reader on a tour of the first twelve cards in the major arcana. Alchemy created the basis for modern chemical processes today.

Alchemists align the Chariot card with the process of Sublimation. In alchemy, sublimation is the first stage of Coagulation. It is vaporization of solid material, followed by the condensation of vapor in re-solidified form. Thus, we revisit the #0 Fool's purity: The

---

79 Plath and Hughes conversed with a spirit named Pan in her poem, "Dialogue Over a Ouija Board" (*CP*, 275-286).

"Tulips" as a Microcosm of the Major Arcana's First Twelve Cards:

Plath has a bit of fun with "Tulips," broadly infusing each stanza with ordered major arcana tarot card properties within the poem's greater tribute to the Chariot card.

1st Stanza: Plath invokes the "excitable" mood of both The Fool and The Chariot. Plath associates herslf with The Fool card's nobody-ness and number, zer, as well as the snow in his picture.

2nd Stanza: reflects the learning of the Magician card #1, a "pupil" with an inclination toward overconfidence, and The High Priestess' white cap, silent gestures, and mystery.

3rd Stanza: "Tulips" addresses the #3 card, The Empress,' motherhood.

4th Stanza: illustrates The Emperor's stubbornness and lack of loving association, followed by the purity, nun-like demeanor, and name recognition of tarot card #5, The Hierophant.

5th Stanza: reflects the flowers, freedom and peace of The Lovers, as well as the closing in and shutting of the Chariot.

(Cont.)

winter, whiteness, and snow images of the first and second lines reflect the first, previous White phase of alchemy. "Snow" is an alchemical name for "white foliated earth," the "Salt of Nature." The white powder collects on the vessel walls, can easily fly into the air and onto the hands of the alchemist. One must learn to be peaceful to manage it. The white powder, Plath's "light," is on her hands, vessel, and its walls. The alchemical vessel is also called a "bed," fitting the bedridden patient of the poem.

When Plath says "I am nobody," she is stripped of ego and pure as The Fool. She is not interested in laboratory explosions. In the second stanza, Plath as tarot card #1, the alchemist-Magician, learns to wait for results. Her head is propped up; "head" another name for the alembic vessel. Open bottles are likened to open eyelids without stoppers or seals. The Magician begins as "stupid pupil," and becomes a detached tarot card #2, the High Priestess-like nurse; "Nurse" is another term for alchemists. With white-winged hats, they pass like gulls. Alchemical drawings often portray eye-like designs of a large circle with the self in the center, as the pupil (Roob, 156). As alchemist, Plath makes the ritual hand sigils, or signs in the air, for each substance added, seen in the second stanza.

The third stanza alchemy-Empress, and tarot card #3 correlate gently and tenderly: Plath's language of water, tending, and smoothing, as well as the family and smiling all apply. Plath draws the parallel between tending and perfecting the physical human body with the philosopher's stone. In alchemy, smoothing and prodding with needles causes properties to settle. The subtle matter separates from the gross form; it is the poem's lines of sleep, losing oneself, and baggage. The stone is washed after impurities are burned away. There is "numbness" and peace.

To lose oneself references the ego, properties of tarot card #4, The Emperor. Abraham

66

6th Stanza: returns to union, intensity, and correspondence of the Lovers.

7th Stanza: introduces the forthcoming tarot cards: Justice's redness, action and consequence, as well as being supervised, behavior enforced, and daily routine.

8th Stanza: contains the watching and self-effacement of the Hermit.

9th Stanza: bears the coming and going of tarot card #10, the Wheel of Fortune, with its happiness and play. Plath continues with #11 Strength's African lion and great power of love. Plath ends this poem as a stranger in a strange land, physically in peril as is the Hanged Man, card #12, the card before Death.

It is no wonder "Tulips" feels so magical!

von Franckenberg, pupil of the alchemist Böhmes, wrote that all illnesses are based on false, self-centered imaginings. Plath is sick of the illness and baggage-weight of worldly troubles. The word *patent* has interpretations beyond leather: it can mean something is obvious and out in the open, one of The Chariot's reversed meanings. The "leather overnight case" is the human body, temporary, from a soul's perspective. The body as a case in the third stanza, and disease symbolized by rust in the eighth, are images found in alchemical poetry (Greer, 9-10). Plath's simile of the pillbox is the old body blackened through trials and burnings. Her "husband and child" are important to include here. They are not only the other parts of her, but "husband" is the alchemical expression for Mercury, to unite with for the chemical wedding. The "child" is the term for the philosopher's stone resulting from this unity.

Plath's fourth stanza therefore expresses the stubbornness and coldness of the Emperor, as well as his alchemical ascendancy from human form into purity. In medieval times, monks and nuns were often alchemists. Water dominates much of this alchemical process, and so the alembic vessel is sometimes called the "ship," or "boat." Plath speaks of the ego and the stuff of the world, the Emperor's domain, when she writes, "Stubbornly hanging on to my name and address."

The fifth stanza moves into tarot card #5, the Hierophant's, spiritual focus. The alchemist has stripped her spirit from its source, the physical body. The "green plastic-pillowed trolley" is alchemically relevant: the color green signifies the infant stone is alive and maturing in the vessel. The word "plastic" has been embraced by hermeticists to describe the malleability of the human body (Steiner). Yet, a "plastic pillow" is a balloon, another name for the alembic vessel during distillation, when its globe catches rising vapors. "[T]rolley," of course, is the moving Chariot, the physical body for travel.

Plath takes inventory of her alchemical laboratory in the fourth stanza. The word "sink," which begins the sixth line, can be read as a noun. Plath is baptismally washed pure into the White phase. Slowly, she moves into tarot card #6, the Lovers, daze of peace, the Garden of Eden. Worldly concerns and possessions, name tags or trinkets, hold no importance. Yet before the fifth stanza is complete, card #7, the Chariot closes in, stopping up the mouth of the alembic vessel.

The sixth stanza of "Tulips" shows red seep through the white in the Rubedo phase, an alchemical unity of form and spirit. This process takes place through tongues of fire until the stone transforms, and is symbolized by various red flowers, including tulips. When Plath states, "in the first place," in the sixth stanza, she is the white stone, exposed to the active red Sulfur. The "gift paper" is papyrus and old writings revealing alchemical secrets. Her "awful baby" might be phonetically read as "awe-full." Plath's use of the word "corresponds" suggests the many metaphoric and symbolic associations throughout the Hermetic sciences. Plath continues with the alchemical term of "subtle." She addresses the stone physically floating in the vessel, as well as spiritual floating. The weighing down in this stanza is her necessary return to the heaviness of the body. The corresponding, the subtlety, the weighing, and punishment of a neck bound with sinkers of lead, the base metal, all represent the next in the major arcana after the Chariot: tarot card # 8, Justice. In Jungian alchemy, lead represents the fragmented, chaotic state of the psyche that must be separated from the body to gain equilibrium and receive illumination.

"The tulips turn to me" in the seventh stanza might be interpreted as "turn into me," as the two become one. The window is behind Plath at this stage; there is no way out. She judges herself in Justice's negative light, calling herself ridiculous. Her position between the sun's eye and the tulip's eyes is between the stage of Rubedo and gold. At this time, the red Sulfur violently devours the stone, bringing redness and eating all of the oxygen in the process. When the air is fixed, the body of the stone can be penetrated by Sulfur, sometimes called the "Red Man" or "Red Lion" (Abraham, 4). This hearkens to Plath's closing line in the preceding poem, "Lady Lazarus": "And I eat men like air."

Tarot card #9, the Hermit, watches and meditates, launching Plath's seventh stanza. He concentrates his attention, as Plath writes in her eighth stanza. However "concentrate" serves a double, alchemical meaning of reduction through distillation. The circular effacement and sun's eye images of card #10, the Wheel of Fortune, continues in the eighth stanza with its "Coming and going," and "round them," moving into the happiness of card #11, the Strength card. Strength's images of warmth and its dangerous cat, the "Red Lion" of Sulfur, complete the last stanza. As the entire vessel reddens in this phase, "The walls, also, seem to be warming themselves" in the final stanza. The vessel is sometimes called "a prison" to confine the experiment and force the union of opposites. This explains why the "tulips should be behind bars."

Prison and bars bring us into card #12, the Hanged Man's outward character of being a prisoner, and his inner qualities of self-awareness, his heart, and his connection with the *Infinite Continuum*. The Hanged Man and Plath are both aware of impending physical death in order to become perfected. Perhaps she took this alchemical concept literally a couple years after writing "Tulips." When Plath writes of tulip blooms in the bowl, "blooms" should be read as a verb and not as a noun. For Plath, the entire bowl is red, not only the blooms, as she did not use the verb "are" after "blooms." The red bowl is the alembic vessel, blooming into the Rubedo phase. This cannot be obtained without purity of heart and Plath's "sheer love."

Water is a closing image of "Tulips." It is "the water of life" to first kill impure metal, then revive and regenerate it. One of the four elements, water is considered to be "the mastery of which brings peace" (Abraham, 213). Plath's "Salt" is alchemy's third principle, with Sulfur and Mercury. Salt is said to be the body, Mercury the spirit, and Sulfur unites the two. Salt is synonymous with the White stage and the soul. The alchemist prizes tulips as symbols for seeking the light, and attaining spiritual awareness. Tulips are a perennial bulb, returning each year like the daffodil. They symbolize resurrection and determination.

Third Mirror: Mythology

The charioteer pictured on the Chariot tarot card is said to be the Greek god of war, Ares. He drives through a mostly dry, desert landscape. The land symbolizes his lack of feeling; his focus and disconnection propel him to victory. Emotion does not slow him down, and this feeling of disconnection is the same mood that gives Plath's "Tulips" its otherworldliness.

Ares is said to have had a passionate affair with Aphrodite, goddess of love and sex. Instincts of Ares' force and Aphrodite's passion are seen as opposites of the same fierce drive, explaining the sexuality revealed in the tarot/Qabalah mirror of "Tulips."

The Chariot is also connected to two Greek myths: one of Myrtilus, a coachman, who took the axle-pin out of his master's chariot wheel, causing the King's death (Plath's "I have let things slip"). The cursed Myrtilus, son of Hermes, was turned into the constellation Auriga, the Charioteer (Grimal, 300).

There is also the myth of Phaeton, son of Helios, the Sun god. Foolhardy and undisciplined, Phaeton took the sun chariot out alone one day and soon lost control. Helios had to stop Phaeton from destroying the earth with a thunderbolt. Plath's entire eighth stanza of "Tulips" illustrates Phaeton well, with Phaeton playing happily until he becomes snagged and sinks by the red setting sun.

The goddess Olwyn[80] is the Welsh version of Aphrodite, and she is connected with the wild apple and its white blossoms, Plath's whiteness at the beginning of the poem (Graves, 42, 248). In Welsh legend, the wild apple has the power of salvation for poets. The Greek goddess Nemesis, meaning "grove," was celebrated with cider and said to hold an apple bough in one hand, and carried a wheel in her other hand to represent the turning year, and that vengeance will come around to the sinner—a fine fit for the Chariot card, and support for the next mirrors of the poem, "Tulips."

Fourth Mirror: History and the World

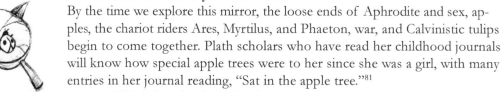

By the time we explore this mirror, the loose ends of Aphrodite and sex, apples, the chariot riders Ares, Myrtilus, and Phaeton, war, and Calvinistic tulips begin to come together. Plath scholars who have read her childhood journals will know how special apple trees were to her since she was a girl, with many entries in her journal reading, "Sat in the apple tree."[81]

In 1797, John "Appleseed" Chapman left his Massachusetts home, Plath's home state, to travel across America like the Chariot, planting apple seeds, the fruit of Aphrodite. Wandering his entire life, he moved along the small tributaries and rivers in a canoe loaded with seeds. Chapman's squeaky clean reputation, courtesy of Walt Disney, is not quite the truth. Chapman was a pantheistic healer, a Christian mystic, evangelist, philanthropist, and a peacemaker with the Indians, which was scandalous in those times. The apple trees he planted produced bitter apples, good for concentrating into hard cider. Chapman's river journeys, the concentration, and happiness are represented in Plath's eighth stanza. Each spring, Johnny Appleseed scouted out land, planted nurseries and fenced them in, reinforcing the enclosure idea of the Chariot card. Johnny Appleseed dressed in rags and denied himself all of life's luxuries, effacing himself as in Plath's third through seventh stanzas.

If one holds a red apple upside down, it is much like a tulip in shape. To slice an apple in half produces a model of the female genitals; to cut it crossways produces a perfect pentagram. Robert Graves' believed the pentagram to be the symbol of the infamous White Goddess, another incarnation of Aphrodite/Isis, present in nearly all forms of early literature and culture, in her five stations from birth to death, and reborn again.

The second line of the second stanza of "Tulips" might regard apple seeds within the core. The core of the half-sliced apple is much "Like an eye between two white lids that will not shut." The apple's seeds become pebbles in Plath's imagery; the skin its overnight case, as shiny as patent leather. As the Chariot contains the war of Ares and the love of Aphrodite, apples contain both sweet fruit and bitter seeds; the seeds contain cyanide bringing the numbness in the third stanza.

---

80 "Olwyn" is coincidentally the name of Ted Hughes' only sister.
81 The first notation, "Sat in the apple tree" is recorded on August 12, 1944 in Plath's childhood journal. This journal is held at the Sylvia Plath Archives in the Lilly Library, Indiana University-Bloomington.

The true apple was not known in the biblical Mideast. It was likely to have been the quince, also sacred to Aphrodite (Graves, 261). The quince tree produces tulip-like flowers that circle back around to Plath's poem once again. In European literature and folklore, the apple represents consummation. It is the Chariot's conquest after the headiness of the previous Lovers card. When the biblical Adam and Eve reached Europe, the fruit of the Tree of Knowledge was reinterpreted as an apple; despite the fact the couple covered themselves with *fig* leaves in shame (Graves, 253).

The tulip flower was brought to Europe by the Ottoman Empire during the Dutch Golden Age, and produced almost too much excitement, as Plath's "Tulips" suggests. "Tulipomania" has been long been researched by psychologists, economists, and historians evaluating the causes of the madness of crowds. The first documented case of an economic bubble, the excitement over tulips seemed to be that a flower so brilliant and colorful could bloom in winter. Tulipomania has been used as a parable for utopianism and communism, subjects that interested Plath (Pollan, 94).

Tulipomania began in the Calvinist's homeland of Holland. The acronym TULIP defines the five points of Calvinism: Total depravity of man; Unconditional election; Limited Atonement; Irresistible grace of God; and the Perseverance of the Saints (Whitlock). The 18th century Puritan Calvinist theologian, Jonathan Edwards, held his Great Awakening revivals at his church in Plath's Smith College town of Northampton, Massachusetts. Plath knew of Calvinism, at least since her Calvinist Hungarian boyfriend, Attilla, in her teens (*UJ*, 139). Her former boyfriend Richard Sassoon also playfully bashed Calvinism in an undated letter to Plath.[82]

It is no surprise that Plath didn't want tulips, when speaking of this kind. Recent converts can be over-zealous and are known as "Cage Stage Calvinists," so excited it might be best to cage them until they calm down, and sounding like Plath's animals that belong behind bars. Calvinistic thinking was responsible for New England's witch trials and more. It was practiced by the pilgrims who traveled from England to the new land. Plath's image of a head propped between a pillow and a sheet-cuff sounds much like a female pilgrim's coif or bonnet, and a high-necked bodice. The small white coif made pilgrim women look like today's nurses, another image in "Tulips." The unflattering female garb is presumed to have been mostly black and white. It might make Plath look as flat, ridiculous and shadowy as she writes in the seventh stanza. Those subscribing to repressive Calvinistic doctrine certainly efface themselves. The tulips would have suffocated Plath and killed all passion.

In "Tulips" Plath contrasts all this with the famous anti-Calvinist healer, Mary Baker Eddy, who had turned to spiritualism for physical healing before founding the Church of Christian Science.[83] In "Tulips," Plath's air becomes snagged and "eddies" twice in the eighth stanza. Eddy believed in "malicious animal magnetism"; that people could harm one another telepathically and were as dangerous as Plath's "great African cat." Boston was home to Eddy for many years and the location of the Mary Baker Eddy Library for the Betterment of Humanity.

Classic and modern Persian literature has also given special attention to tulips. The plant's place of origin is in the steppes of Central Asia in Kazakhstan, bordering the Siberian lowlands. There, after harsh winters, spring tulips grow wild on the barren land. They are considered to be a symbol of life and fertility (Gäckler). Plath knew of the Russian steppes. In 1955 she dated a Russian Jew and studied Russian history and literature, and she mentioned the steppes in a journal entry (*UJ*, 193). She also read the Russian-set novel, *Dr. Zhivago*, in 1959.

---

82 This undated letter from Richard Sasson to Sylvia Plath may be found in the 1955 correspondence of the Sylvia Plath archives of the Lilly Library, Indiana University-Bloomington.

83 Plath had read from Eddy's book, *Science and Health with Key to the Scriptures* with Bob Cochran, a boy she met in the summer of 1952 as a mother's helper. Plath wrote of silently mocking the Christian Science Sunday School, pretending to be devout while believing that she had a devil in her heart.

The center of the tulip flower might be likened to an eye with two lids around it that do not shut, seen in the second stanza. The dusty golden pollen, analogous to male sperm, becomes Plath's husband image, and the dark curved seeds with their little hooked points are future children, seen in the end of the third stanza. The tulip flower resembles an empty hand turned up to the sky---Plath's fifth stanza. A blossom resembles the shape of the human heart as it opens and shuts---ninth stanza. In the language of flowers, the tulip symbolizes love in its most passionate and thornless vulnerability. As a flower, it is a rare bloom, because it continues to grow after it is cut.

Another historical traveling figure corresponds with the Chariot card, the steppes, and a different kind of mania: Communism. Plath referenced the steppes in 1955 in her journals (*UJ*, 193). Grigori Rasputin (1869-1916) was the Russian mystic and healer often blamed for bringing down the Romanov dynasty. At about thirty years old, the age of Plath's "Tulips" narrator, Rasputin practiced *The Way of the Pilgrim*, a 19th century Russian work about a journey of unceasing prayer. Performing miracles, he eventually moved in with Tzar Nikolai II and his family in the St. Petersburg Winter Palace, echoing Plath's winter imagery. The royal family believed in Rasputin's powers to heal their son of his hemophilia. Rasputin was rumored to have been one of the banned Khlysty, a Christian sect of flagellants as the metaphoric red wounds of "Tulips." The Khlysty wandered Russia in Chariot-fashion, free of ego and belongings. They called the people of God "ships," as Plath refers to herself as a boat. The Khlysty initiation begins when the red sun has set in a solemn service that breaks into "sudden tongues," convulsions, and sexual orgies.

In *Rasputin: The Holy Devil*, written in 1927, author René Fülöp-Miller summarizes, "Only in this mad intoxication of the senses are earthly consciousness and self-will completely extinguished, for in the 'sinful encounter' the earthly ego has no more influence, but only the will of the invisible spirit" (Fülöp-Miller, 29-32). This ego-less freedom from trappings of the world appears in Plath's first, third, fourth and seventh stanzas of "Tulips." Both the Khlysty ritual and Rasputin's reputation for a wild and unrestricted sexual life evokes the Golden Dawn rite in the first tarot/Qabalah mirror of this poem.

The Romanov's Winter Palace is protected between the Palace Embankment and the Palace Square. The Bolsheviks' Red Army stormed the palace on Bloody Sunday in 1905, at the onset of the Russian Revolution that removed Tzar Nicholas II in 1917. For seven years, seven being the Chariot's number, the Bolshevik Red Army fought against the conservative White Army, which was against the rebellion. This red-versus-white feeling is throughout "Tulips." The Romanov family were forced to move out of the Winter Palace and lived for six months as prisoners until they were exiled to Siberia. Bolshevik leader Yakov Sverdlov ordered their execution, and red tulips have been a regular part of Sverdlov Square for decades since. The whole Bolshevik (later, Soviet) idea of communism is one of effacing the individual personality.

The Romanov family was executed by firing squad in the cellar of the Siberian Ipatiev house in 1918. Mysterious graffiti appeared on the walls soon afterward: pornographic drawings of the Empress and Rasputin, lines were quoted from Heinrich Heine's poem in German, "Balthazar." The unknown vandal equated the Tzar with the ruined King of Babylon, and therefore was a person educated both in literature and in German to make this connection with Russia.

In "Tulips," Plath subtly associates the Calvinistic over-excitability of the Bolsheviks with the Nazis a few decades later. Empress Alexandra, of German descent, was despised by many of the Russian people. Known to have studied philosophy and ancient religions, she used the swastika symbol as a reminder of God's presence and protection. Relating Alexandra to her German roots, it is fascinating that Heine surfaces in "Tulips" once again.[84] Heine, a German Jew, prophesied

---

84 Heinrich Heine was mentioned as one of Emma Lazarus' great works of translation in the *Fixed Stars Govern a Life* interpretation of Plath's "Lady Lazarus."

the Nazi regime ninety years before it took place. The Nazis attempted to erase Heine from history by burning his complete works, and attributing the few remaining as written by "anonymous," swabbing *him* clear of names and associations, as Plath wrote in "Tulips." Plath wrote of her knowledge and appreciation of Heine (*LH*, 192), and her 1958 poem, "A Winter's Tale" celebrates Heine's satire of the same name.

Fifth Mirror: Astrology and Astronomy

The astrological symbol associated with alchemy's Sublimation is the constellation Libra, the scales. In the *Atlas Coelestis*, the balance pans of Libra are held by chains affixed with tulip blossoms. In ancient times, the area of the sky considered to be Libra was occupied by the Scorpion, Plath's zodiac sign. Their word for these stars was *chalae*, meaning "claws." The ancients decided a tulip blossom is like a scorpion's claws in shape; the two claws, side by side in the sky, reflected the balance of heaven. The idea of balance in this part of the sky is as old as the Babylonians. The only constellation depicting an inanimate object, Libra was later matched with Virgo, goddess of justice, who held these scales. In Chinese astrology, *Zhenche*, with three of Libra's stars, forms a triangle of battle chariots. Nearby stars in *Tianfu* are said to be a pile of spare spokes for mending broken wheels. These all fit Plath's symbol of tulips, or else the Chariot card's movement she infused across the whole poem.

The constellation of Libra is difficult to see, as it is far south and quite weak; it is how Plath herself was no doubt feeling in hospital. Libra is best viewed for a short period on bright northern spring nights, and not during Plath's white winter landscape of the poem.

Plath nods toward Libra, but also to other constellations she no doubt learned of through her astrologer husband: Auriga, the Charioteer constellation, reflects the story of Myrtilus first seen in the Mythology mirror of this poem. In the northern sky, its stars shape the form of the charioteer's helmet. In Chinese astronomy, Auriga is divided into three sections: Purple Forbidden Enclosure, a nice fit again for the Chariot card's idea of enclosure; The White Tiger of the West, which sounds like Plath's African feline in "Tulips"; and the Vermillion Bird of the South, vermillion being a rich red color. One of the stars in the constellation, AE Aurigae, is a runaway star, moving through space at an abnormally high velocity. Because the Milky Way runs through Auriga, which also has many open clusters of stars, they cannot be counted, like the nurses in the last line of second stanza of "Tulips."

Sixth Mirror: Humanities and the Arts

The chariot from the Book of Ezekiel is portrayed in the great work of art, "Ezekiel's Wheel" (1836), part of a large fresco painting in the St. John the Baptist Church in Kratovo, Macedonia by an unknown painter. Swimming in an oceanic sky, the wheel can be compared to Plath's rusty red engine, sunken in the sky. The wheel bears many open eyes upon it that do not close, again like Plath's second stanza of "Tulips." Little white wings turn the wheels, resembling Plath's nurses' hats.

Ezekiel's vision of the chariot was also captured by Raphael in the oil painting "Ezekiel's Vision" (1518), including cherubim in their white swaddling clothes, in the same way Plath describes the roses in her sixth stanza. The mystic poet and artist William Blake portrayed this vision in his "The Whirlwind: Ezekiel's Vision of the Cherubim and Eyed Wheels" (1803-1805). A Blake pen and watercolor of the same time, "Satan in his Original Glory: 'Thou wast Perfect till Iniquity was found in Thee" (1805), depicts the fallen ("sunken") angel Satan, with wings of red rust against whiteness. His double-set of upward-pointing wings present him as a giant tulip. His sheet-draped body stands, or, if the viewer is omniscient and looking down from above, it would be lying down with its "hands turned up," flat against stars and pebbles. Ribbony "tongues" of darker red and orange color wraps around his shoulders. He bears a necklace that could be described as Plath's sinkers made of red lead. Beneath the cross-bearing orb in his hand, a small body clings to a Plathian communion wafer. Blake's Satan has a face so calm and peaceful that it is almost no face at all, as in the seventh stanza of "Tulips."

The light and dark sphinxes on the Chariot card are meant to echo the light and dark horses, the noble and ignoble impulses discussed in the philosopher Plato's *Symposium*. In her personal library, Plath owned Plato's *Lysis, Symposium, Giorgias, The Republic, Five Dialogues*, and many critical studies of Plato, whom she loved studying in Cambridge under Dr. Dorothea Krook. Kabbalah has some alignment with Plato's *Symposium*,[85] including the idea that bodies wholly male *and* female were the original "global" individuals. These beings were divided by an angry Zeus/God, creating attraction between the two halves. Eroticism emerged as an attempt to counteract this act of divine anger, to heal the damaged whole, and express as spiritual attraction to the other corporeal half (Idel). In *Symposium*, most valued as a document shedding light on love and sexual behavior in ancient Athens, a series of speeches are given by seven men. Oh yes, there is that number again.

Symposium's seven speakers:

Plath conveys the mood of the first speaker, Phaedrus, in the first stanza of "Tulips." He speaks of sacrifice and the closeness of death. As Phaedrus, Plath has given up her body, her name, her memory, and all possessions.

Pausanias, the legal expert, is mirrored in the second stanza, lecturing on complexities of Athenian law regarding love. The other men are his pupils, as Plath refers to herself.

Plath's third stanza of "Tulips" echoes Eryximachus' speech evoking a medicinal definition of love including the humors of Hippocratic medicine illustrated in "Tulips." This same stanza eases into Aristophanes' speech of comic relief with its "little smiling hooks."

Agathon speaks next about love being for the youth and an enemy of old age. It is in the fourth stanza where Plath muses over her own aging. Agathon claims love never settles where there is "no bud to bloom," lending a new understanding to Plath's fifth stanza opening line.

Socrates begins his questioning. The men correspond, as Plath says redness does to her speaker's wound. Drunken Alcibiades becomes excited and tempted by beautiful young boys not ready to be lovers, those awful babies, in Plath-speak. After a scuffle, there is upset and "sudden tongues." Alcibiades speaks against Socrates; Socrates restrains him like Plath's lead sinkers.

In an attempt to learn Socrates' weakness, Alcibiades futilely tries to seduce the old man. He ends up falling in love with Socrates and being rejected, feeling ridiculous and other qualities in the seventh stanza. *Symposium* closes with a drunken group showing up, going to bed, "Playing and resting without committing itself." The final stanza of "Tulips" parallels Socrates going off alone to the Lyceum to wash and think (Plato, 202e).

"There was no one around, neither family nor people whose judgment you respected. At such a time you felt the need of committing yourself to something absolute--life or truth or beauty--of being ruled by it in place of the man-made rules that had been discarded. You needed to surrender to some such ultimate purpose more fully, more unreservedly than you had ever done in the old familiar, peaceful days, in the old life that was now abolished and gone for good."

— Boris Pasternak,
Doctor Zhivago

---

85 Kabbalah with a "K" has Ancient Jewish origin and is considered to be the first brand of this religious practice (Idel).

In 1960, a year before Plath wrote "Tulips," the poet W.D. Snodgrass won the Pulitzer Prize. Over that year, Plath had selected a poem by Snodgrass, "Operation," for the closing poem in the 1961 *American Poetry Now* collection she edited. With its anesthesia, attendants, carts, snow, and images of solitude, it must surely have inspired Plath. Snodgrass' "Operation" even ends with a bowl of flowers blooming in the window.

German-Jewish author Heinrich Heine suffered a great deal of state censorship, almost a century before the Nazi party. One of his most famous books, *A Winter's Tale*, begins with an imaginary journey befitting the Chariot card. It is a story of Heine's exile as a writer from his homeland, in the time of Germany's reformation led by Protestants such as John Calvin and his TULIP principles. He contemplates the nationalistic babble of German identity; identity being a key theme of Plath's "Tulips" poem.

In *A Winter's Tale*, Heine muses over the transformation of Europe after Napoleon Bonaparte. Because *A Winter's Tale* criticized Germany's militarism and nationalism, it was called shameful, and Heine was accused of betraying the Fatherland. As the Russians went from bad to worse when the Bolsheviks toppled the tsarist regime, so too did Germany with reformation and its accompanying fascist censorship. *A Winter's Tale* was translated to English in 1844 by Herman Salinger, a mystic Jewish poet who wrote a series of books that questioned war, and challenged ideas of nationalism. His poem, "Sunday," ends with the line, "Who lose, now that quiet wins?" It is another connection to themes within Plath's "Tulips."

The surname *Salinger* opens yet another connection to literature that may at first seem arbitrary, but is actually a key interpretation of this "Tulips" mirror: the reclusive author, J.D. Salinger, whose novel, *The Catcher in the Rye,* was one of Plath's great inspirations for *The Bell Jar.* Plath wrote in her journals of being "increasingly enchanted" by Salinger's *Seymour: An Introduction* (UJ, 492). In J.D. Salinger's "Franny," from the 1961 collection of short stories, *Franny and Zooey,* the character of Zooey Glass was a genius with "a vocabulary on an exact par with Mary Baker Eddy's"echoing Plath's use of "eddies" in the eighth stanza (Salinger, 55). *Franny and Zooey* was first serialized in *The New Yorker*, with "Franny" published in 1955 and "Zooey" published in 1957.

When John Updike reviewed *Franny and Zooey,* he wrote of Franny, "In the first story, she arrives by train from a Smith-like college[86] to spend the week-end of the Yale game at what must be Princeton" (Updike). As a Smith College alumna herself, this would have been a significant detail for Plath. Franny carries Rasputin's same inspirational text, *The Way of a Pilgrim,* everywhere with her, mouthing the Jesus Prayer. At the end of "Franny," she faints and is last seen lying face-up in silent prayer. By the end of the following story, "Zooey," Franny lies quietly by herself, echoing Plath's first and last stanzas. Franny's Jesus Prayer has become a part of her being and "For some minutes, before she fell into a deep, dreamless sleep, she just lay quiet, smiling at the ceiling" (Salinger, 202). It is just as Plath begins her poem "Tulips."

Franny's words might be straight from Plath's poem and journals. For instance, "I'm sick of not having the courage to be an absolute nobody" (*Franny*, 30). Plath continually faced ego in her journals, as Franny and Zooey also do battle with their egos, shut away in bathrooms or their family living room. Updike points out the risk Salinger takes, like Joyce, in writing so much of the internal world. Salinger's novel of two stories at first appears to condemn American culture and materialism, as communism does, yet in the end it is portrayed somewhat positively.

86 Smith, Vassar, Bennington and Sarah Lawrence colleges are all mentioned by name in "Franny" (*Franny and Zooey*, Little Brown, Boston, MA. 1961. p.9).

Chapter Nine: A Woman Scorned
Card #8   Justice   Corresponding Poem: "A Secret"

Sylvia Plath's "A Secret" was one of a wave of poems she produced while separated from Ted Hughes. At first glance, the poem is about a secret that is difficult to hide; one that takes on a life of its own and eventually gets out. The secret, of course, was Hughes' affair with their once-mutual friend, Assia Wevill (and her subsequent pregnancy). Plath also nods to the wandering gods Zeus and Odin, as well as their bastard children and alchemy's philosophical child; to King Henry VIII's Tudor dynasty; to the powers of amber and femininity; to author Lawrence Durrell's *The Alexandria Quartet*; and other secrets.

 **First Mirror: The Tarot/Qabalah**
In Qabalah, old tarot texts, and decks such as the Tarot de Marseilles, the Justice card is positioned as number VIII. At the turn of the century, the Hermetic Order of the Golden Dawn moved this card to position XI in its Rider-Waite deck, considering Justice and Strength as interchangeable; two aspects of power that the purified, disciplined personality uses to discern right from wrong.[87] Evidence suggests that Hughes and Plath held the traditional view and rejected this repositioning, considering Justice as the eighth card. The meaning of this card is that justice will be done; it is an impartial weighing of sides or ideas; settling conflict; law; equilibrium; balance; Karma; cause and effect. It can signify arbitration through courts of law, and rational, logical solutions through balance. It is the power of the mind, intellect, and logic over fiery battles. Transcendent wisdom is another meaning, which is why some tarot decks depict King Solomon on Justice.

The number eight was a favorite of Pythagoreans, who believed this number "is the ruler of forms and ideas, and the cause of gods and demons" (Graves, 251). Its two halves are in perfect balance, the symbol for infinity tipped on its side. Plath wrote "A Secret" in quatrains, half of eight. The Golden Dawn allied the Justice card with the Hebrew letter *Lamed*, meaning, "the goad which pulls our acts in towards the needs of the inner self" (Tarotpedia). If Wevill's pregnancy wasn't a "goad" to Plath, what else could be?

In Hermetic Initiation, the Justice card represents the spiritual "semen" of the adept's *secret* ideas, irresistibly drawn from their hell by the love of his angel. Golden Dawn text states:

> "It is said among Men that the word Hell deriveth from the Verb helan, to hele or conceal, in the tongue of the Anglo-Saxons. That is, it is the Concealed Place; and this, since all things are in thine own Self, is the Unconscious" (Crowley, LA).

Weirdly, a solar-phallic hippopotamus is the Hermetic ritual symbol to represent the female; "conceived as invulnerable, reposeful," and "of enormous swallowing capacity" (Crowley, *LS*). One should therefore not be surprised to find a hippopotamus referenced in the first line of the fourth stanza of Plath's poem.

---

87 See the interpretation for tarot card #11, Strength.

The legal authority of Justice is expressed in Plath's first stanza lines. Her fourth stanza "square, stiff frill" is the square clasp at the collar of the judge in the card's picture, as well as a descriptive image of collared slaves up for auction; the ultimate injustice and the meaning of this card, reversed. Like the Libran scales of judgment and authority, Plath weighs the players in the poem: "One a fool, the other a fool."

The fifth stanza's mention of an extra finger points to that awkward, protruding finger on the hand holding the scales on this tarot card. It is a *brandy*-brown color.

"A Secret" is Justice's dispassionate, efficient method of seeking quick resolution. Plath suspected Hughes' affair for some time, seeing the faint mark of it before definitely knowing. Weakness expressed in the second-to-last line refers to the Strength aspect of this card, when reversed: lack of strength. She is also overcome, having released the secret—the alchemical spirit—into the world ("The secret is out").

Second Mirror: Alchemy

In an earlier draft of "A Secret," Plath wrote of feeling powerful, and expressed the idea of largeness appropriate to the judge in this card's picture. Before she had written the lovely echo of "You are blue and huge," Plath had spoken of redness, drawing inspiration from the judge's robes and the alchemist's final color of transmutation before gold. Blue is said to represent mercurial water and alchemical quintessence, Plath's faint watermark in the second stanza. The most famous alchemist ("huge"), Paracelsus, on whom Plath's mother wrote her master's-degree thesis, introduced the blue sapphire as the "arcane substance" into alchemy (Abraham, 15). Arcane, defined, means "secret." Paracelsus studied smallpox in the 1500s, and was one of the first to declare that it spread through agents outside of the body, such as bacteria. The fourth-stanza square represents the four elements and the necessity of transforming a square into a circle, or the fifth element, or the Philosopher's stone.[88]

Plath's amber is a loaded detail: Associated with witches, amber is not a true stone, but fossilized resin considered to be a gem. In alchemy, amber is synonymous with gold. When rubbed, amber produces a negative electrical static, explaining the gemstone's Greek name, *elektron*, from which *electricity* is derived. In Norse myth, amber came from Freya's tears when Odin wandered out into the world. The metaphoric possibilities are endless when placing Plath in Freya's role: viewing the wandering husband's lover as a false stone and a witch, feeling the negative electrical charge of emotion, and of alchemy. The alchemist typically distills pure alcohol from strong brandy. English texts call alchemy's seven compounds "spirits of wine." One of these compounds, *aqua vitae,* is brandy that has been repeatedly distilled.

The cooing dove in the fifth stanza sometimes represents the White stage. It is followed by the blackness of putrefaction and creation of a purified new "You." Other alchemical birds that roost and coo include the cock (rooster) and hen, symbolizing the sun and moon, or male and female aspects. Both the words "dwarf," and "baby," in "A Secret" are metaphors for the homunculus, or the philosopher's stone (Abraham, 102). The secret of alchemy is producing this child, Plath's "illegitimate baby," so called because it is without biological parents.

88 A.E. Waite mentions in *Brotherhood of the Rosy Cross* (p 473) that the circle within the square represents the four elements coming from the unity.

The Emerald Tablet is part of the larger *Book of the Secret of Creation*, written by the first-century pagan mystic, Apollonius of Tyana. Because of religious and social persecution, politics and other reasons, the secrets of alchemy have been kept hidden for two thousand years, yet this Hermetic Science remains alive. In the seventh stanza of "A Secret," something is secretly living, tucked away in a drawer. In the poem, Plath writes of *levering* dirt, not leveling it, as one might expect. "Lever" is a gilding term for an instrument to apply gold leaf. Turning dirt to gold is the alchemist's wish.

Excised lines from earlier drafts of this poem describe the three spaces of yellow across the top and sides of the Justice card. Plath also removed mention of a lack of anemia, pertaining to the flushed complexion of the lady of Justice. Salt represents the human body, and fish are a symbol for Isis and female power.[89] The eighth stanza references both, as well as insulting Wevill's female cleanliness and calling the child a bastard. Alchemically, the eighth and ninth stanzas weigh Plath's drive and force to leave the physical body and dwell in the spirit, versus remaining as a tainted part of the world. The spirit gains strength and frees itself in the ninth stanza.

Plath's "My god" is not just a colloquialism. As alchemist, she faces her God within, bursting free and out of her control in the tenth stanza. A stopper makes an alchemical vessel airtight, and the image of a bottle exploded suggests a laboratory chemical reaction; as well as the Golden Dawn's "spiritual semen," when taken in the context of foam in one's lap. Plath has released her own spirit, yet it stumbles out, betrayed with a knife in its back.

Third Mirror: Mythology

In the second line of "A Secret," Plath plays with the idea of female strength and superiority, demonstrated by the Greek goddess Athene, pictured on the Justice card. Athene, a.k.a. Athena, or her Roman counterpart, Minerva, represents Justice, wisdom, war, and poetry, among other arts. Athene teaches moral lessons, and weighs truth with her scales. The goddess Athene raised Erechtheus, the bastard child from the foiled rape of Hephaestus, to become King of Athens. Athene, sometimes called *Hippia*, "of Horses," returns us to the Golden Dawn's Solar Phallic Hippopotamus, the word "hippopotamus" meaning "water horse."

The rooster in "A Secret" both roosts and coos. His randy nature is where the slang *cock* is derived, and therefore also suggests Hughes' unfaithfulness. Roosters are considered to be hermetic solar symbols and signs of illumination (as is the hippopotamus), yet Celtic and Norse mythologies consider the rooster a messenger of the underworld, calling out danger. In Christianity, the rooster crowed three times when Peter denied Christ, as if pointing and accusing Plath's words, "You, you"! The rooster signifies pride, honesty, courage, strength and other characteristics of the Justice card. Cooing is also a trait of the dove, Athene's bird, and synonymous with motherhood as it produces milk to feed its young. The ancient Celts believed to hear the coo of the dove was a mourning call. The Japanese war god, Hachiman, claimed the dove as a symbol of peace after conflict has ended.

The idea of illegitimacy might have been Plath's premonition of Hughes' illegitimate child Wevill would soon be carrying (Koren, 114). Hughes and Wevill decided to abort that pregnancy (Koren, 119-120), suggested in the eighth and ninth stanzas. In Greek myth, Athene, Aphrodite, and Hera were said to have squabbled over the "apple" of desire, and a stabbed apple makes an appearance in the eighth stanza. Apples were the fruit of Aphrodite, and so it makes sense that Athene, with her sword, would be the one doing the stabbing.

---

89 See *Fixed Stars Govern a Life*'s interpretation of "Nick and the Candlestick" interpretation for more about fish.

Fourth Mirror: History and the World

The first settlement of Roman London, "The Square Mile," was a trading port, Plath's ideas of square and export in the fourth stanza. "The Steelyard," as London's port is called, was famous for its medieval scales to balance measurement. Excavated in 1954 within the City of London's Square Mile were ancient temple ruins that included white marble likenesses of the goddess Minerva, Athene's Roman name. Plath references the digging out of this great archaeological discovery with the first three lines of the sixth stanza. The sword held by Athene, the judge of Justice, also fits for Plath's knife.

"A Secret" hints of illegitimate children, London, and smallpox which point directly to England's King Henry VIII. The blueness and size in "A Secret" represent this obese, powerful, misogynistic blue-blood ruler of the Tudor dynasty. The style of the Tudor royalty is perhaps best known for the *Tudor Ruff*, starched, crimped and pleated circular collars worn by both men and women. It is Plath's "stiff frill."

The first wife of King Henry VIII, Catherine of Aragon, was rumored to have been murdered by poison. Her heart was found blackened during embalming, seen in the detection of black in the third stanza. King Henry had first wanted to divorce Catherine for Anne Boleyn; the public support remained with Catherine as she had solidified England's alliance with France, referenced in the tenth stanza.

Henry married his second wife, Anne Boleyn, in secret while he was still legally married to Catherine. Anne Boleyn was believed to have six fingers on one hand, Plath's extra finger in the fifth stanza. Boleyn liked fashion, poetry and literature, as Hughes' mistress Assia Wevill did (Fraser, 121). Anne Boleyn became pregnant right away and gave birth to Queen Elizabeth I, before miscarrying several times after. She was thought to be a witch because she had a strawberry birthmark on her neck, the stamp and watermark in Plath's second stanza. King Henry VIII blamed Anne Boleyn for seducing him into marriage with a *sortilège*, a French term for a witch's spell, and she was beheaded at the Tower of London on flimsy charges of adultery, incest, witchcraft and treason; another reason to exclaim over a big blue head.

"Bloody Mary," Mary I of England, was daughter of Henry VIII and Catherine. She was called "illegitimate," as her parents' marriage had been annulled. She had smallpox in 1527 and lost her eyesight, fitting the fifth stanza. Mary was known for her terrible persecution and executions of Protestants, as in the eighth and ninth stanza's lines condemning one to execution. Queen Mary I was the inspiration for the old nursery rhyme, "Mary, Mary, quite contrary."

Elizabeth Blount fathered King Henry's only son illegitimately, and so this label shows up yet again. Henry did claim him, naming him Henry FitzRoy, meaning "Son of the King." FitzRoy became the first Duke of Richmond, Somerset, and first Earl of Nottingham, but died of Tuberculosis at age 17. Coincidentally, Plath's place of residence was 23 Fitzroy Road, in London.

King Henry VIII significantly improved the British Navy and sea trade, and large merchant ships carried England's export of "salt cod" to Spain and Portugal (Millais, 160). The words "My god," here pay the necessary deference to the King, in order to keep one's life.

The reason for King Henry III being unable to bear a lineage of sons was his own female-strong sex chromosomes, but this was not known at the time. The narrator of "A Secret" appears to be male, as a man would be likelier to say, "Is that lingerie, pet?" A male, therefore, feels weak at the end of the poem. The "X" has been used since the earliest times to represent an individual or identity, and could be related to the pronoun for the self, "I"; Plath often used its homophone, "eye", in poetry.

The Place de la Concorde, mentioned in the tenth stanza, is a section of Paris, France, full of white stone government buildings with pillars, much like the one pictured on the Justice card. Having visited Paris often, Plath was familiar with this site and its history: There, executions took place within its square front of cheering crowds, as well as the stampeding French Revolution, mentioned in that same tenth stanza. Executed in this square was Queen Marie Antoinette, a woman who feared her Athene-like ruling, overbearing mother in a way to which Plath also might have related.

Marie Antoinette was a beautiful, cool, and fashionable blonde and many portraits show her wearing stiff and frilly gowns. She was known for her perfumes and sachets, mentioned in the eighth stanza. Antoinette was favorable to freemasonry and praised the good works of the masonic sisterhood, such as providing dowries for poor girls. Her father, Emperor Francis I, as well as Sylvia Plath's father, Otto Plath, was a freemason (Webster, 237-238). In 1790, Marie Antoinette attended a play in Paris. When she got up to applaud, she was pelted by apples from the crowd, including one containing a pen knife, the apple-stabbing in Plath's eighth stanza.

> *"Authority in science exists to be questioned, since heresy is the spring from which new ideas flow."*
>
> — John C. Polanyi

Antoinette was accused of various adulteries and deviant sexual acts, and these unfounded rumors were used to justify her execution. Marie Antoinette suffered frequent hemorrhaging, probably from uterine cancer, which stained her clothing. It fits Plath's "watermark," and "lingerie" images. Regarding faint marks on the skin, Antoinette's father-in-law, King Louis XV, died of smallpox, but she herself had survived the disease in her childhood. Her daughter and son were both rumored to be illegitimate. Marie Antoinette had her children educated in secret, against the traditions of Versailles.

The tenth stanza of "A Secret" describes the French Revolution and its mobs descending upon Versailles and the royal family. Antoinette turned to her brother Leopold II of Austria for help. Leopold was more interested in taking advantage of France's chaos to benefit himself, a proverbial knife in her back. Both Marie Antoinette and her husband Louis Charles XVI were beheaded at the Place de la Concorde, more big blue heads to match Plath's poem.

Fifth Mirror: Astrology and Astronomy

Astrologically speaking, the world has just left the paternalistic age of Pisces, the fish pictured in its constellation with one eye and one *i*, and moved into the Age of Aquarius, when feminine power is believed to resurge and dominate. The picture for the constellation of Aquarius holds up one palm as in the first stanza of "A Secret." The flow of Aquarius' water runs into the mouth of Pisces Austrinus (note its two *i*'s). This mark is faint and undulant, as well as "Wavery, indelible." Do not forget that some believe astrology to be "true," including Plath's husband. The African giraffe and Eden point to the Nile. According to author Robert Graves, the water pourer Aquarius represented the Egyptian god of the Nile.

The mythological epitome of masculine power was Hercules, Zeus' illegitimate son. The constellation of Hercules visualizes his head, easily blue in a dark night sky. Its proper name, Ras Algethi, means "head of the kneeling one." Mythologists tell that the Milky Way was formed by a trick Zeus played on his wife Hera, so she would suckle the infant Hercules in her sleep to make him immortal. She awoke in a rage, and milk squirted across the sky, forming the Milky Way and matching Plath's exploded stout bottle.

An alternative vision of the constellation of Hercules features his body, with one leg kneeling. This constellation, *Engonasin*, means "the kneeling one" in Greek. Hercules ultimately became weak and wounded, illustrated in the last stanza of this poem (White, 199ff).

Astronomically speaking, "A Secret" is about the planet Venus transiting the Sun every 105.5 years, or 121.5 years, at the opposite node of Venus' orbit (NASA). Astrologers believe when Venus transits the most powerful women made and make history. Likewise, Venus' eclipse invokes misogynistic acts such as the Salic Laws that prohibited women from inheriting land. It should be noted as well that Venus connects to the Sun on the Qabalah's Tree of Life.

While Plath never professed to be an expert in astrology, her husband Ted Hughes took the practice seriously and had been casting charts since he had been a young man in school, as well as sending out poems only on astrologically auspicious days. A correspondence with Greek myth and repetition of astronomical/astrological cycles of female power and vengeance probably intrigued Plath, as these themes are throughout her poetry.

Sixth Mirror: Humanities and the Arts

The Alexandria Quartet is a complex study of love, passion, deception, shifting alliances and sexual entanglements in all forms. Author Lawrence Durrell wrote that the four novels are an exploration of reality and the notions of continuum and subject-object relation, using modern love as the subject. The collection is said to be a convergence of Eastern and Western metaphysics, based on Einstein's overturning of the old view of the material universe (Andewski, 26-27). Carl Jung affects the book as well with his libido, anima, and shadow reflected in the hero, heroine, and villain respectively (Frye). Durrell, Plath and Hughes certainly knew of each other, sharing the publisher Faber & Faber, and Hughes and Durrell were published in some literary journals together.

Lawrence Durrell believed "the capital, the heart, the sex organ of Europe" is located in the "central point. The pivot," of the Mediterranean, in Alexandria (Diboll). Alexandria, one of the most famous cities of ancient times, has a large seaport and was founded by Alexander the Great. Alexandria gave rise to some of the greatest mystic poets and philosophers.

The first three books in *The Alexandria Quartet* tell essentially the same story from different perspectives, as Plath's "A Secret" has a narrator and two speakers. The collection explains the theosophical systems from Neo-Platonism, gnosticism, Kabbalism, Sufism, and alchemy that swept over the Egyptian city (Plath's "African") between the wars and into World War II. The books connect literature as diverse as Cavafy, Forster, de Sade, Freud, traditional Arab folklore, and Paracelsus' alchemy.

Plath surely saw the correlation between Ted Hughes' lover, Assia Wevill, and the *Quartet*'s leading character, Justine: a beautiful and mysterious Jewish woman with whom all the male characters were erotically obsessed. In real life, Durrell had met Eve Cohen, connecting to Plath's Eden in the third stanza. Cohen became Durrell's model for Justine, and he left his wife for her in 1942. The similarity of this relationship with Plath and Hughes is uncanny. The first book in Durrell's *The Alexandria Quartet* is entitled "Justine," corresponding with the Justice card. In *The Alexandria Quartet*, Justine has a stroke that leaves her with a drooping eye. The story's narrator calls Justine "the primitive face of mindless Aphrodite" (Durrell, 27). Justine, whose name should therefore not be taken lightly, is also an illustration of the personality resulting from Venus crossing the Sun. As in Plath's first stanza, the original cover design of *Justine* has a blue handprint spanning the cover; the spines of all four books have one handprint on them.

Durrell's character, Clea, fashionable and blonde as Marie Antoinette, is an artist who loses a hand after an accident. The faint stamp or watermark represents smallpox, this time in the *Quartet*'s character Leila. The third stanza of "A Secret" refers to the famous scene in *The Alexandria Quartet* when the character of Mountolive approaches the African green city of Alexandria by sea during a wartime blackout. "Wavery" is Leila's smallpox again, which come in waves, both on the body and as epidemics. "Indelible" refers to smallpox marks that cannot be erased, and Mountolive's indelible memories of war. Plath's associations of Morocco and Africa are important, as much of ancient alchemy, art, and language first developed in this region of the world. It might suggest Plath's use of African Black Magic in revenge on Hughes, as her editor, A. Alvarez, once suggested (Alvarez, 203-4).

In *The Alexandria Quartet*'s book *Mountolive*, the narrator mocks both himself and the character of Pursewarden, who is brought in for comic relief, suiting the fools of that last line of the fourth stanza. The *Quartet*'s character Liza suffers blindness, reflecting nothing but Plath's monkeys. The monkeys also fit the characters being slaves to their primitive natures, most especially the character of Justine. It appears Plath believed Hughes and his lover were slaves to their lower selves, their "monkeys." She uses metaphor that suggests picking them out as old slave traders once viewed blacks.

The character Melissa has an illegitimate baby that dies. The baby is featured in this unforgettable scene:

> "Clea's account of the horrible party; driving with Justine they had seen a brown cardboard box by the road. They were late so they put it in the back and did not open it until they reached the garage. Inside was dead baby wrapped in newspaper. What to do with this wizened homunculus? Perfectly formed organs. Guests were due to arrive, they had to rush. Justine slipped it into drawer of the hall desk. Party a great success (Durrell, 211).

In another scene from *The Alexandria Quartet*, Justine spills a bottle of perfume all over herself, reminiscent of Plath's stopper image. The smell is sickening, as Plath's eighth stanza echoes. In a parallel scene in a later book, the character of Leila, now an old woman who has had smallpox, runs into her former lover. She is drenched in a sickening perfume.

Beyond the suggestion of male ejaculation to Plath's images of exploded stout and foam in the lap, these lines and "Dwarf baby" refer to the *Quartet*'s alchemist character Capodistria, who studies Paracelsus' *De natura* and claims he has seen homunculi himself: "this Baron had…*actually produced* ten homunculi which he called his 'prophesying spirits'. They were preserved in huge glass canisters. […] They dangled lazily in those stout glass jars" (Durrell, 809).

As lovers reconnect and re-injure each other throughout the *Quartet* books, Plath's "knife in your back" image fits well too.

The precept on the Hermetic Emerald Tablet that correlates with "A Secret" is: *Thus was the World created*. This means that there is life in everything: every plant, animal, rock, or creation of man, and all life should be honored and treated with equal respect. Sylvia Plath used "A Secret" to reveal the secret of women's power, good and evil, for justice and revenge. It is the meaning of the tarot card Justice.

Chapter Ten: Doing Time as a Nobody
Card #9   The Hermit   Corresponding Poem: "The Jailor"

A popular interpretation of "The Jailor" is that the poem shows Plath's exaggerating her suffering during her marriage to Hughes, likening it to torture. When Sylvia Plath was in high school, she visited a prison and watched an inmate build a church from matchsticks, and astute scholars might have noticed this detail in Plath's poem. Plath uses the British spelling, "Jailor," in her title in the restored edition of *Ariel*. In *The Collected Poems*, edited by Ted Hughes, it is spelled as the Americanized "Jailer." This poem was not included in the first publication of *Ariel* in 1965. Seen through the Hermit tarot card, there are real tortures built into this poem, some mythological, some historical, and others happening in the world on the very day Plath composed this poem.

First Mirror: The Tarot/Qabalah
The Hermit card represents soul-searching, withdrawal, isolation, enlightenment, and all that is solitary. In its reversed position, it denotes suffering and cruelty, and negative qualities of isolation. *The Painted Caravan* states the Hermit symbolizes "the rewards and penalties of the lost soul. No emotion of pity or compassion enters here." The Golden Dawn assigns the Hermit to the Hebrew letter *Yod*, meaning, "within its hand the potential to create." The Hermit is said to be Cronos of Greek myth. His number in the tarot is nine, the number of completion of a cycle. In numerology, nines are revered. Add all of the numbers of the major arcana journey: $1+2+3+4+5+6+7+8+9=45$. Reducing the result, numerologist-style, $4+5=9$, returns it to the beginning. Furthermore, multiply nine by any number and the product's digits always add up to nine. Plath wrote "The Jailor" in nine stanzas.

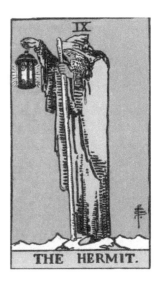

THE HERMIT.

In "The Jailor," Plath is both her own jailor and a prisoner of the dark forces of her subconscious.[90] Like The Fool, The Hermit is a traveler; however The Hermit has seen life's hard times and is no longer carefree. He is alone in the barren mountaintops, searching within himself. In reverse, he has lost the wisdom of introspection, filling his life with empty chatter and denial. This reversed Hermit is false and hidden behind masculine defenses of fake armor and amnesiac masks of Plath's sixth and seventh stanzas. The Hermit has been likened to St. Jude, the patron saint of hopeless cases, who is invoked when all else has failed.

In "The Jailor," Plath works with the rape, wet dreams, and impotence suggested by The Hermit's phallic staff. The staff also condemns wrong-doing as a jailer might enforce it. Plath feels punished, yet "The Jailor" is the one who has done wrong.

Managing Self-Harm: Psychological Perspectives states that in forensic psychotherapy, "the victim and perpetrator co-exist in the same person" (Motz). Plath's psychiatrist, Dr. Ruth Beuscher, speculated that Plath had a subconscious need to be punished, either by her own means, such as cutting her skin, or taking shock treatment as her punishment from society.

---

90 Plath's husband, Ted Hughes, wrote his own take on "The Jailor" in his collection *Birthday Letters*, with "The Blackbird." Hughes' poem helps to explain this interpretation of the subconscious.

Easton's 1897 Bible Dictionary explains that the Roman jailer in Acts 16:23 was "insensible as a rule and hardened by habit, and also disposed to despise the Jews, who were the bearers of the message of the gospel." This and Plath's jailor therefore represent the ego, suppressing and even punishing truth and self-actualization in effort to keep or imprison the status quo. He is the proverbial "keeper of the keys," rattling them as a taunt, setting no one free.

"The Jailor" poem has many visual tarot images from this card, such as "blue fog," "high, cold"; and the "black sack," like the Hermit's garments. In addition to the lantern's light, Plath's "gimlets" describe the hatch marks the artist used for The Hermit's shadings. The Hermit's isolation says it all; best captured in Plath's fourth stanza line: "I am myself. That is not enough."

Second Mirror: Alchemy

"The Jailor" is full of symbolism and chemistry terms straight out of the alchemy lab: a prison, or torture chamber, are terms for the alchemical vessel during putrefaction, the Black Phase; "sweats" pertain to the beads of liquid that accumulate on the sides of the glassware during the fire of distillation and purification; "grease" is characteristic of mercury's oily appearance. There is the sacrificial laboratory "plate"; blue vapors; and to wheel something into a position might be moving a cart, or referencing the alchemist's circular work of the elements (Abraham). The first stanza's "trees" address the Qabalah's Tree of Life, with its headstone-like Sephiroth marking the attributes of God. Other alchemical links include the timing of seven hours, as within the seven alchemical phases; the sack, the lever[91]; wetness; the observation that something has gone missing; capsules; drops, as from an eyedropper; the act of spreading; creating holes; comparison to paper, as a quality of the stone, or reference to alchemical papers; the burning process; noting of color; grassiness; rippling; to glue something; burned matchsticks; high; cold; masks to protect the face; dying in different ways; the impotence of the stone after it has endured its blackening; eating a ration; being drugged; cutting with a knife; feverishness; trickling; stiffening of a substance; and questioning what might have been ingested, because potability is important to alchemists.

Through the psychological interpretation of Jungian alchemy, "The Jailor" represents the deadly grip of the subconscious, with which the ego-consciousness must do battle (Jung *Symbols*, 348). Death of the ego is essential to the move toward individuation and standing Hermit-like, wholly on one's own. It is Jung's term for self-actualization: the philosopher's stone. This might disappoint those wanting to believe Plath's torturer was Hughes.

From *Man and His Symbols* by Carl G. Jung:

> "The actual processes of individuation—the conscious coming-to-terms with one's own inner center (psychic nucleus) or Self—generally begins with a wounding of the personality and the suffering that accompanies it. This initial shock amounts to a sort of a 'call,'[92] although it is not often recognized as such. On the contrary, the ego feels hampered in its will or desire and usually projects the obstruction onto something external. That is, the ego accuses God or the economic situation or the boss or the marriage partner of being responsible for whatever is obstructing it" (Jung *Man*, 169).

Jung referred to what we today call the *subconscious* as the *unconscious*. Jung called this dark side

---

91 See *Fixed Stars Govern a Life*'s interpretation of the Sylvia Plath's poem, "A Secret" for "lever" and its association with gold leaf.

92 It is almost impossible not to hear Sylvia Plath's line, "I guess you could say, I've a call," from her poem, "Lady Lazarus," here.

"the shadow self," explaining much of Plath's poetic shadow imagery. When subconscious rules, it makes its presence known primarily in dreams: thus the "night sweats," if they are unpleasant. Sleep itself becomes Plath's blue fogginess as it wheels into its time on the clock to take her over. "[T]rees" and "headstones" become a wooden bed frame and pillows. In the second stanza, Plath gets seven hours of sleep from her sleeping pill, during which she is taken advantage of by the unconscious mind, powerless to defend herself and likening it to rape. Nighttime is a "black sack," reminiscent of the expression, "hitting the sack."

The first stanza's "rattler" holds snake associations if disassociated from metal keys. In alchemy, the serpent represents a dark, destructive force with the power to kill the corrupt metal or matter, dissolving it into its first, pure matter in preparation for the philosopher's stone. It is also a metaphor for the Grim Reaper who rattles bones as he harvests souls and continues the circle of life. He teaches that nothing is allowed to live past its time, and nothing remains unchanged. Likewise, his "keys" may be taken to mean "answers."

In the second stanza, Plath sleeps either in fetal position, or with an arched back, like a cat. "Fetal" and "cat" are alchemical terms for the philosophical child and the lion of Sulfur.

Plath imagines herself victim of her own unconscious, under a lever of perverse fantasies. Wet dreams are of course a man's nocturnal emissions. Like Plath's vulnerability at night, a man is powerless to control them in sleep. This also hints of the alchemist's sperm or semen metaphor, the seed of metals from which silver and gold are grown.

"Something is gone," is Plath's ego-self, a smashed carapace by the stanza's end. The "sleeping capsule" is both the bed and the unenlightened trip through life. The capsule is red and blue, mirroring the *Rubedo* phase and blue mercurial water. Alembic glassware has a round end, or "balloon." "Sack" is another name for the alembic, and all are synonymous with zeppelins. The Grim Reaper is in action, destroying the carapace in the Black Phase.

Jung said birds are symbols of transcendence. When Plath spreads "to the beaks of birds," she is taken up into the greater collective unconscious (Jung *Man*, 147). Jung's individuation is not isolated, but a process to become one with the whole of consciousness.

Plath asks, "What have I eaten?" and later announces she consumed her "ghost ration," suggesting the alchemical process *cibation*, nourishment of the philosopher's stone. Another metaphor for cibation is to devour; it is the paradoxical nature of destroying in order to be reborn (Abraham, 40, 53). Plath is not starving, she devours herself; "ration" becomes the rational mind.

The "fever" in the fifth and last stanzas nod to Nicolas le Fèvre, a famous 17th century alchemist who wrote *Traicté de la Chymie*, *A Compendious Body of Chymistry*, and *A Discourse upon Sr. Walter Rawleigh's Great Cordial* (leFevre). Likewise, in the fifth stanza, Plath has two lines starting with the word "Surely." Was this homophone fun with alchemist writer John W. Shirley's name, and an equally well-known alchemist, Sir George Ripley ("rippling")? One of Shirley's famous texts was *The Scientific Experiments of Sir Walter Raleigh, The Wizard Earl, and the Three Magi in the Tower*.

The "gluing" in Plath's sixth stanza is an alchemical term for uniting opposite qualities and states. Glue is the alchemical "sperm" or "semen." Sometimes during the Black phase, the vessel is referred to as "burnt," "dead," "prison," "headstone," "coffin," or "churchyard." Plath's "church of burnt matchsticks" is an amalgam of these terms.

Plath's "negress" references *nigredo*, and its paw color clarifies it as a panther, the alchemist's metaphor for the swollen matter in the alembic (Abraham, 201). Indeed, those "eyes to knife" may be *I*'s; the self. After release from the body to a spiritual formless state, it is back into the fire to become a new being, the other person Plath dreams in the sixth stanza.

In "The Jailor," Plath dies many ways, yet none are bloody. This is important, as Jung points out in *Symbols of Transformation* that all gods going on to eternal life have been stoned and hung in relatively bloodless deaths: Christ, Odin, Attis, and others. Jung sees hanging and hooking up of the gods, shown in the seventh stanza, to have symbolic value of unfulfilled longing and "suspension" (Jung *Symbols*, 383). Likewise, Plath's "variety" of death fits all alchemical processes for killing impure base material in the pursuit of the philosopher's stone.

Third Mirror: Mythology

The Greek god Chronos' name means *time*. Chronos teaches the lesson of time and the limitations and continual changes of mortal life, including aloneness and ultimate death. He presides over cyclical laws: the passage of seasons, birth, growth, death, and gestation to rebirth. Chronos is depicted as the man turning the zodiac wheel in Greco-Roman mosaics, and the wise, old hermit; his semen was said to produce the first generation of gods. Chronos is sometimes called Aeon, meaning "life" or "eternity," or "one billion years" to geologists, astronomers, and cosmologists. Hermeticists designate an aeon as 2000 years, an Age. From *aeon* has come the word eon, meaning roughly a thousand years. Plath's "seven hours" are her seven years of marriage, feeling like Chronos' eons of jail time.[93]

Chronos is often confused with the Titan's Cronus, the Grim Reaper, and Plath plays with both characters. Cronus' symbol is the sickle, relating to Plath's knife image. Cronus used this sickle to castrate his father Uranus, at the urging of his mother. According to Hesiod's *Theogony*, Uranus had prisoners in a dungeon of torment and suffering called Tartarus. Hesiod wrote that an anvil took nine days to fall from heaven to earth, and another nine days to fall from earth to Tartarus. It is Plath's drop from great altitude, and reinforces The Hermit's number, nine. In the Old Testament Book of Daniel, and in the ancient Jewish Book of Enoch, Tartarus is where the fallen "watchers" (angels) are held. The Hermit, looking down from his mountaintop, is a watcher.

Cronus is the patron of harvest, and has comparable identities in Roman, Sumerian, Akkadian, Babylonian, and Phoenician myth. The Greeks viewed Cronus as cruel, with a tempestuous force of chaos and disorder. The Romans saw him more favorably, renaming him Saturn and crediting him with harvest and the Saturnalia festival. Matching Cronus with seasons turning to harvest, he became known as the god of time, and thus the confusion with Chronos.

Cronus married his sister, Rhea. Rhea means "pomegranate," a red and purple-blue fruit. Some might call it a capsule of seeds, and it is certainly zeppelin-shaped. Rhea's daughter, Hera, wore a pomegranate calyx on her head instead of a crown. In Orphic myth, when Rhea gave birth to Zeus, her name was changed to Demeter. Rhea/Demeter gave birth to Persephone, who was tricked by Hades into imprisonment in the underworld by eating six pomegranate seeds, thus creating the torturous and cold season of winter.

"The Jailor" also fits the grandson of Cronus and son of Zeus, Hephaestus, god of fire and metalworking. Hephaestus is also equated with The Hermit tarot card, and both walk with a stick. When Plath wrote of being "hung, starved, burned, hooked," this could be Hephaestus' blacksmithing. Hera, Hephaestus' mother, threw Hephaestus out of heaven in disgust because he was born lame. Hephaestus fell nine days and nights. As an adult, he made himself a wheelchair, Plath's wheels in the second line of "The Jailor." He was said to have made his mother a magical

---

93 The span of seven years is mentioned again in the poem "Daddy." Plath was actually married for six years and into her seventh with Hughes. She might have stressed seven for mystical importance.

golden throne that trapped and imprisoned her when she sat down in it, another fit for "The Jailor." Hephaestus was given Aphrodite's hand in marriage by Zeus, but Aphrodite had an affair with Ares, who carried a phallic staff certainly apposite with Plath's wet-dream lever. Hephaestus built an unbreakable net of chain to trap them both.

Fourth Mirror: History and the World

Mentioned in the Mythology mirror, the pomegranate's "carapace" must be "smashed" to get the fruit inside. The pomegranate's pulp is considered to be astringent, a property of the Hindu god for Saturn, Shani. Mentioned in the Bible, the Homeric Hymns, and many ancient texts, the pomegranate is tolerant of difficult desert conditions that would kill most other fruit-bearing plants. In ancient Greek mythology, the pomegranate was known as the "fruit of the dead."

In the tarot, pomegranates fill the background of the temple of the High Priestess card. The two pillars of Solomon's temple were said to be engraved with pomegranates representing the fertility of the Promised Land. Jews believe the pomegranate has 613 seeds, corresponding with the 613 commandments of the Torah. In Qabalah, pomegranates represent the mystical experience itself, the "garden of pomegranates," or paradise.

In nature, pomegranate seeds are eaten and dispersed by birds, as in the end of the poem's third stanza. The shape and interior of the pomegranate is often compared with the poppy's narcotic capsule, Plath's drug reference.[94] We know Plath knew this about poppies due to her "Poppies in July" poem's line, "Where are your opiates, your nauseous capsules?"(*CP*, 203). Opium can be smoked, and was often used in earlier times as a substance added to tobacco by cigarette makers, to make cigarettes more addictive. The cigarette burnings in Plath's fourth stanza now becomes the opium talking.

Early drafts of "The Jailor" offer a new perspective from cut lines: the speaker is light itself, caged within the Hermit's lantern and about to be let go. In the final version of the poem, the trapped light references sky, a zeppelin, altitude, gimlets, and burning. When Plath wrote "The Jailor," *Who Destroyed the Hindenburg?* by A. A. Hoehling had just been published. A popular book, it was first to suggest that an anti-Nazi saboteur destroyed the luxury German airship in 1937. The Hindenburg was a "black sack" phallus, floating through the sky, tilted like a lever in its last minutes. The airship appeared to be strong and invincible, but it was the false armor of the sixth stanza, with the height and cold of the seventh. The third stanza describes the drop to the ground, and the following three illustrate the burning and the girder "ribs." Plath notes that the sky is black, not the color it should be.

Another phallic tilted lever in the sky is a missile, and "The Jailor" was written the day after the Cuban Missile Crisis was announced. The poem well describes the positioning of the missiles aimed at the United States.

Plath's church of burned matchsticks is part memory of a prisoner she met on a youth group trip to the Charles Street Jail in November 1947.[95] The trip made a great impression on the then fifteen-year-old Plath. In her diary she paid special attention to a young burglar who constructed a delicate model of a cathedral from burned matchsticks. Plath's burned church of course also references Germany's destruction of France in World War II. Her contained light is hydrogen breaking

---

94 For more on Soma, see *Fixed Stars Govern a Life*'s interpretation of Sylvia Plath's poem, "Morning Song."
95 This journal is kept in the Sylvia Plath archives at the Lilly Library, Indiana University-Bloomington.

free, its inevitable destruction. "The Jailor", therefore also reflects the people imprisoned on the dirigible twenty-five years earlier, and the missiles in Cuba.

The Tower of London inspired the setting for much of this poem too. There is the height of Tower Hill, and the enormity of the castle itself. The castle, with its tapering turrets of blackened stone, may be compared to a church made of burned matchsticks. For much of its history, the Tower of London had been used as a prison, with neighboring Tower Hill as the location for executions. In modern London, historic sites are marked with blue placards, referenced in the second line of "The Jailor." Plath's last residence had a placard proclaiming it as a building in which W.B. Yeats once resided, and this unheated place with bursting pipes was a kind of a torture too in her last days in the hardest winter England had seen in 100 years. The foggy setting in this line pertains to London. The Wheel put in place fits the Catherine Wheel, a torture device of the time found in the Tower. When prisoners were not beheaded or burned at the stake, there was always the lever-controlled executioner's rack.

Beginning in 1485 A.D., Europeans endured an epidemic known as "the English Sweate" which accounts for the fevers mentioned in the fifth and last stanzas. King Henry VIII's second wife, Anne Boleyn,[96] who was imprisoned in the Tower of London and later executed, had this sickness herself, referenced in Plath's first line. Used as a prison, palace, and government building, the Tower also served as a military armory, as in the sixth-stanza; and it has been the home of the royal zoo, befitting the panther in the alchemical interpretation. There were many famous prisoners and executions at the Tower, especially the wives of King Henry VIII. Plath's fourth-stanza gimlet image may refer to the direct, knifelike and penetrating stare of King Henry, seen in Holbein's famous portrait of him from 1537. The charges against Henry's wives were almost all flimsy, and the question Plath asks in the first stanza addresses this. King Henry VIII had difficulty fathering male children, and Plath's mention of impotence is a playful dig at this condition, for which he blamed his wives. Prisoners such as Anne Askew were charged with the "subversion" seen in Plath's sixth stanza, and Askew bravely refused to change her faith, facing accusers with "Lies and smiles."

To lie and smile through imprisonment calls to mind the grinning mask of another famous Tower prisoner/execution victim who gave his name as "John Johnson," until the truth was tortured out of him. He was the infamous Guy Fawkes, responsible for the Gunpowder Plot, an attempt to blow up Parliament in 1606.

The fourth stanza's cigarettes connect to yet another Tower of London prisoner, the great explorer, poet, and Renaissance man, Sir Walter Raleigh. Raleigh was imprisoned in the Tower for thirteen years, although it appeared to be a comfortable stay, living with his family, growing tobacco, fathering children, doing alchemical experiments, and writing *The History of the World* (1614 A.D.). Raleigh, his poet and scientist friends met regularly in what became known in 1592 as "The School of Atheism," often called "The School of Night," where they were said to be worshipping pagan gods, an act of treason. Raleigh was eventually released, but imprisoned again later and executed in 1618. Moving ahead a few centuries to World War I, a group of German spies was shot in the Tower. During World War II, the last Nazi German spy executed and the last execution in the Tower of London, was Josef Jakobs, who had parachuted into England and was injured upon landing.

Curiously, "The Jailor" is full of symptoms of arsenic poisoning, an occupational hazard for metalworkers like the hermit god Hephaestus, who blamed the often crow-black metalloid for his lameness. Plath's fifth stanza question about what she had eaten is apt, as deadly arsenic has been

---

96 Anne Boleyn and her King Henry get a great deal of attention in the *Fixed Stars Govern a Life*'s interpretation of Sylvia Plath's preceding poem, "A Secret."

a favorite murder weapon since the Middle Ages, often going undetected. The narrator of "The Jailor" suffers all symptoms of arsenic poisoning: fever, weight loss, sleeplessness, foggy confusion, drowsiness, sweating, and traces of arsenic can be found in a victim's hair, stiffening it. Poisoning might happen if the chemical were falsely presented as a sleeping pill, as in the third stanza. Drawing parallels with The Hindenburg, missiles, and the Hermit card, arsenic burns in the air and can be used in laser diodes and LEDs to directly convert electricity into light.

Some important historical figures fell to arsenic: Napoleon Bonaparte suffered and died of arsenic poisoning during his imprisonment on Saint Helena.[97] The painter Vincent van Gogh died ultimately of arsenic-induced depression and insanity. His last work, "Crows on a Field," fits Plath's third-stanza birds and the many crow connections. The Grim Reaper, Cronus, sometimes has an arsenic-black crow on his shoulder, and a staff with a crooked blade like a crow's bill. The name of the Welsh crow-god, Bran, equivalent of Cronus and Saturn, means "crow" or "raven." The head of the Celtic king who took his name is said to be buried at Tower Hill as protection against invasion. It was linked with the wren, "Bran's crow," as a prophetic bird, and crows are historically important to the Tower of London; a superstition holds that "If the Tower of London ravens are lost or fly away, the Crown will fall and Britain with it."

The oldest tale of the crow/wren comes from Pausanias in his *Description of Greece*. Trochilus, meaning "wren," and "of the wheel," returning to Cronus' wheelchair and Plath's first stanza, fled Argos for Attica when his city was seized by Syrian invaders. Afterward, it became customary on the twelfth day to carry a crow caged in a box with glass windows, decorated with a wheel and colored ribbons. The crow becomes the jailbird. The British expressions, "Crow Station," and "To the crows with you!" derive from from Cronus' place of damnation. The Night-Crow brought terror to the Celts. The crow is also known as a rook, jay, or raven, and a flock is sometimes also called *a murder*, also apropos to this poem.

Fifth Mirror: Astrology and Astronomy

The crescent moon is said to be the blade of Cronus' scythe, symbolizing the cycles of time. The Romans called Cronus *Saturn*, the outermost of the classical planets visible to the naked eye. In astrology,

"The public is a bad guesser."

–Thomas de Quincey

Saturn is the severe god who radically changes a person every 29-½ years. His tests last for a period of seven and one-half years. Saturn, like the other planets in our solar system on the zodiac wheel, fits Plath's second-line wheel image. As Saturn is far from the Sun, it is high, cold and dark: all descriptions Plath gives to her jailor.[98]

Babylonian astronomers grouped Saturn with the seven *Mashi*, constellations older than the signs of the zodiac. Saturn is connected to the godship of *Ninib*, resembling Cronus in description and myth. In Hindu (Vedic) astrology, the seven known planets of the time, along with the north and south lunar nodes, are known as the *Navagraha*, the nine "seizers" or "influencers" related to the Sanskrit word *graha*, for holding (as in a prison). The Navagraha points out the karmic influence on living things, and Sanskrit astrological writings refer to graha as evil spirits born of anger.

---

97 Plath studied Napoleon and Josephine, and might have been amused to learn that in 2005, it was discovered that 18th-century British King George III, who defeated Napoleon, suffered arsenic-caused madness.

98 On January 28, 1946, thirteen-year-old Sylvia Plath wrote in her journal, "Miss Walker and about ten other girls and we went to the Wellesley college observatory....I will never forget my first view of Saturn through the telescope!" This journal is held in the Sylvia Plath archives in the Lilly Library, at Indiana University-Bloomington.

Shani is the Hindu name for Saturn, lord of the day Saturday, a primary celestial being. He is dark blue and black in color; the blue sapphire is associated with him is seen in the first stanza. He is dressed in a black, sack-like garment, fitting Plath's second stanza. His element is air, and his direction is west, where the sun sets into darkness. Shani is the god-metaphor for the hard way, and his name means "the one who moves slowly," as the planet Saturn takes about thirty years to revolve around the Sun.

Planetebücher, a popular 15th-century German text on astrology, attributed the qualities of melancholy and apathy to Saturn. Along with Cronus, *Planetebücher* gives control to his wife Rhea, or her Roman counterpart, Cybele. She is connected to the pomegranate and flanked by lions, as we see in both the cat in the second stanza, and the paws in the fourth.

Sixth Mirror: Humanities and the Arts

As with the name "Salinger" in the preceding poem, "Tulips," there is irony matching Nazi German spy, Josef Jakobs (1898-1941), against the same-named Australian literary and Jewish historian, *Joseph Jacobs* (1854-1916 A.D.), who emigrated to London, graduated from Plath's and Hughes' alma mater of Cambridge, and then went on to the University of Berlin. Jacobs collected English and Celtic fairy tales and folklore in five different collections. His story, "The Golden Ball" is the basis of the famous old folk ballad, "The Gallis [Gallows] Pole."[99] In it, a maiden is to be hanged for unknown reasons. Her family members come, one by one. She hopes that they will bribe the executioner, but they have nothing. That is the question Plath's narrator asks in the last two lines of her first stanza.

Opium made an appearance in an earlier mirror of this poem, and a famous opium user was 19th-century English poet, William Wordsworth, also an alumnus of Cambridge University. Wordsworth was famous for many great works, including an unfinished poem for his friend, transcendentalist poet Samuel Taylor Coleridge, called "The Recluse," a perfect fit for the Hermit card. T.S. Eliot wrote of Wordsworth's "persistent metaphor [that life is] a circular journey whose end is 'to arrive where we started / And know that place for the first time'" (Eliot, *LG*). Should this sound like The Hermit's position on the Qabalah Tree of Life, you might recall that Eliot was a member of the Golden Dawn.[100]

Coleridge turned to opium to deal with anxiety and depression, and his own extreme addiction to opium eventually tore the two friends apart. Coleridge's great work, "Kubla Kahn," is said to be opium-inspired. Coleridge's "Kubla Kahn" was written in Plath's Devonshire and intended to be a three-part epic to rival Milton's *Paradise Lost*.[101] "Kubla Khan" portrays the violent, barbaric and uncivilized Tartars, connecting them to ideas of original sin and the garden of Eden, as well as to Cronus' anvil drop from earth to Tartarus. In the poem, an Abyssinian maid cries for her demon lover. Abyssinia, now Ethiopia, explains Plath's mention of a "negress."

Thomas De Quincey is best known for his work, *Confessions of an English Opium-Eater* (1821), which first appeared in *The London Magazine*. It speaks of his hard beginning as a homeless youth in

---

99 "The Gallows Pole" is a song later famously covered by the rock band Led Zeppelin in the 1970s, who also borrowed the Hermit tarot card image for their fourth album. How interesting that Plath presciently used the word "zeppelin" here.
100 There are some scholars who do not believe that there is enough satisfactory evidence to prove that T.S. Eliot was a member of the Golden Dawn. Any in-depth study of T.S. Eliot's work against Hermetic text should satisfy the most skeptical of readers that Eliot was most certainly greatly influenced by the group, at the least.
101 For more Plath references to Milton's *Paradise Lost*, see *Fixed Stars Govern a Life*'s interpretations of "Ariel" and "Fever 103°".

the streets of London. Like Plath's "The Jailor," it includes details of London, the torturous sickness of addiction withdrawal, and visions of being alone atop high, cold, mountains. In *Confessions*, De Quincey wrote of Coleridge's "Kubla Khan," and De Quincey uses Plath's images of wheels, levers, and more. Plath once wrote of understanding the desire to escape into opium, to admit to original sin, and even to follow Hitler (*UJ*, 150). She seems to say that opium, love, and dictators release one of his or her own responsibility, and that these are painful and terrible addictions.

One who painted in "gimlets" is Dutch post-impressionist painter, Vincent van Gogh. Vincent van Gogh was known for his waving "rippling" lines, bright colors, and feeling of movement. Diagnosed as mad, his neurological disorders were blamed on arsenic poisoning from absinthe, as well as his lead pigments and mercury-based paints and solvents. Van Gogh suffered the fever and stomach troubles of "The Jailor's" first and fifth stanzas; hallucinations and nightmares, a quality throughout the poem; anxiety, stupor and forgetfulness, as seen in the third and seventh stanzas; impotence as in the eighth stanza; and insomnia, as in the third stanza. Van Gogh's missing ear, and self-mutilation in a seizure or fit, also fits Plath's notion of something taken in the third stanza.

To read "The Jailor" with van Gogh in mind, his famous painting, "Starry Night," becomes the first stanza's foggy blue placard, with its golden stars wheeling around and as big as greased breakfast plates. He painted the same cypress trees often, and Plath's "wet dreams" now become van Gogh's wet paint; his hand becomes the "lever."

Van Gogh's stars in the famous "Café terrace on the Place du Forum, Arles, at Night" and "Starry Night Over the Rhone" could easily be modeled after cigarette burns. Vincent van Gogh was known to be feverish in his work, as well as gaunt, seen in Plath's fifth stanza. With his brush strokes of lines, Van Gogh's buildings, such as "The Church at Auvers," looks like burned matchsticks. Dark paintings portraying the hopelessness of starving peasants, such as "The Potato Eaters," evoke Plath's eighth stanza. Vincent van Gogh's paintings have been hung and hooked as in "The Jailor," and the "Vase with Five Sunflowers" was burned in a fire during World War II. The artist himself was starved and malnourished most of his years painting, making the list of adjectives closing Plath's seventh stanza an accurate description. Van Gogh wrote to his brother lines such as "I'm such a nobody," and "I wish they would take me as I am." These words are full of Plath's "I am myself. That is not enough."

Chapter Eleven: Song of the Onion
Card #10 The Wheel of Fortune Corresponding Poem: "Cut"

In the autumn of 1962, Sylvia Plath accidentally lopped off the tip of her thumb cutting onions at home in her kitchen. She was with her children and the nanny, the latter to whom the poem "Cut" is dedicated. Like so many of Plath's poems, "Cut" begins with that seed of autobiography, yet it has as many layers as an onion.

First Mirror: The Tarot/Qabalah

The meaning of the Wheel of Fortune card is rotation, circulation, spinning and luck. This is the wheel of life, death, and rebirth, a perpetual mill of motion. Issues in the cards zero (The Fool) through 10 (Wheel of Fortune) in the tarot correspond with the personal life. The tenth card signifies triumph or failure, depending upon how it falls in a spread. The next eleven cards hold more universal themes. Plath used ten stanzas for her number ten tarot card's corresponding poem. The Golden Dawn assigned to The Wheel of Fortune to the Hebrew letter *Koph*, meaning "hand," or "palm of the hand," in which a fortune may be read. The Golden Dawn explains it as "the fist which, when its inner potential strength is expanded by directed and broadened motion, can change the direction of events for good or ill."

A hand or fist may be near to the image of Plath's poetic thumb in "Cut," but there is much more to this match-up than that.

The first line's "thrill" is the vibratory change many mystics assert takes place when our ego confronts the blood of its body form. True freedom of the will is believed to be attained through the unity of the greater outside life forces with the inside self. Hermeticists teach that when we bleed and feel this thrilling feeling, consciousness alters (or, in extreme cases of blood loss, leaves us), and the spirit is able to step away and view the body objectively.

Pilgrims are on a spiritual journey. Plath's third-stanza pilgrim image represents her traveling in a new America of mysticism. The Indian reference could symbolize Native Americans, or the eastern Yogis. Consider the famous magic carpets of the Middle East, and that "Turkey," taken now as the country, is so near "Carpet rolls" in the poem. Plath's metaphors in "Cut" reinforce The Wheel of Fortune card's design many times over: The Wheel looks very much like an oriental rug in its design.[102] One of the definitions of Plath's word "trepanned" in the last stanza is to cut circular discs. This, in addition to the standard meaning of amputation, fits the poem. Plath's onion, round like The Wheel, is a qabalistic and mystical symbol for countless existences and the higher self, with its seven principles represented by the spokes of the wheel.

There are no sides to a wheel, and so Plath shows confusion as to what side one is on. In "Cut," Plath's body is threatened by the "redcoats"; her spirit expands into an experience of occult initiation, allowing her essence to flow into the whole of humanity through self-sacrifice. Note the line break after "O my": The Homunculus, a being within, is hers indeed, but she shows surprise and even fright.

---

102 Plath removed her original metaphor of a pith helmet from an earlier draft of the poem "Cut"; a pith helmet is also an apt picture for the shape of The Wheel.

The feeling of paper in the seventh stanza suggests either burnt ash, or possibly a reference to an earlier Plath poem not found in the *Ariel* collection, called "Apprehensions." An excerpt reads:

"This red wall winces continually
A red fist, opening and closing,
Two gray, papery bags—
This is what I am made of, this and a terror
Of being wheeled off under crosses and a rain of pietas." (Plath, *Winter*, 3)

The continual wincing in "Apprehensions" is understood to be blood pulsing. "Apprehensions" has the same images as those in "Cut": the hand, the feeling of paper, and the wheel. Written in May 1962, "Apprehensions" is an earlier working of the ideas and process of "Cut," written October 24th of that same year. Plath likely chose "Cut" for the *Ariel* collection because the imagery is more powerful and works across so many levels (DiBenedette).

Plath used the word "balled" in a poem to come, "Death & Co.," and as a homophone for the "bald" image in "Morning Song," and "Barren Woman." This time, "balled" may be those same ideas of birth and purity, but also the round ball of The Wheel itself. Plath closes "Cut" with the observation that she feels small in the face of God. Her last stanza image of dirtiness is the wound from the darkness of humanity. *The Painted Caravan* reads:

"The body and the soul had to be, as it were, slain and desecrated, or at least soiled and scarred, before contrition and absolution were of any value."

This same book claims the onion symbol "penetrates into the secret recesses of God's nature and unveils his many countenances," and "…the veils of the hidden side of life, its spiritual essence, could be rent ["cut"] apart by those who had the perseverance to undergo the trials and sacrifices ordained by the secret societies" (Rákóczi, 45-46).

The Wheel's number ten is highly significant. There are ten fingers on the hand, and ten stations on the Qabalah Tree of Life. In the Bible story of Jacob's ladder,[103] Jacob vows to give a tenth of his blessings to God. As a kind of illustration, the Tree of Life projects notions about how the one (individual) is related to the many (the ten, whole). Ten, in the tarot, is also the number in the tarot where issues stop being personal and cross into universal meanings. The form of the Tree of Life is a 1:10 ratio, comparable to Egyptian obelisks with a base width 1/10 of their height. Obelisks look like the number one and the letter I, loading it with meanings of the individuation, as well as the phallus, a symbol underlying many qabalist teachings. In Qabalah, Creation is viewed as a falling, overflowing, or emanation from the throne of God, beginning at the top of the Tree of Life, sphere number one, and proceeding downward in stages, through the sun, moon, and to the earth or world.

Second Mirror: Alchemy

Alchemists assign The Wheel of Fortune to the "Fixed and the Volatile," representing fate, transformation, and change. Plath's third line about the top gone refers to the alchemical metaphor of beheading; the entire second stanza illustrates a scalping. During *nigredo*, the black color is transformed to white. Alchemist Nicolas Flamel wrote of the metaphoric "blacke man" losing his head, and a "sharp ax" to do the job and drain it of color. These fit Plath's "dead white," and "Ku Klux Klan" (Abraham, 21).

---

103 Jacob's Ladder is a metaphor for the Tree of Life and first seen in *Fixed Stars Govern a Life*'s interpretation of Plath's "Tulips" poem.

The reference to white in the second stanza suggests a communion wafer.[104] The plush of red matches the blood from a scalping, but also symbolizes Eucharistic wine. Red and white are the colors of alchemy representing salt of body and Mercury of spirit. Thus, the rolling and mill imagery of "Cut" is blood circulating and flowing, and the turning Wheel of Fortune.

In the third stanza, the turkey is known as a *philosophical bird* of alchemy, praised by alchemists like Benjamin Franklin for its giving to man. Jonathan Allen, an early feminist and educator who lectured on spiritual alchemy said, "Thus the selfsame sacrificial turkey will come to high or base ends, just according as the human absorbing it is motive by noble or ignoble aims" (Allen, 256). The steps in alchemical transformation are to coagulate the lower and higher self into a transformed being.

The bottle Plath clutches in the fourth stanza holds her stone in the beginning stage of *rubedo*. The white, purified stone first turns pink and then reddens in a fizzy chemical reaction as it reunites with the spirit (the chemical wedding). As the heat of fire increases, the color deepens. When one nears the perfection of rubedo, which some equate to eternal life, Plath's fifth stanza celebratory exclamation is absolute.

The word "million" contains that word "mill," a kind of wheel. A million, like infinity, is a number so large it is difficult to fathom. Without actually counting, to grasp the concept we must rely on faith, much like our attitude toward God. Like the spokes of a wheel, alchemists, mystics, and other believers revolve around blind faith that something greater is in control.

A "Homunculus" is another being inside Plath, gaining power and coming into consciousness.[105] The homunculus is the philosophical child. Likewise, "saboteur" is metaphor for the alchemist, and "kamikaze" is the alchemist dying for the cause. The darkening and tarnish of the eighth stanza is the blackening process of *nigredo*. From the Jungian alchemy perspective, the entire ninth stanza addresses the reduction of the Self and ego.

In "Cut," Plath clearly speaks of blood. A pure blood line bears special significance in the occult. German Renaissance alchemist Rudolf Steiner claimed:

"Endogamy preserves the blood of the generation; it permits of the same blood flowing in the separate members as flows for generations through the entire tribe or the entire nation. Exogamy inoculates man with new blood, and this breaking-down of the tribal principle, this mixing of blood, which sooner or later takes place among all peoples, signifies the birth of the external understanding, the birth of the intellect.

"The birth of logical thought, the birth of the intellect, was simultaneous with the advent of exogamy" (Steiner, 55).[106]

Sigmund Freud, whom Plath read avidly, wrote a paper deemed racist today on the subject of inheritance and aggression in bloodlines. In *Civilization and Its Discontents*, Freud sought to prove that civilized society is a substitute-formation for our individual instincts and drives, directed as much by the blood of our original clan or tribe than our conscious egos.[107]

---

104 The communion wafer was seen first in her seventh *Ariel* poem, "Tulips."
105 Ted Hughes' poem, "Tutorial," includes the image of "homunculi" and was published in the November 2, 1962 edition of *The New Statesman*. Plath had likely read the poem, and possibly submitted the poem on behalf of Hughes, for publication.
106 This idea is discussed also in Sir James George Frazer's *The Golden Bough*, a book that Plath owned.
107 Ted Hughes' poems "Childbirth" (from *The Hawk in the Rain*), "Thistles," and "The Warriors of the North" (the latter two from Hughes' *Wodwo*) may be considered meditations on the subject of an ancient bloodline. "Childbirth" is also full of wheel imagery, and Hughes wrote this poem during his time with Plath.

Third Mirror: Mythology

The Wheel of Fortune card is associated with the Greek myth of the Moirai, goddesses of fate. These were fatherless daughters of the night, with whom Plath might have identified. One daughter spins, one measures, and another, Atropos, cuts. Atropos means "she who cannot be avoided." She and her two sisters hold the Wheel of Fortune that spins the thread of fate (Sharman-Burke, 54). Plath's silent mill is the Moirai's wheel with its still center; a constant and unchanging hub despite the whirl of outside activity.

Mythologist Robert Graves wrote in *The White Goddess* that the ancient Greek goddess Nemesis carried a wheel in hand to show that she turned the year, as did Egypt's Isis and the Latin Fortuna (or Tyche, meaning "luck," in Greek). In the Hellenistic world of arbitrary violence and sometimes great misfortune for no just cause, Fortuna/Tyche, pictured holding or standing upon the wheel, was credited for the act. It was understood that the wheel of fate would one day come around and exact its due upon the sinner. Oracular wheels of fortune decorated the temple of Apollo at Delphi and many early European churches. Similar wheels were used by the magi in ancient Babylon and in ancient Egyptian temples.

Egypt's reigning goddess Isis held decision-making power in matters of fate. One of her symbols was the *tyet*, known as the Knot or Blood of Isis. Resembling an ankh with its arms pointed down, it could be compared to a thumb. Isis famously lamented her beloved Osiris, who was cut to pieces by Set. She went to recover the pieces and reconstruct him, but fish had swallowed Osiris' penis. Isis made him a new one, after which they conceived Horus. The Romans and Greeks considered the thumb phallic and an emblem of Venus, connected to Isis, and celebrated in these societies with sexual orgies.

In Druid myth, Mogh Ruith (meaning, "slave to the wheel") flew in a machine called "the oared wheel," causing men to turn to stone, a different sort of silence-mill. Legend held he was the executioner of John the Baptist, bringing a curse upon the Irish people.

The Homunculus figures into myth too: Hindus believe that the innermost self, or soul, is a *thumb*-sized being that dwells in the hearts of all people.

Fourth Mirror: History and the World

The word "onion" originated from the Latin *unio*, meaning "single white pearl." Like pearls, onions are ball-shaped and increase size by adding layers. Ancient Egyptians worshiped the onion's spherical shape and concentric rings, which symbolized eternal life. Onions were found in the eye sockets of the mummy Ramesses IV; ancient Greek Olympian athletes ate onions to balance the blood; and Roman gladiators rubbed their bodies with onions to firm muscles. Onions were given as gifts in the Medieval Ages, and doctors have used onions to cure everything from bowel troubles to snakebites. According to diaries of the early American pilgrims, onions were the first vegetable planted. It is a vegetable packed with history and spiritual power to match its odor.

The onion/pearl connection takes us to Japan, where pearls were first cultured en masse in 1893. The country of Japan is shaped much like a thumb, with its northernmost main island, Hokkaido, cut away like Plath's "hinge." Hokkaido is home to the Ainu race, which has faced much discrimination in line with the KKK and Nazi themes revealed elsewhere in this poem. Plath had an interest in Japan, not only in what happened during World War II, but in their rituals and disciplines, as mentioned in a February 1955 letter discussing the "intriguing" Japanese movie, "Gate of Hell." In *The Golden Bough*, a favorite book of Plath's, the Ainu people's magic and culture is discussed (Frazer, 524-9, 548-9, 684).

Japanese female pearl divers, called *Ama*, wore white gauzy diving wear with matching hoods, fitting Plath's Klan metaphor. The Ama collected oysters from the sea bed, replacing them after a nucleus was inserted to create the pearl. The Ama had to move the oysters to safer locations in times of red tide attack, or typhoon. Understanding this, the first stanza well describes the bivalve of the opened mollusk, with its top gone and only a hinge left.[108] The second stanza of "Cut" describes the raw oyster, garnished with its "red plush" of cocktail sauce. The Native American Indians gave oysters as a gift to the pilgrim settlers. This food, along with turkey, was the Indian welcome, rolling out the third stanza's red carpet. In the fourth stanza, oysters are said to be an aphrodisiac, they are often stepped on as they rest on the sea bed, and often served with champagne.

Red tide is a condition when red algae blooms from a water column of sediments and colors the water red, fitting Plath's gap and redcoat analogies. The algae contaminate shellfish such as oysters with toxins harmful to humans. Plath questions which side the ocean takes as this tide hurts man and animal. Digesting a raw, uncooked oyster poisoned with red tide produces the illness in Plath's "Cut": flu-like symptoms at best; death at worst. The pearl, as it lays in an open half-shell, is much like the pill Plath mentions, in its pillbox. Near the conclusion, "Cut" reflects on the oyster silently creating the ball of its pearl.

Oysters developing pearls are considered female and known as "Mother of Pearl." A pearl is caused by an irritation through inserting a nucleus or, in nature, dirt or sand inside the oyster tissue. It is another association for the girl in Plath's poem who is tainted by dirt.

Plath dedicated "Cut" to her children's nanny with an Irish name and heritage, Susan O'Neill Roe. Almost 100,000 Irish Catholics made the pilgrimage to America in the 1600s, and another 100,000 followed in the 1700s, Plath's pilgrim image once again. Irish cuisine is heavy on oysters and onions. Most of America's Irish immigrants came to work as unskilled laborers in factories and mills. Like blacks, Jews, and other minorities, Irish Catholics faced a great deal of discrimination in the then-mostly Protestant United States.

The original Ku Klux Klan was founded by Confederate veterans in 1866, on the heels of the American Civil War. They claimed to be descendants from the original 18th century British redcoats in the Revolutionary War. Fearing insurrection by former slaves and exploitation by Northern carpet-baggers, another kind of rolling carpet, the group acted violently against blacks, Jews, immigrants and Catholics. Had she been in America at that time, Susan O'Neill Roe would have been a target as an Irish Catholic immigrant. Members of the KKK often hide their identities behind white sheets and hoods. Their name was a corruption of the Greek word, *Kuklos*, meaning "circle," and fitting the Wheel again. A Klan member demonstrated membership by placing the *thumb* and little finger in a pants pocket, leaving the middle three fingers out.

Among other things, "Cut" also becomes a playful study of the hand[109]: The opposable thumb is one of the principle differentiators between man and primates with other animals. Not as long as the other four fingers, the thumb might be looked at as missing its top, and all of the hand's

---

108 In her journals, Plath wrote in detail of oysters attacked by echinoderms, or starfish, as well as notes on mollusks, bivalves, and other oceanic creatures, including a sketch of how these creatures close their mouths (*UJ*, 584-6).

109 The hand as a poetic subject intrigued Plath. In 1961, she wrote "Words for a Nursery," (listed in the 1958 section of *The Collected Poems*). This poem is spoken in the voice of a right hand, structured with five syllables a line, five stanzas, and ten lines to a stanza. "*Very fingery,*" Plath said (*LH*, 410).

digits have hinge-like joints. The base of the thumb is known as the "pulp," which reaches into the "heart" of the palm. The palm side of the hand is hairless, as if scalped. Viewing the palm with fingers extended, the fingers are like spokes on a wheel. The thumb is also able to touch the other four fingers, an exercise Hindus practice in meditation. Children in America outline their hands in school at Thanksgiving time, making the thumb the turkey neck and head, and the rest of the fingers its body and feathery tail. Criminals and prisoners of war are often required to put finger and thumb prints in ink on paper for police. All of these ideas are demonstrated in Plath's "Cut."

The previously mentioned Renaissance alchemist, Rudolf Steiner, was translated and praised by transcendentalist writer Thomas Carlyle, a life-long friend of Ralph Waldo Emerson. After reading Carlyle's biography on Frederick the Great, Adolf Hitler embraced many of Carlyle's ideals, especially those of rejecting Democracy and believing in charismatic leadership. The Nazis were influenced by many occult ideas and practices, and fascinated with ideas of palingenesis (evolving the species) and endogamy.

Political "palingenetic ultranationalism," was seen when Fascist Italy and Nazi Germany sought pure ancestral bloodlines for their nations. This explains Plath's emphasis on racism and male-dominated fascist imagery of war in "Cut." Plath draws the line from man first manipulating bi-valve mollusks, to attempts at manipulating human genetics.

The Golden Dawn wore robes similar in style to the KKK's garments, including the pointy hood. Plath was surely sensitive to this, whether or not she and Hughes ever donned Hermetic robes. Gauze, in the eighth stanza, is used for bandages, clothing, and was originally made of silk. Much of it comes from Japan, an Axis power in World War II. The gauze-wearing KKK is American, and so "Cut" reveals that evil exists on both sides.

"Babushka" is originally a Russian word, and another connection to the Axis. A babushka is a headscarf typically worn by eastern Indian, Muslim, Russian Orthodox, gypsies, and observant married Jewish women for practicality, modesty, and to place morals and character over physical looks. Plath celebrates the pain of the cut as a necessary separation, now of the sexes. In the sixth stanza, she begins to delineate and question sides: Axis and Allies; Good and Evil; Dark and Light; and ultimately, Male and Female. She has killed the paper-thin emotion of the seventh stanza, touring through contracts with untrustworthy fascist alliances, printed religious scripture, or even a marriage license.

The babushka image follows Plath's words about the stained, racist man to whom she is speaking. She is glad to be separate and soiled, rather than supposedly pure, like him. To Plath, to mix blood, destroy endogamy and increase the intellect/self-actualization is to be desired, no matter what pains are necessary to get there.

Another match to the silent mill is the swastika. The swastika design was first based upon the Sun Wheel, or the Wheel of the Year, which as the Wheel of Fortune, marks the change of the seasons and the cycles of death and rebirth,[110] from the womb to the tomb. It has been a religious symbol since prehistoric times. In Kundalini Yoga, which Hughes practiced regularly, the "Swastika Center" dwells at the very top of the chakra system of the Subconscious Mind. Author Robert Graves wrote that the swastika represents "The fullest extent of sovereignty" and it is comprised of the cherubs that drive the fiery wheels of God's chariot. The right-handed fire wheel was considered lucky, and the left-handed one adopted by the Nazis was said to be unlucky (Graves, 410, 445).

Trepanning was a form of brain surgery that originated in prehistoric times. It is an effort to relieve pressure on the brain, epileptic seizures, madness, and other forms of illness by scraping off

---

110 For more on the Wheel of Life, see *Fixed Stars Govern a Life*'s interpretation of Plath's "Morning Song."

the skin and hair on the head, an Indian scalping again, and drilling a hole into the skull. On the heels of the American Revolution's war against Britain, France had their own revolution. The Napoleonic Wars against France introduced the first modern battlefield surgeons, primarily concerned with amputation, another meaning to the title and the soldier.

Continually at war with the British Royal Army's redcoats, Napoleon Bonaparte, Emperor of the French and one of the greatest military commanders of all time, was known to open bottles of champagne with his sabre, cutting off the neck of the bottle in a quick swipe. A lover of champagne, Napoleon was once quoted to say, "Champagne! In victory one deserves it; in defeat one needs it" (Wine). Celebratory champagne is, of course, the first image that comes to mind for Plath's fizzy pink. Plath told an interviewer in 1962 that she was very interested in Napoleon and wars in general. That April, she had reviewed Hubert Cole's biography, *Josephine*, for the *New Statesman*.

Napoleon was an egomaniac and usurper, to be sure. His military symbol was the bee, and the Wheel of Fortune card might also be compared to a hive. Both the bee and hive are symbols of Freemasonry. Much of "Cut" fits Napoleon: The pilgrim of Plath's third stanza may be the bee, Napoleon himself, or both. In Plath's eyes, Napoleon was not all bad: he destroyed feudalism in Germany; emancipated the Jews in all countries he took over; and emancipated Protestants in Catholic countries and Catholics in Protestant countries, viewing all people as equal and refusing to favor one religion. Additionally, Napoleon Bonaparte did a great deal for art and science. He did prove to be a hypocrite to his early ideals of abolishing imperialism when he crowned himself emperor, and it was for this reason that his close friendship with composer Ludwig van Beethoven was broken (Weider).

> *"Every man is more than just himself; he also represents the unique, the very special and always significant and remarkable point at which the world's phenomena intersect, only once in this way and never again."*
>
> --Hermann Hesse (from *Demian*)

Evidence shows that Napoleon was a Freemason, and therefore likely to have been a Hermeticist. *The Encyclopedia of Freemasonry* lists that Napoleon was initiated, passed and raised into an Army Philadelphe Lodge of the Ecossais Primitive Rite of Narbonne between 1795 and 1798. Freemasons consider the bee or hive as symbols of alchemy and industriousness (Grand). Additionally, Napoleon and his wife Josephine were fascinated with the tarot. They had been documented having readings done, and were even painted consulting the cards.[111]

"It is by making myself Catholic that I brought peace to Brittany and Vendée. It is by making myself Italian that I won minds in Italy. It is by making myself a Moslem that I established myself in Egypt. If I governed a nation of Jews, I should reestablish the Temple of Solomon," Napoleon once said (Weider). And so it might well be asked whose side Napoleon was on, for he played all sides, especially with religion. The Russian Orthodox Church renounced him as the Antichrist and Enemy of God. Like Hitler a hundred years afterward, it was the Russian winter, not the Church that defeated Napoleon's Grand Armée. Plath draws the comparison between the two military leaders in her poem, "The Swarm," included in the original 1965 edition of *Ariel*. Ultimately, Napoleon fought two armies at once at the battle of Waterloo, and lost. He was first exiled to the island of Elba, where he attempted suicide with a pill, seen in Plath's sixth stanza of "Cut." He survived. After an escape from Elba, he was exiled to St. Helena, where he died in 1815. In Napoleon's final days, he was quoted as saying, "I must either command or be silent," in the same way that Plath's mill had to be confronted.

---

111 One of several examples is the Russian oil painting "Napoleon and Josephine with the Fortune Teller" (1844) by Josef Franz Danhauser.

French anthropologists in the 1930s lived with the primitive West African Dogon clan ("Klan") and learned of their surprising culture, believed to relate to the ancient Egyptians. Onions are their only cash crop. Sacrifices of blood and pearl millet are made to their ancestors. Their religious mythology includes dismemberment (trepanning) of their gods, called Nommo, who inhabit a world that circles the star Sirius. They believe the Nommo landed in a spaceship called "Star of the Tenth Moon," another fit for this number tarot card with a circular center. The spaceship crashed, spurting out blood and flames before teachers and spiritual guardians came to save them. The Dogon spiritual leader wears a red fez and an armband with a sacred pearl. The tribe practices male circumcision and female genital mutilation, yet another take on Plath's title, the first three stanzas, and the last stanza of "Cut." The Dogon wear swastika-like patterned Kananga masks in ceremony, to create a bridge to the supernatural world (Temple).

Fifth Mirror: Astrology and Astronomy

There is great mystery about how the Dogon people learned their advanced astronomical knowledge, taught through oral tradition, and dating back thousands of years. The Dogon linked the star Sirius with the Egyptian goddess Isis, and they determined that Sirius had a companion star invisible to the human eye. They claimed to have been given this information from ancient Egyptian ancestors. The second Sirius star was not verified by western culture until the 1920s, and remains a mystery how word could have reached this remote tribe, if in fact they were told by outsiders. Sirius, also called "The Star of Isis" is the brightest star in the night sky, with a circle of red around it the Dogon describe "like a spot spreading." The Dogon believe Sirius to be the axis of the universe, a wheel from which all matter and souls are produced in a great spiral motion (Temple).

A large main belt asteroid discovered in 1886 is named 258 Tyche, after the goddess of Fate. Her Roman equivalent, Fortuna, has its own asteroid, 19 Fortuna, discovered in 1852. The constellation Virgo is also sometimes identified with Tyche, the Greek goddess of fortune.

Our galaxy is wheel-shaped, and the wheel of the zodiac has been portrayed across many cultures since the middle of the first millennium BCE as a celestial coordinate system. The word "zodiac" comes from the Greek *zōdiakos kuklos* meaning "circle of animals," and is found in Kabbalistic writings such as the medieval *Sefer Raziel HaMalakh*, which claims the zodiac has magical uses. Additional cosmological tie-ins to the Wheel's Napoleon theme include the faint constellation Apis, the Bee, which was first identified in the 16th century, but renamed to Musca, the Fly. Finally, both the Mississippian and Mayan Indian cultures have a Hand constellation, where Orion's Belt forms the wrist of a cut-off hand. The Hand constellation is said to mark the portal to the Otherworld. Both cultures also refer to the movement of the Milky Way and the wheel-like rising and falling of the night sky.

Sixth Mirror: Humanities and the Arts

The thumb plays a curious and fascinating role in the Humanities and the Arts. In entertainment, we have "General Tom Thumb," a.k.a. Charles Sherwood Stratton (1838-1883). At less than two feet in height, Tom Thumb was one of P.T. Barnum's greatest and most famous attractions. A Freemason and a successful businessman even during the Civil War years, Tom Thumb came from Plath's home state of Massachusetts. Tom Thumb had many costume personalities, but one of his most famous was Napoleon Bonaparte. Red carpets were certainly rolled out for Tom Thumb as he was received by the president of the United States, Abraham Lincoln, and most of the crowned heads of Europe.

Taken from inspiration by real-life little people, Hans Christian Anderson created the character "Thumbelina" in 1835. The real Napoleon had since met his match at Waterloo and French monarchy returned to France, and soon after, General Tom Thumb conquered the world of entertainment. *Thumbelina* is an adventure story from a feminist point of view. Its moral is that people are happiest with their own kind.

It begins with a woman who wants to have a tiny child, the homunculus image of "Cut." Folklorists have drawn parallels between Thumbelina and the Greek myth of Demeter and her daughter Persephone, as well as the Hindu's thumb-sized soul.

Another children's story of English folklore is Tom Thumb, a boy no bigger than his father's thumb, and continuing the homunculus metaphor. *The History of Tom Thumb* (1621) was the first fairy tale printed in English. The story has several versions, and he is most famously swallowed by a cruel giant, like a pill. In another, he is swallowed by a miller and a host of animal characters. Tom Thumb is threatened with beheading for enraging the king's cook, rides a butterfly with paper-thin wings like Thumbelina, and ultimately gets caught in a web and dies of a spider bite, the circular web being another kind of mill.

Tom Thumb's French counterpart is *Le Petit Poucet*, meaning "Hop o' my thumb," or "Little Thumbling." In all these stories, the characters seek transfiguration and redemption, the goal of the Hindu's homunculus spirit. During the Napoleonic Wars, a nursery rhyme warned children that Napoleon ate naughty people, and his last name, Bonaparte, may have originated the name "Bogey-man," likening him with a tiny evil man.

In Plath's personal library were adventure journalist Richard Halliburton's books, *The Glorious Adventure* (1927), *Richard Halliburton's Complete Book of Marvels* (1941), and his *The Flying Carpet* (1932). Plath had been reading Halliburton since sixth grade, when her teacher lent her *The Glorious Adventure*.[112] Halliburton was known for covering the Matterhorn, the Nile, the Orient, South America, Russia, and many distant parts of the world for English speakers, and his myriad adventures no doubt echo through Plath's poem, "Cut." *The Flying Carpet* begins with Halliburton agreeing on a handshake to ride around the world for eighteen months in an open cockpit biplane named "The Flying Carpet." The open cockpit also fits the missing top in the first stanza. The Flying Carpet aborts a roll maneuver, the rolling of the third stanza. Beginning in America, they toured Europe, India, Africa, the South Pacific, and gave a ride to Sylvia, wife of the White Rajah of Sarawak in Malaysia, making her the first woman of that country to fly. Flying was something Plath loved to do as well, and she once had the chance to copilot a plane (*LH*, 101).

Halliburton was celebrated for his ability to evoke a place or famous historical character around his own adventures. He was a man who believed in assuming the culture of the people, wearing traditional clothing, and even adopting a slave child, which complicates national allegiance and even morals. One might have wondered whose side Halliburton was on. Halliburton dropped racist comments into his work, which was not unusual for the time, and especially appropriate to the eighth stanza of "Cut."

Reading Plath's "Cut" from the Freudian perspective, the "thrill" takes on orgasmic meaning. The clitoris becomes Plath's skin flap to a plush reddened vaginal opening. Interpreting thusly, the

---

112 Halliburton's book is found in Sylvia Plath's journals, March 2, 1944. This journal is kept in the Sylvia Plath Archives at the Lilly Library, Indiana University-Bloomington.

pilgrim with the axed scalp and turkey wattle could be viewed as a circumcised penis, circling back to the Dogon tribe's circumcision. Readers of Plath probably can't help but associate the famous scene from *The Bell Jar* when Esther sees her boyfriend Buddy in the nude, and all she can think of is "turkey neck and gizzards" (*BJ*, 69).

In the art of music, apopular military ballad of the French Republic and First Empire was "Le Chant de l'oignon," which translates to "Song of the Onion." The song was a favorite of Napoleon's Imperial Guard when they mounted an attack on the enemy, singing as they beat drums and bayonets against their cannons.

The Wheel of Fortune has been a common literary image since Greek and Roman times. Fortune's wheel is the basis for Chaucer's "The Monk's Tale" (from *The Canterbury Tales*), it appears in Dante's *Inferno*, and William Shakespeare wrote of the Wheel of Fortune in *Hamlet, Henry V, King Lear*, and *Macbeth*. The image also appears in much medieval art, including the great stained glass rose windows in cathedrals of that era.

Plath's poem "Cut," with its many onion-like layers of stumpy thumbs, turning circles and perfect pearls, is remarkable from all sides of the wheel.

Chapter Twelve: Who Put Bella In The Wych Elm?
Card #11   Strength   Corresponding Poem: "Elm"

Plath wrote "Elm" in April of 1962, before any apparent trouble in her marriage. Hughes has commented that the poem referred to a giant Wych elm that overshadowed their Devon property. Hughes claimed that "the *Ariel* voice emerged in full, out of the tree" (*LTH*, 192). Darkening the elm image, Plath's desk was also made for her by Hughes from an elm coffin plank. One could stop there to explain this poem's dark mood, yet Plath seems never to have been content with one meaning.

First Mirror: The Tarot/Qabalah
The Strength card is numbered either XI or VIII, depending on the deck used. The Justice card, matched with Plath's earlier poem "A Secret," bears the number XI in the Rider-Waite deck. Evidence suggests Plath and Hughes held fast to the original positioning, but used the Rider-Waite deck, whose creators, the Golden Dawn, repositioned these cards. Medieval and Renaissance decks sometimes called this card "Fortitude." *The Painted Caravan* attributes the Strength card as the great cosmic force *Kundalini*, the serpent-power. To mismanage this force is to create human wrecks and derelicts, and drive others to madness and obsession; Strength can be used for destruction as well as integration. From early drafts to the final poem, "Elm" embodies these qualities. When Plath's narrator breaks into pieces and flies "about like clubs," this illustrates elm tree seeds in the air, and the lemniscate shape pictured over the woman's head.

The woman on this card represents the Kundalini subconscious. She has the lion in control, unless the card is read reversed, which is Plath's intent with this poem. Strength reversed suggests hatred and fear. It is the cry inhabiting Plath in the tenth stanza; dependency in her search for love in the third and tenth; suffering in the sixth; intolerance and violence in the seventh; submission in the ninth; and of being prey, in the eleventh stanza especially. In the third stanza, Plath expresses a need and hunger to be loved, yet longs for a love greater than that of a man. She wants divine love; the drive takes her on a quest to find it. The fourth stanza's stone and turf is a gravesite. Plath understands eternal love may only be found in death.

The sixth stanza, with filaments burning and standing, red in color, like a handful of wires, is pictured on the Strength tarot card as the woman strokes the wiry mane of that enormous gingery cat. Her own hair is also wiry and bright. The word *filament* takes us back to "Lady Lazarus" and her "million filaments." Here, Plath again masterfully milks every meaning, using it to represent hair, the heating element of an electric bulb, tree branch and root systems, and a solar flare or prominence.

There were many early revisions and cuts from "Elm." Most point to the Strength card's imagery, usually in reverse meanings. In the early drafts, Plath tested lines about hatred, unease and lack of peace; she wrote of a hill, and a line about the blue north suggesting the card's background mountain; and she noted the ideas of largeness and beautiful antiquity. Plath also tried language about animal nature, hunger, and savagery.

A second set of revisions includes cut lines about trees, the cycle of life and infinite renewal, emotion and love, and atavistic ideas of engineering whiteness and purity.[113]

In later drafts, Plath wrote of bony pellets at her foot, both tree seeds and lion claws. She had other leonine images of hunger, savagery, and satiety, and lines of mothering, gentleness, love, and averted eyes.

In *The Painted Caravan*, the Strength card pictures a tree with the full root system. A direct reference to the Qabalah Tree of Life is found in an excised line from the fifth draft, claiming another tree of great power holds her. In that tree, she wrote that the dead bloom like orchids. On the Tree of Life, Strength connects opposite poles of God's energy: Mercy and Severity. It is taught that those believing life should always be kind and gentle fail to see the imbalance and danger that degenerates into cowardly creatures with no power or force. The reverse is true, as well: Kundalini energy out of control is summed up in the last line of Plath's final version of "Elm," with its repetitive killing. About the Strength card, *The Painted Caravan* reads:

> "He has been subject to all manner of occult tests to ensure his reliability and the tempered quality of his character. Now he is being prepared to face utter disillusionment and despair, and his faith and knowledge will be taxed to the uttermost. [...] But he must also have the power to draw from the depths the hidden forces of the earth, the nature Gods and their elementals…"

Hughes practiced Kundalini yoga and taught Plath exercises and meditations from this practice, if not all that he knew (*UJ*, 167). Across the world Kundalini power is known by different names. The Japanese call it "ki," the Chinese "chi," and the Mesoamericans worshiped the serpent-god Quetzalcoatl. Kalahari bushman call this same power "n'um." The Sanskrit word "Kundalini" means an awakening of the root consciousness, the Shekinah, which is exiled, creative, feminine power.[114] The word Kundalini is a composite of a series of other Sanskrit words with collective meaning of feminine power. Broken apart, these short Sanskrit words are all incorporated in Plath's poem, "Elm":

Kh' – meaning hollow, cave, sometimes symbolized by the open vagina to represent the feminine. "Elm" reflects this in the hollow Elm, as well as cave and bat imagery.

u' – meaning the moon calling to the sun, seen in the "Elm" eighth and ninth stanzas.

N' – meaning ocean wave, ebb and flow of consciousness seen in the second stanza.

Dh' – meaning virtue, inner focus and receptivity, seen in first and eleventh stanzas.

A' – meaning going inward, the feminine "first-sound" from which all words are formed and all life emanates. Cries and shrieks are throughout the poem, as if giving birth, and the second stanza mentions the sound of the sea, from which all life was born.

Li'—to rock, sway, tremble; best illustrated in the seventh stanza.

N'—the lotus plant, the pearl, nakedness. The lotus has deep roots, like an Elm. She is also "barren," a word synonymous with being stark or bare, as well as infertile.

I'—to go beyond, grow, or evolve. Plath's narrator has reached the height of her knowledge and strength in the thirteenth stanza.

Western languages and scripture do not have a word equivalent to "Kundalini." A feminine power equal to the masculine God of the western world is difficult for westerners to grasp, as is

---

113 Atavism is first seen in Plath's poem, "Cut."

114 Plath had a part-time job in 1958 working for the Department of Sanskrit and Indian Studies at Harvard. Sanskrit literature and symbolism began to creep into Plath's work at this time, beginning with her 1959 poem, "Goatsucker," about the Nightjar bird (found in *The Collected Poems of Sylvia Plath*).

the idea of her excommunication, suffering, and even death. Her existence is not acknowledged in western culture. Qabalists believe that unification with Shekinah and the male God energy will bring about perfection, and blockages create psychological and physical distress and disease. However, when repressed blockages begin to flow, results can be terrifying. Kundalini is an awakening to the truth of one's power, and bringing to consciousness one's repressed beliefs and limiting decisions. Christianity is uncomfortable with Kundalini's beginning and return to the sinful area of the base chakra: The point of penetration, conception, and governance, to Hindus. Many speak of the journey up the spine, shunning mention of the return cycle back down to complete an Ouroboros, the acceptance of a dark side and an orbit toward wholeness.

The message of the Strength card is to create balance between our spiritual and carnal natures. It is the art of alchemy, the transformation of one thing into another. In some card designs, this idea is symbolized by a lion with a serpent's tail. The Golden Dawn attributes the Strength card to the Hebrew letter, *Teth*, meaning: "the snake which tempts our lower passions to guide our will and actions." It is Jupiter acting through Leo (the lion) upon Mars.

Most tarot readers interpret the Strength tarot card to mean physical or emotional strength, and bravery. With this in mind, the second and third lines about facing fear in "Elm" convey the epitome of strength.

Second Mirror: Alchemy

From the first line in "Elm," the narrator draws from the depths of the soul. Almost every culture has its version of the Tree of Life. The Tree of Alchemy symbolized the plantlike growth of metals, dependent upon a single trunk of solar life, such as Jakob Böhme's Divine Tree in Man. With roots in the heart, Böhme's tree rises through the sphere of understanding into the sphere of the senses. Its face represents day, and its back is night (Böhme).

At her home at Court Green in Devon, Plath's study looked out over a great Wych elm. This tree is special to alchemists. With hermaphroditic flowers, it represents alchemical union of opposites and completion. Old English for "Elm" is "Wice," meaning "weak," the Strength card in reverse.

From the first stanza of "Elm," the speaker seems to change from line to line. It is an eerie sensation: multiple voices, separate and yet all within, suggesting Plath's ego is unraveling in as many directions as a root system. Numerous alchemical texts depict the philosophical tree growing with roots in the sea (Abraham, 179). The sea represents the *prima materia*, or raw matter from which life began. The spiritual, higher self, the voice of infinite inspiration and wisdom, is within the second stanza's vast, dissatisfied sea. The narrator cannot quite reach wholeness for fear of the darkness that engulfs her worldly life. Through the eyes of the ego, she is terrified that death is truly oblivion; it is a nothing-voice that drives her mad. This nothingness also fits Plath's shadow image in the third stanza.

Alchemists compare the shadow to night, defining the day and without which the day would lose its value. The "voice of nothing" correlates with alchemy's adage, "The sun is the tongue, the shadow is the language." If love is perfection and God, Plath's, "Love is a shadow," echoes the famous alchemical motto, "The sun and its shadow complete the work" (Abraham, 195). Just as destruction is needed for perfection, the alchemist Ripley referred to the Black phase as "the shade of night" to define the day (Abraham, 134).

The echoes in the fourth stanza are the voices of the alchemists who have spoken for centuries or even thousands of years. Their words can still be heard.

Plath's reference to poison is the alchemical union of opposites, metaphorically expressed as a union of male and female, and of the sun and moon, and is first seen as undesirable, corrosive, and poisonous as in the fifth stanza. Plath's rain in that same stanza is the washed stone after the Black phase, representing the integration of the feminine unconscious. Likewise, her "big hush" not only contains poetic alliterative beauty, but refers to the secretive nature of the alchemist's work.

The last line of the fifth stanza presents the purified matter on its way to completion. It bears a fruit white as tin; she compares it to arsenic.[115] Plath as alchemist has reached the White phase. She suggests that death, symbolized by arsenic, goes hand-in-hand with purity. When Plath writes of the "atrocity of sunsets" in the sixth stanza, this is a reference to the sun being eclipsed by the night and the dark side. The scorching in the sixth stanza is the alchemical burning process.

The alchemical snake makes itself present in the description of acids in the last stanza. Alchemists often use the snake/serpent metaphor to describe the acids of sulfur. The symbols of the medical caduceus originated in alchemy: Serpents entwined around Hermes' wand. The snake ring of eternity, the Ouroboros, was used often in texts to illustrate the circulatory process of death and birth, and the notion of cosmic time. It means that there is no end and no beginning. Additionally, in "Elm" words like "petrifies," "isolate," and "slow" all have chemistry associations. Finally, the last line of killing represents both the Black phase, and the need to kill animal urges on the quest toward Individuation, the goal of Jungian alchemy.

Third Mirror: Mythology

The Greek/Roman myth associated with the Strength card is that of Hercules, who killed his wife and children in a mad rage. In the twelfth stanza of "Elm," they are unable to be retrieved. His murderous acts are in the thirteenth stanza and insanity in the second. The myth and tarot card both are about controlling the dark animal instinct that lives inside us.

Hercules grieved over his family, as seen in much of "Elm." To make amends, he had to labor for an evil king. The first job was to slay the man-eating Nemean Lion, said to be the lion pictured on this card. An early draft of "Elm" had a cat reference. Plath, however, decided upon a bat image in the tenth stanza. The bat has been a symbol of Kundalini and its hidden, frightening qualities. Bats symbolize facing darkness, understanding grief, and transformation of the ego into rebirth.

Hercules shot arrows at the lion; they bounced off, becoming no better than wires in his hand. He used a sword that bent as easily as tin, and his clubs shattered into pieces on the lion's head, all matching Plath's fifth through seventh stanza verses. Hercules lost one of his own fingers choking the lion. Its maned face might have been described as Plath's thirteenth stanza, with its murderousness and hair like wild branches strangling the animal. Hercules eventually killed the lion with one of its own claws, fitting the last line of "Elm."

Hercules fought the Hydra as his second labor. Hydra's poisonous breath caused others to die in agony. Hercules smashed one of its many heads with his club, referencing the seventh stanza again. When one head was destroyed, two new ones grew in its place. Adding insult to injury, a huge crab called Cancer attacked his heels. Hercules crushed and flattened it, as Plath shows in the eighth and ninth stanzas. In the end, with the help of his charioteer, seen in the galloping horse imagery, the stump of each head was burned as soon as it was cut. It is Plath's scorching to the

---

115 See *Fixed Stars Govern a Life*'s interpretation of Sylvia Plath's poem, "The Couriers," for more on tin, and "The Jailor" for more on arsenic.

104

roots. Hercules dipped his arrows in poison from the creature's body, returning to wire as a handful of arrows again.

Tiamat, from Babylonian myth, was the female creator goddess of sea from which all life sprang, and too the monster of primordial chaos.[116] Tiamat is sometimes identified as a serpent or dragon, Plath's snake imagery. "Elm" is full of Tiamat: the idea that chaos is a dark void where creation has not begun is an age-old metaphor for the female womb. "Elm" is distinctly empty with its fourth stanza echoes, and Plath's pronoun "she" in the first line is feminine. Tiamat was killed by the storm god Marduk, who overtook her using arrows of wind, Plath's violent winds and arrow imagery. Marduk also used a net, seen in the dragging of the eighth stanza; a club, as in the seventh stanza, and an invincible spear, in the releasing action of the ninth stanza. Older Sumerian tablets show the god Enlil slaying Tiamat. Mythologist Robert Graves believed this was the first shift in power from matriarchal to patriarchal societies.

Another monster in Greek myth is the gorgon, a female with venomous snakes for hair: Medusa is the most famous. The description of the murderous face and strangling branches fit her well, and her name entitles a later poem in *Ariel*. One look upon Medusa turned a man to stone, a new meaning for Plath's stone head in the fourth stanza. In each of these cases, the idea of female power is fearsome.

Ophiuchus, the snake charmer, controls the snake in the same gentle way the woman tames the lion on the Strength card. The Greeks called him Asclepius, god of medicine. He was the son of Apollo and Arsinoë, conjuring Plath's arsenic image again. Asclepius' mother was unfaithful, and a crow, with his "feathery turnings," told Apollo the news. Apollo was so upset that he turned the once "tin-white" crow to black. Apollo as sun god explains the sunsets' "atrocity"; angry Apollo shot his wife with a fiery arrow, Plath's wires and filaments again. Apollo snatched baby Asclepius from his mother's womb, fitting the cruelty and barrenness of the eighth stanza. A centaur raised the child, teaching him medicine. Asclepius was said to raise the dead with tree bark, a gift from a snake; tree bark and shed snakeskin have since become symbols of healing and rebirth. Others say Asclepius received the blood of Medusa and thus could raise the dead. As the story goes, Hades, god of the underworld, complained to Zeus that not enough men were dying, blaming Asclepius. Zeus therefore struck Asclepius down with a thunderbolt, angering Apollo. Apollo in turn killed the three Cyclopes who forged Zeus' thunderbolts, corresponding with the three repetitions of the word "kill" at the end of "Elm."

A Persian legend tells of two speaking trees that grow on the Indian border. They are guarded by frightening, fire-spitting birds in the daytime: Plath's malignant feathery creatures. The creatures disappear at night; in "Elm" they flap away. The tree, like the hermaphrodite, is said to have two parts to the trunk: male representing the day, and female representing the night. One of these trees told the great conqueror, Alexander the Great, he would die at the height of his notoriety, which came true (Mystical).

Norse myth holds that the first woman, Embla, was created from the elm tree and that a World Tree sprang at the beginning of time from the primordial slime and ashes. The World Tree's roots represent past, present and future, fitting Plath's first stanza claim of not fearing, because she has already been to that place. The roots spread to reach wells, Plath's tap-root.

The first branch of the World Tree reached over the universe and was a home of the gods. Its leaves were the clouds in Plath's twelfth stanza. Its fruit was the stars, white as tin and pictured in the fifth stanza. The second branch held the three Fates, and two swans, seen in the feathers and

116 See *Fixed Stars Govern A Life*'s interpretation of Sylvia Plath's poem "Morning Song" for more on Tiamat.

the triple-kill at the poem's end. The second branch also held the sun and moon, Plath's sunset imagery, and the moon in the eighth stanza. At the top of the tree sits an eagle with a hawk, fitting Plath's flapping and feathers again. Coiled at the bottom of the tree is the familiar serpent, kin to the Kundalini snake. It represents inner torment and waiting to take over the earth. A squirrel runs up and down, between the eagle and the serpent, trying to bring peace and salvation between the two. It is another galloping creature of "Elm."

Salvation is represented by snow and rain, the latter being present in "Elm." A wise giant dwells in the second fountain of the tree, providing wisdom for man who cannot improve himself more than he has, seen in the first line of the thirteenth stanza. At the time of the final conflict between the gods and men, a horn will be sounded like Plath's shrieking image, announcing doom that fits her last line (Mystical/Worldtree).

The Native American Omaha people had a variation of this myth with the "Mystery Tree." It was home of the Thunder Bird and the center of the four winds, reflecting that violent wind of Plath's again (Mystical/Mystree).[117]

Ancient Egyptians believed the lunar god Osiris was killed by his brother Set, the destructive, angry sun. Set tricked Osiris into a coffin and threw him into the Nile, where it washed out to the sea, echoing Plath's sea image, and the atrocious act of this sun: Set. The goddess Isis searched everywhere for the body, mourning her husband as Plath's third stanza reflects. After a time, the trunk washed upon the shores of Syria, and a tree grew with a wonderful fragrance. The King and Queen requested the tree be cut down and the branches lopped off to be used as the central pillar in their palace. Isis demanded the pillar be returned to her. On the way home she placed her dead lover in a

"Any man who is attached to things of this world is one who lives in ignorance and is being consumed by the snakes of his own passions"

— Black Elk,
from *Black Elk Speaks*

boat, turned into a bird like Plath's flying creature, and flew around him, returning him to life long enough to impregnate her "for something to love." Evidenced by their child Horus, Osiris defeats death in his love of Isis. Ancient Egyptian festivals raised a pillar in Osiris' honor, representing resurrection and the Tree of Life (Cashford).

The Wych elm has been associated with death since the ancient Greeks. An elm grove is said to have sprung up when Orpheus played a love song on the lyre for his wife Eurydice. In other myths, the maiden Erytheia transformed into a Wych elm, Homer wrote that these trees were planted on the burial mound of the King of Trojan Thebes, and Virgil said the spirit of dreams slept in a Wych elm guarding the entrance to Hades. The Wych elm was sacred to Dionysus as it supported grape vines planted for wine. It has been used as protection against witchcraft.

Trees of wisdom and life are throughout mythology and religion. The Buddha was enlightened beneath a Bodhi tree, and Christians recognize the Tree of Good and Evil, also called the Tree of Knowledge. Shamans in the Amazon use a vine tree to access medicinal knowledge for their tribe. The Celts worshiped trees, assigning a Tree Calendar and Tree Zodiac. The Celtic Tree of Life is said to have roots deep in the earth, its trunk within this realm, and branches extending to the Otherworld. Celtic myth equates Adam and Eve with the ash and elm trees, respectively. It makes sense that Plath would use the elm to represent the frightening aspects of female Kundalini power, as female as the strangulating Hydra.

The fall of man from the place of God, representing a complete lack of strength, is depicted

---

117 Plath certainly knew of Thunder Birds. She referred to them in her early poem "Mad Girl's Love Song," which she wrote at age nineteen (*BJ*, 207).

in various manners throughout religious scripture. In the story of Jacob's dream in the book of Genesis 28: 10-22, Jacob sees a ladder from earth to heaven. When Jacob awoke, he "took the stone that he had put for his pillows," and he set it as a pillar for God's house and proclaimed he would give one tenth of all he had to God.[118]

Fourth Mirror: History and the World

"Elm" was dedicated to poet Ruth Fainlight, one of the first true feminists to whom Plath was close. Fainlight wrote that she and Plath acknowledged each other as "sister-spirits" from their first encounter (Fainlight, 12) and "sister-mother-muse-friend." Plath wrote in a letter to Fainlight and her husband Alan Sillitoe on April 16, 1962: "…How I loved Ruth's poem in Encounter! It is a real White Goddess poem, and a voice on its weird fearsome own."

"We were two poets, Sylvia Plath and Ruth Fainlight," Fainlight wrote. "…not Mrs. Hughes and Mrs. Sillitoe, and our friendship was centred on this crucial reality" (Fainlight,13).

The fearsome feminine power is Kundalini in action; it is tortured and repressed, agitating the personality until it is terrifyingly released for the purpose of self-actualization.

Fainlight is a Jew who has written about female oracles and prophets. Much of Fainlight's work uses tarot, Kabbalah, and Plathian imagery and words. In a 2008 interview with *Contemporary Poetry Review*, Fainlight is quoted: "I also relate the poet figure to the shaman, or someone like that—the village wise-woman or maybe idiot, the person who is marked from birth and is both more powerful and less powerful" (Fainlight).

Trees represent the Qabalah's Tree of Life and the journey of the soul; they are simple, pure systems of life, uncomplicated by thought or sin. The elm species of tree lives hundreds of years and produces one of the strongest kinds of wood, echoing its association with Strength. The elm resists decay and is often used for coffins, breakwaters in the sea, and boats. It is associated with melancholy and death in folklore, possibly because elms are known to drop large branches without warning. The bark of the slippery elm (also called the red elm, suggesting the sixth stanza) was used as a natural way to induce miscarriage. It was a common method in Plath's 1950s, when abortion was still illegal in the United States and Britain. The fifth and eighth stanzas perfectly reflect the feminine moon's 28-day cycle and destructive feminine strength. In an early draft of "Elm," Plath also experimented with the idea of unwanted children.

The elm is susceptible to both Dutch elm disease, which arrived in New England in 1928, and elm phloem necrosis, a destructive bacteria and a neat metaphor of Kundalini power: It girdles the tree and stops the flow of water and nutrients. The eleventh stanza of "Elm" illustrates this disease well.

Plath knew the American elm tree well; her native New England was full of them. In fact, her personal addresses were full of them: Her childhood home was on Elmwood Road in Wellesley, Plath's Haven House address was on Elm Street at Smith, and Plath and Hughes had an Elm Street address in Northampton. Hughes even came from the area of Elmet. Elms were undoubtedly noticed by Plath as a kind of totem.

New World settlers planted an elm in Sheffield, which became "The Liberty Tree," and up to 500 townspeople met beneath its tall boughs. British troops cut down the Liberty Tree in 1775. At Boston Common, another elm "Liberty Tree" served as a rallying point for the resistance movement

---

118 Plath had underlined Thomas Hobbes' telling of this Bible story in her own copy of *Leviathan*, held in the rare book room at the Washington University library, St. Louis, Missouri.

against the rule of England over American colonies. The Great Elm of Boston Common had been there before the city was established. George Washington was said to have taken command of his troops under an elm in Cambridge, and William Penn signed a treaty under an elm with the Native American Indians in 1683.

The Wych elm is the most common variety of the species in Britain. There is great mystery around the tree on Wychbury Hill, in Worcestershire, England. A favorite spot for pagans, it is near the Wychbury Ring Iron Age fort, the Wychbury Obelisk, and an ancient sacred grove of yew trees. In 1943, the body of a woman was found stuffed into a hollowed tree. Having not been pruned, the tree was indeed "murderous in its strangle of branches." Soon after the body was found, regular graffiti began to appear on the obelisk over the next fifty years, reading "Who Put Bella In The Wych Elm?" The woman had one of her hands cut off, and a theory suggests this was a black magic execution. A rival theory in 1953 suggested that the woman knew too much about a German spy ring during the war (Haughton).

Remembering the Strength card number was changed from eleven to eight, it is interesting to note that in 1188 A.D., "The Cutting of the Elm" took place in Normandy, France. Some say "The Cutting of the Elm" is a metaphor for the separation of the Knights Templar and the Order (or "Priory") of Sion, both freemasonry orders. If one counts the total chapters in the King James Bible of that time, the chapters total to 1188, the year of the fall of Jerusalem and this separation. The shortest chapter of the Bible is Psalm 117, composed of 33 words, and the longest is Psalm 119, featuring all 22 letters of the Hebrew alphabet, correlating with 22 chapters in the Book of Revelation, and the 22 major arcana cards in the tarot. In the Bible's center is Psalm 118:8: "It is better to trust in the Lord than to put confidence in man."[119]

Others believe "The Cutting of the Elm" was a literal cutting: King Henry II, "The Lion of Justice," or King Richard the Lion-hearted, depending on the version of the story, demanded to meet France's Phillipe II in a neutral open field where only a large elm tree stood shading both kings' territories. The two men failed to agree on returning the dowry of Phillipe's widowed sister, and "Phillippe ordered the tree cut down and hacked to pieces, sending the message that he would offer no quarter to the English." In another telling of the story, King Richard fits the tree with bands of iron, but the French persist and break through, felling it. In both stories, it is the female tree that suffers, "Diminished and flat," by the hands of men.

Fifth Mirror: Astrology and Astronomy

Hydra, the female serpent, is the largest of the 88 modern constellations. She resembles a twisting snake, winding a quarter of the way around the sky. Her head is south of Cancer, the crab. Plath's eighth-stanza moon is associated with this zodiac sign, and Plath's image of surgery in "Elm" references breast cancer. Hydra's tip lies at Centaurus, the Centaur, whose gallops and hooves are found in the third and fourth stanzas of "Elm." Hydra corresponds to one of two ancient Babylonian constellations, the other being Hydrus, or Serpens, a mythological hybrid of serpent, lion, and bird, and an excellent fit for the Strength tarot card and Plath's snake metaphor.

Holding the Hydra is Ophiuchus/Asclepius, the Snake Charmer. All stars, of course, are Plath's "tin-white," affected by sunsets, and witness to clouds passing and dispersing.

The bat is another obvious image in "Elm." Plath's headstone, turf, shrieking, and poison imag-

---

119 Two aces (ones) and two eights are also considered the "Dead Man's Hand" in the game of poker, after Wild Bill Hickok was murdered holding it in the wonderfully fitting town name of Deadwood, South Dakota.

ery in "Elm" conjure the legend and myth around death by poisonous vampire bats[120]. The Bat was one of the most important constellations to the Mayan Indians, found in the Milky Way, believed to be the creator of all things and the path of the dead. The Bat was located in the mouth of the Heavenly Reptile, corresponding to Ophiuchus at the center of the galaxy. It represented an entrance to the underworld.

An obvious pictorial correspondence to the Strength card is Leo the Lion, found between Virgo and Cancer. Leo is the Nemean Lion, slain by Hercules and said to be an offspring of Selene, the Moon goddess. The constellation's brightest star, Regulus, marks the Lion's heart. It is called "The Little King" and corresponds well with Richard the Lion-Hearted.

Sixth Mirror: Humanities and the Arts

Plath deftly interwove legends of both Saint George and Robin Hood into "Elm." Saint George is the Patron Saint of England, a country symbolized by a lion. He rode a horse (third and fourth stanzas), was a soldier (see the violence of the sixth and seventh stanzas), and he was said to have slain a serpentine dragon to save a princess. George was a Christian martyr, tortured for his faith. Several great churches have been built in his name, and many have also burned down ("Scorched to the root").

In Palestine three great religions share a shrine at what is believed to be Saint George's birthplace. Arabs believe Saint George can restore mad men to their senses. From this the colloquialism, "sent to Saint George's house," has come to mean a mental institution (Finn, 46-47). Often confused with Saint George was George of Laodicea, who was strangled by an enraged mob and thrown into the sea. It is Plath's branch and sea images again.

The legend of Robin Hood came from a 14th century poem. The dashing outlaw robbed from the rich to give to the poor, and kept a base camp with his Merry Men in a huge tree in Sherwood Forest. Robin Hood's gravesite is in West Yorkshire, Ted Hughes' home country. Recorded in *Sylva*, a 1679 alchemical text subtitled, "A Discourse of Forest Trees," is a memoir of taking a drink at Robin Hood's well in South Yorkshire (Evelyn). This well undoubtedly contributed to that first line of "Elm," creating a link from the elm to Robin Hood. Robert Graves also connected Richard the Lion-Hearted and Robin Hood in, *The White Goddess* (Graves, 396).

Robin Hood's gravesite has been neglected and overgrown for centuries; it is another strangling of branches. Robin Hood was cursed by a witch and then fell ill on the way to a nunnery, where he sought healing and refuge from the Sheriff of Nottingham. Accounts say he was treacherously bled to death; others say he was poisoned by the wicked prioress. Both images are present in "Elm." On his death bed, Robin Hood shot an arrow, telling Little John to bury him where it landed. "Lay me a green sod under my head," he said in *The Death of Robin Hood* (Barton), which coincides with Plath's pillow of turf.

A Yorkshire man like Hughes, Robin Hood was a great swordsman and archer, the latter fitting the handful of wire and turning feather images of "Elm." The gravesite of Robin Hood has long been considered haunted, and Plath and Hughes may have visited it in their traipsing around the moors after literary landmarks. It is said that his ghost has been heard calling out for his love, Marian, as Plath's poem is full of loss and crying out for love. The apparition of a mad woman in white believed to be the prioress has also been seen there, Plath's images of madness and scathing radiance. In the legend, Robin Hood never hurt a woman. His faithful companion, Little John, while

---

120 For more on bats, see the *Fixed Stars Govern a Life* interpretation of "Thalidomide."

angry toward the prioress, therefore did not seek revenge and freed her, as in the ninth stanza of "Elm."

16th century tales hold that Robin Hood served King Richard the Lion-Hearted, who was a bad king despite a chivalric, dramatic image. King Richard was responsible for anti-Jew violence in London, a new meaning for something white and arsenic-like. Richard famously and perhaps rightly claimed that England was "cold and always raining," rain being another image found in "Elm."

Perhaps when Plath wrote in her journals of her "crazy eye for anagrams," such as the way she admitted to fictionalizing Dido Merwin's name to "Dody" (*UJ*, 311, 332), she might have been thinking "Elk" for "Elm." An early title of the poem was "The Elm Speaks." Plath's "Elm" covers a lot of ground from the mystical classic *Black Elk Speaks*, a book by John G. Neihardt about Native Americans from a life of freedom to reservation culture and the massacre at Wounded Knee during the Westward Expansion. It is the story and spiritual experience of the Oglala Sioux medicine man, Black Elk, as relayed into English by Black Elk's son to the author. Psychologist Carl Jung read the book in the 1930s and believed it was so important he had it published in German in 1953, and reprinted in English in the United States in 1961.[121] "Elm" was written in April of 1962.

There are many correspondences in *Black Elk Speaks* and Plath's "Elm," beginning in the third paragraph of the story, when Black Elk tells of a mighty vision "of a holy tree." It is his hope through the entire story for the tree to bloom again after the white man had taken their land and changed their ways of life. In the beginning of the story, a powerful female spirit arrives with a lesson, matching the poem's feminist theme. "Elm" is full of Black Elk's Indian life with horses galloping and feathery turnings of arrows. White men are scarily like Plath's arsenic to the Indians, with their madness over land and gold.

One of the main reasons for the Westward Expansion and pushing the Indians off their territories was the Gold Rush. Images of the Gold Rush "madness" begin in the second stanza, continuing through the poem. There are high levels of arsenic where gold is found, and arsenic is a product of smelted gold. Gold is highly conductive and used as filaments in electric wiring, becoming reddened when turned on, as in "Elm's" sixth stanza. The word "filaments" may also refer to fibers of clothing. It would suit a Native American to be "red," as well as to have him "fly about like clubs" and "shriek."

There has been considerable violence and crime over gold, both toward the Native Americans who saw no use for it, and to others. The settlers panned for gold, letting the cloudy sediment "pass and disperse" as they "agitate[d]" the watery pans in streams. A lot of the western American gold was panned along the Snake River, which begins in western Wyoming and stretches into central southern Washington State (Dee). Another snake reference touching on Plath's last stanza is Black Elk's continual referral to the white men as speaking with a snake's forked tongue, making promises not kept. Finally, gold dissolves in acid ("snaky acids hiss") and is found in the shattered rock near fault zones: Plath's "slow faults" (Alleby).

Black Elk has a vision of riding with the storm clouds and he comes to earth as rain. He is turned into an eagle and flies over the land and all his people (seen in Plath's tenth through twelfth stanzas), taking in the tragedy as the sun goes down and the great tree dies. As a younger boy, he was afraid of the vision, his queer feelings, and his psychic powers, echoing the dark thing growing within in Plath's eleventh stanza. In chapter nine of *Black Elk Speaks*, "The Rubbing Out of Long Hair," the Indian Standing Bear speaks of the battle during the Moon of the Snowblind (March).

---

121 Ted Hughes had a great interest in the Native American Indians and later wrote his own tributes to them, such as "On the Reservations," in his collection, *Wolfwatching*.

Bad dreams indeed take over, as in Plath's ninth stanza. In the story, everyone cries out to break camp when more soldiers are coming, shouting, "We will leave and let it go!" as Plath repetitively lets "her go"). The "radical surgery" of "Elm" also sounds like the scalpings from that war scene.

In chapter ten, "Walking the Black Road," warrior chief Crazy Horse isolates himself from his people, living in caves like a bat, before he is tricked by the white man and murdered. After forcing the Indians away from their land and starving them, General Nelson A. Miles' telegram complained to a general in Washington DC of the "Indian problem" and their "dissatisfaction" (as worded in the second stanza of "Elm"), just a week prior to his command at the massacre of hundreds at Wounded Knee. The story ends at Wounded Knee, and the final line of *Black Elk Speaks* is, "There is no center any longer, and the sacred tree is dead."

Plath's father Otto lived in the state of Wisconsin during the Indian relocations and as a pacifist, Otto Plath witnessed Native American culture being destroyed with imposed boarding schools for Indian children. Ted Hughes' Uncle Albert had been known for his stories of the Wild West and Red Indian wars, stories that may have also made their way to Plath beyond the likelihood that she read *Black Elk Speaks* (G. Hughes, 114).

Plath's final home in London was once the residence of writer and occultist William Butler Yeats. Using bibliomancy, Plath felt strengthened by a quote from one of Yeats' plays: "Get wine and food to give you strength and courage, and I will get the house ready." Ruth Fainlight wrote of Plath sharing this story of how she got the apartment (Fainlight, 14). At the time, Plath needed to lean on the Strength card's qualities and female support. In 1962, Plath explained to an editor at *The New Yorker* that the "she" in "Elm" is a female, and she speaks to another woman of anguish that the two share (Crowther, 27). It is that feminine Kundalini submission of the Strength card, reversed.

Chapter Thirteen: Nihilism and Funereal Lilies
Card #12   The Hanged Man   Corresponding Poem: "The Night Dances"

"The Night Dances" is variously interpreted by scholars and readers. Hughes claims that Plath wrote it after watching their baby Nicholas tossing and turning in his crib. It has also been read as a sexual poem. Keen observers have recognized the abundance of lilies and details about this flower, but it does not stop there.

First Mirror: The Tarot/Qabalah

The meaning of The Hanged Man is reversal, delay, being emptied, upside-down, or getting nowhere. Sometimes called "The Scapegoat," other meanings are indecision and wasting resources through ignorance. In a positive light, The Hanged Man signifies voluntary sacrifice, waiting, and the triumph of spirit over the flesh.

Both "The Night Dances" and The Hanged Man show the self as a disintegrating structure swallowed up in a dark, unconscious space. It is presumed that hanging upside-down is not fun; this is why his smile has fallen into Plath's poetic grass. The Hanged Man knows that on this journey of life he will never return to what he once was; it is an irretrievable condition reflected in the second line of "The Night Dances."

The lesson of The Hanged Man is that he must hang until he finishes his great work of regeneration within. Numerology is a key component of tarot, reflecting Plath's math in the second couplet. The Hanged Man must stand upon his feet to surmount the four-stations of the cross. Hanging, his legs create an upside-down number four. His torso forms a triangle, representing the Holy Trinity and the number three. With his head blazing like a comet, he is just over the halfway point of his journey, with a long way to go, as in Plath's eighth couplet. When the Hanged Man is turned right-side-up, with his bent knee across a straight leg, he is in the position of the World card's *dancing* figure of eternity, corresponding with the poem's title and Plath's line, "The world forever."

THE HANGED MAN.

The Golden Dawn attributes this card to the Hebrew letter *Mem*, meaning:
"the Water of baptism that enables the intellect to focus upon the needs of the spiritual dimensions. […] On a human level, initiation can only take place once the purification rite has been undergone. Only then can we think and communicate with the Higher Will."

Second Mirror: Alchemy

In alchemy, the Seal of Solomon, best known as the Star of David, represents the unity of masculine and feminine, God and earth. It is the combination of the upward triangular fire and downward triangular water symbols representing this combination of opposites: alchemical transmutation. The position of The Hanged Man's arms and legs echo these triangles. Alchemically, Plath's expression, "night dances," might be a delicate phrasing of the act of sexual intercourse, a metaphor for the chemical wedding of disparate elements, and/or the loss of self in the second couplet as one material becomes the other. In the center of the triangles is a perfect hexagon, representing the earth. Plath's "mathematics" is also an important part of an alchemist's chemistry computations.

Perhaps Plath had a particular chemical in mind: Coronene, a.k.a., Superbenzene, shares a mystical hexagonal structure with the Seal of Solomon. Coronene occurs naturally as flakes within sedimentary rock. Coronene is a molecular hexagon and a luminous mineral that gives off fluorescence under UV light; it is Plath's flakes, pinkness and light from the poem. Coronene can also cause DNA damage in mammals, echoing the tenth couplet's blood and peeling.

Plath's fourth couplet muses on an everlasting world. This is the panentheistic[122] idea of God reflected in everything, and everything being a gift of God. Elements among these lines add up to the burning of material ("emptied of beauties") and the valuable present of Green Vitriol, the most important liquid in alchemy and one in which all other reactions take place. Plath's images of breath and grass are heated vegetable matter releasing a steam of essence. The first distillation of Vitriol smells like rotten eggs from Sulfur, reflecting the smell image in the fifth couplet. Heated Vitriol, a.k.a., *Flower of Copper*, describes the Tiger Lily here. Heated vitriol is dark lead-grey with a metallic luster. It becomes black and dull upon exposure to light, further supporting the poem's title. Plath's fifth couplet is therefore death and resurrection from the blackness to the new self. Lily flowers are associated with funerals and Easter, and the white lily symbolizes alchemy's *albedo*, or White stage.

The first line of the sixth couplet is the philosophical child, the perfect being who is created and not of impure human nature. To fold the cold ego turns control over to a transformed spiritual being through the lily phase, white as the calla. As the being grows toward the pure, perfected self, the white lily reddens to its *rubedo* phase like Plath's tiger. Red is echoed in the next line's word "hot" and spreading petals suggest Rosicrucian roses.

The flaking off of gestures in the ninth couplet is the body and matter crumbling away in the alchemical vessel. The body is no longer of consequence when the reddening stone is revealed to be growing within. Thus, Plath's tenth couplet qualities of humanity and warmth are the heated matter in the laboratory, and the imperfect shell containing the spirit.

As Vitriol easily dissolves human flesh, its effects are seen in the tenth stanza. Vitriol's crystals are six-sided prisms, mentioned in the thirteenth couplet. It is a soft mineral and can be cut or scraped off with a knife, like Plath's flakes. The pink lighting, blood, and peeling of "The Night Dances" are also part of the impending Rubedo phase as the physical body dissolves. Heaven's black amnesia is the old, blackened body, now forgotten. The second line of the twelfth couplet is a weighty one, with meaning in astrological stars, qabalistic snowflakes[123], and the alchemical White phase.

Third Mirror: Mythology

The Hanged Man is considered to be the Titan Prometheus in Greek myth. The Titans warred against the classical gods, and ultimately lost. Prometheus, the bringer of fire, teaches the dark night of the soul. Prometheus means "foresight" and his brother Epimetheus' name means "hindsight," both names being apposite to The Hanged Man. The gift in Plath's fourth couplet is Prometheus' fire, stolen from Zeus to give to mankind. Prometheus knew he would suffer greatly for his actions.

Prometheus was said to have made man from earth; therefore human flesh was not related to the gods, addressing the sixth couplet. Zeus decided to destroy mankind through a flood, drenching

---

122 Panentheism is the belief that the divine is within all nature and timelessly extends beyond it. Panentheism differentiates from pantheism, which is the belief that the divine is synonymous with the universe. Qabalah is panentheistic.
123 Six Qabalah Tree of Life images, placed with their lowest ends touching, create the "cosmic snowflake." It represents the Body of God, emanating out from a central point.

the grass and all land, as in the fifth couplet. Prometheus warned his son, who built an ark. Zeus gave mankind a break, but he had Prometheus hang for thirty years, where every day an eagle tore out and devoured his liver, and every night it regenerated for the torture to continue. This is shown in couplets nine and ten of "The Night Dances." After thirty years of punishment, he was freed by Hercules and made immortal, reflecting the eternity of the fourth couplet.

Prometheus represents willingness and acceptance to sacrifice for the greater good. He is in suspension, but finds immortality at the end because he trusts in something greater than ego. Plath knew this story, as she owned a copy of Aeschylus' *Prometheus Bound*, and her Dr. Beuscher encouraged her to read William H. Sheldon's *Psychology and Promethean Will* "for sustenance." Sheldon's book associates psychological growth with alchemy, divination, and telepathy.[124]

Religions of every culture and era are fundamentally based upon allegorical expressions of the universal Sun myth; the sunset represents the power of a dying God and mythological crucifixion; the sunrise is resurrection. Here is why the Hanged Man is universal: The Norse god Odin hung on the World Tree. The Christian Jesus, the Sumerian god Dumuzi, the Egyptian god Osiris, the Phrygian god Attis, the Syrian god Adonis, the Roman god Mithra, and Greek god Dionysus were all put to death, hung on a cross or tree, and resurrected. The hanging, dying god is an allegory for total absolution, returning to the Creator, and losing a false human self in favor of the eternal. Plath's "The Night Dances" is the beauty of crucifixion in myth. It is destruction of the ego to become something eternal for the greater good of mankind.

Prometheus was a son of Saturn, from whom the Roman festival Saturnalia was named. Saturnalia was a time when all social restraints were abandoned. Punishment, the main theme of the Hanged Man card, belongs to Saturn, god of Judgment and Duty. Most of the Titans were portrayed as savage and less kind than Prometheus. It was standard for the Titans, whether killing the Sabazian Dionysus, or any of their other victims, to tear them to pieces (Graves, 336). Plath's "The Night Dances" reflects this destruction of the flesh in its ninth and tenth couplets.

Fourth Mirror: History and the World

Ted Hughes said that the poem "The Night Dances" is about Plath watching their infant son asleep and moving about in his cot. This appears to have been a red herring, or at least a gross understatement. Most anyone can see that the poem is also about the beauty of the six-sided blossoms of lilies: Calla, Tiger, and white lilies, which are not-so-subtly mentioned throughout the piece. A certain kind of lily, however, the Amole, or "Soap Lily" (*Chlorogalum pomeridianum*) opens its six petals at dusk, a lovely correlation with this poem's night theme. It has been widely used by the Native American Indians of the Sierra Nevada Mountains for soap, medicine, and food. The dainty ("small breath") Soap Lily is found in grasses ("drenched grass") in the foothills. It does not resemble the larger, more common lilies of the poem's sixth couplet. The Soap Lily's bulbs may be slow-cooked to destroy their soapy nature, which is said to bleed out. Then they are peeled like a sweet potato to be eaten, both seen in the second line of Plath's tenth couplet. The roasted bulbs are also used as a poultice for sores.

The lily blooms in the pink light of sunset, as Plath describes in that same tenth couplet. Like The Hanged Man tarot card, the flowers of the Soap Lily appear to float in mid-air. The stamens are a tigery yellow and orange, and the petals are "Six-sided, white." This is another hermaphroditic flower,

---

124 Notes from Dr. Beuscher's session with Plath are found in Plath's Day Planner entry for November 27, 1954, held in the Sylvia Plath Archives at the Lilly Library, Indiana University-Bloomington.

prized by alchemists for its wholeness and ability to self-fertilize, Plath's seventh couplet's image of self-embellishment (Palomar).

Also once thought to be in the lily family, King Solomon's Seal, or the Seal of Solomon, is a plant with medicinal properties, expediting healing of cuts, bruises, acne and skin troubles, as seen in Plath's ninth, tenth, and thirteenth couplets. Its tubular flowers resemble little hanging "lamps," dangling like The Hanged Man himself. The Seal of Solomon name recalls the hexagonal structure of Coronene seen in the alchemical mirror of this poem, a shape to be revisited shortly.

In the 15th century, traitors were often painted as hanging men. This was the "Shame Position," when the ego must fold and be humbled. It is Plath's sixth couplet again (Moakley). Here, "calla" feels kin to the word "callous." The calla is not a true lily, and every part is toxic. It symbolizes the spirit unfolding out of the toxic ego-body, to become something greater.

Mythologists speculate that Prometheus hung from the Alder tree as pictured on the Hanged Man card. When in flower, its pink catkins, a slim, cylindrical flower cluster, look like hanging smiles, Plath's first line of "The Night Dances." It has light pink buds that grow in spiraling designs on the male catkins. The alder belongs to the birch family, which are trees with peeling bark. Alders are most often found in "drenched grass" near water. Most unusually, the alder appears to bleed crimson when cut, like wounded human flesh. The British Alder god is "Bran," equated the Greek's Cronus, with Saturn, and with the fiery Titans Phoroneus, and our Hanged Man here, Prometheus. The Alder is considered to be a tree of fire and a token of resurrection (Graves, 171). The Greek word for Alder means "I confine," yet another association with The Hanged Man.

The name of the six-sided crystal "Quartz" means "cross-vein ore" and fits Plath's six sides and the crossing of space. There are many types of quartz: citrine is suggested for the tiger-ish color; milky quartz for white; rose quartz with pinkness; and smoky quartz, with its blackness. These are all colors found within "The Night Dances." Citrine is also a birthstone associated with Plath's astrological sign of Scorpio. Considered to be a mystical stone for thousands of years, quartz was sacred to Druids and used in religious, Wiccan, and shamanistic systems worldwide. Quartz is considered a goddess symbol, and is the national gem of Scotland (Jewels).

The ancient Romans considered quartz to be a kind of ice, Plath's comment on the cold in the sixth and ninth couplets, and likening quartz to Plath's six-sided snowflakes of the last two couplets. Quartz is also often white as are Plath's falling flakes.

The "six-sided" hexagon is an important part of "The Night Dances." First, the hexagon is the shape of the Qabalah's Tree of Life. The bee's honeycomb is made of hexagonal wax cells in nature, and Plath's first seven couplets might easily address bees.[125] Friedrich Nietzsche wrote, "Our treasure lies in the beehive of our knowledge. We are perpetually on the way thither, being by nature winged insects and honey gatherers of the mind" (Nietzsche).

The hexagon is one of the crystal structural systems; crystals were first identified by their geometry, Plath's "mathematics," and snowflakes are comprised of ice crystals.

The six-pointed star, or hexagram, is best recognized as the Star of David and the Seal of Solomon. It is a symbol of the Jewish people, also seen in Hinduism, Islam, Occultism and other religions. It is comprised of two equilateral triangles, one said to represent the Hebrew letter "D" for "David" written in Greek as a triangle and positioned upside down and backwards, as The Hanged Man hangs. The Star of David probably originated in the writings of Aristotle, who used these superimposed triangles to represent combining the elements of fire (triangle pointing up) and water (triangle pointing down). The Star of David is part of the emblem of the Theosophical Society, an

---

125 Bees were an important image to Plath: she kept hives herself; she wrote her Bee poems, to be addressed in volume two of *Fixed Stars Govern a Life*; and her father was an expert on bees.

organization of mystics in the late 1800s. The six-pointed star is sometimes called the "Talisman of Saturn" and used to conjure spirits in witchcraft (Stewart, 304).

In the Bardo Museum in Tunisia, a large Imperial Roman mosaic displays images of the twelve zodiac signs and seven days of the week within a hexagram. The central figure is Kronos or Saturn, god of time and judgment, and representing the day of Saturday. Hexagrams have been used in Kabbalah as early as the third century, and in Kabbalistic textbooks on magic from medieval times and the Renaissance.

A hexagram contains the shape of a hexagon, another six-sided shape, at its center. A hexagram's perimeter can be changed from a star to a hexagon by drawing straight lines from each point to the next, closing the shape. The hexagon creates the illusion of a cube, making it an important symbol in Freemasonry, Islam, and other religions. The most sacred site in Islam is the Kaaba ("cube" in English), in the center of Mecca. Inside the Kaaba is the Black Stone, a holy relic believed to be a meteorite and expressed here as Plath's comets crossing through space and the black heavens. The relic is said to have originated in the time of Adam and "descended from Paradise whiter than milk, but the sins of the sons of Adam made it black" (Tirmizi, 49). In central rituals venerating the stone, pilgrims (Plath's "they travel") must walk seven times around the Kaaba building in a counter-clockwise direction ("spirals"), reciting words full of the sounds of Plath's "lilies": *Bismillahi Allahu akbar wa lillahi-hamd*, meaning, "In the name of God, God is great, all praise to God" (Iqbal, 21). Over the centuries, the stone has suffered desecrations and significant damage, Plath's images of flaking and peeling.

The cube/hexagon relationship is also important to Qabalists, Freemasons, and occult practitioners. First, the cube has six sides, six containing the two irreducible prime numbers 2 and 3, representing male and female. There are six directions: north, south, east, west, up and down. There are six spellings for the Holy name of God in Hebrew. Finally, the Qabalah's Cube of Space has the six sides of wisdom, wealth, seed, life, dominance and peace.

Leonardo Da Vinci's famous drawing "Vitruvian Man" reveals the sacred geometry of the ages and the golden ratio of phi, studied since the ancient Greeks. It has enchanted biologists, artists, architects, musicians, scientists, mathematicians and mystics over the ages. The tarot's Hanged Man card, aside from echoing the golden ratio in his halo of enlightenment, is another mathematical study of the human body. He hangs from the dividing line deemed the "extreme and mean ratio" (the golden section); and his head, feet, and elbows create six points like a hexagram. The golden ratio is the natural ratio found in nature, from the arrangement of stems and branches in plants to the design of the human body. The Fibonacci numbers relate to the golden ratio and map out natural cubes and spirals found in nature, such as the nautilus shell or the arrangement of a pine cone. Finally, the Poincaré Recurrence mathematical theorem states certain systems will return to their original state, or very close to this state, after a period of time.

The Sikh mystic Kabir, who harmonized Hinduism with Islam said, "Why wander in the outer garden? In your body there is a garden, an endless world…There the lamps of a million suns and moons are shining…" Perhaps that best sums up "The Night Dances."

Fifth Mirror: Astrology and Astronomy
Astrology views the heavens as lamps and planets guiding the way. The planets are said to mirror organizing principles in the universe, and reflect the ebb and flow of basic repeating human impulses and patterns, geometric and otherwise. Cosmologists have calculated through mathematics that the universe is receding, that there may be identical "multiverses" because the universe continues to exist

beyond the scope of observation, and that the universe will ultimately end in collapse. It is a Nietzschean nihilistic forecast, indeed. With its words like "spirals," "forever," "lamps," "planets," and more, "The Night Dances" seems to support the 1930-published theory of an oscillating universe and eternal recurrence.

Some researchers theorize that the Star of David was the astrological chart at the time of David's anointment as king. The hexagram is called "The King's Star" by astrologers, and it appears in cosmological diagrams of the Hindus, Buddhists, and Jainists. It symbolizes man's position between earth and sky, and the mystical union of masculine and feminine.

To ancient astronomers, planets wandered against the fixed (unmoving) stars of the zodiac. With the naked eye, astrologers were able to observe the movement of the Sun, Moon, Mercury, Venus, Mars, Jupiter and Saturn. Evidence suggests the Star of Bethlehem, the Christmas star marking Jesus' birth and also known as the Star of David, was the brilliant alignment of the giant planets Jupiter and Saturn (Levine). Saturn is the sixth planet from the Sun and the second largest in the Solar System. It has slow movements, taking about 30 years to revolve around the sun, and has been observed and recorded since Babylonian time. Saturn has a ring system composed mostly of ice particles, the poetic cold of "The Night Dances."[126] Romans considered Saturnus equivalent with Greece's Cronus, the god who punishes the undutiful. It is a match for the Hanged Man once again. The Hindus knew Saturn as "Shani," judge of deeds in life, and bringer of bad luck and hardship. The rings of Saturn are said to reflect man's limitations, restrictions and boundaries, as well as practicality, reality, crystallizing, and structures. Astrologers believe the planet governs ambition and career, feeding Plath's embellishment image; it affects a person's sense of duty, discipline and responsibility, addressing Plath's symbol of ego; one's physical and emotional endurance; and long-term planning, as in the fourth couplet.

In 1944 it was discovered that Saturn's moon, Titan, had an atmosphere of icy methane.[127] Discovered in 1655, Titan is the biggest of the 53 moons, larger than Mercury and Pluto, and has a planet-like atmosphere denser than Mercury, Earth, Mars, and Pluto. At about -290 degrees Fahrenheit, it is comprised of half-water ice and crystals, applying again to the space, the cold, and the six sides of which Plath writes. It is orange-pink in color, giving it the human-ness and light of the tenth couplet.

Plath's "lamps" in the twelfth stanza are a celestial body giving off light. "Lights" and "lamps" were both terms for stars and planets in the Middle Ages. Comets, in Plath's eighth couplet, were described by Aristotle as "stars with hair," fitting the long golden-haired haloed head of the Hanged Man. The metaphor of a grassy meadow was used by early astrologers to describe a comet, as in Plath's fifth couplet. One of the meanings for "comet" is "men of dissolute"; it is another good fit for the Hanged Man's guilt (Liddell).

Sixth Mirror: Humanities and the Arts

There may be no better Hanged Man in literature than Friedrich Nietzsche's Übermensch, or "overman," a higher being, from his mythical/philosophical novel, *Thus Spake Zarathustra* (1885). Plath was given this book as a Christmas gift from her mother in 1949, and it became very important to her, inspiring poems and her outlook on life.[128] Most famous for his statement, "God is Dead,"

---

126 It is fascinating to note that in 2006, well after Plath's death, the Voyager 1 photographed a persistent hexagonal wave pattern around Saturn's North Pole.
127 The hexagonal molecule Coronene has also been identified on the surface of Saturn's moon, Titan. This however was not known during Plath's lifetime.
128 For more on *Thus Spake Zarathustra*'s influence on Plath, see Andrew Wilson's biography, *Mad Girl's Love Song*, pp 84-86. © 2013 Scribner.

Nietzsche warred against God in the way of the Titans. His character Zarathustra is based on the Persian mystic prophet Zoroaster, who is explored also in Plath's treasured books, *The Golden Bough* and *The White Goddess.* Plath wrote a poem in 1955 called "Notes on Zarathustra's Prologue,"[129] and in her scrapbooks housed at the Lilly Library at Indiana University, Plath took the paper cover sleeve from her copy of *Thus Spake Zarathustra* and made it central to a collage, demonstrating also a visual artistic importance. Nietzsche's protagonist turns morality upside-down, as The Hanged Man might see it. Known best as a nihilist, Nietzsche had emptied himself of all that was beautiful, seen in Plath's fourth couplet, and found nothing of meaning in the world. Embracing the war between poetics and philosophy, Nietzsche did not trust poetics for their inexactness, connotations, and incongruences.

Plath's math, in this case, is Euclidean geometry, the tool with which Zarathustra charted the heavens. It is characterized by precise definitions and clarity. Plato's famous Academy had posted over its door, "Let no one enter here who has not studied geometry." Plath uses the term "lamps" in a later *Ariel* poem, "Magi," presenting Plato to represent philosophers showing the way.[130] The perfection of Zarathustra's poetic meditations is lost in the exactitude of mathematics, as Plath suggests in the second couplet of "The Night Dances." Plato observed that all language has baggage, group-think, and subjectivity that make it indefinite. Nietzsche embraced this concept, claiming that to merely say something like, "I think," makes large claims about the ego. His suggestion, "Thinking is going on in my body," does not tempt us to claim an independent ego. Plath's cold folding of ego in the sixth couplet is a nod to this.

Zarathustra's idea of time is viewed as cyclical with events eternally recurring, as in the tarot, Hinduism, Buddhism and many religions. Nietzsche knew *Thus Spake Zarathustra* was a different, more powerful book than anything else he had written. In its warmer, more humanistic language, it lacked the chill of his other philosophical works. He wrote in his preface that *Thus Spake Zarathustra* was "the highest book there is, the book that is truly characterized by the air of the heights—the whole fact of man lies beneath it at a tremendous distance." Zarathustra instructed in his prologue that being human is something to be overcome. He calls man "A laughingstock or a painful embarrassment,"—all corresponding to The Hanged Man card, and the disintegration and weakness of the human body in Plath's "The Night Dances."

In his chapter XLVIII, "Before Sunrise," Nietzsche begins, "O heaven above me, thou pure, thou deep heaven! Thou abyss of light! Gazing on thee, I tremble with divine desires.

Up to thy height to toss myself—that is MY depth! In thy purity to hide myself—that is MINE innocence! The God veileth his beauty: thus hidest thou thy stars. Thou speakest not: THUS proclaimest thou thy wisdom unto me." Plath's "The Night Dances" encapsulates Nietzsche here, as well as the picture and meaning of The Hanged Man tarot card. With the sky above and the darkness all around, the speaker is strung up from a height and at the depths of his own personal darkness. As The Hanged Man is sometimes called "the scapegoat," he may be said to be innocent of his said crime. He does not speak. His job is to learn, and to be enlightened.

Nietzsche continues: "Together did we learn everything; together did we learn to ascend beyond ourselves to ourselves, and to smile uncloudedly:—". Smiles of course are a part of Plath's poem and The Hanged Man's demeanor. It is also a summary of Plath and Hughes' relationship which, after all they had been through, was to end nowhere.

Nietzsche wrote, "Whoever is the wisest among you is also a mere conflict and cross between plant and ghost. But do I bid you become ghosts or plants?" Plath seems to wonder this herself.

---

129 A copy of the unpublished poem is held at Smith College.
130 Plato is also significant in the *Fixed Stars Govern a Life* interpretation of Plath's "Tulips" poem, and Plath's *Letters Home* is full of excitement about learning of this philosopher at Cambridge University under Professor Dorothea Krook.

"The Night Dances" shifts from the lilies, a plant making its first appearance in Plath's fifth couplet, to the ghost-like attributes of her final five couplets. For Plath to end her own poem on the word "Nowhere" could not fit Nietzsche better.

Nietzsche's idea of the eternal recurrence, when man lives patterns he cannot escape, is throughout *Thus Spake Zarathustra*, as well as the Nietzschean concept of the will to power, which is man's struggle with and reasons for living in an environment. When Plath writes of being forgetful in the ninth couplet and amnesia in the eleventh, she refers again to Nietzsche, who believed that society experiences a kind of productive amnesia, forgetting the past in order to move forward. In his essay entitled "The Use and Abuse of History," Nietzsche stated productive forgetting, or amnesia, comes from the need to separate ourselves from history. Forgetting, he claims, is necessary to live productively. Without it we, "destroy present existence and thus impresses [a] seal on the knowledge that existence is only an uninterrupted living in the past" (Nietzsche, 3).

Artist David Malek put Nietzsche's eternal recurrence idea into context in an interview in *Dossier* about his series of paintings, most fascinatingly called *Hexagons*, in 2011:

"Nietzsche talks a lot about an 'a-historical sense'. From my understanding, this is a notion of history that is non-chronological, where ideas, or works of art, share […] a common plane and echo across time and space outside of linear time. He came to this conclusion after his study of the ancient pre-Socratic philosophers whose ideas were shockingly modern. For example they deduced the atomic theory of matter and were skeptical of the existence of the gods. Heraclitus, standing in the river, proposed that the universe is in perpetual flux, which influenced Nietzsche's concept of the 'Eternal Return' and shares similarities with contemporary physics. When he read these old Greek texts, he felt as if he were reading the work of a contemporary, someone with whom he shared a great deal, although they were in fact separated by thousands of years. I mention all this to illustrate the idea that if we are talking about melancholy or the sublime, maybe there exist key concepts that don't actually change. A simple way to put it is maybe there is nothing new. And so maybe there isn't a 'contemporary' sublime or 'contemporary' melancholy, but rather these emotional states persist unchanged across time." (Malek)

Here, Malek has essentially summed up the wonder of Qabalah, and he provides an explanation for the concepts embedded within Plath's "The Night Dances."

The word "irretrievable" stands out in "The Night Dances," and in Plath's preceding poem, "Elm." It is not the everyday word, yet "irretrievable" is often used regarding lost ancient secrets of the Kabbalah. This word surfaces in the 14th verse of Nietzsche's Zarathustra Chapter XXXIII, "The Grave-Song," as well as tree images corresponding with the previous poem, "Elm," and this poem, "The Night Dances".

In *Zarathustra's* "The Grave-Song," Nietzsche wrote, "And once did I want to dance as I had never yet danced: beyond all heavens did I want to dance." "The Grave-Song" is preceded by the chapters "The Night-Song" and "The Dance-Song." In *Thus Spake Zarathustra*, there are many references to dancing, to lilies, to The Hanged Man's punishment and absolution, and to Plath's never-ending nowhere world.

"Man is something that shall be overcome.... Man is a rope, tied between beast and overman -- a rope over an abyss... What is great in man is that he is a bridge and not an end."

— Friedrich Nietzsche,
Thus Spake Zarathustra

Allusions to Nietzsche's theme of eternal recurrence appear in novels by P.D. Ouspensky, the writings of Tolstoy, Dante Gabriel Rosetti, and others. James Joyce's *Finnegans Wake*, a book Plath originally considered for her thesis at Smith College, was structured in this same repeating cycle and studies have been made of aligning it with Qabalah (Brivic, 7).

The dissolution of the ego-body in Plath's "The Night Dances" is an age-old literary trope. Dante Alighieri believed, like Nietzsche later on, that humans might "transhumanize" when experiencing a "beatific vision." Alighieri defined transhumanizing as to "go outside the human condition and perception." Plath's copy of Dante's *The Divine Comedy* is well-annotated.[131]

Plath's spirals and leaping echo when Dante wrote that the traveler "moves in one absolute spiral direction which is to the left as he descends and to the right as he ascends, after having turned upside-down at the earth's center."

Because of Dante's traveler's inversion into the center of the earth, the direction can no longer be described as a descent, but now, rather, *ascent*. Up seems to be down, and left seems to be right. This is also the case of the newly incarnate soul in Plato's *Timaeus*, which was Dante's inspiration: The circles of reason and passion in the soul are disrupted when yoked to a mortal body. In viewing these opposites, Plath might ask: *Why not give a striped tiger spots?* By turning upside-down at the center of the universe, from the perspective of Hell, Satan seems right side up.

Plath's eighth couplet begins the second half of the poem. "The Night Dances" is written in two equal sections of seven couplets, seven being a divine number.[132] Likewise, after crossing the cosmic starting-point, Dante sees Satan from God's perspective. Satan is planted head downward with respect to the celestial abode from which the angel fell. Plath's comets crossing space are Dante's falling angels, and, in Plath-fashion, the word "cross" holds an alternate religious weight. In *Inferno*, the first book in *The Divine Comedy*, Prometheus' kind, the Titans, stand around the edge of the lowest circle of Hell for their treason against the gods.

The first step of the mystical journey is correspondingly an inverted perspective. Saint Augustine, whom Plath studied at Cambridge in 1956, wrote, "Descend so that you may ascend" in *Confessions* IV, xii. The Bible's *Ephesians* 4:7 reads, "He also descended first into the lower parts of the earth."[133] Saint Peter was said to have been crucified in an inverted position, by his choice, to have complete knowledge. According to Dante and St. Peter, the inverted (hanged) man can finally see and understand things the way they really are.

Of Plath's "no relation," but not to be missed, is Dante Gabriel Rossetti (1828-1882 AD), an English poet, illustrator, painter and translator most famous for his sonnet sequence, "The House of Life," which includes the poem "Nuptial Sleep." Rossetti's father was an alchemist and mystic, and both men's work is full of such symbolism. Dante's work was often attacked as erotic and of the "fleshly school of poetry," with his warm, revealing, and very human paintings of pink-lit women, echoing the tenth couplet of "The Night Dances" especially.

In the 1860s, Rossetti lived near where Plath and Hughes settled in London, close to the London Zoo at Regent's Park. Rossetti's wife, Elizabeth Siddal, often modeled for Rossetti as Dante's Beatrice. Siddal struggled with opium addiction, and Rossetti himself was addicted to a sedative and hypnotic drug, chloryl hydrate, sometimes called "knock-out drops" (Marillier).

The subject of chloryl hydrate opens "The Night Dances" to even more intriguing layers. Chloryl hydrate is the drug that ends the life of the protagonist "Lily" Bart in Edith Wharton's famous 1905 novel, *The House of Mirth;* its title is similar to Rossetti's, "The House of Life." *The House of Mirth*, like Plath's poetic lost smile and The Hanged Man's expression, is a story of America's gilded age. The

131 Some of the books owned by Sylvia Plath may be viewed at the Sylvia Plath Archives in the Lilly Library at Indiana University-Bloomington.
132 See discussion of the number seven in *Fixed Stars Govern a Life*'s interpretation of Plath's "Tulips."
133 Smith College's Mortimer Rare Book Room lists Saint Augustine's *The Confessions of St. Augustine* as part of Sylvia Plath's personal library. They claim "underlining and annotation throughout."

protagonist Lily denies true love to marry well in society, and the cold ego triumphs over the heart. Lily has a gambling addiction, losing herself in mathematics. Like the tarot's Hanged Man, Lily becomes the scapegoat for society scandal. Her reputation is ruined and the amnesia of death appears to be her only option.

The Nobel Prize-winning Edith Wharton was a major female author from Massachusetts who left America for Europe, as Plath had done. Plath owned her book *Ethan Frome*, and was likely to have read Wharton's other works in school. Wharton used much of the same symbolism in "The Night Dances" in *The House of Mirth*: blood and bleeding appears on eighteen occasions. Lamps and lamp-posts appear nine times and are deftly used to set the scene in the same astrological way Plath uses them (Wharton). Plath's leaping and spiraling references Wharton's literary technique of *chiasmus*, or the symmetrical crossing-over through a reversal of structures to make a larger point. Chiasmus inverts motif, structure, and ideas as The Hanged Man is inverted.

The character of Lily has a long physical and mental decline, and the novel addresses Nietzschean ideas of fatalism and predetermination. Lily uses the motto, "Beyond!" throughout *The House of Mirth*, connoting transcendence from the literal world and the limits of social convention, both Nietzschean ideas explored in his book, *Beyond Good and Evil*.[134]

In fact, "The Night Dances" seems to simultaneously praise and unite Wharton and Nietzsche's work, as they come from the same spiritual and psychological place.

Wharton wrote:

> "That Lily was a star fallen from that sky did not, after the first stir of curiosity had subsided, materially add interest in her. She had fallen, she had 'gone under,' and true to the ideal of their race they were awed only by success by the gross tangible image of material achievement" (Wharton 2:461-462).

In *The House of Mirth,* "Lily, in order to escape her depression and insomnia, overdoses on that same substance, chloryl, which took over Rossetti's life. In *The House of Mirth*, it is not clear as to whether Lily intended to commit suicide, as her debts were paid, she had new inspiration in her life, and she had a man who loved her. This is most interesting, because like Lily, Plath also had depression, insomnia, and reasons to live before taking her own life.

An earlier draft of Plath's "The Night Dances" includes references to astronomy, as well as inhalation, one of the ways to administer chloryl.

Finally, *The Painted Caravan* speaks of decomposition before a spiritual rebirth, which is the essence of this poem, best seen in Plath's tenth couplet. "The Night Dances" echoes the nowhere place beyond, wherein lies the peace of an amnesiac eternal perfection.

---

134 Authors Janet Gabler-Hover and Kathleen Plate explore Nietzsche's idealism all throughout this story in their article, "*The House of Mirth*' and Edith Wharton's 'Beyond!" *Philological Quarterly* 72.3 (1993): 357-78.

Chapter Fourteen: A Tribute to the Whodunit
Card #13   The Death Card   Corresponding Poem: "The Detective"

Autobiographically, it is easy to consider "The Detective" as directed toward Ted Hughes' philandering, with Plath casting herself as his victim and the hausfrau in the kitchen. Careful readers of her journals and letters will realize that Plath also loved the occasional murder mystery. She read them while shut up in hospital for appendicitis in 1961, and she caught a live performance of Agatha Christie's *The Mousetrap* in London with Olive Higgins Prouty in 1962. The black crow is the sole survivor at the end of "The Detective," a bird that would later become Ted Hughes' alternate poetic identity. The crow is famously a metaphor for death, and the Death card.

First Mirror: The Tarot/Qabalah

The meaning of the Death card is rarely a physical, literal death. Instead it is a new start or a radical change. The scene in the card's picture is not sunset, but sunrise. The Death card does not represent the end, but rather, change, motion, and transformation. The tarot's major arcana is divided into three sets of seven: 0-6 for the physical world; 7-13 for the emotional and mental needs; and 14-21 for spiritual experiences. As seen previously, the number seven represents perfection within the tarot and numerology. In "The Detective," Plath's "Over the seven hills, the red furrow, the blue mountain" represents the qabalistic and Rosicrucian journey to the paradise of a New Jerusalem, the city in the background, pictured on this card. Rosicrucian white roses adorn the grim reaper's banner, the bishop's cloak, and the woman's hair. Plath's third stanza smiling man is most certainly the skeleton knight/grim reaper here.

The milk in the seventh stanza of "The Detective" comes first as yellow and next blue. This describes the ground on the Death card; the foreground is mostly yellow, and there is the yellow sun, a yellow pontiff, and the yellow bones of the dark knight. Yet everything in the background is in icy blue water that blends into land of the same color.

Plath and Hughes had two children, who are referenced in the poem, and two children are pictured on the Death card. The two towers in the background are the same as on the Moon tarot card, cross-referencing to The Moon, and supporting the lines about the moon in the seventh and eighth stanzas. Plath's word "embalmed" is an apt choice for Death.

Beyond tarot, it is well documented that Plath and Hughes regularly attempted to communicate with the spirit world through the Ouija board, using a glass as a planchette. This is another meaning for "arranging cups." The Golden Dawn allots to the Death card the Hebrew letter Nun, meaning "the fish, symbol of Christ dying and resurrecting in Death is the Victorious (Netzah) Self (Sun)."

The poem "The Detective" most obviously addresses the death of Sylvia Plath's old life and the beginning of her new one. On the surface, "The Detective" reflects upon a slow killing of that old life; first with lies, then the absence of speech, neglect of affection, and the over-hard work of motherhood. The different figures pictured on the card—male, female, old, young—show that death can happen to anyone.

Qabalists believe death is necessary for transformation. Plath's line about having to face pointed fingers refers to the worldly-minded masses caught up in ego and unwilling to transform to new life. The Golden Dawn writes of this card's teachings: "I have finished my work. I have entered into the invisible" (Regardie, 264). Plath corresponds with a body-less case turning to vapor.

Second Mirror: Alchemy

In alchemy, the Death card represents Putrefaction, when decomposing essences are reabsorbed. Viewing "The Detective" through the lens of alchemy, the first line's "blew in" is the bellows that keep the fire going in a laboratory. There are seven phases in alchemy. Two corresponding alchemical colors, red and blue, are given full attention in the second line, and Plath's first stanza cup arrangement may also refer to lab work.

As in Plath's second stanza, the alchemical vessel is sometimes called a "garden," where the philosopher's stone is grown. The pipe, smoke, and burning years are all good images for the blackening of Putrefaction, and "kitchen" is an alchemical term for the laboratory.

Like Buddhists, the alchemist believes the material world is illusion. Surroundings therefore are merely lies and deceits, tacked up before us like Plath's photographs. When Plath wrote that no one was dead in the third stanza, she refers to the impossibility of spiritual death. Likewise, to have no body in her house means she is only spirit.

The "blades" the sun plays with are knives in the laboratory, to cut away the gross matter from the pure philosophical stone. Here, "Bored" may have a double meaning of being full of holes. Plath's fourth stanza "hoodlum" in his red confinement is another name for the alchemist's "fugitive servant." *The Golden Tract*, an ancient alchemical text, claims the true philosopher would not "extract the quicksilver from any but the red slave" (Abraham, 125).

"[W]ireless" is a disconnected feeling alchemists have to the world, feeling both special and alone. The "elderly relative" represents generations of preceding alchemists. The alchemist is known to work with highly toxic substances, especially mercury and arsenic, in pursuit of the philosopher's stone. With this in mind, Plath's fifth stanza's poison fits right in.

Plath's image of phosphorus is the only compound with the apparent ability to contain light, and pure phosphorus spontaneously burns in the air. Phosphorus was the ancient name for the planet Venus, seen just before sunrise and correlating with the Death card's picture. This planet/morning star is also called Hesperus, Flame of Eos (the Dawn), and Lucifer.[135] Phosphorus is a nerve agent, Plath's images of curling nerves and convulsions. Discovered in 1669 by the German alchemist Hennig Brand, phosphorus resulted from an attempt to create the philosopher's stone from urine. Brand produced phosphorus by distilling the salts after evaporating urine, Plath's sixth stanza's vaporizing.

In alchemy, the mercurial worm devours the old, corrupt body in the vessel, reducing it to prima material. It is both a devouring worm of death and nourishing worm of new life, and like the butterfly from the chrysalis, alchemy is considered a divine metamorphosis. It was also believed Ovid's *Metamorphoses* contained secrets to the philosopher's stone (Abraham, 128).

The first draft of Plath's "The Detective" included the word "Sulphurous." Sulphur (also *Sulfur*), is the stone that burns. Alchemy cites that inside gold is the alchemical Sun, and inside the Sun is Sulfur. Therefore, Sulfur is the spirit of life, equivalent to the Sun. It represents the philosopher's stone, the perfect solid. To create this stone, the alchemist's soul must also be refined and purged for purity; one process is the mirror and visible symbol of the other.

---

135 For more on Lucifer, see the *Fixed Stars Govern a Life* interpretation of Sylvia Plath's "Lady Lazarus."

Third Mirror: Mythology

In Greek myth, Hesperus was the son of the dawn goddess Eos, and brother to Phosphorus, a.k.a., Lucifer. Hesperus personified the evening star, the planet Venus. Phosphorus/Lucifer is the same planet, only seen in the morning.

In a myth of St. George, George rescued a princess tied to a tree in much the same way that Longfellow had his maiden tied to the mast in his poem, "The Wreck of the Hesperus," to be discussed shortly. St. George was called "The Lion-Hearted," and Leo the lion, the constellation corresponding with the Death card, was his emblem.

The rider on the Death card is Hades, who abducted Persephone and took her to the underworld. It is Plath's mysterious case with no body. The rising sun on this thirteenth card suggests the future, although the grieving people are unaware of it, and Plath makes use of the sunlight in her fourth stanza. Hades was known as "the Invisible," the unnamed murderer in "The Detective." Hades is in constant procession; he is the irrevocable ending and death of the old ways of life, best shown in the third stanza of this poem.

In Navajo Indian myth, "Changing Woman" was the goddess of the order of the universe and cycles of the seasons. She had two twin sons, Monster Slayer and Born for Water, as there are two children in "The Detective": Monster Slayer and Born for Water. Changing Woman also abducted two children of another god with the help of a sunbeam, hinting of the fourth stanza's criminal sun again. The two children were taught the Blessingway Ceremony and were eventually returned to teach it to their people. Changing Woman and her holy people disappeared soon after, in the way Plath's poem indicates, but their presence was manifest in Mother Nature, sounding like the furrows and estate of Plath's eighth stanza. Navajos believe crows are helpers of evil spirits. In their culture, things of darkness and the night, such as the moon, are to be avoided. Thus, Plath's last stanza in "The Detective" is full of Navajo omens (Bulows).

Mars is the Roman god of war, a fine fit for the Death card as its corresponding planet with Leo as its constellation. Mars stood for masculine aggression, anger and violence. The Greeks called him Ares, and by either name he represented military power. Leo the lion was the man-eating Nemean lion, killed by Hercules. Because the lion ate its victims, bodies were not left. The lion's mother was Selene, the Moon goddess, explaining why Plath's moon smiles.

Ares' mother Juno became pregnant with him by a goddess' flower, the garden image of Plath's second stanza. The flower was first tested on a heifer for potency, corresponding with Plath's thriving cow image. Mars was said to have two infant sons, Romulus and Remus, who were left exposed to the elements by a jealous uncle fearing they would usurp him. They were suckled by a she-wolf and saved, fitting the poem's lines about nursing. The wolf is an animal known to howl at the moon, also an image in "The Detective."

The Norse equivalent to Ares/Mars is Týr, meaning "god of the hanged"; it is a reference to Odin and good fit with Plath's sixth stanza line of hanging punishment. Northern Germanic myth holds that the gods decided to shackle a wolf, but it broke free of every chain. They created a magical silken ribbon, as in Plath's second image of stanza silk, but the wolf sensed their lies to trick it into captivity. The brave Týr wrestled the wolf into bondage, but lost one hand doing so. It is a new way to be "Unable to face the fingers."

The Tiwaz rune was named for Týr. It is marked like the arrow image in Plath's fifth stanza. This rune design was later used as an insignia for the Nazi party's Third Reich. Also named after Týr is *Týrhialm*, a plant better known as Aconitum. It is one of the most poisonous plants in Europe, guaranteeing certain death. Plath noted "yellow aconites" in her pocket calendar on January 30, 1956, so we know that she was knowledgeable about these flowers.

Fourth Mirror: History and the World

 One of the most famous Sherlock Holmes stories is *The Hound of the Baskervilles*, largely set in Devon's Dartmoor, England, near Plath and Hughes' home.[136] Plath wrote of witnessing a foxhunt with "a pack of spotted, sulphurous dogs" in the area (*LH*, 436) and of taking baby Frieda on a trip there (*LH*, 441). *The Hound of the Baskervilles* is inspired by local legend of a demonic hound, associated with the real-life old squire, Richard Cabell. Cabell had a passion for hunting, was said to have sold his soul to the devil, and rumors abounded that he had murdered his wife, who disappeared without a trace. Cabell had an evil reputation until his death in 1677, when spectral hounds were said to have come and escorted his soul to Hell. Some believe they can still hear "shrieks echo" in the night. Cabell's Dartmoor tomb is a building secured with heavy stone, referenced in Plath's seventh stanza of "The Detective." Iron bars were installed, Plath's gate image, to prevent his soul from escaping, a kind of walking "on air."

The nearby Holy Trinity Church is known for its trees full of crows, referenced in the last line of "The Detective." Many are said to notice a strange red glow through the iron bars of the Squire's crypt, the poem's red room with its hoodlum. Legend claims that if a visitor sticks a finger through the iron bars, the Squire will bite them ("Unable to face the fingers").

This graveyard was a frequent target for 19th-century body snatchers, returning to the poem's missing-body theme. The Holy Trinity Church was badly burned in May 1849, connecting with Plath's years going up in smoke. The church lost its original spire to lightning in 1884, Plath's image of electrification, and it was damaged by German bombs in World War II. It is believed that black magic rites have been carried out at that church, especially at the site of the Squire's tomb, for hundreds of years. The Holy Trinity Church, now a shell of itself, is in a valley, as in Plath's first stanza. There is a lovely vast landscape view in which one can see her "seven hills, the red furrow, the blue mountain" (Legendary).

In the 19th and 20th centuries, matchsticks contained phosphorus and were dangerously toxic. This substance was traced to many murders, suicides and poisonings. Those who had to work with phosphorus sometimes suffered "phossy jaw," a condition in which jaw bones glow in the dark. It is an eerie echo of the Death card's skull, and fits Plath's images of missing lips, bones that show, and a smiling moon. Phosphorus is plentiful in Dartmoor and used for agricultural purposes (Royal, 11). Dartmoor's dark skies are also an apt image to match Plath's idea of walking on air, because it is sometimes difficult to tell where the horizon ends and the sky begins.

In 1822, a railway was built from Plymouth to Princetown. This giant steel worm crawled across the country, putting its mouth (Ply*mouth*, in this case) first. The successful venture expanded because of increased demand from operations at Dartmoor Prison, as in the sixth stanza lines of insatiability and punishment. Sir Arthur Conan Doyle made reference to the fictional "Princetown Prison" in four stories he wrote between 1890 and 1903, based on Dartmoor Prison. Dartmoor Prison was built and first occupied in 1809, in an area of dense fog, colder and rainier than anywhere else in England. It has been written that the prison's existence alone was "an act of positive cruelty." By April of 1813, it held 1700 American prisoners. On April 6, 1815, after the treaty of Ghent was signed, the prisoners were not immediately freed. They rioted, and guards shot as many as 72 unarmed men, at least seven mortally (I.H.W.).

---

136 Plath references Sherlock Holmes in her poem "Dialogue Over a Ouija Board," where she writes: "Your Sherlock Holmesing steered to a blank wall" (*CP*, 280).

"Hesperus is Phosphorus" is a famous sentence by the mathematician, logician, and philosopher, Gottlob Frege. It is a linguistic exercise that distinguishes sense and reference.[137] Frege was anti-Semitic and a supporter of Adolf Hitler, using his analytical skills to assist in the removal of Jews from Germany after World War I. "The Detective" therefore takes on new meaning of learning the truth of Nazi extermination camps into which the trains rolled full of Jews who had been lied to about where they were going. These camps were in the countryside, Plath's deathly valley with its thriving cattle. Plath's "egotists" are the Nazis, believing their kind to be superior. The "smoke rising" becomes the ovens for cremation. There were no proper graves to mark their deaths, and these deaths were widely denied, as in the end of the third stanza. The Nazis lived comfortable lives at the camps, as polished and plush as Plath's fourth stanza suggests. The wireless radio reported the news, yet the Holocaust was rarely considered a front-page story, even in America. Most Nazis did not speak of the truth of what was happening; this is the missing mouth image. The last three stanzas show the physical decline of a mother who might have remained alive in a camp with her children, wasting away to skin and bone. The last stanza takes into account "the whole estate" with its "dry wood" and "gates" as presented on the news reels Plath watched as a girl in school and at the movies. Plath's "furrow" is the graves where the bodies return to mother earth. Only the moon has the dignity of being "embalmed," and the black crow of course is a bird of death. "Make notes" is Plath's directive that this episode of history should not be forgotten.

There is another kind of Holocaust to which "The Detective" applies, being the fate of the Native American Indians. The Navajo recognized Mount Hesperus in Colorado as their sacred mountain of the north, the direction in which the winds blow. Hesperus is one of seven mountains, like Plath's seven hills, delineating Navajo territory: four mountains represent the cardinal directions and three are inner mountains. Their First Man (God) was said to have fastened Mount Hesperus down with a rainbow, Plath's red and blue, from one end of the color spectrum almost to the other. He then covered it in darkness. Mount Hesperus is full of the mineral jet and is associated with the death color, black. As this is Badland territory, much of the wood is dry (Hesperus).

"The world is full of obvious things which nobody by any chance ever observes..."

— Arthur Conan Doyle, *"The Hound of the Baskervilles"*

Navajo legend speaks of two blackbird eggs in an obsidian basket at Hesperus' peak, the two stones in Plath's poem. Trains shrieked past and settlements slowly moved west with the white man's expansion of territory. This is the poem's side-moving, slug-like killer. The white "egotists" decided their ways were superior and should be taught to the Indians.

The Native Americans considered Mother Earth to be female, and the Navajo goddess, "Changing Woman," was honored every time a girl had her first and second menses, officially becoming a woman. With the white man's ways, the Indian celebration of the feminine was tamped down as Plath's poetic woman is sealed in a wall (Lapahie). The pipe and smoke of Plath's third stanza is now Indian; the deceits are unkept promises of the white man. The white man attempted to shut the Native Americans away on reservations, believing white ways were more civilized and that Indians needed to be taught how to be fully human. It infuses Plath's fourth line of the third stanza with a degrading tone. The white man excused his own behavior, since on the reservations, physical lives were not lost. On these reservations, Indians were unable to make a sufficient living of any kind, and forbidden to

137 For more on Gottlob Frege and "Hesperus is Phosphorus," see the *Fixed Stars Govern a Life* interpretation of Sylvia Plath's poem, "Lady Lazarus."

practice much of their own culture. Boredom brought on alcoholism and crime, the "hoodlum" image again and their red skin is therefore the color of the reservation room. The arrows and knives Plath mentions are traditional tools and weapons of the Native Americans.

In 1864, during the Civil War, Kit Carson imitated the Southeastern Trail of Tears and made the Navajo suffer The Long Walk, over 300 miles to a confinement camp called Bosque Redondo, in New Mexico. Many Navajo died or were killed by white soldiers along the way. Conditions were deplorable at the camp, and the Navajo's four years there were marked by hunger and disease, the bones of the seventh stanza.   —

The San Juan Basin, where Mount Hesperus is located, is known for its large amounts of coal, uranium and natural gas   the poison, nerve gas, convulsions, and electricity in the "The Detective." In the 1940s, despite their forced removal, the Navajo were denied welfare relief because of their separate nation status. Many went hungry. Meanwhile, lung disease and cancer were rampant from mining and industrial environmental contamination.

The Death card's holocaust cloak shadows nations and races, and even animals, plants, and insects. Interestingly, the last three stanzas of "The Detective" also fit the Milkweed plant *Asclepias Tuberosa*, hardy enough for the UK and deadly to the native milk-producing Grayface Dartmoor Sheep, which suffered their own sort of holocaust with decimating foot and mouth disease through the 1950s (Sheep). This event took place a few short years before Plath and Hughes moved to the Devonshire countryside. Up to 35% of the sheep were exterminated and Hughes, being a countryman, would have surely known of it.

Milkweed was used by the Hopi Indian women to stimulate milk flow; by the Chippewa to make charms; and in ancient times to poison arrows. The Milkweed plant secretes a milky juice and is known for having "foot" and "mouth" parts to its flower.[138]

Milkweed's transition from flower to pod is well described in the sixth stanza of "The Detective." Rose Milkweed is considered to be a "Moon Plant" to alchemists and beloved by witches for its silvery silky white fluff and a watery, juicy stem. Milkweed is damaged by caterpillars and slugs, seen in Plath's second stanza. This opens up still another amazing interpretation for the poem, as moths and butterflies are an alchemical symbol for metamorphosis, the meaning of the tarot's Death card.

A common European plant named after the Norse god, Týr, is Aconitum, a garden flower whose name means "without struggle." It is a sad metaphor for the murder of peaceful peoples. Other names for Aconitum include "Wolfsbane," "Monkshood," and "Devil's Helmet," the former corresponding with mythological Ares' children suckling the she-wolf, and the latter with the armored skeleton of Death on this tarot card. Its cup-like flowers are often blue or purple and grow in the mountains, as in Plath's first stanza.

When monkshood roots are touched to the lips, they produce tingling—Plath's seventh stanza. When any Aconitum species is taken internally it reacts severely on the nervous system—Plath's fifth stanza. Traditional eastern medicine used Aconitum to increase the Ares/Mars-like fire or heat in the body, but the plant is highly toxic and large doses are almost always fatal to humans. It is used for food by several *Lepidoptera* (butterfly and moth) species.

"The Detective" is loaded with *Lepidoptera*-appropriate phrases, words, and symbols: The arrival on the wind; the arrangement of cups, which may be floral cups; the garden image; the shaking off of silky cocoons; larvae or caterpillars, as they kill plants, moving along like slugs; the body in the pipe, which now becomes the cocoon; the notion that "No-one is dead," despite the missing larvae; an empty cocoon as a house with no body in it; the body only leaves the cocoon, it does not "come into

---

138 Plath mentioned milkweed in the second stanza of her later poem, "The Bee Meeting": "Now I am milkweed silk" (*Ariel*, 81).

it"; butterflies and moths chew their ways out, explaining why the mouth would be first; arrows represent flying, knives represent hatching out; poisons represent how many are poisonous to eat; Plath's image of absence and the second year also fit the cocooning process, as well as insatiable appetite, the hanging like fruit, and the wrinkling and drying; the veins of butterfly wings are like bones that show; the moon might certainly smile at moths in the night; and certainly these creatures "walk on air." Even "Watson" applies, as a Robert Watson bequeathed the famous Watson collection of British Butterflies and Moths to the Natural History Museum in London in the 1950s.[139] Finally, the glowing colors and dust on the mature creature's wings might be compared to phosphorus.

Fifth Mirror: Astrology and Astronomy

The planet corresponding with the Death card is Mars. Named after Mars, god of war, is the red planet in our solar system is marked with craters, Plath's furrows of red. Mars has volcanic mountains with blue striations which in Plath's time were thought possibly to be water, suggested in the first stanza of "The Detective." The symbol for Mars is a circle with an arrow, an arrow being mentioned in the fifth stanza. Mars is the only planet in our solar system with two moons; these may be either Plath's white stones or the children in her seventh stanza. Phobos, meaning "fear," is the moon nearest to Mars. Many geological features on Phobos are named after Jonathan Swift's Lilliputian characters from his famous work of fiction, *Gulliver's Travels*. The name "Lilliputian" is in itself a funny play on the idea of missing lips. Mars' moon Deimos, meaning "dread," has its two largest craters named after the writers Swift and Voltaire, who speculated on the existence of Martian moons before their discovery.

The idea of life on Mars was an obsession for many, including the astronomer/writer Percival Lowell, founder of the Lowell Observatory in New Mexico. He was of the Boston Lowell family, related to Plath and Hughes' friend, poet Robert Lowell.[140] Percival Lowell perpetuated Mars excitement with the publication of three books on the subject, addressing his theories, publishing drawings of surface canals, and more. H.G. Wells' *The War of the Worlds* was created in the heat of this excitement. Wells' description of the aliens was famous:

> "There was a mouth under the eyes, the lipless brim of which quivered and panted, and dropped saliva" (Wells).

It is another absent lips image. Plath knew that despite enthusiasm about finding life on Mars, or fear of Martians finding us here first, wars and death happened already in our own world, among the same species.

Inventor Nikola Tesla believed that the repetitive radio signals he received from the atmosphere might have been communication from Mars, Plath's wireless in the fourth stanza.[141] There had been five attempts to either fly by or land on Mars before Plath's death, and these attempts were all within the last two-and-one-half years of her life ("The Detective" was written in 1962).

The astrological constellation Scorpio corresponds to the tarot's Death card. Scorpio the scorpion, Plath's zodiac sign, is a symbol of darkness and bad luck, which gains its power when the sun is in decline after the autumnal equinox. Dante's *Purgatorio* referred to Scorpio as rising in the cold hours of dawn, fitting Plath's vaporization. The claws of Scorpio are called the Yoke of Balance, devoted to Venus and uniting persons under the yoke of matrimony (Allen, 364). Pliny assigned the color brown to Scorpio, Plath's brown fruit, and the portent of plagues of insects fits the cocoon,

---

139 One who is interested in butterflies used to be called an *Aurelian*. The name Aurelia, Sylvia Plath's mother's name, is derived from this word.

140 Robert Lowell wrote a foreword to Plath's original version of *Ariel* in perfect Qabalah ordering. See *Plath Profiles* vol. 5.

141 For more on Nikola Tesla, see the *Fixed Stars Govern a Life* interpretation of "The Couriers."

caterpillar, and silk imagery. The Chinese called some of Scorpio's stars Fu Kwang, the Basket with Handles, presiding over the rearing of silkworms.

Sixth Mirror: Humanities and the Arts

Plath's poem, "The Detective" celebrates famous mystery novels and authors. First and foremost is Sherlock Holmes. Plath's poem is structured as a series of Holmesian questions and deductions, and his pipe is seen in the third stanza. The author of the Sherlock Holmes stories, Sir Arthur Conan Doyle, had two children with his first wife, Louise. He became a spiritualist in his adulthood, fascinated by psychics, mediums, séances and fairies. Doyle wrote a great deal about these subjects, and toured the world as a lecturer. His book, *The Land of Mist*, written in 1926, is a spiritualist story featuring his Professor Challenger character.

Doyle killed off his Sherlock Holmes in the story, *The Final Problem*, a title that sounds very much like "The Final Solution," the Nazi program to annihilate the Jews of Europe. Under intense public pressure to revive his hero, Doyle wrote *The Hound of the Baskervilles*, setting the story before Holmes' death. In 1903-1904, Doyle published thirteen "Return of Sherlock Holmes" tales, coinciding with the Death card's number. In Doyle's *The Adventure of the Empty House*, Holmes fakes his own death; it is a missing body as in "The Detective." Plath's "valley of death" appears to be Dartmoor, where so many of Holmes' murder cases took place.

"The Detective" predominantly addresses the story, *The Hound of the Baskervilles*. In the tale, a hellish hound is sent to attack in the setting of Dartmoor. *The Hound of the Baskervilles* has been listed by the BBC as the United Kingdom's "Best-Loved Novel." In the story, the Baskerville family is cursed. Two centuries prior, Hugo Baskerville became infatuated with a young woman and kidnapped her, shutting her in his bedroom, as in Plath's fourth stanza. She escaped and Baskerville offered his soul to the devil if he could recapture her. He lured her to a desolate moor. Both the girl and Baskerville were found dead; the girl died of fright, and Baskerville had his throat torn out by a hellhound that cursed the family from then on. Doyle said he based this on Devon's real-life Squire Richard Cabell.

Generations later, Holmes is called in to solve the mystery of the recently deceased Charles Baskerville, a superstitious bachelor in poor health. The killer is revealed to be a naturalist in search of the Dartmoor butterfly *Cyclopedes* and long-lost relative who committed the crime in order to take Baskerville's fortune. The hell-hound is ultimately a dog painted in phosphorus to give him a frightening glow, Plath's second to last line of the poem. Sherlock Holmes' assistant is Dr. Watson, who is named in the last stanza of "The Detective."

The second most-famous fictional detectives also have a Dartmoor connection: Agatha Christie's Hercule Poirot, and Miss Jane Marple. Born in Devon, the *whodunit* author Agatha Christie was a frequent visitor to the Hay Tor area of Dartmoor, and wrote her first novel at the Moorland Hotel in Dartmoor. Plath knew Christie's characters, making a reference in her journals to "An Agatha Christie housefrau" (*UJ*, 637). Plath read Christie's novels in the hospital recovering from surgery, and noted that she and Hughes saw a London live production of Christie's "Mousetrap" with a visiting Olive Higgins Prouty (*LH*, 459). Christie's heroine, Miss Marple, was frequently pictured pulling weeds from her garden as she worked out her mysteries. Christie's Dartmoor series includes *The Sittaford Mystery*, which touched on the author's own interest in the supernatural, séance, and spirits (Christie).

In Christie's 1932 short story collection *The Thirteen Problems* (Death's number thirteen once again), each story touches on at least one line of "The Detective." In the first story, "The Tuesday Night Club," a pregnant girl is tricked into murdering her lover's wife—Plath's woman in the wall. In "The

Idol House of Astart," there is a house on the edge of Dartmoor called "Silent Grove," with a moonlit orgy to the goddess of the moon—Plath's smiling moon. A character in her story "Ingots of Gold" is in a place called Princetown Prison, remarkably similar to Dartmoor Prison—Plath's hoodlum again. In "The Blood-Stained Pavement," an artist paints the tell-tale hint of a future murder. "Motive v. Opportunity" is about a spiritualist and séances. In it, a young boy tricks a woman into writing a will in disappearing ink, another Plathian "vaporization." "The Thumb Mark of St. Peter" features an elderly insane man—Plath's fourth stanza. In "The Blue Geranium," a mysterious fortune teller predicts a full moon and flowers turning blue to precede a death, suggesting the first four lines, the second line in stanza two, and the second-to-last stanza of "The Detective." In "The Companion," a body is missing after a drowning. In "The Four Suspects," a species of Dahlia are rearranged to spell "Death," fitting the Death card itself, as well as references to a garden. In "A Christmas Tragedy," corpses are switched. In "The Herb of Death," a character named Sylvia dies of poisoning from the foxglove flower, affecting the nervous system, causing convulsions, and shocking the heart; this sounds very much like Plath's fifth stanza nerve-curling and convulsions (Sowerby, 129). In "The Affair at the Bungalow," a crime has a lack of evidence, and in "Death by Drowning," a young girl is pregnant and ashamed, much like the story of Kitty Jay, to follow shortly.

Agatha Christie's real life had mystery, too. On December 3, 1926, soon after discovering her husband Archibald was having an affair (Plath's "deceits"), Agatha Christie disappeared. She and her husband's eight married years had burned down to nothing, as in the third stanza. Christie's car was found abandoned with no trace of its owner. Sir Arthur Conan Doyle, among others, was sought to help the police solve the mystery. Christie turned up eleven days later at a hotel, suffering from amnesia and a suspected nervous breakdown. Some say she received shock treatments soon after, as in Plath's fourth and fifth stanzas. Many believe Christie's novel *Unfinished Portrait* (1934), written under the pseudonym Mary Westmacott, is autobiographical. In the story, a woman is driven to suicide when her husband demands divorce.

As further testament to Plath's purposeful intention of Dartmoor images and symbols, Christie's *The Thirteen Problems* was dedicated to Sir Charles Leonard Woolley (1880 – 1960), knighted in 1935, a famous British archeologist. Woolley spent much time on Dartmoor's ruins.

After admitting she created him in the Sherlock Holmes tradition, Christie killed off her star detective, Hercule Poirot, in 1960. Christie called Poirot "a complete egoist" and a "detestable, bombastic, tiresome, ego-centric little creep" (BBC). Doyle's Sherlock Holmes was recognized as equally arrogant, self-obsessed and pretentious, as Plath's second stanza references.

Other Dartmoor legend figures into "The Detective" too: Dartmoor is famous for pixies, or little elves, said to create harmless mischief around the house, such as rearranging cups. They have been immortalized by poets such as Samuel Taylor Coleridge, and Mary Elizabeth Whitcombe. The Dartmoor region is also known for its great archeological remains dating back to the late Neolithic and Early Bronze Age, appropriate to Plath's question about arrows and knives in the fifth stanza. Additionally, the famous Dartmoor knife is known by hunters and outdoorsmen around the world.

A sad and often-visited spot in Dartmoor is Kitty Jay's Grave, burial site of an orphan teen who was raped by a farmhand and impregnated. A child herself, yet another take on Plath's idea of "two children," she had nowhere to turn and hung herself in shame, seen in the end of Plath's sixth stanza. Kitty was buried at a crossroads between two churches.

Author Beatrice Chase (1874 – 1955) is known as "My Lady of the Moor," and regularly put flowers on Kitty's grave. Born Olive Catherine Parr, Beatrice Chase was considered to be egotistical. She was directly descended from William Parr, the brother of Catherine, the sixth wife of King Henry VIII.

Chase wrote many Dartmoor-based novels, including *Through a Dartmoor Window*, echoing Plath's first stanza. Chase's home is open to the public, and its polish and plushness is well described in the fourth stanza of "The Detective" (Legendary)[142].

A BBC radio program, *The Goon Show*, was at its height of popularity from 1954-1959, with a large listening audience and the actors' names being household words. It is Plath's wireless image again. Their "Tales of Old Dartmoor," first aired February 7, 1956, while Plath was ttending Cambridge. The skit included jokes about a bored guard in this empty prison with such a bloody past. He is the "Bored hoodlum." The guard has a scheme to sail the Dartmoor Prison out into the Atlantic, Plath's poetic blue water. An excerpt from the script contains most elements of the fourth stanza of Plath's "The Detective," plus a bonus mention of hounds at the end. "Seagoon" is the bored prison guard:

> Seagoon: It's all very well for him to talk, but nobody's committing any crimes. Here I am working my fingers to the bone, sweeping out empty cells, oiling unused locks, polishing handcuffs and giving transfusions to blood hounds! (Milligan)

The Goon Show was written by Spike Milligan, a writer, poet, playwright, comic, and painter. Plath listened to Milligan's popular radio show, "Beyond the Fringe" (Peel, 22), and got tickets to his show in January 1963 (*UJ*, 633). In the last months of her life, she even contributed a poem for a Milligan event (Peel, 250). Like Plath, Milligan suffered mental breakdowns and manic depression through the 1950s. Plath might have seen in him a kindred spirit. Milligan was a regular correspondent with Robert Graves, whom Ted Hughes greatly admired (Scudamore).

Yes, Plath had her own red room at Court Green. However, Plath's "red room" carries a lot of historical artistic weight: August Strindberg, of whom Plath read a great deal at Cambridge,[143] is famous for his 1879 novel *The Red Room*, which skewers literary critics with their own hypocrisy. In 1894, H.G. Wells wrote his own "The Red Room," a gothic ghost story. Painter Henri Matisse painted *The Red Room*, a portrait of a woman at her kitchen table with a window looking out onto hills and gardens, just as in Plath's poem.

Finally, "The Detective" would be incomplete without the Hesperus imagery as it relates to Henry Wadsworth Longfellow's poem, "The Wreck of the Hesperus." The poem commemorates a famous shipwreck off the coast of Plath's home state of Massachusetts. The pipe-smoking ship's captain had brought along his lovely young daughter for company. A sailor warned that a hurricane was on its way, with its killer eye and sidelong movement of Plath's second stanza. In Longfellow's poem, the moon had a ring around it, as Plath's moon is awash in phosphorus. As the storm came in, the captain bound his daughter to the mast for safety. The storm washed everyone overboard and broke off the mast with the girl tied to it, leaving the schooner empty ("a case without a body"). Longfellow begins and ends with her beauty and perfect white breasts, ending frozen and caked with salt, like Plath's white stones.

From the 1950s to the 1970s, it was a popular colloquial term in the U.K. to say, "You look like the wreck of the Hesperus!" The Death card grins throughout Plath's "The Detective," a study of homicide and mystery around Dartmoor, and genocide by egotists around the world. "Make notes" was Plath's command to herself to write the details down, and she did so beautifully.

---

142 Beatrice Chase, a contemporary of Plath's American Smith College professor Mary Ellen Chase, was buried in Dartmoor. Local legend says that she was taken to a hospital in a straitjacket after the loaded revolver she kept by her bed was removed.

143 Strindberg's works consumed much of Plath's school readings in January 1956 at Cambridge, as noted in her pocket calendar. This calendar is held in the Sylvia Plath archives of the Lilly Library, Indiana University-Bloomington.

Chapter Fifteen: Arrow Into the Apocalypse
Card #14   The Temperance Card   Corresponding Poem: "Ariel"

Plath told the BBC that her poem "Ariel" was "Another horseback riding poem [...] after a horse I'm especially fond of" (*Ariel*, 196). She did ride a horse by that name in Devon. Hughes elaborated that "Ariel" was about her runaway horse in Devon, who once took her on a terrifying ride. Hughes may have been confusing another horse-riding incident Plath had years earlier at Cambridge, when her horse, Sam, went out of control. That event on July 9, 1958 was the first seed for her poem "Whiteness, I Remember." The autobiographical story is the popular interpretation of this poem and little else is explored, as has been true with most of Plath's work.

First Mirror: The Tarot/Qabalah

The Temperance tarot card symbolizes tempering passion or strength; bringing balanced, adaptable influence; repentance and baptism; equality and equilibrium. The card also foretells of a safe journey and health. Reversed, passions are set free, even out of control. Shown is an angel at the beginning of the path to the great mystical journey begun by its predecessor the Death card. Temperance lies on the central path of the Qabalah's Tree of Life and represents the alchemical process of Distillation. It is essentially a process of concentration, no matter which level (physical, mental, or spiritual) it occurs. There are two Hebrew correspondences with "Ariel" and Temperance: The Hebrew word ARYH, for *Leo* or *Lion*, is designated feminine, as it ends with an H. *Auriel*, derived from this root word, means *Lion of God*, *hero*, and *Hearth of God*. Plath wrote her intention, clearly knowing the Hebrew meaning because she had written "Lioness of God" on a typescript draft of this poem.

In Gematria, linking the English alphabet with the Hebrew alphabet's numerical correspondence and its relation to Qabalah, words have values that equate with numbers. The value of Temperance's Hebrew letter *Samech* is 60, connecting it with Hebrew's BChN, meaning to *try by fire*, and MChZH, meaning *vision*. *Samech* is therefore the mystical Path of the Arrow, the straight shot of true vision.

Plath's second stanza of "Ariel" steers us toward a qabalistic initiation called Liber Samekh, an occult ritual full of words and images portrayed in the poem.

Liber Samekh represents the Sagittarian union with God. This merging is echoed throughout the poem, in images of growing into one and being one with the drive. The Golden Dawn assigns the color blue to Sagittarius, reflecting Plath's blue in the first stanza (Regardie). The ritual, part of an initiation to become an adept in the *magickal*[144] arts, is said to have come from Hermes, god of literature and poets. The Liber Samekh union is passionate; God is described as both an angel and a lion-serpent in this text that makes "voice" the magical weapon to produce "words" as the wisdom of God. God is said to be the "unconscious Will."

---

144 The Hermetic Order of the Golden Dawn preferred the spelling as "magickal."

The text reads:

"Let him now imagine, at the last Word, that the Head of his will, where his consciousness is fixed, opens its fissure [...] and exudes a drop of clear crystalline dew, and that this pearl is his Soul, a virgin offering to his Angel, pressed forth from his being by the intensity of this Aspiration" (Crowley, F).

Here is one of the meanings for Plath's flying dew in the last full stanza of "Ariel." The Liber Samekh's "offering" in the text above becomes Plath's "Suicidal," in the quest to become joined and one with the angel. The ritual text continues:

"the author of the infallible impulse sends the Soul sweeping along the skies on its proper path with such impetus that the attraction of alien orbs is no longer sufficient to swerve it,"

The text states that the physical body and its worldly ego must be abandoned "because it is not yet his whole being which burns up before the Beloved"(Liber, Ff, Line 4). This sounds very much like Plath's "Ariel," as well as her earlier *Ariel* poem, "Lady Lazarus."

The "orbs" then become Plath's red eye image. This suicide, as writer Judith Kroll wrote in her *Sylvia Plath: Chapters in a Mythology*, "expresses mystical union or transcendence, 'sui-cide' in that it represents the death of the (personal) self—the little 'I'" (Kroll, 184).

"Ariel" therefore is a fine paraphrase for the Liber Samekh, and an understanding for Plath's inclusion of suicide. The goal was to kill her worldly, small, ego self and become part of a larger consciousness.

The poem "Ariel" is loaded with images from the Temperance card's picture: Yellow irises are said to represent passion, pictured behind the angel on this card. Plath's "Stasis" is a condition of stability in which all forces are equal and opposing, thereby canceling each other out, and representing the card's balance and equilibrium aspects.

The crown rising as a sun on the card is *Kether*, the highest point on the Tree of Life and the goal of all mystics. The picture shows a pouring, to work with the "Pour of tor" in Plath's third line. "Tor" is the rocky piles and core of ancient mountains, as Ted Hughes explained in *Winter Pollen* (Hughes, 203). Both Plath's tor and images of distance are pictured on the Temperance card.

The yellow-haired angel fits both Plath's Godiva and leonine symbols, with her white gown and her mane-halo emanation. She has one foot on land and one in the water, a pivoting position of heels and knees.

A "furrow" is shown on Temperance's picture, a distant path with the split and pass of Plath's third stanza. The angel dips her foot into glittering water, like the seas in Plath's eighth stanza.

Returning to Gematria, the numeric value of a word also equates it with other words of equal value. "Lioness of God" reduces to the number 840, which also equals *magnum opus* and Conjuration. The name Sylvia Plath reduces to 870 and is equivalent to "Flame of the Sun." Considering that the Temperance card is one of balance and equilibrium, Plath took advantage of every possible way to echo this idea. No matter how the numbers added up, Plath couldn't go wrong with "Ariel." Ideas within "Ariel" of passion set free, art, and untamed temperance were to be Sylvia Plath's new identity and possibly her greatest poetic achievement.

The Centennial Review's Mary Kurtzman pointed out that "unpeeled" is a curious word, meaning the same as "peeled," and suggesting this might have been a game for Plath, to make "PLATH" un-PL'd. If she had done this intentionally, reading her name from right to left would be the Hebrew for *Aleph*, meaning a "beginning," plus *Th* for *Tav*, the last letter, or *Omega*, in the Hebrew alphabet, meaning "end." To play the Gematria game again, "unpeel" equals number 438, also meaning "goddess," "perfect," and "union."

Another name for berry is "gog" in England, meaning both "eye" and "sun" (the sun being God's eye). Gog is referenced in the Hebrew Bible, the New Testament, and the Qu'ran as either a fallen angel or fallen city destroyed by fire from heaven (the sun). Gog almost always refers to end times. Plath owned a book in her personal library entitled *Was Jesus Gog?* by Walter Donald Kring. Just southeast of Plath's Cambridge University was the Gog Magog Downs, a site of archeological significance with ancient hill figures of gods and goddesses. Plath certainly knew these Gog connections, and it is dizzying to entertain the associative possibilities.

The Temperance card's angel has red wings, as does Eros of Greek mythology and supporting Plath's flight into red in the last full stanza. The circle with the center point is the alchemical symbol for gold, the end of the quest, or perfection. It is a bull's eye for an arrow.

Of Temperance's letter Samech, the Golden Dawn claims it is:

> "the prop[145] through which the Self [represented as the Sun] can enthusiastically [a Sagittar-ian trait] reflect [the Moon's trait] itself. [...] When the Self correctly mixes the elements, it reflects the higher will onto the lower spheres. On a human level, any action of significance must be allowed to be guided by the inner Self in order that a correct balance be achieved, and reflected in one's own psychological make-up - The depths of the unconscious need to be in agreement with the proposed movement in order that they truly move."

There is no argument that Plath's "Ariel" truly moves. "Ariel" reigns and rides passion to its fullest potential at the risk of all. This poem is absolutely Temperance, in its upright and reversed positions. It is the card occultist Aleister Crowley renamed "Art" in his Thoth tarot deck, published in the late 1960s.

Second Mirror: Alchemy

In alchemy, "stasis" is the state of putrefaction, or the Black Phase. This dark-ness in the first stanza is spiritual, a lower, human place of waiting. Plath's second line depicts the sky as the sun rises from that spiritual darkness. This is the beginning of purity and a washing free of blackened matter. The angel conducts Plath's "pour" from one cup to another as alchemical equalizing.

The lioness symbolizes the green lion of alchemy: ore from which philo-sophical mercury is extracted. She is green because she is fertile, growing, and her virtue and force create all things. She has not yet ripened to red (*rubedo*) and then gold.

In Brittany and parts of Wales there once was a taboo against eating blackberries, a fruit of the Goddess (Graves, 395). When alchemists speak of the green lion devouring metals, they liken it to mercurial blood dissolving and reducing material to the first matter, like a mouth full of black blood in Plath's fifth stanza. The green lion has also been illustrated consuming the sun, dissolving, and coagulating (Ashmole, 278-290). This dissolution, called *nigredo*, is symbolized by the eclipse ("Nigger-eye"). It is essential for the sun's raw gold body to be dissolved to release the active male seed, Plath's berry image, in union with the female moon (Abraham, 94).

The violent male Red Lion (the sun, or sometimes "King," or "Brother") then takes over, devouring feminine Sulfur (known as "Moon," "Green Lion," "Queen," "Silver," or "Sister")[146]. Plath's unpeeling is synonymous with this dissolution, as are the body pieces and flakes of the sixth and seventh stanzas. The alchemist Ripley wrote of the "Whyte Woman" in the chemical wedding that is Plath's Godiva becoming one with the Red Man. They dissolve together, creating the

---

145 "Prop," as in "to prop up." The shape of the letter Samech represents a rough stone set up on end, and its meaning is "a support."
146 The language of alchemy usually evolves from lions as metaphor of the base or primitive, evolving to man, as the operation becomes more refined.

new individual in the eighth stanza; it is the perfect, pure hermaphrodite or philosophical child crying out at his birth (Abraham, 167).

From the psychological Jungian Alchemy perspective, Plath's complete surrender to passion and who she must become requires her to drop all cover (unpeel), to transform into the pictured angel, the mythic White Goddess of Love and Death[147]. In the Godiva legend, the goddess defies her husband, traveling naked on her horse.

The White Goddess was connected to the death of the Sacred King, also alchemical allegory. Early drafts refer to Plath/Godiva shedding dead men. Either act of shedding or peeling suits the Temperance card's need to remove falseness and recreate into something better.

In alchemy, dew is the beneficial, healing aspect of mercurial water that transforms black *nigredo* into white *albedo*, bound for *rubedo*. These are clear connections to Plath's blackness and the infamous N-word; the whiteness of Godiva; and Plath's missile *into* the color of red. The sun's evaporative heat and descent of dew represents sublimation and distillation of matter in the vessel, sometimes called a cauldron, as in Plath's last line. Dew precedes the chemical wedding, preparing the body for reunion with the animating spirit/soul. Dew is symbolic of divine incarnation or manifestation from above. Alchemists believe natural dew contains divine Salt (thoughts of the One Mind) that can transform Sulfur and Mercury, the Elixir or contents of the cup of God, the Holy Grail. Distillation, the alchemical phase corresponding to Temperance, is the transformation from one form to another, through action. Plath's poetic suicide drive is the fusion of all three aspects of alchemy: practical, psychological, and spiritual. The "Eye" becomes the *I*-- the individual, the God within, the philosopher's stone. The alchemical morning is sunrise, when the philosophical stone, or *magnum opus*, is born.

Third Mirror: Mythology

The ancient Greek's Iris is associated with the Temperance card. She is the goddess of the rainbow, and female counterpart to Hermes. Iris is a beautiful, winged woman, another kind of flying dew, as rainbows are created by moisture. Iris serves the great mother with her feelings, the intelligent process of emotion. She represents a balance of heart and mind, the feminine over masculine.[148]

Plath's reference to foam in the eighth stanza suggests the goddess Aphrodite, who rose from the foam of the sea. "Foam to wheat" may suggest female sexuality, as wheat is symbolic of procreation in the tarot and Qabalah.

"Ariel" also corresponds with King Arthur's Glastonbury at the Isle of Avalon. The "Tor of Glastonbury" is world-famous, rising high on blue Jurassic sandstone, reminiscent of the first stanza. The lioness of God is England herself. The River Brue surrounds Glastonbury on three sides, Plath's furrow and glittering seas. During King Arthur's time, the River Brue formed a lake at Glastonbury. There resided Vivien, "The Lady of the Lake," a water fairy sometimes called "Cerridwen" or "The White Goddess." Vivien refused to give her love to Merlin the magician until he taught her all his magic secrets. Her powers became greater than her teacher's, and she sealed him inside an oak tree. Vivien also gave King Arthur his sword, and boasted to King Mark that she would return with the hearts of Arthur's knights in her hand. Sir Thomas Malory's hero Tristram, in the late 15th century prose account of the rise and fall of King Arthur, *Le Morte d'Arthur* (Malory), was a native of the lost land of Lyonnesse, a

---

147 The White Goddess symbol shows up a great deal in Plath's husband Ted Hughes' work, as well.
148 Justice is Temperance's complement, with its masculine reason balanced over feminine emotion.

place for which Plath wrote a poem in October 1962. Lyonnesse was said to be a rocky stretch of ground connecting Cornwall with the Scilly Isles in the English Channel. It was engulfed by the turbulent sea. It is Plath's tor, with a split and pass, swallowed up by the blue and glitter of the seas.

Saint Brigit of Irish myth was a woman of poetry, whose name means "a fiery arrow." One side of her face was said to be beautiful and one side ugly. She ruled all things lofty: flames, highlands, hill forts, as well as the psychologically uplifting: wisdom, excellence, intelligence, perfection, craftsmanship, healing, druidic knowledge and warfare. The Haitian's Voodoo *loa* (spirit) Maman Brigitte is traced to her. It is not a stretch to recognize these fiery women embodied in Plath's "Ariel."

In Celtic mythology and folklore, the cauldron symbol provides infinite sustenance or artistic inspiration. In Wiccan ritual, the cauldron represents the feminine source of life, the womb. Most often it holds fire or water elements, but the cauldron is sometimes employed for gazing, for mixing herbs, for consecration, for alchemy, or to hold the ingredients for a spell.

Pagans consider the cauldron to be the cosmic mother's womb. Ancient Babylonians believed that Sirius, Mother of the Stars, stirred the mead of regeneration in a cauldron called "The Blue Heaven." Odin, the Norse god, obtained his powers by changing into a phallic snake and entering the earth's cave-womb to reach its three cauldrons (Buckland, 77-79).

Transformations of all kinds are an integral part of Celtic mythology, and at the center of these myths is often a cauldron. In ancient Celtic tradition (reflected in the tarot's Cups suit), there are three types of cauldrons: for transformation, rejuvenation and rebirth, and inspiration.

Cerridwen, one of the megalithic pre-Christian goddesses and another identity of the White Goddess, had a cauldron that symbolized the merging together of these three aspects. According to Welsh legend, Cerridwen was Keeper of the Cauldron, and like Plath, she had a son and a daughter. As the tale goes, Cerridwen entrusted a young boy to watch over the cauldron, but he carelessly spilled some of the magic potion on himself.

It is here where the "Ariel" poem mirrors much of this legend too: The drops were seen as sparks which ran through him like wild fire, until he became aware of all the knowledge of man, originally intended for Cerridwen's son. The boy was reborn as a famous poet. Cerridwen flew into a rage, pursued this boy, and a great chase ensued. Cerridwen's cauldron held the secret of immortality: the ability to see death as integral in the cycle of life; every death brings rebirth, and every ending a new beginning (White).

White Goddess author Robert Graves wrote in *Seven Days in New Crete* (1949)[149] that a future world would discard monotheistic religion and return to worshipping a triple goddess as primitive civilizations all over the world have done. The Celtic triple goddess was a composite of the Latin Diana (the huntress, represented by the arrow), Phoebe the moon goddess, and Hekate, goddess of the underworld. Ovid's Medea called Hecate a triple goddess, and Hesiod wrote that her triplicity had a share in earth, sea, and starry heavens. Here is another reflection of the word "sister," and explanation for why Plath chose three-line tercets throughout "Ariel."

The Catholic Encyclopaedia reads: "The altar of holocausts is called the 'ariel of God'... on this altar burned the perpetual fire that was used to consume the sacrificial victims (Lev. 6:12)."

---

149 Also known as *Watch the North Wind Rise.*

Fourth Mirror: History and the World

Plath takes us in two directions with the "Lioness of God." The first matches this title to the queen bee in a hive; bee symbolism appears repeatedly in Plath's work, and bees are symbolically important creatures in alchemy, as they turn pollen into golden honey. Plath's father Otto was an expert on honey bees, and Plath herself was a beekeeper after her son Nicholas was born. "The Bee Poems," as they are called, show up at the end of the restored edition of the *Ariel* collection, providing some literal translations of these facts, in addition to their symbolism of the tarot suits and other qabalistic mirrors. Still, no poem besides "Ariel" so describes the lion-yellow queen bee's early morning consummation in mid-air, devouring her mate and flying solo into the sun. In her journals, Plath wrote of a dream of police chasing a swarm of bees with "ariel nets" (*UJ*, 396). She misspelled "aerial" as *ariel*, favoring consciously or subconsciously the Ariels of fiction and myth over the atmospheric homophone.

In an older poem, "Blackberrying," Plath called berries "dumb as eyes." It is these blackberries again, an alchemical fruit of knowledge with sharp thorns, to which she refers in the fourth stanza of "Ariel." And blackberry wine can be made from them, suggesting the first line of the fifth stanza. It is yet another temptation for the chalices of the passionate Temperance reversed.

Remembering that Ariel is one of the planet Uranus' moons leads us to consider the "aerial" homophone of Ariel, coupled with the idea of *uranium*, which can only be the atomic bombing of Hiroshima at the end of World War II. When Plath was twelve years old, on August 8, 1945, she wrote in her diary of that world event. It both horrified and left her in awe at that young age. When Plath wrote "Ariel," it was her thirtieth birthday, on October 27, 1962. This was at the height of the Cuban missile crisis. For thirteen days in October 1962, ending the day after Plath's birthday, the world was on the brink of nuclear war. Plath wrote put every bit of anger and fear into this work, probably believing there would be another Hiroshima and Nagasaki[150], or worse. Her other poems written during this time, "The Jailer," "Stopped Dead," "Fever 103°", "Amnesiac," "Lyonnesse," "Cut," "By Candlelight," "The Tour," "Poppies in October," and "Nick and the Candlestick," and some poems afterward, are infused with war imagery, nuclear winters, and missiles.

Stanza by stanza, "Ariel" is the story of the atomic bombs dropped on a quiet Japan one dark morning from the "substanceless blue" sky, over the "Pour of tor and distances"[151] in August 1945. Certainly the roar of nuclear power could be compared to a lion as it grew into its great mushroom cloud, Plath's second stanza. Heels and knees were sure to have pivoted as the Japanese citizens ran for cover toward any furrows they might have found.

The cities of Hiroshima, Kokura, and Nagasaki were the targets for the American atomic bombs in 1945. They are sister cities, reflected in the third stanza. Kokura lies at the narrow "neck" of land where the island of Japan nearly splits. The curve of the land forms an arc of brown earth, all well described in the third stanza. The primary target was Kokura's military arsenal, but attack upon that city was abandoned due to adverse weather conditions. The neck of Japan could not be caught.

The Japanese are usually brown-eyed, and U.S. war rhetoric at this time was quite racist. The N-word is a touchy one; Plath's use of it here, as well as her Jewish references in other poems, has caused some to think her a racist. This was definitely not the case, as she wrote repeatedly of idolizing Jewish writers and mentors such as Dorothea Krook, Alfred Kazin (*LH*, 149), and of her "dearest friend" at Cambridge, African-American writer Nathaniel LaMar (*LH*, 194, 211).

---

150 Nagasaki was bombed with a plutonium atomic bomb.
151 Seventy-three percent of Japan is mountainous, the meaning of "tor."

The mortar, shells and shrapnel of war become the hook-filled berries, leading soldiers of both sides to the bloodiness of the fifth stanza. Famous photographs after the bombing showed Japanese citizens with mouths full of blood. Some of the citizens had vaporized completely, leaving only traces of their shadows on the wall.

The horror of the initial blast is through the fourth and fifth stanza, and then the "Something else" introduces the shock waves of radiation and the blast winds, many times greater than the strongest hurricane, hauling one through the air. There is a great and terrible power to this fearsome white Godiva, the mushroom cloud.

"Godiva" means *gift of God*, a dark joke on Plath's part, as well as a likening to the legend of the woman who rode naked through the streets of Coventry in order to gain her people freedom from the oppressive taxation imposed by her husband. At the time, America saw this military action against Japan as a necessary sacrifice to end the war without another D-Day type of invasion. In Lady Godiva's Medieval England, it was customary for penitents to make a public procession in sleeveless white underwear,[152] another meaning for the color white, if one looks beyond meanings of race or the more obvious symbol for purity. America would *force* Japan to repent! It is a fine correlation with the tarot's Temperance card, as the water signifies baptism.

With the mushroom cloud's subsequent radiation, the reader understands the unpeeling to now mean human skin. Widely published photos of the dead, and useless hands and limbs of the injured fit the last line of Plath's seventh stanza. Every horrible and gory detail of the bombings is somehow beautifully rendered within this poem, as the wheat fields and land turned to foam surrounded by sea. In that terrible blast, the cry of a child would have melted into nothing.

"It is perfectly obvious that the whole world is going to hell. The only possible chance that it might not is that we do not attempt to prevent it from doing so."

—Robert Oppenheimer

In 1942 before the atomic bomb drops, American aviation hero James (Jimmy) Doolittle, a US Army Air Corps lieutenant-general, led a bombing raid against Japan, known as "The Doolittle Raid" ("Doo" now as homophone for Plath's flying dew). The purpose of this mission was to shake the faith of the Japanese after the Pearl Harbor attacks, and to boost American morale. This was considered a suicide mission. The flight crew's aircraft carrier, USS Hornet, a hornet being a cousin of the bee, was deep in enemy waters with each of the 16 aircraft pilots having only enough gas to reach their targets in Tokyo before intentionally crash-landing in enemy territory (Chun).

Plath gave her intention away at the end of "Ariel" writing, "Into the red / Eye." A red eye is the perfect visual metaphor for the flag of Japan, and certainly Japan was a cauldron of fire on those terrible mornings in 1945. The United States used no Temperance in ending the war.

Flying dew is also a fine reference for Gwen Dew, one of the first twenty-five American women to get her pilot's license, an accomplished writer and photographer. Born 1903, the year the first powered and manned airplane was invented, Dew was just the type of historic female Plath admired, and fits well with the Temperance card's meaning of equality. Dew served as a war correspondent in World War II who wrote popular books and many newspaper and magazine articles about her time as a prisoner of war in Japan. Dew had a passion for the Orient prior to wartime, and was the first female foreign correspondent permitted into Japan after the bombings. Plath had once pictured herself becoming a foreign correspondent in high school (Rollyson, 21).

---

152 This sleeveless undergarment was probably what Lady Godiva actually wore (and not the total nakedness that literature has romanticized), if the story is true.

"If I had any hatred for the Japanese, it disappeared when we pulled into Yokohama," Dew once said. "Seeing the nearly total devastation, you could only feel sorry for them." Regarding Hiroshima, "Never could you imagine such death, such fearful death. I saw it and I literally could not speak for days" (Passic).

As an adult, Plath also wrote against the atomic bomb and nuclear weapons testing (*UJ*, 46), and was known to have actively protested against nuclear weapons in 1960, taking her two-week-old infant Frieda on her first outing to a Ban the Bomb march in London. She was proud that this was her baby's first outing, and wrote of being moved to tears by the marchers over "the insanity of world-annihilation" (*LH*, 378).

Plath had also written *The Nation* in response to an article called, "Juggernaut, The Warfare State" declaring that she was preoccupied with "the incalculable genetic effects of fallout" and the "terrifying, mad, omnipotent marriage of big business and the military in America" (Alexander, 271).

Plath was horrified over the United States selling un-equipped missiles to Germany, and awarding former German officers medals. She believed England would be obliterated in a nuclear war, and she was very much in favor of disarmament (*LH*, 437-438). In August of 1962, troops in East Germany sealed the border between East and West Berlin, shutting off the escape route for thousands of refugees with a 12-foot, 66-mile wall built of barbed wire and concrete blocks. Also that year, five Britons were accused of spying for Moscow; exiles had invaded Cuba at Bay of Pigs; Russia was soon to explode the world's largest nuclear device; and the Soviets were winning the space race. Sylvia Plath, and the world, was terrified.

Plath and Hughes had a map of the relationship between nuclear waste dumps and the rate of leukemia across England, southern Scotland, Northern Ireland and Wales. They wanted to be as far from it as possible (*LTH*, 518-519). Plath also worried over dangerous radioactive levels of Strontium 90 in the milk supply from fallout (*LH*, 434). The isolation in Devon was especially important to Plath. On the occasion when two American professors visited and offered Hughes a lucrative position teaching in the United States, Plath was outraged, regarding them as saboteurs of their writing plan, and perhaps even saboteurs of her family's safety.

Author Tracy Brain considers Plath's poem "Fever 103°," also in *Ariel*, to reflect postwar and Cold War concerns with the effects of nuclear explosions on the human body. Brain states that Plath's friend and editor, A. Alvarez, believed the 1959 film *Hiroshima Mon Amour* greatly influenced both "Fever 103°" and "Elm" (Brain, 118).

Fifth Mirror: Astrology and Astronomy

Many readers interpret the "Ariel" poem's horse imagery to be about Plath's literal horse, missing the idea of the Sagittarian centaur's half-horse body. The astrological designation for the Temperance is Sagittarius, and there are many Sagittarian aspects in "Ariel": Thighs and hair, for instance, are symbolically Sagittarian physical features, and arrows are symbolic of the Sagittarian archer. The starry sky itself fits the description of a glittery sea.

Sylvia Plath was a Scorpio, the sign positioned just before Sagittarius on the zodiac wheel. In "Ariel," she moves out of her old form, Scorpio, to become the next new sign, the Sagittarian arrow. Remembering that Ariel is a moon of Uranus, many of the stanzas, and especially the first, describe characteristics of these satellites.

Viewing "Ariel" through its astrological lens, this is a poem about the end of an age, and the beginning of the new, represented on the Mayan calendar as December 21, 2012. The Mayan prophesy is one of awakening; moving away from Pisces' age of greed and materialism and into an Aquarian phase of love.

The first stanza of the poem "Ariel" is an accurate depiction of the skies as seen from the Earth. The Milky Way is the lioness of God, which has been slowly been devouring its black mouthfuls of our smaller galaxy until the two finally merged on the 2012 Winter Solstice. This lion is female, because the Mayans foretold that this shift of planetary stewardship would fall into the hands of the feminine, as Temperance's Iris serves the mother. Mayan symbols for this date include lion-like representations.

Ancient Babylonians identified Sagittarius as a centaur with his bow and arrow, except theirs bears a panther's head, a leonine cousin. Two major stars of Sagittarius, Alpha Sagittari and Beta Sagittari, mean "knee of the archer" and "the archer's Achilles' tendon" respectively; it is Plath's knees and heels. The archery bow is an arc of brown, and in the sky it is comprised of three stars. Notable objects within Sagittarius include the Lagoon and Trifid Nebulae, two clouds of gas lit up by stars within, a constant atomic explosion. Sagittarius' arrow points toward the star of Antares, the "heart of the scorpion" (Ridpath). It is a symbolic union with God, described previously in the Liber Samekh initiation. Plath would have seen this as a metaphor for destruction of her physical and ego self, born under the sign of Scorpio, and moving into the new Age. On July 31, 1945, Plath wrote of being overwhelmed by the Milky Way's beauty as a girl. In her journal, she wrote a poem (unpublished) about it called "The Fairy Scarf."

The centaur represents the struggle between the animal and civilized self. In stories such as *Ovid*, other ancient Greek literature, and Shakespeare's *King Lear* (all studied and translated by Ted Hughes and which Plath knew well), female centaurs ("centaurides") abound. They are the sisters and wives of the males on Mount Pelion. *Ovid*'s centauride, Hylonome, committed suicide when her husband was slain in battle. Some centaurs are said to be white and naked from the waist up, as is Plath's horse-riding Godiva. Also applicable to Plath's suicide end is the story of the wise and noble centaur Chiron of Greek myth, who gave up his immortality and sacrificed his life for mankind to obtain the use of fire.

The Milky Way has its infamous Dark Rift, a kind of furrow in the sky with a split, and an almost perfect likeness to the shape of Japan. From ancient times this rift was considered to be the entrance to the underworld and a haven for evil. It is through this same rift that the sun aligned on December 21, 2012. The colors of the Milky Way appear to have an arc of brown, and its swirl, with the dark center, becoming the "Nigger-eye" again. The Mayans echoed this astrological design in their Pyramid of the Sun. The closest neighboring constellation to the Milky Way is Sagittarius. Because of the Milky Way's advancement, Sagittarius is losing stars, specifically its heels and knees as they are enveloped.

Sixth Mirror: Humanities and the Arts

The name "Ariel" is loaded with literary connections, and many of them have already been explored by other scholars and will just be summarized here.

Ariel is an angel in Judaism, Gnostic Christianity, and occult lore. In Milton's *Paradise Lost*, Ariel is an evil angel and pagan god. Ariel is one of the names for Jerusalem, and it is the brightest of the five major moons of Uranus, which are all named after characters from Shakespeare and Alexander Pope. In Pope's classic poem, "The Rape of the Lock," a parody of alchemy, Ariel is the chief sylph (defined by the famous alchemist Paracelsus as a mythological, invisible being of the air). Pope expanded the sylphs' characters to consist of mystically concentrated humors of difficult women whose spirits were too full of dark vapors to ascend to the sky after death. It is an interesting metaphor for a nuclear explosion more than two hundred years after Pope's death. Sylphs are throughout Rosicrucianism, Hermeticism, and because of their association with the ballet *La Sylphide*, fairy tales. Plath may have enjoyed the closeness to her first name, and she at least once used the pen name "Sylvan Hughes" (*UJ*, 366).

The Hermetic Order of the Golden Dawn cites the angel Ariel as "the Ruler of Air." Ariel was the blithe spirit who yearned for release in Shakespeare's *The Tempest*. In the tale *The Little Mermaid* by Hans Christian Anderson, Ariel is the little mermaid who ultimately decides to kill herself by jumping into the ocean and becoming the foam of the sea, as she cannot allow herself to choose to kill someone she loves. She becomes a daughter of the air.

Plath's great poem "Ariel" then, is so much more than a ride on a runaway horse. "Ariel" is a poem about the end of the world, or at least the end of the paternal, warring world. It is a poem of mythology and history, as they both teach terrible lessons of violence and celebrate feminine power. It is the dark dissolving into the light, the male dissolving into the female, and the rise and flight of women in a new age.

Chapter Sixteen: As a Man Is, So He Sees
Card #15   The Devil Card   Corresponding Poem: "Death & Co."

On the surface, "Death & Co." is a poem written directly as a slam on Ted Hughes' character after Plath learned of his affair with Assia Wevill. Archival material suggests that Plath wrote this poem after a visit from two homosexual professors from America who approached Hughes with a job offer and a plane ticket; Hughes' family was not invited to join him. Plath later told the BBC that this was a poem about "the double or schizophrenic nature of death." She imagined aspects of death as "two men, two business friends, who have come to call" (*Ariel*, 197). This may all be true about the moment that inspired "Death & Co.," yet further study reveals there is a great deal more.

First Mirror: The Tarot/Qabalah
The meanings of the Devil card are bondage, sensual and material goals, obsession, lust, selfishness and overwhelming physical desire. The Golden Dawn attributes the Devil card to the Hebrew letter *Ayin*, meaning "the eye which allows one to see beneath the surface

structure. It is also the eye which imprisons us to focus on the surface structure." That surface structure is superficiality. Plath's words from "Death & Co." are pictured here well in illustration and meaning. We see two people, one looking down, unsmiling, with lidded eyes (*Ariel*, 35). Interestingly, in Hebrew the word *Binah* is a homograph to *Ayin*. Binah means "Wellspring of Forms" and reflects a preoccupation with the superficial. The poem's examples of bad photographs and babies' appearance contribute to this superficiality.

The Gematria/numerology student has much to reckon with in "Death & Co." The Devil (NChSh in Hebrew) and the Messiah (MShYCh) both equal 358; and the Hebrew letter *Ayin* spelled out equates with the word for *Deliverance* (Hebrew). Plath wrote "Death & Co." in five-line verses, perhaps with the Devil's five-pointed pentagram in mind.

The naked couple on the Devil card is chained together and exposed (Plath's "nude"), an analogy for a bad marriage. In *The Painted Caravan*, the hands of the Devil are described as "Taloned," Plath's condor image in this poem, as are the Devil's feet pictured on this card (Rákóczi, 55). On the Tree of Life, the Devil card's path falls between Splendor and Beauty. However, this path is not beautiful, but cold, under the influence of Capricorn, the Earth sign of Saturn and like Plath's frosty flower.

Second Mirror: Alchemy
There is a great deal of alchemical wording in "Death & Co." In the laboratory, pots and vials may be lidded, and there are trademarks, scaldings, beakers, iceboxes, fluted necked test-tubes, gowns, smoke, and of course the creation of something from its seeming opposite. The experience of alchemy—practical, psychological, or spiritual—could be said to be masturbatory as it relates entirely to the self.

"Verdigris" is "the true first matter" in alchemy, to process the philosopher's stone. Verdigris is what the V stands for in "Vitriol"—the alchemists' code name for the Latin Visita Interiora Terrae Rectificando Invenies Occultum Lapidem Veram Medicinam, which is believed to mean, "See into the interior of the purified earth, and you will find the secret stone, the true medicine" (Krummenacher).

Dew is symbolic of divine incarnation or manifestation from heaven, and thus its connection with stars is apt. Alchemists believe natural dew contains divine salt, the thoughts of the one Mind, transforming the sulfur and mercury of the First Matter. In many ways, dew represents the elixir, or contents of the cup of God or the Holy Grail, because it has completed the entire circulatory process of rain, becoming part of the earth, and rising up again through evaporation. In alchemy, the eagle (soon to be discussed) symbolizes *Volatilization*. An eagle devouring a lion indicates a fixed component overtaken by a volatile component. Alchemists believe the devil corresponds with the last operation in alchemical transformation, *Coagulation*.

In the sixth stanza's first line both meanings of "stir" are implied. The poem's speaker does not move. Nor does the alchemist stir the mixture, suggesting a waiting for change toward peace. Alchemists and mystics use the cold winter as metaphor for physical death and this waiting.

Third Mirror: Mythology

Zeus, the king god of appetite, was born in midwinter, when the sun entered the sign of Capricorn. His foster-brother was the goat god, Pan, whose myths almost all have to do with chasing lovely nymphs. The lecherous Pan was made cognate with other gods of egotistic and devilish temperaments born at the winter solstice, such as Dionysus, Apollo, and Mithras. The intention of celebrating Christ's birthday at this time was to directly counter the profane rites of the heathens (Graves, 319).

Pan, whom Plath and Hughes regularly conjured and spoke with over the Ouija board according to her letters, journals, and poems, was said to have learned masturbation from his father Hermes. This fits Plath's fifth stanza. Pan is the god of lustful, natural impulses and devilish desire. Being half-goat, half-man, Pan was so ugly he grew up in the woods, and was consequently worshiped by the mountain people of Arcadia. In myth, the goat is associated with lechery and filth, as well as being the root of the term "scapegoat," a person blamed in order for someone else to feel self-righteous. Excluding Asclepius, Pan is the only Greek god who actually dies, suggesting the death bell in the last full stanza of "Death & Co."

Dew forming a star suggests Eos, the Roman goddess of the dawn. The alchemical text *Dawn, De Aurora Libellus Apollonii* reveals that she is daughter of Hyperion, the One Above, Who Travels High Above the Earth. This is fitting for the condor in this poem. Eos carried pitchers with which she poured the dew on the earth, causing our great star, the sun, to rise.

Traditionally in myth, bells are a connection between heaven and earth, between the high and the low, announcing the presence of the holy while scattering the powers of the base and profane. The tolling of bells was often viewed as the voice of God himself. In older times, bells were relied upon to measure the hours and to divide the day into its parts. Bells toll for people only three times: at baptism, marriage, and death. The motions of bells are said to describe the cosmic dance of the elements. In Hebrew lore, bells are called the Quintessence, the fifth element in alchemy: the *magnum opus* or philosopher's stone. And of course, the gown of death brings immediate association to the ancient Greek tragedy of Medea, discussed in the sixth mirror of this poem.

Fourth Mirror: History and the World

The condor is an important symbol in shamanism and alchemy. This bird circles high above the Andes and is believed to be a messenger of the deities, carrying souls of the deceased into the Realm of the Dead. The Condor Dance has been performed for thousands of years by shaman of the Amazon and Andes, in Mayan, Aztec, and Hopi cultures, and by natives of the Bering Strait and Asian Steppes. The dance symbolizes the mysteries of life and death, and is said to manifest a shaman's inner alchemy, uniting and melting the male and female sides together. The dance celebrates and fulfills the Native American prophesy that when the condor of South America (symbolizing feminine Mother Earth) and the eagle of North America (symbolizing masculine Heaven) unite, it is the beginning of a new age; a unity of the mind and the heart.

With this in mind, "Death & Co." takes on a whole different feeling, becoming a poem of hope. Who would never look up, except for one who is already there? The female condor gazes down, representing the subservience of her sex. She has "lidded" and "balled" eyes, the "birthmarks" of her vulture species, and "nude" legs and neck.

Condor and eagle nests are up high where it is cold, like Plath's "Icebox" babies. Nests, of course, are where these baby birds are found. The eagle represents the male in the Native American prophesy. He is described well in Plath's fourth stanza, with his frilly neck, and legs like fluted Ionian gowns. Eagles have stern expressions. It is the lack of smile in the fourth stanza; quite different to the vulture-like grin of the condor in the fifth. The long, "plausive" hair may reference shaman tradition. An earlier draft compared him to a shaggy dog.

Plath's first draft tried out ideas of the male wearing yellow gloves, and she labeled him a homosexual. These lines are telling, for they show both the yellow feet and legs of the American eagle. Plath sees homosexual preference for men in line with a paternalistic society. Both Germany and America, Plath's countries of heritage, bear the eagle as their emblem.

American Indian prophecy held that in a 500-year period beginning in the 1400s, the eagle of North America would become so powerful it would virtually destroy the condor of South America, as male would dominate female. This has long been considered a metaphor for America's power and wealth ("Masturbating a glitter") as birds cannot resist objects that shine. The line also fits with the Devil card's selfishness and giving in to desire, as well as a blatant negative sexual reference.

"[D]ead bell" has many associations, and Plath surely wanted them all to apply: Rosicrucians tell a tale of Frater Gualdi, who was found lifeless after ringing the Death Bell (Rituals). An early draft of "Death & Co." followed Plath's "Death-gowns" with images of Christmas roses, the Rosicrucian's Rosy Cross. Plath's "Death & Co." shows the demise of the male American eagle, to be replaced by the female condor.

The Devil card's corresponding Neptune, a.k.a. Poseidon, was the god of horse-racing and the Devil's gambling. With horse-racing in mind, the jockey/horse team is Plath's couple in the introduction. They keep their heads down; and a running horse often has an intense "balled" eye expression, fitting the first stanza of the poem. Horses are exhibited, as this first stanza suggests, and breeding, shown in Plath's birthmarks and trademark, is important. Horses are sometimes eaten or used for animal feed, the second stanza's red meat. A jockey's legs might be compared to a beak clapping sideways; certainly the crowds in the stands applaud this way.

"I am not his yet" is the anticipation for a win. Horse racing is known for a close photo-finish, seen in the third stanza. A winning horse sometimes is adorned with a frilly wreath at its neck, and its long legs might be likened to "flutings." Horse racing goes back to the Ancient Greeks, Plath's

Ionian reference, and the sport can be deadly to both horse and rider, explaining Plath's gowns of death. The feet in the fourth stanza belong to the jockey, who neither smiles nor smokes. A horse's mane is the "long and plausive" hair to which Plath refers. As offspring of a stud, a male horse is likely a "Bastard," and a sexually charged pursuit of glitter is going after the money. The bell begins a horse race. Plath's "dead bell" and her last line recognize everyone who lost, or was possibly even killed in the race.

Goats, relating to goat-god Pan, usually give birth to twins, returning to Plath's pairing in the first line of "Death & Co." Goats have round, ball-like eyes, with three eyelids, apposite to Plath's comment on the lids. The inverted pentagram, used in satanism, resembles a goat's head; and goat is a kind of red meat eaten globally.

Mountain goats have feet called "dewclaws" on their feet, enabling them to hold their grip on steep, rocky slopes. Young goats must be protected from eagles, the highest flying North American bird comparable to Plath's condor. Less than half of goat offspring live to maturity due to falls, severe weather, and predatory birds. Mountain goats are aggressive, and destructive of their environments, very much in line with the devil. In the heights of the Rocky Mountains, the babies, or kids, may be said to be in icebox-like temperatures, as Plath's babies in this poem. Goats also have a neck frill, and the hairier mountain goats' white straight legs might be compared to Ionian fluted columns again. Goat skins have been used for coverings and gowns since ancient times. Their cloven hooves are like "two little feet" in one. Goats are known to love and pursue glittery objects, and like the evil, they love attention. These qualities make them good animals for petting zoos and fit the fifth stanza line about wanting love.

Fifth Mirror: Astrology and Astronomy

The Devil is assigned to the zodiac sign of Capricorn, the sea-goat. Capricorn is located in the part of the sky that is called the Sea, or Water, with the other water-related constellations, as in the watery second line of the second stanza. Plath's sidewise clap also fits the idea of a claw better than a beak.

The Greeks identified Capricorn with Pan, the devilish goat-horned god from whom the word "panic" originates. Pan was famous for playing his flute of reeds, fluting now corresponding with music rather than architectural detail. On the advent of the winter solstice, apropos of Plath's icebox and frost imagery, the Tropic of Capricorn is at the latitude at which the sun appears at noon.

"Without a certain continuity of effort— without a certain duration or repetition of purpose—the soul is never deeply moved. There must be the dropping of the water upon the rock."

–Edgar Allan Poe

The bluish ("Verdigris") planet Neptune was discovered within the constellation Capricornus. In 1612, Galileo mistook Neptune for a fixed star; it appeared in conjunction with Jupiter. It may be said all astronomers' eyes are "balled," as seeking planets defines their careers.

There were two men, as Plath introduces in the first line, known for the discovery of Neptune: the Frenchman Urbain Le Verrier, who did correctly calculated the planet's position within one degree, and John Couch Adams, who was twelve degrees off and worked on it with varying interest, eventually receiving equal credit with Le Verrier in the discovery. Couch is another version of Plath's bastard, stealing fame and fortune. Le Verrier did all of his work on paper, seen in the third line of the poem. He appealed to Berlin's astronomer Johann Galle to search for the planet from his better equipped observatory. Le Verrier and the French almanacs wanted to call the planet Leverrier, but the name Neptune was later decided to keep with the planetary Greek/Roman mythological nomenclature. Appropriate to the Devil tarot card, this is a story of egos, reputation, fame and competition.

Western astrologers attribute some of Neptune's negative characteristics to be illusion, confusion and deception. Neptune governs hospitals, mentioned in the third stanza, among other institutions and especially places of isolation.

In "Death & Co." the planet Neptune declares himself red meat, as everyone wants a piece of him. Also, the planet photographed poorly, given its distance and verdigris color. The baby image could be said to be Neptune's moons (not all 13 were known in Plath's time).

Sixth Mirror: Humanities and the Arts

In his *Letter to Revd Dr Trusler*, August 23, 1799, poet and artist William Blake said, "As a man is So he Sees. As the Eye is formed such are its Powers" (702). This may have been what Plath was referring to when she wrote of Blake's balled eyes.

The god Pan has been likened to the character of Puck, a faun-like prankster who appears in Shakespeare's *A Midsummer Night's Dream*, in John Milton's *L'Allegro*, in Goethe's *Faust*, and in Rudyard Kipling's *Puck of Pook's Hill*. Variations on his name and character are throughout German, Celtic, Norse and Icelandic literature.

Peter Pan of children's literature is partly based on the god Pan. Author James Barrie wrote that Peter Pan was created by violently rubbing five young brothers together. This is full of sexual implication befitting the Devil. Peter Pan is a bragging, selfish boy with a devil-may-care attitude, unaware of danger and death. He lives in Neverland, a place of no rules, with the little fairy Tinker Bell, and Peter Pan's aim is never to grow up. He says, "To die will be an awfully big adventure." Tinkerbell's cohorts were Pixie-Hollow fairies. Two of them were the frost fairy Periwinkle (the name of a flower), and Silvermist, a fairy of dew.

The villain in Peter Pan is Captain Hook, with his sidekick, Smee. It is Plath's two characters once more. Smee has round "balled" eyes, and always looks down in deference to Hook. Hook wears a frill at his neck, and he kidnaps the children with the sweet talk of the third stanza. Additionally, his hair is long and "plausive."

"Death & Co." also echoes the famous Ancient Greek story of the devilish Medea. Medea realizes her husband Jason has two women, herself and Glauce, the princess of King Creon. He wants to marry the princess for her birthright and riches, as in the second and fifth stanzas. Jason assures Medea that Glauce's money and lineage will be good for her and their children too. Medea is in a rage and sends her two children with a gift for the princess: a poisoned gown and tiara, which kills both the princess and her king father in a horrible way, befitting Plath's last line. A variation of this tale is told in Sophocles' tragedy, *The Women of Trachis*, when Hercules' wife Deianira gives him a shirt smeared with poisoned blood to ensure he remained faithful.

Early drafts of the "Death & Co." poem show that many more lines were cut entirely.[153] These lines are loaded with imagery and meaning from the Devil card, as well as eagles and birds. There are also references to horns, slaves being sold on the market, and all the Devil card traits of indul-

---

153 Early drafts are found in the Plath Collection at the Mortimer Rare Book Room, Smith College.

gence, shallowness and superficiality, as well as unease. A reference to America returns to the Indian prophecy.

Plath's own tarot book, *The Painted Caravan*, defined the Devil card as:

> "a disruption of character, the crumbling of power achieved through cruelty, domination by animal passions and mental perversity. It is the card of the sadist and all who have sold their immortal souls for temporary gain while on earth, [...] The dark forces of nature are to be understood for what they are and respected as such" (Rákóczi 56).

If this doesn't sound like the history of post-war United States of America, what does? Sylvia Plath herself described this poem as "concerning the double or schizophrenic nature of death," symbolizing the two sides of death by picturing them as contrasting men and ultimately, "Somebody's done for" (Alexander 308). Yet it seems that one of these men is the rich United States of America. Or, perhaps Plath was only talking about the physical, the devil's domain: some *body*.

Chapter Seventeen: Babble of the Golem
Card #16   The Tower Card   Corresponding Poem: "Magi"

The popular interpretation of the poem "Magi" is that Plath was offended when visitors suggested her baby Frieda was not developing fast or impressively enough. Such comments would be enough to infuriate any mother, and they were probably the starting point for Plath's aligning this poem with the Tower card, a card of upset.

First Mirror: The Tarot/Qabalah

The Tower tarot card is sometimes also known as "The Tower of Babel." It features the only man-made structure in the tarot's major arcana and symbolizes the inner and outer structures of man, error, and ignorance, struck by the lightning of spiritual comprehension. The Tower card's meaning is one of anger, a flash of clear vision and total disruption. On the path of the major arcana, it is the Devil card that leads to this dark place; now is the time to destroy that which is false and start again. The person receiving this tarot card in a reading is finished with the social facades to impress, and any sort of foundation of lies or pretension. The crown knocked off of the top is will power, but it is a false crown representing the personal will of the ego. The lightning therefore purifies and refines what is good. Thus, what is really overthrown is the delusion that we exist as separate personalities. This concept, embraced by many religions, is understood to be the cause of all human suffering and limitation. The falling figures are the two modes of personal consciousness: self-consciousness and the subconscious. The four-cornered rock tower pictured corresponds with Plath's fourth stanza of "Magi."

The Hebrew letter for the Tower card is *Peh*, meaning "mouth," the organ of speech. The Golden Dawn attributes that "word alone has the power of destroying any human creation." From the mouth comes both breath and speech. Another manifestation of *Peh*, therefore, is oracular speech; it is a combination of natural utterance and learned knowledge.

In numerology, *Peh* breaks down to the number 8, equating with the Hebrew words for "Breath" (NShMH), "Precepts, Laws" (PKVDYH), and "To Prophecy" (NAB).

The soul's journey on the Qabalah Tree of Life is called "the Lightning Flash." In *Revelation* 1:16 from the Bible, the double-edged sword issues from the mouth like a lightning bolt.

In the previous poem, "Death & Co.," Poseidon/Neptune appears as the god of horses and horse racing. In the fourth stanza of "Magi," the six-month-old colt or filly is "on all fours." "Magi" continues the horse theme with the Enochian chess game and the Qabalah's corresponding horse-like chess piece of the Knight. Chess is an abstract strategy game, which attempts to minimize luck. Nothing revealing is to be given over in facial expression, shown in the first stanza of "Magi." The white in the second stanza is the white side's pieces. Now, knights "rock" on all fours, moving four squares each time. Magi, as travelers, now become analogous to the traveling chess pieces that move across the board.

Second Mirror: Alchemy

Plath's poem, "Magi," is also an easy metaphor for the three Magi following their star to the Christ child. However, this is very much an alchemy poem, beginning with the "abstracts" that must be calculated. In alchemical treatises an *angel* symbolizes purification of the volatile principle, Plath's first line of "Magi." On Plath's working surface, she pushes around only white powder, seen in the second stanza. Alchemists assign the Tower card to correspond with the alchemical process of Dissolution, dissolving a solid in a liquid, or the reduction of a dry material in water.

An alchemical whiteness comes from dissolution. While Plath is pleased with the purity of her elements, seen in the last line of the second stanza, the tone reflecting the other interpretation of this poem is that she is not pleased with these Magi. "Magi" is plural for *Magus*, a Latin term, derived from the Greek *magos*, referring to one of the Medean tribe, who were purported to be enchanters. The word "magic" is derived from this same root.

In alchemy, multiplication is the process of distillation, in which the power of transmutation is concentrated. This explains Plath's third stanza line of multiplication's lovelessness, for distilling is work to reduce and make stronger.

A naked child symbolizes the innocent soul in alchemy. The child is the result of marriage or union and known as the philosopher's stone, or the Great Work. Plath's idea of rocking on all fours is to move through all four elements: air, fire, water, and earth with her alchemical rock of lead in its transmutation process.

In Carl Jung's studies of alchemy, he claims that the fourth century Egyptian text about alchemical dreams, *Visions of Zosimos*, presents the homunculus concept for the first time in literature. Zosimos fights a spiritual being that impales and dismembers him, skins him alive, mixes his eyes with blood, and he melts into another being, the opposite of himself. Zosimos dreams of a man boiled alive for purity and distillation, reflecting Plath's second and third stanzas. There is certainly no love there, as there is no love in the punishments and unendurable torment reflective of the Tower tarot card. Jung believed that the tormented homunculi represent transmutation from one phase to another through great pain and sacrifice.

Third Mirror: Mythology

Some say that The Tower on the tarot card portrays the Tower of Babel, believed to have been in Babylon. The tower was built as a act of hubris by Nimrod who wanted to reach the heavens. God decided to put an end to that, but not through a great flood, as he had just done earlier. Rather, God's solution was to confuse languages and spread people across the world all with different tongues, unable to communicate and finish the job. Variations of this story are found in the Bible's Book of Genesis, the Jewish Midrash, the Sibylline Oracles, the Islamic Qu'ran, the Greek's Third Apocalypse of Baruch, the Kabbalah, and more. In many versions of the story, God destroys the tower with lightning and earthquakes.

Indigenous legends of Africa, Central and South America, and Asia tell similar tales, almost all with man wanting to equal or pursue God, to conquer him. Man is torn down in the process. Stories explaining the multiplicity of languages are just as prevalent worldwide, and Plath's first stanza of "Magi" reflects this confusion and misunderstanding.

When Plath wrote of "papery godfolk," in "Magi," she referred to more than Bible paper and its people of God. She also referenced the mythological Greek and Roman gods. The Tower card is sometimes also said to represent the labyrinth of the Minotaur, which has a Poseidon connection. In Greek myth, Poseidon was angry with King Minos for not sacrificing a beautiful white bull, corresponding to the snow and chalk images in Plath's poem. Poseidon believed that after he had done so many favors for Minos, he was owed that much. The second line of "Magi" shows he did not get so much as a nose or an eye. It is not an accident that Plath used the word "Bossing" in the first stanza, as "boss" as a noun means a cow or a calf. Additionally, "bossing" can be a raised ornament in architecture, or an enlarged part of a shaft, appropriate to the Tower tarot card.

The love-goddess Aphrodite helped Poseidon with his revenge on King Minos by putting a spell on his wife, Pasiphae. A bewitched Pasiphae fell in love with the white bull and had a cow body built for her to make love to it. The lack of relation refers to bestiality, and more erotically, she must "rock on all fours." Pasiphae became pregnant with the Minotaur, the heavy and evil notion of the fourth stanza. The Minotaur was a man-eating creature with a human body and a bull's head. King Minos hid the shameful creature in a labyrinth he had built to contain it. Poseidon's son Theseus came and killed the Minotaur, and Poseidon rose from the ocean in a rage, demolishing the labyrinth, King Minos, and the body of the beast. At this time, all of King Minos' slaves were set free, Theseus was made the new king of Crete, and the labyrinth's rubble symbolized the end of an era.

The doom of the Tower card is connected to Poseidon, god of the ocean, earthquakes, drowning and shipwrecks, and Plath's boiled water. Poseidon's trident, or pitchfork, is a symbol of the lunar crescent, linking him to the powers of instinct and the night. Three is Poseidon's number for his three-pronged trident and the belief the world was divided by three, with Zeus ruling the sky, Hades ruling the underworld, and Poseidon ruling the ocean. Plath chose three-line stanzas for "Magi."

"Power floats like money, like language, like theory."

-Jean Baudrillard,
Simulacra and Simulation

A crumbling stone structure hints of Ancient Greece, and Plath mentions Plato in the last stanza of "Magi." Poseidon was said to have a fish's tail, making him cold-blooded. In Plato's dialogue, *Cratylus*, Plato translates Poseidon's name to mean either "foot-bond" (bound by the water), or else, "he knew many things." Poseidon therefore had some of Plato's brain power in addition to boiling water.

"Magi" begins with descriptions of the statues of Ancient Greece, especially the blank faces of the great philosophers, Socrates and Plato. In the second stanza Plath asks the questions of Philosophy: *What is real? What is right? What is good? What is true?*

The ruins of the Greek Temple of Poseidon at Cape Sounion, built around 440 BCE, is rectangular with a series of Doric columns on all four sides, although only fifteen stand today. The temple looks very much like a baby's "crib." In myth, Poseidon and Athena were said to have competed for the title of patron of Athens. At Plato's "crib" of the Acropolis, Poseidon offered a gift of water from a spring he created by stabbing the ground with his trident. It was salty however, and not useful. Athena offered an olive tree, from which the people got food, wood, and oil. Athena was the chosen patron of the people, angering Poseidon and causing a great flood. Plath's question at the end of "Magi" is the perfect retort.

Like Pasiphae, Poseidon had a bestial side and mated with a creature that produced the first horse (Burkert, 136-39). The Ancient Romans built two temples and a racetrack for him in

Rome. Poseidon/Neptune was one of three gods to whom it was appropriate to sacrifice bulls.

In the Bible's New Testament Gospel of Matthew, three magi followed a star to the Christ-child in Bethlehem. Plath's fifth stanza mentions this star.

Fourth Mirror: History and the World

"Magi" was a term to denote a priestly caste of followers of the Persian prophet Zoroaster, a.k.a., Zarathustra.[154] Pliny the Elder considered Zoroaster the founder of astrology and magic.[155] Greek philosopher Heraclitus of Ephesus cursed the magi for their improprieties with rites and rituals against the dogma and tradition of the time. The god-following Heraclitus was not open-minded enough to accept the magi ways. Heraclitus strictly adhered to the laws on paper, as in Plath's fifth stanza.

The three wise men following a star in the Gospel of Matthew were considered to be magi, or Zoroastrian astrologers (Boyce, 10-11). This is a turn away from the more negative meaning for magi of "magician or trickster." Two of the gifts of the magi to the Christ child in the New Testament were the aromatic resins frankincense and myrrh, documented as valuable as long ago as 345 BCE by Theophrastus, father of Botany.

Frankincense, from the Boswellia sacra tree, is so named as it was the incense favored by the Franks.[156] The tree has a lot of similarities to the Tower's meaning of pain and violent upheaval. It is tapped from its tree by slashing the bark, allowing the resins to bleed out and harden. These resins are known as "tears," apropos of the Tower. Frankincense trees grow in the most unforgiving climates and sometimes directly out of solid rock, as the pictured Tower stands. The trees endure violent storms and grow strong bulbous bases to prevent being torn away.

Myrrh, a thorny plant, derives from an Arabic word meaning "was bitter," and also grows in dry, rocky soil. It is often used in neo-paganism and ritual magick. Both plants provide healing and medicinal benefits, Plath's image of being salutary and pure.

When frankincense or myrrh is burned, the smoke hovers "like dull angels." Hebrews consecrate frankincense and myrrh, and use it in services described in the Talmud and Hebrew Bible. In the Hebrew's Exodus 30:34, it is named *Levonah*, meaning "white" in Hebrew and reflecting the second stanza of Plath's "Magi." To cultivate the frankincense is said to "milk" the tree, cognate with the fifth stanza. In Christian, Jewish and Muslim faiths, newborn babies were anointed with frankincense oil, returning to Plath's baby symbol in the poem (Segelberg, 48).

In Plath's last stanza of "Magi," the word "crib" also suggests the strategic game of cribbage, sometimes called "crib" for short. It was invented by the 17th century English poet Sir John Suckling, Plath's fifth stanza nursing mother image. The English court of law was called the Star Chamber, echoing Plath's star as well as god-like social status. The Star Chamber ordered Suckling to his country estates for absentee landlordism. Shut away there, he devoted himself to writing. This was not difficult punishment, seen in the fifth stanza. The term Star Chamber came from the Hebrew *starr*, meaning a contract or an obligation to a Jew. Like the Tower card's meaning, the Star Chamber punished reprehensible, if technically legal, actions.

Nazism is a widely-recognized theme throughout Plath's poetry, if not fully understood before

---

154 Magi also appear in *Fixed Satrs Govern a Life*'s interpretation of Plath's "The Night Dances."

155 The book Plath used to learn tarot, Rákóczi's *The painted caravan,* credits the prophetic gypsies with possessing the secrets of Zoroastrianism (Rákóczi, 13).

156 See the first mention of the Franks, a mystic Judeo-Christian sect, in the History and the World facet of *Fixed Stars Govern a Life*'s interpretation of "Lady Lazarus."

relating Plath with tarot and Jewish mysticism. Her poem, "The Night Dances" contains the line, "Their flesh bears no relation." In Plath's "Magi" is seen "Their whiteness bears no relation to laundry." It is doubtful that a perfectionist such as Plath would carelessly repeat a phrase. Beyond the mythological Minotaur seen earlier in this interpretation of "Magi," an atavistic theme of racial purity surfaces.[157] Plato, named in the last stanza of "Magi," wrote of racial purity, and believed in the theory of forms, that there was only one true creation of anything in God's mind; the rest were simulacra, from *simulacrum*, which is defined as an image or representation of something (Merriam-Webster). Plath's fifth stanza suggests rejecting a theory. In his *Sophist*, Plato used Greek statues as an example of intentionally distorted form, created to be perceived as correct from the viewer's perspective, but out of scale. Nietzsche also wrote about distorted form, as man is limited by imperfect language and reason.

French social theorist Jean Baudrillard saw four steps in the creation of a simulacrum. The simulacrum might be viewed as a kind of child or alchemical homunculus itself: simulacrum is only an abstract idea when there is no model, as seen in the "Magi" poem's first stanza; Baudrillard claims the simulacrum "bears no relation to any reality whatsoever" (Plath's second stanza); it is a perversion of reality (third stanza); it is a basic reflection of reality (fourth stanza).

In myth, mandragora are little demonic men, thought to be dolls, poppets,[158] or homunculi-like creatures created by a shaman or magician ("Magi"). These effigies are said to transfer feelings to the subject they represent; they are what most people know as *voodoo dolls*. They were sometimes created from the bulb root of the mandrake plant, which is often said to look vaguely human and has been compared to a homunculus, the first stanza of "Magi." The mandrake has paper-like star-shaped flowers, and has been used for many centuries in magic and pagan rituals. It was believed to grow under the gallows from the semen ejaculated by men after they were hanged. Its hallucinogenic properties have been tapped for love potions and to enhance fertility, referred to even in the Bible's Book of Genesis and Song of Songs. Witches who copulated with the mandrake root were said to become pregnant with children incapable of love or feelings and without souls (Plath's poetic lovelessness). When the leaves of the mandrake are boiled in milk, touching upon Plath's third and fifth stanzas of "Magi," they can be used as a poultice for ulcers, and when boiled for six hours with ivory, referring to the whiteness of the second stanza, the ivory is malleable and able to form whatever shape the artist would like. When the mandrake root is pulled from the ground, it is said to scream. While poisonous, the ancients used it as an anesthetic, a purgative, and to aid sleep, in addition to warding off demonic possession and mania (Botanical). The mandrake is a native of southern Europe and does not grow well in chalky or overly wet winter soil, the whiteness described in Plath's second line of the second stanza. "Grimm's Saga No. 84," from *Grimm's Fairy Tales*, proclaimed that the mandrake had oracular powers to answer questions about the future. On July 4, 1958, Plath wrote in her journals of translating *Grimm's Fairy Tales* from their original German.

Fifth Mirror: Astrology and Astronomy
Astrology and astronomy are studies of "abstracts" and measurement of the sky. The constellations are crude depictions of figures, without the detail of noses or eyes, Plath's second line. Astrologers may be said to be acting like the bosses of these blanks, as the third line of "Magi" suggests, assigning stars to certain constellations. The second and third stanzas of "Magi" describe the white stars themselves.

157 These are more fully explored in this book's interpretations of Plath's poems such as "Cut" and "Daddy."
158 Poppets, or small human figures used in sorcery and witchcraft, are not the same thing as puppets, which can be representations of all people and animals, and usually have no mystical purpose.

Sky activity, as seen from Earth, actually took place about six months before it was witnessed, fitting the first line of the fourth stanza. The sky is divided into four quadrants, representing the four seasons, and the fours rocking in Plath's poem. The Milky Way was thought to be a pool of cow's milk to the Ancient Egyptians, and the Greeks believed the milk was from Hera, Plath's fifth stanza mother. Zeus tricked Hera into suckling his illegitimate child Heracles/Hercules, the no relation in "Magi," to give him godlike powers. Older Greek myth held the Milky Way to be a herd of cows with bluish glowing milk, the symbol of bleached white laundry of the second stanza.

In the Gospel of Matthew, the Star of Bethlehem guided the magi (also called the "three kings" or "wise men") to the Christ child. The book does not say that the child was found *in* Bethlehem, rather, that they followed the star and found the child *near* it. The name Bethlehem translates to "House of Flesh" or "House of Bread." This is another name for Virgo, the constellation of the virgin holding a sheaf of wheat. There are three stars in the constellation Orion's Belt, which have been known since ancient times as "the three kings." On December 24th of every year, these stars align with Sirius, the brightest star in the eastern sky, pointing to the sunrise. This is why the kings are said to follow the star in the east. Virgo's ancient glyph is an altered letter M, which explains why the Virgin Mary and many other virgins of other religions have names beginning with M, such as Adonis' mother, Myrra, and Buddha's mother, Maya. Many other major ancient religions such as Mithra of Persia (1200 BC), Krishna of India (900 BC), Dionysus of Greece (500 BC), and Attis of Greece (200 BC), share this story of virgin birth, the three kings following a star in the east, the ideas of crucifixion, resurrection, and more. Perhaps this is why Plath wrote that these god-folk are mistaken over their star.

During the time of the three magi and the birth of Christ, King Herod the Great was said to have felt threatened that he may be usurped, and so he demanded that every male child under the age of two should be killed in and around Bethlehem. Herod was known to have murdered many, and so he well fits Plath's fourth stanza's heavy evil notion.

Neptune, the Roman's name for Poseidon, was the first planet found by mathematics rather than through observation, Plath's hovering abstracts and theory. Galileo had in fact sighted and documented his observation of Neptune in 1612; however, he mistook it for a fixed star, as Plath's fifth stanza echoes.[159]

The fourth planet, Mars, is made of rock, suggesting a noun instead of a verb for the rock in the fourth stanza. Mars was named after the Roman god of war, another good match for the anger of the Tower card. On Mars is Olympus Mons, Latin for the Greek's Mount Olympus, home of the gods and Plato's crib. One of the tallest mountains in the solar system, Olympus Mons was discovered in the early 19th century. Since the late 19th century, Olympus Mons was considered to be an albedo feature on Mars, albedo being an alchemical term defining the mountain's whiteness, seen in the second stanza of "Magi." The mountain was formed from the pressure of a volcano, Poseidon's disastrous domain.

Sixth Mirror: Humanities and the Arts

If one looks closely at the faces of the falling figures on the Tower tarot card, they resemble the blank oblong expression of terror in the famous painting by Norwegian artist, Edvard Munch, "The Scream." Plath's first stanza of "Magi" describes these faces in both the painting and on the card perfectly, and "The Scream," of course, fits the Tower card's meaning, as well as the legendary sound of the mandrake root pulled from the ground.

---

159 Neptune's discovery is also part of the *Fixed Stars Govern a Life* interpretation for Plath's "Death & Co."

The idea of the homunculus or simulacrum appears throughout fiction, and in much of "Magi." Examples are found in Ovid's *Metamorphoses*' character, Galatea, whose name means, "she who is milk-white." Galatea and her lover Acis were surprised by a jealous Cyclops, the facial vulgarity of the second line of "Magi." The Cyclops killed Acis with a boulder. This tale inspired several stories by Dostoevsky, including "Golden Age," "A Raw Youth," "The Devils" and "The Dream of a Ridiculous Man."[160]

The golem in Jewish folklore is an unfinished human made of mud, as Adam was. A golem is dumb and helpless, or else huge, strong and brainless, and sometimes hostile. A holy word is inscribed upon its forehead or placed inside its mouth to animate it. In the earliest of golem stories from the Talmud, a golem is proclaimed created by magicians and commanded to return to dust, supporting the "Magi" idea once again. The entire "Magi" poem, with its abstracts, blank face, lack of relation, lovelessness, lack of ability, and the mistake of it is now Plath's brilliant take on the man-created monster.

The Magician is a 1908 novel by W. Somerset Maugham based on occultist Aleister Crowley. Plath had two other books by Maugham in her personal library, and so it is likely she knew of this one as well. *The Magician* features much romantic drama between a magician and others, ending in the discovery of a laboratory where the magician has been murdering the living to create homunculi. Crowley reviewed the book for *Vanity Fair* under the fictional protagonist's name, claiming it plagiarized from several books on the Qabalah, alchemy, Rosicrucianism and also from H.G. Wells' *The Island of Dr. Moreau*.

The Life and Opinions of Tristram Shandy, Gentleman is a 1759 novel by Laurence Sterne and also mirrors multiple themes and correlations in Plath's "Magi." Plath had this book in her personal library. Tristram narrates his story, telling of distractions and annoyances while he was a mere homunculus in the womb. Tristram's nose was crushed by the forceps of Doctor Slop. Noses are therefore very important to Tristram, who was raised to believe that a large and important nose leads to success. Shandy speaks on obstetrics and babies. He plays with and mocks philosophical ideas as Plath does with Plato in "Magi." Tristram refers to whimsical obsessions as "hobby-horses," touching again on Poseidon's animal. He was supposed to be named for the great Hermetic deity, Hermes Trismegistus, who is a synthesis of the Egyptian Toth and the Greek Hermes, but his name was mangled and confused with "Tristan." If Plath and Hughes were indeed the Hermeticists the evidence suggests they were, she must have enjoyed that detail. The book *Tristram Shandy* was admired by Arthur Schopenhauer, Johann Wolfgang von Goethe, Karl Marx, and Friedrich Nietzsche.

Tristram Shandy was inspired by a Robert Burton novel called *The Anatomy of Melancholy*, one of the first stream-of-consciousness books, originally published in 1621. It begins with an astrological calculation of the author's nativity, Plath's first line of "Magi." The story also has all the images found in "Magi": whiteness, Neptune, Plato, evil, and the idea that insensitive, never-satisfied people continue to multiply.

In 1941, Jorge Luis Borges wrote a short story called "The Library of Babel" that has also been available in a collection entitled *Labyrinths*, connecting to the Minotaur and Tower of Babylon as they relate to the Tower tarot card. Borges' story is about a vast library with interlocking hexagonal rooms. These rooms contain the conception of the universe, and the tale begins with the "abstracts" of its shelves and railings. It sounds very much like the hexagonal Qabalah Tree of Life. Mundane details are given a strange importance in the story. Borges wrote of the lamps providing light as a "spherical fruit," like stars.

---

160 Plath was an avid reader and lover of Dostoevsky, and had written her college thesis on his theme of the Double.

Borges illustrates the scene on the Tower card in this line from "The Library of Babel": "Once I am dead, there will be no lack of pious hands to throw me over the railing; my grave will be the fathomless air; my body will sink endlessly and decay and dissolve in the wind generated by the fall, which is infinite."

Borges' fictional library contains all useful information, future predictions, biographies of every person, and translations of every book. The books however are unreadable gibberish (babble), and the librarians are in a state of suicidal despair, fitting the Tower card. There are the "Purifiers" (Plath's "Salutary and pure") who arbitrarily destroy books they deem useless in a quest for perfection and truth. The story opens with a quotation from *The Anatomy of Melancholy*. Borges has many other Kabbalistic and Hebrew-themed writings informed with the knowledge only a Kabbalist would have, including the poem "The Golem," the stories "The Aleph," "Death and the Compass," and "The Secret Miracle," and four short stories concerning labyrinths. Interestingly, women are almost entirely absent from Borges' work. Plath might again ask her final question about what girl would flourish there. Several mathematicians have written of the complex and elegant mathematics in Borges' stories, and that Borges had at least a cursory knowledge of set theory, hinting at Plath's images of abstracts and theory once again.

The homunculus-like magical mandrake plant is found throughout literature, in much of Shakespeare (*Othello, Antony and Cleopatra, Romeo and Juliet, King Henry VI*), in Machiavelli (*Mandragola*, or, "The Mandrake"), in D.H. Lawrence, and in Samuel Beckett (*Waiting for Godot*), all writers revered by Plath. Beckett appears again in the Arts and Humanities mirror of this poem.

The homunculus is throughout 20th-century literature, too. The famous 1911 novel by Hanns Heinz Ewers and the 1928 movie of the same name, *Alraune*, German for "Mandrake," is about a laboratory-developed woman, created from the semen of a hanged murderer and implanted in a surrogate mother prostitute. The girl conceived has no concept of love, reflected in Plath's third stanza of "Magi." She seduces many men and kills without conscience.

Mary Shelley's *Frankenstein* contains a twist on the man-made golem, and it is interesting to note that one of the themes is a parent/creator's responsibility to his creation. This draws a parallel between Plath's feelings about Hughes and their children, and Shelley's personal life; her husband, Percy Shelley, had an affair with Mary's stepsister at the time their child, two months premature, died two weeks after its birth (Spark, 39).

Carlo Collodi's *The Adventures of Pinocchio* is another literary golem, and so beloved that even Tolstoy later wrote a Russian version of the story called *Burattino*. Whitewashed into a Disney movie in 1940, the original Pinocchio "bears no relation" to the friendly puppet boy with whom most of us are familiar: Disney features a woodcarver named Geppetto, who creates a boy out of wood and wishes upon a falling star for him to be real. The puppet Pinocchio is directed that he must be brave, truthful and unselfish, sounding just like Plath's last line of the second stanza, if he is to ever become a real boy.

Collodi's original Pinocchio however, was a nasty, impish character who was humiliated, hanged, robbed, kidnapped, stabbed, whipped, starved, jailed, punched in the head, had his legs burned off, and was emotionally abused for his sins. Pinocchio was dunked in flour until "he was white from head to foot and looked like a puppet made of plaster," echoing the second stanza of Plath's "Magi." Pinocchio was terrified of thunder and lightning, pictured on the Tower tarot card, and under stress, the boy-puppet's nose grew. Pinocchio was collared and strapped like a dog in a kennel, rocking on all fours like a baby in a crib. He was also made to dress like a girl and dance absurdly, causing more emphasis on the "What girl" part of Plath's last questioning line. The Blue

Fairy advised him, "Try and do better in the future and you will be happy," which sounds like a paraphrase of Beckett's, "Try again. Fail again. Fail better."

The showman takes pity on Pinocchio, and says, "Your lamentations have given me a pain in my stomach!" like Plath's belly ache. Disney's "Pleasure Island" was originally Collodi's "Land of Boobies," a hedonistic place of never-ending desserts and summer vacation all year long, with its name suggesting breastfeeding, as in Plath's fifth stanza. Ultimately, *Pinocchio*'s author Collodi chose to write for children because "grownups are too hard to satisfy," sounding much like the last stanza of Plath's "Magi" (Rich).

Friedrich Hölderlin, 18th-century German poet. is another surprising fit to the Tower card and the idea of "Magi." He wrote pantheistic, Neoplatonic poems celebrating the universe and divine oneness. Philosopher Friedrich Nietzsche had a deep appreciation for him, as well as Martin Heidegger, who interpreted Hölderlin's work. Hölderlin had an intense relationship with his mother ("And Love the mother of milk") who controlled his finances until her death. The French Revolution was a turning point in Hölderlin's life, and emulating his favorite philosophers of ancient Greece, he dreamed of inner freedoms from which a free society with Athenian ideals might emerge. In his book, *Holderlin, 'The Poet in the Tower,'* reviewer J.M. Coetzee wrote:

> "The Revolution, said Hölderlin, gave an intimation of how the gap could be bridged between ideas and reality, between the realm of the divine and the world. En kai pan: what had once been whole and good, and had then fallen apart, could be put together again. To search out traces of lost unity in the chaos of appearance we have only the aesthetic sense to rely on; to philosophy and poetry falls the task of healing what was broken" (Coetzee).

This is essentially the meaning of the Tower card, and Coetzee even calls Hölderlin "The Poet in the Tower" in his review's title, referring to the madness Hölderlin faced in later years.

Hölderlin obtained the degree of Magister, close in sound to "Magi," and meaning "master." However, Hölderlin's fits of rage, also very much in line with the Tower card and Plath's "Magi," made him unsuitable as a teacher of young children. A century after his death, Hölderlin was viewed as German prophet/poet and his work embraced by the Nazi's Third Reich. He was said to break apart good poems and rebuild them from the ground up, or sometimes abandon projects completely, all portrayed in the Tower card (Coetzee).

It might be said that there are three kings, or "magi," in the history of Irish literature who all reflect the Tower tarot card: W.B. Yeats, James Joyce, and Samuel Beckett. These three Irishmen were friends, Jungians, poets, novelists, and playwrights battling terrible, debilitating depression and dark temperaments. Plath and Hughes idolized all three writers.

A derelict 16th-century Norman stone tower was an important place for the mystic poet and visionary, W.B. Yeats. In 1917, he purchased Thoor Ballylee ("Thoor" is the Irish word for "tower") near Coole Park in Galway, Ireland. Yeats restored it and spent many of his later summers there writing poetry. Plath's journals are full of mentions of reading Yeats, criticism of Yeats, and her own comparisons of William and Georgie Yeats with herself and Hughes. "As we know from numerous occult notebooks and papers," writes a biographer, "W.B. could cast a horoscope, trace Hebrew letters or astrological symbols, or copy a kabalistic drawing with the best of his fellow adepts in the Order of the Golden Dawn" (Brown, 264). Not surprising, then, Plath's poem, "Magi," reflects Yeats' work, "The Tower."

Yeats' Thoor Ballylee was a significant place for Plath, because it was on a vacation here that she and Hughes tried to heal their marriage. Hughes, however, abandoned Plath there in Ireland to run off with his mistress, Assia Wevill. Shortly thereafter, Plath, believing bibliomancy guided her with words from one of Yeats' plays, moved into Yeats' Fitzroy Road house in London. It was the apartment in which Plath endured one of the worst winters London had ever known and where she committed suicide.

Plath's second line of "Magi," with its "nose or an eye" echoes Yeats' seventh line in the first stanza of his poem, "The Tower": "Imagination, nor an ear and eye." Plath's Plato reference connects to Yeats' same stanza line that he must "Choose Plato and Plotinus for a friend," and his second-to-last line of that stanza, "In abstract things; or be derided by" reflects Plath's image of abstracts.

In 1914, Yeats wrote "The Magi," a poem about the unsatisfied ones on their search for meaning. In Yeats' poem, the magi not only witness the birth of Christ, but his crucifixion on Calvary. Some readers relate this poem to Yeats' "Second Coming," believing both poems address the birth of the anti-Christ and the Biblical end of the world. In this view, Yeats sees the second coming as a means of resolution through destruction, like the Tower tarot card.

Yeats' life was full of Tower card-like emotional tragedy. He was famous for his many proposals to, and rejections by, the love of his life, Maud Gonne. This was followed by rejection from her daughter, Iseult. It was an astrologically propitious time, so he married the young Georgie Hyde-Lees. The two settled into what biographer Terence Brown called "An Occult Marriage" of automatic writing, alchemy, astrology, tarot, meditation, and other magic practices (Brown). It was essentially the same kind of marriage that Plath and Hughes built together fifty years later.

In 1914, Yeats wrote "The Magi," who not only witness the birth of Christ but his crucifixion. Some have related this poem to "The Second Coming," thinking Yeats addresses in both poems the end of the world and recreation through destruction, the meaning of the Tower card.

Yeats considered his greatest literary work to be *A Vision*, a 1925 mystical treatise documenting his qabalistic occult system used in literature. Yeats' phrase, "moments of crisis," an important element of his automatic script technique, is symbolized by a qabalistic lightning flash, akin to the Tower card in picture and meaning (Yeats).

The next in the trio of Irishmen, Samuel Beckett, was born on Good Friday in 1906, a day also reflecting the Tower card. Beckett wrote the play, "Of the Clouds," inspired by the last verse of Yeats' poem, "The Tower." Beckett once remarked, "I had little talent for happiness," and like a golem, considered himself dead and without human feeling. Beckett's characters are known for their unending grief and bewilderment.

A mentor and friend of Beckett's was James Joyce, another of Plath and Hughes' favorite writers. Their wedding day was intentionally scheduled for June 16th, Joyce's famous "Bloomsday," the day on which *Ulysses* takes place. Joyce suffered from keraunophobia, or fear of thunder and lightning, seen on the Tower card. In Dublin, Ireland stands a 19th-century Martello tower built during the Napoleonic Wars, and officially known as the James Joyce Tower and Museum. Joyce spent six nights in this tower, leased from the British War Office by a friend. The opening scenes of *Ulysses* are set here.

Pain always accompanies the Tower tarot card, as it does in the plotlines of much great literature. When this card turns up in a reading, it is time for the questioner to tear down the foundation, to question who or what one has been serving or attempting to please, to do away with the golem and use one's own magi powers in the quest for wholeness. Plath knew that she, or any girl, could not flourish otherwise.

Chapter Eighteen: Diamonds are a Girl's Best Friend
Card #17   The Star Card   Corresponding Poem: "Lesbos"

On the surface, Plath's "Lesbos" is disgust with marriage, motherhood, and the failings of what had once been the family dream. At the time of this poem's creation, October 18, 1962, Hughes had just left Plath for good. After Hughes had come by to retrieve his clothes, Plath packed up the children and two kittens and went on her first independent excursion to the emerald beaches of St. Ives, Cornwall, to visit a lesbian couple she knew there (*LH*, 469). Hughes omitted this poem from the original UK version of *Ariel*, so as not to offend them. "Lesbos" has been considered one of Plath's most venomous poems; readers often miss its overt references to Hollywood fame and stardom, and especially how this affects women.

First Mirror: The Tarot/Qabalah
The meaning of The Star card is one of hope, dreams and expressions of love. It can emphasize feminine sexuality and also celebrity. Reversed, it may indicate delayed or unfulfilled dreams; pessimism and doubt; lack of trust; insecurity with sexual identity; and inability to express love and affection. The Golden Dawn assigns the Hebrew letter *Tzaddi* to The Star card, meaning: "the fish-hook that plunges itself into the depths of the unconscious (Moon) in order that beauty and order (Venus) be recovered for the greater whole—the world, or humanity (Aquarius)." This card is another metaphor for moving out of the Age of Pisces and into the new Age of Aquarius, an idea first visited in Plath's "Ariel" poem. The Hebrew correlative fishhook symbolizes fishing for truth and spirituality in the murky depths of the psyche. *Tzaddi* consists of the letters that mean "hook," "door," and "hand" in Hebrew. A close look at "Lesbos" shows that Plath presents all three: She is hooked to a husband; she talks of peering from the door; and the false life closes on her like a baby's fist.

The "Lesbos" poem matches the description of the Aquarian water bearer well. The water washes away the past, leaving room for a fresh, new start. In The Star card's picture, the pouring water breaks into five separate rivulets. Correspondingly, in Plath's "Lesbos," there are five people in this poetic kitchen: two mothers and three children. Plath's puppet image reflects the woman's position in the picture on the tarot card, looking like a marionette with cut strings. She dips into a pool like Plath's well of cement; Plath would have been more accurate to say "concrete," but cement is a *binding* agent, another prison metaphor.

Sometimes The Star signifies a trip to the country, and a need for contact with nature. "Lesbos" is a lack of contact, The Star reversed: the women are shut inside with the children. The kittens are outside in the well where they cannot be heard crying. The smell of cooking and dirty diapers opening the second stanza suggests that they all really need some fresh air.

When The Star card relates to work, it concentrates on human rights and equality of the sexes, the subject of which "Lesbos" complains most about. The woman on The Star card is alone, the double orphan of the second stanza's sixth line.

Other moments in the poem point to details in the card's design: "In New York, Hollywood" are places for movie and theater stars, and corresponds to the pictured seven stars of Pleiades, or Seven Sisters. The Romans believed the Pleiades were "Virgins of the Spring," arriving in May, the most fertile time of the year. "Lesbos" is full of images of femininity, fertility, and sexuality, although most of these pictured are negative. Plath herself had her "tubes blown out" by a gynecologist to increase the chances of her fertility in the spring before she and Hughes left for Yaddo artists' community (*LH*, 352). Finally, in the eleventh line of the second stanza, Plath accuses someone, possibly herself, of acting and pretending she is someone she isn't.

Second Mirror: Alchemy

Alchemists ascribe The Star card to the alchemical phase of purification. In *The Secret Tradition in Alchemy*, Arthur Waite wrote: "The revelation comes in a stillness which is as if after a tempest: it is then that the darkness dissolves, the sun rises and the treasure is found" (Waite, 285).

Plath's tempest is throughout the poem "Lesbos" from its very first line. When one looks more closely at "Lesbos" however, this woman friend Plath complains to is her physical self, stuck in the world. "Lesbos" then becomes a schizophrenic battle with the self, named in the tenth line. There are urges to lash out in upset, with suggestions of drowning kittens and children to escape it all. In "Lesbos," Plath embraces the alchemist's sulfurous, fiery aspects of her ugliest self. It is her shadow rival, as Dostoevsky did battles and conversations with his own ugly doubles. The spirit has only itself to worry over. Plath's body self is the speaker of the poem, made clear with her counting babies (bodies) in the twenty-eighth line.

Plath's eighteenth line of "Lesbos" lets go of the past and the voices within that keep her rooted in the negative. It is a line about future dreams, which The Star card and alchemy represent. The Star card is "schizophrenic" in its upright joyful meaning and reversed meaning of frustration and lost dreams; its inability to alchemically unite the two psychological selves; and its inability to cast off the body and become pure spirit form. Reversed, this card well reflects the last line of "Lesbos." Plath's higher and lower selves are unable to meet in that Zen Buddhist heaven where everything is a gift and the world is mere illusion.

The alchemical need for the unity of self presents its face again in the poem's suggestion of meeting in a different life, somewhere more ethereal.

"Through?" is an interesting question to be asked by Hollywood, the land of the stars. The reader assumes men asked her if she was finished, either in the sex act or her acting career. But this word is also about bursting through, finding both the true self of Jungian Alchemy and the spiritual world.[161] "Lesbos" therefore is a poem much about alchemy and the alchemical marriage. As all elements are within us, the alchemist's job is to heighten his or her consciousness to gain an understanding of the universe. Outwardly, the alchemist uses animal, vegetable, and mineral in an effort to transmute and purify. Inwardly, the alchemist uses symbolic language and images to point to a personal and spiritual transformation. This inner alchemy, based on intuition, mysticism and imagination, is said to be the feminine force.

"Lesbos" therefore acknowledges the alchemical stage of "Blackening." Considered the most difficult stage, it is about separating oneself from appearances, and drowning in the cosmic feminine nature, as Plath is directed to drown kittens. Consider that "kitten" is sometimes a slang term for a woman; childlike and getting no respect. Blackening is considered to be death, marriage, separation, and descent into hell simultaneously. It is the bad marriage of "Lesbos."

---

161 "Through" is the final and most powerful word of Plath's famous poem "Daddy."

Alchemical transcendence is achieved through the physical union of King and Queen. He is the red man of fire, she the white woman of water or Mercuric Quicksilver. Plath includes these colors in her eleventh line. In early alchemical texts, this union was often incestuous and depicted by a mother taking her son back into her body, Plath's twenty-fifth line of eating up a little boy. Jung described this symbolic mother as the unconscious, and the boy as consciousness. The mental must be reabsorbed into the potentiality of the soul; man enters the symbolic woman to be dissolved before he can be reborn as pure.

Alchemists personify animal, vegetable and mineral, to gain insight into the human psyche. Plath's journals reflect this mindset of life in all. She practiced the godlike perspective of breathing life into everything, and of sharing the experience of "being" inanimate objects (*UJ*, 307). In "Lesbos," alchemical personification is alive, i.e., "The potatoes hiss" like dangerous creatures. Plath's poetic kitchen is now the scientific laboratory, windowless, with paper strips, tubes, smells, stink, the smog of cooking, a lightning rod, and acid baths.

"[S]tink of fat" results from making Liquor Hepatis, a.k.a., Balsam of the Soul, a substance created by alchemists with wax and fat to capture the essence of a liquid. Likewise, burning Sulfur smells like "baby crap." The union with the double is evident in the second stanza. Plath's images of heads floating, and the bones and hair around these "two venomous opposites," give the impression of bodies being dissected in some kind of experiment.

An alchemist endures ulcers from chemical burns and coughing fits from fumes, the second stanza's seventh line. When Plath writes of the husband lumping downhill on the cobbled road, it is metaphor for the lump of stone after repeated doses of acid in an acid bath, dropped on it from above, as seen in the second stanza. The disintegrating stone slowly works its way down the slant of the alchemist's pan like Plath's "Flogged trolley."

Alchemists work with gems and minerals, Plath's second stanza comment on rarity. There are sometimes sparks, as seen in the last two lines of that stanza. Additionally, the proper cutting of a gemstone with long rod-like crystals is called a "Star," relating to this tarot card. Using a single light source, Plath's lightning pole, a jewel's reflection produces lines in even numbers with a common center. It is the valuable jewel that opens the third stanza. Minerals and gems are cleaned with acid baths to remove rust and debris, another good analogy for the dirty body seeking purification.

The Moon represents silver and water in alchemy. A "blood bag" is the physical body; it is nothing but a "sick / Animal." In "Lesbos," Plath is eager to be done with this physical misery and move into the alchemist's second phase of *Albedo,* or whiteness. This is represented by salt, the third element in the trinity that constitutes the philosopher's stone. Plath addresses the material body reaching this phase in the third stanza's seventh line. She works sand "like dough, a mulatto body, / The silk grits." This is the third phase, the Red Elixir. Arab alchemists referred to this phase as simply "elixir," meaning "yeast." As yeast makes dough rise, "multiplication" of spiritual energy heals the imperfect and impure, represented by the mulatto image. Silk grits are small pieces of talcum. Talcum, a word of Arabic origin, means "little sparkling Stars," apt for this tarot card. Talcum is a label given by metallurgists to stone composed of layers or flakes and impervious to fire. Sometimes these flakes are called *scales*, they are dense, fragile, and sometimes sparkling. It is the sheen of Plath's sand in the third stanza.

Plath's acid vase in the fourth stanza is Vitriol, or Sulfuric Acid, the most important liquid in alchemy. When distilled to its pure form, it is severely corrosive. Plath incorporated both meanings of vitriol in "Lesbos," as liquid and emotion. The alchemical 'vas' or vat, sometimes called "the chalice," symbolizes the feminine body. The man in Plath's life, whether Hughes or a masculine half of herself, is in love with base, lowly behavior represented by lead, the base metal, as a "ball and chain." She is sick and tired of working for him.

The work of Blackening prepares Mercury in a way that it begins to congeal, the double thickness of the third line in Plath's fourth stanza. Psychologically, the alchemist detaches from his or her separate existence, extracts vital force from mental and bodily attractions, and painfully and quietly recollects within the self as still water. It is Plath's comment of being silent and up to her neck with hatred.

Salt is considered bitter in alchemy, yet it is a symbol for knowledge and wisdom. Self-knowledge is bitter, painful, and sometimes symbolized as sea water. "Lesbos" is loaded with bitter self-knowledge and plenty of the sea in its fourth and fifth stanzas.

In "Lesbos," Plath seems on the brink of transmutation, peering from its door. In the last lines of the fourth stanza, she is disgusted with her earthly, impure body, likening herself to a hag and a whore. It is imagery of both the crone and maiden, yet Plath does not look down upon the mother, the other aspect of the triple-goddess. Plath wants to talk to God in that last line of the fourth stanza, and yet feels she cannot.

Alchemists of Ancient Egypt and Sumeria revered prostitutes, Plath's whore image, as holding a path to enlightenment. Isis herself was known as both virgin and sacred prostitute. These women exemplified merging of sexual and spiritual energy, known as Kundalini. Male initiates believed they were able to transform and heal through sacred sex. Women were the transformers, not necessarily in need of transformation themselves. This is also in line with Jewish Kabbalah, which holds that women do not need to pray in the temple; not out of sexism, but because females naturally communicate with God. The womb therefore represents the alchemical vessel for transformation. This is why motherhood, through all of its trials in "Lesbos," is not mocked in the same way as aging and sexuality.

Writer Maurice Aniane states that the Blackening stage reverses "the cosmogenic process of Genesis," dissolving the "hardened earth into the unity of primordial water." The goal is to perceive nature and the body as playing with the illusion of individuality, and to rise above this illusion. "The discovery of this interplay is a marriage in which cosmic femininity prevails over masculine objectification. It is a liberating dissolution, which draws the virile force back from separative modes of action and of knowledge in order to bathe it in the baptismal water of universal life" (Aniane).

Alchemy uses the raw materials of nature, and it is both inner and outer, hard and painful, matching Plath's rawness in the last full stanza of "Lesbos." Plath knows that when she achieves alchemical transmutation, she will never return to what she was, the "That is that" repetition in the fourth stanza. At the end of "Lesbos," Plath weakly comforts her body, pretending she might return to the old life, knowing it is a lie.

Third Mirror: Mythology

The woman on The Star tarot card is considered to be Eve, representing the feminine side of human nature. In the Bible, Eve was unable to resist the temptation to eat of the fruit of knowledge from the Tree of Life.

Matching Eve in Greek myth is Pandora, a dazzling virgin created by the gods. She probes for the truth despite the consequences, and she releases all the Spites, evil creatures, from a forbidden box. Plath's "Lesbos" might be said to be a spiteful poem from the very first line. The god Hermes had given Pandora a treacherous heart and a mouth full of lies, reflecting Plath's seventh line of

"Lesbos." Pandora was soon married off to Epimetheus, whose name means "hindsight." Marriage is a key theme in "Lesbos." Pandora arrived to Epimetheus, with this locked chest of Spites and a warning that the chest should not be opened.

Pandora was as foolish as she was beautiful, however. She could not resist and opened the chest, releasing the terrible afflictions Zeus had gathered upon mankind: Old Age, Labor, Sickness, Insanity, Vice, and Passion, all qualities present in Plath's "Lesbos." Only Hope, the meaning of The Star card, which had somehow also been put in the chest, did not fly away. Hope is therefore shown as the female figure, the irrational and intuitive side, which sees the star of Hope through a dark cloud of Spites. For Pandora and The Star card, nothing is corrected, there is no plan, the Spites do not leave, and yet Hope remains.

The Pleiades is a star cluster in the sky pictured on this tarot card. In Greek myth, the Pleiades are said to be the seven daughters of the Titan Atlas and the sea-nymph Pleione. The Pleiades sisters were all mothers. Myth holds that all seven were so sad for their father, who was forced to carry the heavens on his shoulders, Plath's "Flogged trolley." In their grief, the sisters committed suicide, the ultimate loss of hope. Zeus immortalized the girls by placing them in the sky, but only after having raped most of them and had them bear his children.

One of the Pleiades daughters was Alcyone. According to mythologist Robert Graves, Alcyone and her husband Ceyx, meaning "sea-mew," another name for seagull, dared to impersonate Hera and Zeus. As punishment, Zeus drowned Ceyx. Alcyone drowned herself in grief. The sea-mew/gull is sacred to Aphrodite, goddess of love and the sex-kitten of Mount Olympus. This "sea-mew" drowning explains Plath's drowned kittens and girl in "Lesbos."

Another daughter was Maia, honored at marriages by the Greeks. Marriage, however, was abhorrent to this goddess. Maia was raped by Zeus, and from this event conceived Hermes. Maia's name in Greek refers to an older mother, sometimes a midwife. Her month was May and Romans never married in this month as it was considered unlucky. May was also the month Romans threw puppets into the river in offering to Saturn, seen in Plath's puppet image (Graves, 175).

The Pleiad Electra was also raped by Zeus. She gave birth to Dardanus, the founder of Troy. She was said to be the lost sister, disappearing in grief after the destruction of her son's great city. This myth was created to explain her diminishing light since ancient times. About Electra, diminished by marriage, poet Elizabeth Worthington Fiske wrote: "Thy beauty shrouded by the heavy veil Thy wedlock won" (Allen, 406). The Pleiad sister Merope was said to be less bright than the others because she hid her face in shame for marrying a mortal man. Another myth tells of her going to Hades with her husband.

The ancient poet Sappho's Fragment 58, a nearly complete poem about old age, refers to the Greek myth of the plight of Tithonus who fell in love with the goddess Eos. Eos requested that Tithonus be immortal, but forgot to ask for him to remain forever young; this is a problem for mythological stars as well as Hollywood ones.

Celtic mythology also makes an appearance in "Lesbos," with reference to Morveren, the Mermaid of Zennor, a village off the coast of Cornwall. The mermaid was a once-beautiful woman who bewitched a man so that he let her pull him underwater. He was never seen again. Plath's lines about keeping the husband in, dragging a "blood bag" and a sick animal all echo this tale. It is a twist on love and marriage ruining her life, with the man pulled down instead.

Fourth Mirror: History and the World

The Greek island of Lesbos has been home to poets and philosophers since ancient times. Perhaps the best-known resident of Lesbos was Sappho, the first female poet in recorded history, who wrote emotionally charged poems of love, lust, loss and more to other women. In the way that Hughes connected the Tree of Life cycle from one poem to another in his own work, Plath's closing line in the previous poem, "Magi," "What girl ever flourished in such company?" launches into "Lesbos." There is also the "Little unstrung puppet" phrase, suggesting *Pinocchio* in both poems. "I can't communicate," as we have seen, is reminiscent of the Tower of Babel in "Magi."

Born between 630 and 612 BCE, little is known of Sappho's life beyond fragments of her poetry, as the clear historical voices and static of the eighteenth line of "Lesbos." Plath knew of Sappho, as this is the name she gave her cat in Boston, and in her journals she considered Sappho to be a historical poetic rival (*UJ*, 360).

Sappho wove Greek myth, such as scenes from Homer's *Iliad*, into her work. It is presumed that most of Sappho's work was lost by barbarian attacks on the library in Alexandria, or more likely, lost through book burnings by the Catholic Church, who did not approve of her pagan hymns to goddesses, and suggested promiscuity and eroticism. In the 19th century, Sappho's lesbianism fell into the Church's disfavor. Homosexuality was quite normal in her culture, and many ancient Greek men were openly homosexual or bisexual (whether it was equally approved of for women is not certain). In any case, Homeric Greek became the most studied, and Sappho's difficult Aeolic Greek dialect was considered ancient and arcane, even by the time of the Roman Empire. In correlation with the paternalistic turn in society and the loss of goddess worship, Plath might have identified Sappho's work as squashed by masculine ideals. Plath's "Lesbos" is full of female disdain in lines such as the fifteenth and sixteenth calling the girl "bastard," and the twenty-first line suggesting drowning her.

Ovid wrote of Sappho mourning the death of at least one parent by age six, Plath's second stanza orphan imagery. The Suda, a 10th century Byzantine text on the ancient Mediterranean world, purports that Sappho was married to a wealthy trader. This however is thought to be a poetic joke, as the husband's name, Cercylas, means "Penis, from Men's Island." Plath has her own penis jokes in "Lesbos." Some are direct, as "The impotent husband," and others playful: "An old pole for lightning." It has been theorized that Sappho might have been a priestess of Aphrodite, and therefore a ritual prostitute. In Fragment 87, Sappho wrote that she couldn't keep her mind on her weaving because she was in the mood for sex.

Sappho's literary style was groundbreaking, being one of the first to use first-person narrative voice in poetry, and to address deep and erotic emotions.

Sappho was exiled from Lesbos for political reasons, and Plath's packing up of potatoes, babies, and sick cats in the fourth stanza echoes this. The Greek dramatist Menander wrote that Sappho committed suicide for the love of a ferryman. The blue-sparking trolley of the second stanza may be seen as the ferry on water. Plath's last full stanza of "Lesbos" and the poem's final hopeless line of never meeting again now reflect Sappho's suicide.

If one takes Sappho's poems as biography, Fragment 98 bears reference to a daughter. Plath also first refers to her own daughter in "Lesbos." Fragment 58 indicates that Sappho lived to an old age, demonstrated in Plath's poetic references to widows, lost beauty, and a hag. Sappho has been pictured painted in red ("Her face red") on ancient Greek vases ("O vase") with her contemporary, the lyric poet Alcaeus of Mytilene.

In the 17th century, the famous Hope Diamond first appeared, seen in Plath's praise of a valuable jewel that opens the third stanza. Its name could not better fit The Star tarot card. Along with the diamond came the superstition of a terrible curse to anyone who owns or wears it. The Hope Diamond was originally called the "French Blue" for its color, sounding like the second stanza's last three lines with their sparks of blue and split like quartz. The diamond came to be owned by France's King Louis XV and Marie Antoinette, but was stolen during the French Revolution. It was 69 carats and the size of a pigeon's egg, addressing the second stanza's line about rarity. The stone was most likely recut into two smaller stones, the larger piece being the Hope Diamond, now at 45.54 carats. The stone has been stolen a number of times, the kleptomania in the last full stanza.

Plath's vicious kitchen opening "Lesbos" is a nod to Hell's Kitchen, a gritty concrete and warehouse district in Manhattan, New York. It was once a lower-class Irish-American neighborhood, thus "potatoes hiss." Hell's Kitchen is near Broadway and the Actors Studio, considered to be the most prestigious acting school in the nation. This fits Plath's New York, Hollywood, and acting references. The Actors Studio was founded in 1951, and was home to Lee Strasberg, founder of the Method school of acting. Strasberg was coach to Marilyn Monroe, whom he said was one of the best actors he had worked with, second only to Marlon Brando (Kazan). Plath's first ten lines of "Lesbos" describe acting and the theater setting.

> *"Hollywood is a place where they'll pay you a thousand dollars for a kiss and fifty cents for your soul. I know, because I turned down the first offer often enough and held out for the fifty cents."*
>
> --Marilyn Monroe

The famous Brooklyn Theater Fire of 1876 resulted in the death of almost 300 people, most in the family section of the theater where there was only one exit. This sounds like Plath's image of trapped kittens in the well. At first sign of the fire, the actress Kate Claxton tried to calm everyone, telling the crowd it would soon be out and trying to keep them in, as Plath's second stanza attempts to keep the husband home. After a burning timber fell at her feet, panic struck. This fits the idea of trying to disappear by kicking, a schizophrenic change in behavior, and panic of the first stanza. The production was called "The Two Orphans," Plath's double orphan wording in the second stanza. The play was also a 1915 silent film, as the first line of the fourth stanza states, starring Theda Bara. It is now lost to history, but was remade as "Orphans of the Storm" in 1921 with Dorothy and Lillian Gish.

"Two venomous opposites" describes the intertwined snakes facing each other on the caduceus, a symbol of medicine since the 18th century, originally a symbol of Hermes/Mercury. They are wound around "An old pole for the lightning." The "trolley" Plath speaks of may now be seen as a doctor or nurse's cart moving down a hospital corridor. The caduceus was often pictured on vases of Sappho's time, and is a symbol of alchemy.

Finally, there is another kind of orphan to weigh in on "Lesbos." Until recently, Lupus was considered to be an "orphan disease," meaning that it is rare, and fitting Plath's orphan, illness, and rareness comments in the second stanza. Its symptoms most commonly include a red rash on the face, the eleventh line, and skin ulcers from sun and painful breathing that fit the seventh line of the second stanza. It affected the great American early feminist / lesbian writers Louisa May Alcott and Flannery O'Connor, mentioned shortly.

Fifth Mirror: Astrology and Astronomy

The Star card is assigned to Aquarius, the water bearer. Plath's "Lesbos" women serve this role as women at work, symbolically and eternally giving life and spiritual food to the world. The kitchen and the pitcher in "Lesbos" both fit Aquarius. The water from the vessel washes away the past, leaving room for a fresh new start.

Ancient Babylonians called Aquarius "Ea," whose vase poured a single stream of water into Pisces the fish. Aquarius is found in the area of the heavens known as The Sea, due to its abundance of water-creature constellations. Plath's "Lesbos" has both the vase and plenty of the sea in it. Ancient Greeks and Romans believed that the bearer of the water pitcher was the beautiful boy Ganymede who was also carried off and seduced by Zeus. This myth was used to support the gods' approval of homosexuality (Graves, 320).

In Sappho's Fragment 48, she wrote, "The moon has set, and the Pleiades; it is midnight, the time is going by and I recline alone." This fragment reflects both Plath's moon from the third stanza, and The Star card's stars of Pleiades above the maiden. Pleiades is a constellation of star clusters given to the *hot blue emission* star class. Each cluster core's luminous blue nebula, comprised of young, hot blue stars, matches Plath's "blue sparks." Pleiades is mentioned in Hesiod, Homer's *Iliad* and *Odyssey*, and in the Bible, and was revered by the Babylonians, the Hindus, and native cultures around the world. The first rising of Pleiades in May marked the beginning of the navigational year. Pliny wrote that their setting was when the cold North wind blew in with winter, and Robert Graves wrote that Pleiades is connected to the Bronze Age stone circles in the Penzance area in Cornwall, returning to Plath's Cornwall mermaid and also to her two lesbian friends. Cornwall was once called Belerium, after descendants of Apollo, who danced with the seven sisters each year.

In Chinese astrology, the tenth lunar mansion in Aquarius is called Nü, meaning "girl" and representing a maidservant. Two other Chinese mansions within Aquarius represent emptiness, desolation, and darkness. Finally, several stars in Aquarius have names beginning with the Arabic word for luck, "sa'd." Both the English word "sad" and the idea of luck are properties of The Star card, depending on whether it falls right side up, or reversed (Ridpath).

Sixth Mirror: Humanities and the Arts

Sappho recorded culture, emotion, history and myth, as did Homer. But while Homer told heroic tales, Sappho was more interested in the beauty of love ("It is love you are full of"). In Sappho's "Hymn to Aphrodite," the goddess bids Sappho to leave her home and join her. Sappho writes of an unrequited love with a woman and of her "mad heart." When Plath writes "she's mad at two," it may refer to Sappho loving this woman and addressing Aphrodite at the same time (Sappho, 1:VII).

In the second part of this hymn, Sappho writes, "My tongue is useless" (Sappho, 2:II), Plath's "Now I am silent." Sappho writes "my ears ring" (Sappho, 2) to Plath's "Your voice my ear-ring." Sappho's "Hymn to Aphrodite" continues about the sacrifices for love, comparing herself with Helen of Troy "to lead astray when she thinks of no account what is near and dear." Plath wrote, "Why she is a schizophrenic," to match Sappho's, "I know not what to do: I have two minds" (Sappho, 34). Plath's word "hate" which begins the fourth stanza of "Lesbos" fits Sappho's "the thought of me is hateful" (Sappho, 39). Sappho addressed women of no education, dooming them to mediocre, unnoticed lives: "but thou shalt wander, eternally unregarded in the houses of Hades, flitting among the insubstantial shades" (Sappho, 65). It is the housewife's dilemma, as Plath's "Lesbos" illustrates.

When Sappho wrote: "O'er the hills the heedless shepherd, / Heavy footed, plods his way; Crushed behind him lies the larkspur, / Soon empurpling in decay," it matches well to the idea of Plath's "impotent husband" who "slumps out for coffee." The heedless husband of Plath's "Lesbos" "lumps it down" a hill as Sappho's shepherd does. Instead of purple larkspur, Plath gives "blue sparks," conjuring the same sounds and image (Sappho, 91). The idea of the never-ending housework is echoed in Sappho's "Ever shall I be a maid" (Sappho, 93). Sappho's "To the door-keeper" (Sappho, 95) fits Plath's peering from the door in the fourth stanza of "Lesbos."

Sappho wrote several times about the loss of her virginity to a man: "Maidenhood, maidenhood, whither art thou gone from me? / Never, O, never again, shall I return to thee" (Sappho, 104), and it may be this Plath refers to as the valuable jewel of the third stanza. In a 1949 folder of undated notes, Plath had celebrated her own virginity at seventeen years old.

As quoted by Himerius, Sappho wrote, "Thou are the evening star, of all stars the fairest I think." This line is attributed to Sappho's song to Hesperus.[162] Again, he quotes, "Now thou didst appear like that fairest of all stars; for the Athenians call thee, Hesperus" (Sappho, 120). Both lines perfectly fit The Star tarot card.

The Hope Diamond, mentioned previously, leads us to "Diamonds are a girl's best friend." It is the motto of the hyper-sexual Marilyn Monroe, one of the greatest Hollywood stars.[163] Plath had written of liking Monroe and even dreaming about her. Marilyn Monroe spent a good deal of her childhood in the Los Angeles Orphans Home because her mother was mentally ill, and she was an unwanted child. This fits the orphan, schizophrenic, and bastard terms in "Lesbos."

Marilyn Monroe made 32 movies, including the fine symbolic match for The Star card, *All About Eve* (1950). When Monroe married her second husband, baseball player Joe DiMaggio in 1954, she said, "Marriage is my main career from now on." But that marriage did not last, nor did the one to playwright Arthur Miller that followed. Miller was Jewish, and Monroe converted to marry him, Plath's "Jew-mama" wording.

Both a younger Plath and Monroe had modeling photo-shoots at the beach, but Monroe's 1949 photos launched her career. When Monroe made the movie *The Seven Year Itch*, she burned a tiger-striped gown into the memory of millions. In "Lesbos," Plath made the garment more practical for a housewife, writing of tiger pants and having an affair, both ideas fitting Monroe. Monroe suffered a series of miscarriages and abortions that destroyed her fertility and she had an operation on her fallopian tubes, mirroring Plath's seventeenth line in "Lesbos" of blown tubes. Monroe was no longer the wholesome cute girl. The cuteness in fact, was closing in, the babies were not to be, and every director and fan wanted a piece of her. Her end is the last full stanza of "Lesbos." Monroe complained of insomnia and developed alcohol and prescription drug addictions, echoing Plath's thick dope of sleeping pills. Monroe was hospitalized for ten days in 1956 for exhaustion during the filming of her last completed film, *The Misfits*, fitting Plath's exhaustion in the fourth stanza. "Once you were beautiful. / In New York, Hollywood" fit Monroe well then (Summers). As Plath saw her Hollywood heroine's life crumble, the well-educated and perhaps overly-loved Plath might have seen her and Monroe as "two venomous opposites," if only to believe in the possibility of hope

---

162 The evidence also suggests that Plath alluded to Hesperus in the fourth mirror of "Lady Lazarus" and in the fourth and sixth mirrors of "The Detective."

163 See *Fixed Stars Govern a Life*'s Interpretation of Sylvia Plath's poem, "Barren Woman" for more on Plath and Marilyn Monroe. Author Carl Rollyson's book, *American Isis: The Life and Art of Sylvia Plath* explores the Plath-Monroe connection in greater depth.

for herself. Six years older than Plath, Marilyn Monroe died of a suicide on August 5, 1962, seven months before Plath took her own life. Nine days after Plath wrote "Lesbos," on October 26, 1962, Scottish poet Edwin Morgan, published his poem "The Death of Marilyn Monroe" in *The New Statesman*.

Almost eighty years earlier in 1885, American writer James Whitcomb Riley wrote the then-popular poem, "Little Orphant Annie." The poem tells the story of an orphan girl and all the house-work she must do. From this poem, the *Little Orphan Annie* daily newspaper comic strip ("Coy paper strips") was created, which was published from 1894-1968. It is Plath's orphan image once again. The comic dared to take on political commentary on organized labor, the New Deal, communism and more. As most comics starred boys, a girl with spunk and adventure was something new ("The bastard's a girl"). She had big round eyes like windows and frizzy red hair like Plath's sixth line of "Lesbos." One of Annie's favorite words was "Gee," as in the tenth line of Plath's second stanza. Annie's dog Sandy was her constant companion, a "doggy husband." Little Orphan Annie inspired a popular radio show in 1930, seen in Plath's first stanza radio, and two Hollywood films in Plath's time.

Annie's adventures begin in a gloomy Dickensian orphanage, where she is brought home by Daddy Warbucks. Warbucks is kind to Annie, but he and his jealous, spiteful wife are as opposite and venomous as Plath's women in "Lesbos." Annie later does drudge work in Mrs. Bottle's grocery store and is a maid for Mrs. Bleating-Hart. In all of Annie's adventures, older women such as Mrs. Warbucks, Mrs. Bottle, and Mrs. Bleating-Hart are horrible to her, echoing the anti-feminine senti-ment at the end of the fourth stanza in "Lesbos." There was controversy when the comic strip's creator, Harold Gray, gave Annie a black friend, and Gray later made a statement that he was not a reformer and did not believe in breaking down the racial color line ("Hard and apart and white"). Annie later went to Hollywood to try to become a star, fitting The Star tarot card, but failed.

The 1926 episode "Will Tomorrow Never Come?" inspired the famous Broadway song, "To-morrow, Tomorrow." Also epitomizing The Star card in its wishing and hopefulness for something better were the 1927 episodes "Blue Bell of Happiness," and the 1928 "Just Before the Dawn." A 1935 episode is called "Annie in Hollywood," and in 1930, the strip episode bore the same name as the Marilyn Monroe movie of decades later, "The Seven Year Itch" (Smith).

The *Little Orphan Annie* radio show aired on NBC's Blue Network (Plath's "blue sparks"). Captain Sparks, a fictional aviator, was a major character on the radio show.

Finally, "Lesbos" is loaded with feminist, lesbian role models. American author Louisa May Alcott (1832-1888) was a transcendentalist who studied with Ralph Waldo Emerson, Henry David Thoreau, Nathanial Hawthorne, and Margaret Fuller in Concord, Massachusetts. She is best known for her novel, *Little Women*, based on her life with her sisters. As a young girl, Plath's mother, Aurelia Schober, had inherited a copy of *Little Women* annotated by the author. This book might have been Aurelia's, and later, her daughter Sylvia's, first introduction to ideas of feminism and Transcenden-talism, which is affiliated with the Plath's Unitarian church. Most likely a lesbian, Alcott was asked why she remained a spinster for life, to which she replied, "because I have fallen in love with so many pretty girls and never once the least bit with any man."

Alcott took in her sister May's orphan daughter when May died, again fitting the orphan in "Lesbos." Alcott contracted typhoid serving as a Union Army volunteer nurse in the American Civil War. She was treated with mercury for this condition, which may have poisoned her. From this experience she wrote and published *Hospital Sketches* (1863), establishing her name. There is evidence that Alcott also suffered from lupus, fitting Plath's imagery of the red and white face, the illness, the ulcers, TB, and rarity once again (Matteson).

Flannery O'Connor was another great American female writer to suffer from lupus. Both Alcott and O'Connor were once beautiful, as the eighth line in Plath's second stanza of "Lesbos" reads. O'Connor wrote grotesque tales of the South ("The silk grits"), bad men ("your doggy husband"), and what she called the soul's struggle with the "stinking mad shadow of Jesus." "Meanwhile there's a stink of fat and baby crap" might refer to Jesus in the manger here, another connecting line drawn from the previous poem, "Magi." Plath and O'Connor shared a mutual friend in the poet Robert Lowell, and also like Plath, spent several months at Yaddo artists' colony and in New York City (Gordon). Like the *Little Orphan Annie* comic strip, O'Connor was not afraid to take on racially-charged subjects. A devout Catholic, O'Connor never married and had a thirty-year correspondence with her best friend, Betty Hester, a lesbian.

Plath wrote of her near-envy of women who could be in love with other women. To read Plath's journals from when she was a young teen, she appears to have had several intense crushes on some of her female friends, school teachers, and camp counselors. One of her first mentors, Professor Mary Ellen Chase at Smith College, was a quietly open lesbian. It was a solution, as Plath saw it, where a woman did not have to diminish herself as sex kitten, housewife, or both. In her journals she said: "Lesbians, (what does a woman see in another woman that she doesn't see in a man: tenderness)" (*UJ*, 460). A victim of her time, Plath was forced to think of a couple only in sexual terms. She questioned privately in her journals what it must be like for two women to happily live together (*UJ*, 528).

Chapter Nineteen: Escape from Alcatraz
Card #18   The Moon Card   Corresponding Poem: "The Other"

Readers of Plath's biography know that her husband Ted Hughes was a philanderer, and the first lines of "The Other" set this poem up as the angry housewife leaving his dinner out on the doorstep to get cold. The poem takes several weird turns, however; readers grasp the imagery of mirrors, moons and mercury, even if they don't fully understand how it relates to the speaker. And how could they? The Moon tarot card is needed to unlock these meanings.

First Mirror: The Tarot/Qabalah

The meaning of The Moon tarot card is fertilizing, monthly cycles, the shadow self, the dark side, sleep, dreams, imagination, and intuition. Reversed, it is depression, mania, unforeseen peril, nightmares, lies, insomnia, sickness, and insanity. In the card's picture, the pathway of life is full of temptation and danger. The towers represent the boundaries of what is known, and beyond are the heights of consciousness. It is a card of conscious and subconscious knowledge. The Golden Dawn assigns the Hebrew letter *Qoph* to The Moon card, defining it as, "the ear that immerses itself to the harmony of the spheres, thereby causing the cerebellum to respond in tune and empathically." Literally, *Qoph* means "the back of the head," the connecting link between the spinal cord and lower body. The activity assigned to *Qoph* is the function of sleep, and it is on the path of body consciousness.

THE MOON .

"The Other" may be Plath's most obvious match to its major arcana correlation. The Moon is represented in the first five couplets. Correlating with the meaning of this card, the literal meaning of "The Other" is Plath's conscious awareness and depression over having an adulterous husband.

Plath's imagery of smiles, confession, and widened eyes shows the moon as a liar in action, and her distrusting interrogations in return. Interestingly, reducing the words "Old plastic" to their numerical value in Gematria becomes 666, the sign of the Great Beast himself. The Golden Dawn refers to Imagination, an attribute of the Moon, as "plastic energy—the formative power." We now see Plath's inside joke that the adulterous Hughes blamed her suspicions of his behavior on her imagination.

The Moon is assigned to the Golden Dawn's second level in the process of initiation, Theoricus, meaning "beholder" or "onlooker." The element designated for this grade is air, and Hermetic breathing exercises therefore give Plath's "suck breath" another layer of meaning.[164] The planet assigned to Theoricus is Luna, the moon, an orb of reflected and illusionary light.

Plath's discarded lines from earlier drafts include images of divided waters, a dead marsh, and references to two white columns. All fit The Moon card well with its marsh at the edge of the water, and two column-like white towers.

The Theoricus' ritual is a journey through the physical self to the underworld that is said to be both "wondrous and terrifying" (Cicero, 242). The initiate is directed to construct talismanic

---

164 We know from journals and letters that both Aurelia Plath and Ted Hughes instructed Sylvia Plath in breathing exercises since at least 1957 (*LH*, 326).

emblems, including a moon and symbols for each of its phases, painted silver on blue-violet. It is a head on the wall in bluish coloring, seen in Plath's ninth couplet of "The Other."

The arrows Plath rides in the tenth couplet evince the arrows of the Philosophus, a higher grade in the Golden Dawn Order, specifically referring to the lunar deity Artemis, goddess of the moon and night (The moon and the element of silver share the symbol of three arrows stemming from a triangle base). Finally, The Moon card in reverse means sickness, fitting Plath's tenth couplet. A second, unpublished draft of Plath's "The Other" is full of Moon card-like lines of memory, sleep, dreams, fortune telling, premonitions, hidden feelings and nervous tension.

Second Mirror: Alchemy
Alchemists call the Moon the White Stone, approaching the perfection of gold but not yet there. It represents rest, retreat, anticipation, preparation and dreams. In cut lines from an earlier draft, Plath wrote of a "scummy" marsh, echoing alchemy. Alchemists refer to "litharge," the left-over scum, spume, or ashes from metal transmutation.

"It's the moon that makes it so still, weaving some mystery."

— Fyodor Dostoyevsky, *Crime and Punishment*

To many primitive peoples, the female menses were a powerful, positive phenomenon with spiritual significance. Some South American Indian tribes believed that all mankind was created from moon blood. In the Bible's book of Genesis, the name Adam is derived from *adamah*, translated as "bloody loam." It is with this reverence that Qabalists, mystics, alchemists, and many Gnostic traditions regard menstruation, the female reproductive cycle mirroring the moon's 28-day cycle.

The alchemist's "mote" is an old English word for "must." It is frequently used in closing rituals and spells: "so mote it be." Reading Plath's sixth couplet of "The Other," it is now understood that air itself must depart. The following line's corpuscles return us to the physical world. "The Other" becomes a fight over the body and who is in possession of it.

Alchemists liken dew to semen, considered to be an elixir of the moon. Morning dew held symbolic magical properties for alchemists, pagans and others throughout history. It was used to enhance both fertility and beauty, Plath's cosmetic effect in the fifteenth couplet (Cashford, 93-94).

Allusions to the spiritual and physical union of male and female, the alchemical marriage, are throughout early drafts of this poem. The third draft of "The Other" begins with a reference to Apollo's virginal bride who waited for union with her god in a bedchamber on a holy ziggurat seven tiers high.

It is not too surprising that the adulteries Plath speaks of are "Sulfurous." In alchemy, sulfur is one of the three heavenly substances, representing passion and will, and an essential component of vitriol. In the thirteenth couplet of "The Other," sulfur shows itself again as the active agent, grieving over adultery. Sulfur has been used since the times of the ancient Greeks and Romans for treatment of venereal diseases and skin conditions such as scabies, explaining the fourteenth couplet's cat scratching. Sulfur is known for its strong, unpleasant rotten-egg odor, returning to that seventh couplet reference to a smell.

Derived from sulfur, antimony is a toxic metalloid, meaning it resembles but does not chemically react as metal. Its chemical symbol is said to represent the wild animal found within mankind (Venefica). When reflecting light, antimony is black or gray as Plath's "blue lightning."

The antimony pill, or "everlasting pill," was a bullet-sized pellet that was swallowed and recovered in the feces for reuse, to purge the body of ill humors, up until the 19th century. Alchemists used antimony oil to cure breathing ailments and asthma, also fitting Plath's image of sucking breath (Murien). Antimony trisulfide is used in pyrotechnic effects, returning to that fifteenth couplet. Since Biblical times, antimony has been used as medication, and in Islamic and Pre-Islamic times as a cosmetic, best known as Egyptian kohl eyeliner. The prophet Mohammed was quoted saying antimony "clears the vision and makes the hair sprout" (Hassan), fitting Plath's bright hair and widened eyes. Seventeenth century alchemist George Starkey, under the name Eirenaeus Philalethes, wrote in his "An Exposition upon Sir George Ripley's Epistle" that antimony was a precursor to philosophical mercury, and therefore a precursor of the Philosopher's Stone, or perfect creation (Philalethes).

Pliny gave antimony the names *alabaster* and *platyophthalmos*, meaning *wide-eye* (from the cosmetic effect, echoing Plath's second-to-last stanza). Alabaster as we know it today is Moon-white. It was named after the Egyptian cat goddess Bastet, returning to Plath's cat image. Bastet carried the title Eye of Ra, relating to the eyes in the fifth stanza. Bastet was associated with protective ointments, and equated with the moon goddess, Artemis. Alabaster vases have also been found from ancient Sumeria, depicting the moon goddess Inanna.

One of the symbols given by the Golden Dawn to represent the Moon is a mirror, fitting the thirteenth and fourteenth couplet lines about glass. It is a fine metaphor for facing one's true nature, and also a literal alchemical glass in the laboratory.

Third Mirror: Mythology

The poem, "The Other," has a complicated and rich mythological interpretation, uniting tarot and Qabalah, Sumerian, Egyptian, Greek and Roman myth with allusions to the female menstrual cycle, fertility, and synchronization of menses. These female forces are said to all be affected by the Moon.

The Sumerian *Descent of Inanna* (about 1750 BC) is the story of Inanna, the bright Moon goddess, as she enters the underworld and begins her waning phase. Inanna wears the bright jewels of heaven ("White Nike"). Her sister of the underworld, Ereshkigal, the dark moon, lets her enter through seven gates, opened one by one just a crack ("Streaming between my walls"). Inanna must remove some of her garments as she passes through each phase, becoming less and less until she is naked. Erishkigal then strikes her down and kills her, represented by Plath's smiling lightning of blue. Erishkigal then hangs her sister's corpse on a hook, fitting Plath's meat hook image in the same couplet. Inanna's friend has a god help by creating two creatures that pity and cry out with Erishkigal during pains of childbirth, fitting the tenth couplet lines well. It is an interesting solution that the early civilization cultures often proposed: instead of vengeance, they sought to create balance and harmony by blessing enemies and wrong-doers. Winning Erishkigal's favor, they ask for the body of Inanna to resurrect (Cashford, 28). It is the myth of the resurrected moon. This transformation from light to dark to light is seen in many other myths to explain the seasons. Reflecting Plath's ninth couplet, a Sioux Indian elder of Northern America once stated, "All living things are tied together with a common navel cord." This is the great cycle of life that the moon has always represented (Cashford, 98).

The Greek's Dionysus was once a moon god. His dismemberment into fourteen parts echoes the moon phases and other resurrection legends to explain the seasons. It is the burden of all of those parts that Plath mentions in her third couplet. With variations, this resurrection is also the story of Egypt's Ishtar, and Isis and Osiris; Greece's Demeter and Persephone, and Adonis and Aphrodite; the Canaanite Baal and Anath; and the Anatolian and Roman Kybele and Attis.

In a carryover from the last poem's "blue sparks," "The Other" connects to "Lesbos" with the idea of "blue lightning." The important word here is "assumes." What god bearing a lightning bolt assumes that every woman is his? Zeus, of course. In the mythological mirror for the interpretation of "Lesbos," Zeus had had his way, contested or not, with most of the Pleiades, and even the boy of Aquarius. Attractive mortals were all "meat" to him, to hook upon his literal and metaphoric phallic lightning rod. In "The Other," Zeus is at it again.

Knitting may reference the Greek goddess Athena's skill of weaving and crafts. Athena was the goddess of wisdom. It might have amused Plath that Athena was born with the help of Hephaestus, the smith god, who split open Zeus' head with an ax. Smith College, of course, was Plath's under-graduate school.

Sigmund Freud argued that decapitation symbolically equals castration. Plath's head on the wall line is therefore a doubly emasculating message to a man. Freud's posthumously-published essay, "Medusa's Head," equated the serpents on the gorgon Medusa's hair to penises. When a man saw Medusa, or the female genitals that Freud believed triggered castration fears, he became stiff with terror. Freud suggested that the stiffening of a man's penis let him know he hadn't been castrated (Freud). Perseus beheaded Medusa, and then used this serpentine symbol of castration as a weapon against his enemies. The gorgon's head was said to be the face of the moon, representing bringing fear to the consciousness to lose its power. Athena's gift to Perseus was a mirror, so he could see Medusa without beholding her directly. African folklore holds that the moon reflects both on the side of the heavens and on the waters of the earth, fitting Plath's mirror imagery of the thirteenth and fourteenth couplets again (Cashford, 86-87). The mirror is throughout this poem.

Nike,[165] Greek goddess of victory and another epithet for Athena, appears in the second couplet of "The Other." Nike was often seen as a winged figure hovering over the victor in a competition, as the moon hovers over the earth.

The Greek's lunar deity Artemis is associated with the moon, the hunt, and childbirth. Death is brought swiftly by her arrows. She is also credited with healing, a positive note to the moon's sickness, seen in Plath's tenth couplet. Artemis is both a goddess of hunting and a protector of wild animals. This contradiction is a reflection of the cycle of life as menstruation is both a sign of fertility and death of an egg. It should be noted that the Greek god Eros (or his Roman counterpart, Cupid), the god of lust, beauty, love, and intercourse, was made fun of by Artemis' twin brother, Apollo, for his archery skills. Plath's image of belly-shrieks echoes the physical, sometimes debilitating pains of menstrual cramps that Plath herself suffered.

Artemis' name is linked to the word "butcher" in Greek folk etymology, another fit for Plath's "meathook" in the third couplet. When Artemis' mother Leto gave birth to Artemis as the first twin, the baby girl acted as a midwife to deliver her brother Apollo. As the huntress of the forests, Artemis always carried a bow and arrows with her, Plath's arrow image again. Artemis desired to remain a virgin throughout her life and to assist in midwifery and help women with the pains of childbirth, fitting the ninth through twelfth couplets of "The Other," especially if one considers the patterned breathing techniques such as Lamaze today. Plath had great respect for midwifery and was proud to have delivered both of her children at home this way. The Romans called Artemis "Diana," and Shakespeare wrote in *Much Ado About Nothing* that Hero seemed like "Dian in her

165 In Rome, Nike was worshipped as "Victoria." "Victoria Lucas" was Sylvia Plath's pen-name when she wrote *The Bell Jar.*

orb," regarding her chastity. This virgin goddess represented in Roman sculpture fits that Plathian "womb of marble."

Selene was an archaic lunar deity called Luna by the Romans. She was the daughter of a Titan, and her brother Helios served Apollo's role as the sun. Selene's symbol was the crescent, which looks like the smile of the "The Other's" third couplet.

The pre-Olympian underworld triple-goddess Hecate was associated with the moon and darkness, too. Some ancient depictions give her gorgon-like serpents in her hair. Like Artemis, Hecate aided women in childbirth.

The Greek goddess of the night, however, is Nyx, mother of Hypnos (sleep) and Thánatos (death). Nyx is often equated with or as Artemis. Born of Chaos, she was considered to be exceptionally powerful and beautiful. Of her many children, her son Aether rules the Atmosphere, the upper air the gods breathe. This, too, complements Plath's line about sucking breath, and the qualities of these goddesses are all contained in The Moon card's meaning.

Plath's images of stolen horses and fornications refer to the many causes for battle and sexual relations among these gods and goddesses. It also references Odysseus and Penelope in Homer's *The Odyssey*. Odysseus left to fight the Trojan War and did not return for twenty years. Meanwhile, Penelope had 108 suitors vying for her, yet she remained faithful to her husband. Odysseus was less so, and had a son named Telegonus by the sorceress, Circe. Here parallels can be drawn with Plath's marriage to Hughes, and Assia Wevill's pregnancy with Hughes' child. Circe is also very close to Plath's word "circle," the shape of the full moon.

In an earlier version of "The Other," Plath mentions Greece, marshes, and division of black water, referencing the picture of The Moon tarot card and alluding to the Greek tale of Xenophon and his Ten Thousand Men, who fought their way through the Persian Empire that divided the Mediterranean from the Black Sea.

Xenophon and his soldiers became inebriated from honey poisoned by the Rhododendron, a kind of Oleander said to produce the "mad honey" of Dionysian orgies in Pompeii. Oleander contains a powerful poison that can paralyze the heart. In ancient times, honey was mixed with ground medicinal herbs such as absinthe (*Artemisia absinthium*—named for Artemis), to make them palatable. One ancient text lists a vaginal suppository of herbs and honey for pain from uterine contractions (Ebers, 821). This explains Plath's lines, later cut, from the third draft, referencing and describing the rhododendron, ecstatic moments from a drink, and how the moon moves the sea. In a subsequent revision, Plath wrote of a green alcoholic drink, and of the derangement caused by absinthe.

Fourth Mirror: History and the World

A few weeks before Plath wrote "The Other," three inmates escaped from Alcatraz Island federal penitentiary. Over the course of a year ("You come in late") they dug holes with spoons through their cell walls. The escapees then climbed through ventilation shafts ("Streaming between my walls") and quickly left the island on a handmade raft as fast as Plath's lightning on blue water.

A fourth prisoner attempted to escape but did not succeed. In a plea bargain, he confessed everything, sounding like the fourth couplet of "The Other." The night of the escape, the successful escapees fabricated dummy heads with soap, paper, and real hair to convince guards they were asleep in their beds, fitting the hair, polish, and plastic of the fourth couplet, as well as the head on the wall image of the ninth.

Plath's air motes and corpuscles begin a blood stream metaphor that fits these prisoners, too. Air motes, of course, fly about freely. Corpuscles can be said to be imprisoned within the blood stream. As they are "knitting, busily" and hooking onto each other, as in the seventh and eighth couplets, there is a cancerous feeling of a globular mass like Plath's sticky candy. As blood runs, the prisoners' escape is the "dark fruit" of their labor. This fruit, like cancer, is not the kind the world wants running freely. The bodies of these men were never found and it is presumed they drowned, another image for Plath's sucking breath.

The language of "The Other" is full of the imperatives and interrogations a prison guard might yell at a prisoner. The cell blocks in Alcatraz are all connected, and prisoners were sometimes chained together, fitting Plath's hooking image. The island of Alcatraz fits the marble-circled womb metaphor of the eleventh couplet.

The person hiding something in "The Other" appears to be a woman, the owner of a handbag. In a literal interpretation, this poem is less about Plath's interrogation of Hughes than it is about the other woman, Assia Wevill. However, "The Other" seems to be Plath's own escape-from-Alcatraz fantasy. She is both her own guard and a prisoner longing to be free ("Between myself and myself").

Mirrors and the Moon have long been associated with each other as a literary and poetic metaphor, alchemical symbolism, and more. Mirrors reflect light or sound; they can be flat, convex, or concave; and are used for personal and scientific uses. In Feng Shui, the ancient Asian practice of positioning objects in one's home for health, prosperity, and luck, a mirror on the front door deflects bad energy, fitting Plath's doorstep image of the first couplet.

The Bronze Age sculpture "Nike of Brescia" shows familiar Nike again, holding a round disc believed to be a mirror. It is known that the statue was originally of Aphrodite, mirrors being one of her symbols. Wings were added later to transform her into the Roman goddess. A mirror tipped toward light can look like Plath's lightning. Mirrors are usually heavy and hung on walls with a hook, both ideas in the third couplet of "The Other."

One-way mirrors are often used in police investigations, picking up on fourth couplet imagery. Mirrors "confess" the truth of what a person looks like, are used in telescopes and lasers, as well as in cameras to magnify and get a closer look. It should be remembered that in Plath's time, cameras often had a shoe-polish black plastic case and body, fitting the fourth couplet. Mirrors can also be used in microscopes, appropriate to the sixth couplet. A chemical known as "Liver of Sulphur" will oxidize a mirror to produce an antiqued, dirty finish, another explanation for the adulteries Plath compares to sulfur (Finishing).

Mirrors are often made with a silver or metal backing behind glass, as in the thirteenth couplet. They are used for both decorative effect and are helpful in application of cosmetics, both in Plath's fifteenth couplet. Many people smile into mirrors, as in the poem's final couplet. When a mirror is broken, the popular myth is that it brings seven years' bad luck, but "it is not fatal."

Human and animal eyes work similar to mirrors. So too "The Other" mirrors the eye: The simplest eyes work on circadian rhythms of day and night. More complex eyes distinguish shape, color, and depth perception. The "lips" of the eyes would be the eyelids, "untouched on the door-step" to the eyeball itself. The white eyeball, Plath's Nike, is often likened to the Moon, and it can have "streaming" tears. Eyes smile, flash anger and show emotions such as assumption and guilt, all seen in the third and fourth couplets. In that fourth couplet, the eyelashes are Plath's hair, the pupils are as black as shoes, and the entire eye is like plastic. The fifth couplet is all about eyes, and the sixth speaks to blood vessels drifting across one's vision. The two eyes may reflect why Plath wrote "The Other" in couplets. Eyes respond to strong odors such as onions with tears, which fit Plath's smell image in the seventh couplet. The iris, the part of the eyes with color, is a complex "knitting" of pigmented tissue and cells known as the "optic cup," in the way that the Moon was seen as a cup to ancient religions. The colorful irises look like Plath's candy. The optic nerve is a sort of "Navel cord" that anchors and transmits information from the eye's retina to the brain, and the arteries and nerves are exactly as Plath describes in her last line of the ninth couplet. In this way, the bulb of the eye is a kind of belly, as Plath's tenth couplet suggests.

In "The Other," Plath sees only the wrong in the world: her stolen horses and fornications are around that marble womb, a description of the white eyeball. In her journals, Plath wrote on the theme of her short story, "The Eye*Beam": "How one is always and irrevocably alone. The askew distortions of the private eye" (UJ, 283). Inspiration for this story first came when Plath had to see a doctor for a splinter in her eye. This grew into metaphor for the moon beaming alone, as well as the private eye-police detective in the fourth stanza of "The Other."[166]

Menstrual blood has been associated with the moon since earliest times. The limestone sculpture Venus of Laussel is of a naked woman holding a crescent moon in her right hand. Venus of Laussel's crescent moon is marked with 13 lines, suggesting the 13 cycles of the Moon (364 days) in a year. The woman figure places her left hand on her womb, suggesting her 13 menstrual periods throughout the year. The carving comes from the same area of Dordogne, southwestern France, home of the Lascaux cave paintings. Plath and Hughes' friends, the Merwins, had their summer home in this region. In these caves, the moon was painted in these caves going through its phases, and evidence suggests these paintings are the origins of the zodiac. Mythologist Joseph Campbell has written that caves were holy places representing both the womb and the tomb, the cycle of life. We know Plath visited the prehistoric cave paintings, from a postcard she sent.[167]

Plath had a personal battle with her feelings about menstruation. Since puberty, her periods were irregular, heavy, with painful "fruitless" cramps (UJ, 486). She worried about her own fertility, especially after a miscarriage between the births of Frieda and Nicholas. At this time, Plath saw her menses as a sign of failure, yet she seemed to appreciate this symbol of her womanhood, and its importance in ritual.

Looking at "The Other" from this perspective of feminine sexuality, the poem also suggests what a woman's privates might "confess"; perhaps the bright hair on her head is not the same black shoe color of the hair on her privates.

The lies and falseness of the tarot's Moon card appear throughout "The Other." The action of wiping lips is assumed to mean her husband has been kissing other women. Yet this might be metaphor for a late menstrual period finally arriving, and wiping labial lips for personal cleansing. Women in some cultures are sequestered from the general population until menstruation is over, literally untouched and on the doorstep of a community. Continuing with an interpretation of female sexuality and the menstrual cycle in particular, the poem makes a new kind of sense. This powerful white source streaming between her walls becomes the victory of semen between vaginal walls in pregnancy, and/or the moon's power over her menses.

"Metaphors for ovulation and menstrual blood are prevalent in her late work," noted Catherine Thompson in *TriQuarterly*'s "Dawn Poems in Blood: Sylvia Plath and PMS" who states, "the thematic oscillation from suffering to rebirth in these poems appears to follow the phases of Plath's own menstrual cycle."[168]

The Golden Dawn prized menstrual blood, literally and symbolically, calling it the "Oil of Messiah" that makes a Messiah. As the queen bee of a hive has the DNA to birth a kingdom, so it

---

166 Additionally, in 1959 Sylvia Plath wrote a poem called "The Eye-mote," to which "The Other" echoes its motes and horses (CP, 109). The feeling of the narrator in "The Eye-mote" is very moon-like as well, as she looks over the land from a far-off place.

167 Postcard from Sylvia Plath to her mother dated Monday, July 10, 1961. It is labeled "Montignac-sur-Vézeře (Dordogne) Grotte de Lascaux." This postcard can be found in the Sylvia Plath archives at the Lilly Library, Indiana University-Bloomington.

168 See *Fixed Stars Govern a Life's* alchemical mirror of Plath's poem, "Thalidomide" for more about menstruation.

is believed that royal blood (or a cup of wine, as a symbol of the womb holding royal blood) has the DNA to unite its people. This *menstruum* is often compared to the royal jelly of the queen bee, upon which the life of the hive depends. With this in mind, the line about smell is at once a reek of perfume and a crude allusion to menstrual cleanliness; yet for Plath, it also suggests bees again, as a swarm of bees are directed by their queen's scent. With the bee imagery understood, the end of the seventh and the entire eighth couplet are apt bee metaphors for building a hive. The word "knitting" is often used in the Golden Dawn community and scripture as a term to strengthen and reinforce power and shared knowledge.

One of the herbs Qabalists assign to The Moon card is the turnip. In the first draft of this poem, Plath included four lines specifically naming turnips, and there is another turnip reference in the second draft. It seems she made the switch however to the turnip's root vegetable kin, the also Qabalistically important onion, also a primary symbol in Plath's earlier poem, "Cut." The onion comes into season in late-summer or fall, fitting Plath's first line of "The Other." Strong in smell and taste, and often white, it is apropos to call it "White Nike." The onion has walls of layers with juices streaming through and between, fitting the second couplet. When onions are sliced, they fall apart, and the sliced onion looks like a smile as in the third couplet. Onions are known to make people cry, like Plath's confession. The rings of an onion widen from the center outward, as in the fifth couplet, and the scent powerfully fills the air, as the sixth and seventh address. The eighth couplet of "The Other," with its hooking layers and stickiness, describe this vegetable.

The green shoots of an onion sprout from the bulb like Plath's arrows. The onion is moon-shaped, and each layer may be said to circle that same marble womb of Plath's eleventh couplet. When cutting an onion, Plath's breath-sucking might prevent the sulfur-like assault to the sense of smell, fitting the twelfth and thirteenth couplets. Each layer is nearly transparent, as lucent as glass, as seen in "The Other." As something edible, onions may be likened to fruit. Ancient Egyptians worshipped the onion for its spherical shape and concentric rings, which they attributed to eternal life.

The idea of knitting evokes the man on the moon tale, who some say is a person knitting. The moon might also be likened to candy, as the eighth couplet suggests. The bad smelling handbag, according to Plath's first draft of "The Other," was not to hold knitting, but the corpses of seven small children. She may have meant for a possible representation of the seven planets, or even seven miscarriages, as the first draft's preceding line referred to babies and mother's milk, with metaphor of ribbons, like knitting yarn.[169] Plath had written that she and Hughes had originally planned on seven children, in playful hope that the myth of the seventh child of the seventh child would be a rare white witch (*LH*, 255). By July 2, 1962, when Plath wrote "The Other," the dream of these seven children with Hughes was assuredly dead.

Plath's image of something left on the doorstep untouched is first thought of as dinner. However, unobtainable sleep is another meaning, and also correlates with The Moon card. Another supporting theme, explored further in this poem, is the crab, which smiles with his meat hook and carries his many parts as a kind of burden.

The disease of cancer is characterized by malignant cells eating healthy cells, reflecting "The Other's" first line. It is a Nike-brave battle for the patient. Cancer affects blood, tissue, bone or other tissue, streaming past and between cell walls. As cells divide and grow in the healthier parts of the flesh, cancer also fits Plath's meat hook. Some cancers, such as invasive ductal carcinoma, have

---

169 Another possibility may be that this references Assia Wevill's several abortions. Wevill had confessed this to Plath once before her affair with Hughes.

"a pale, crab-shaped mass" at its center. The word *cancer* comes from the Greek *carcinos*, meaning, "crab" or "crayfish," again echoing The Moon card.

Cancer was on Sylvia Plath's mind when she wrote "The Other." Her neighbor, Percy Key, had just died after a terrible battle with it just a little over a week before Plath wrote her poem.[170] Cancer is sometimes called "the great imitator," because it presents symptoms of many other diseases, confessing everything. The fifth, sixth, and thirteenth couplets reflect doctors looking at results or biopsies under the laboratory microscope. The cells invade nearby parts of the body, forming tumors, as seen in the knitting of the seventh and eighth couplets. Radiation can be a cause of cancer, and the moon contains deadly levels of space radiation, Plath's moon-glow (NASA).

As cancer kills its own host and destroys itself, moths risk losing their lives in pursuit of a flame. Moths do not get the appreciation that sunny butterflies do, although some are just as pretty.[171] This might be because they are nocturnal and associated with the moon and The Moon card's characteristics of intuition, psychic perception, and heightened awareness (Venefica). Plath's journals contain notes about using moths, cockchafers, and other creatures as poetic ideas (*UJ*, 594-5). Both moths and cockchafers have a larval grub form that could be compared to Plath's marble circle. One moth, the Luna, is named after the moon. Moths navigate by lunar light and arrive during this poem's late hours. They are ever vigilant in following the path of light, sounding like Plath's tenth couplet. The moth leaves scented trails of pheromones to attract a mate, fitting the poem's smell image. As they feed, moths perpetually wipe their mouths. Moths are often found on the doorstep at night, many are white, and they have wings like the goddess Nike. The moth's body appears to be sectioned into parts, reflecting Plath's third couplet. Many moths have designs upon their wings like the rings of wide eyes to discourage predators and they fly upon the air like motes. Moths busily knit their cocoons, which might be compared to sticky candy, and in the bigger view of continuing the lifeline, could be said to be hooking to other generations as Plath's eighth couplet suggests. Some people mount moths and butterflies for display, as a trophy head is mounted on a wall. Moths and butterflies, however, are inserted between sheets of glass, fitting Plath's thirteenth couplet.

Fifth Mirror: Astrology and Astronomy

Planetary aspects of the moon run wild in "The Other"; according to the Golden Dawn, the moon's colors include pale lemon yellow, red, purple, and violet. Except for yellow, these colors are seen in the final draft of "The Other," and a first draft included reference to an unnatural pallor and yellowness. The moon is said to govern everything in life with its rhythms, including the stomach, fitting Plath's navel image; lungs, fitting Plath's sucking breath; uterus, impregnation, menstruation, and birth, fitting the images of running blood and pain that is not fatal; the nervous system; the nervous system, and the brain. The moon may be said to arrive in the late hours, seen most often at night, and astrologers since ancient times have said it enters different "houses," explaining Plath's doorstep metaphor. Unless one happens to be an astronaut, and none had walked the surface of the moon in Plath's time, the moon is also "untouched" at the doorstep of the planet Earth. The moon is the symbol of the zodiac sign of Cancer the Crab.

The Crab Nebula is the remnant of a supernova found in the constellation of Taurus. First observed in 1731, it looks like a crab, or even a "sticky" candy. It was named "The Crab Nebula"

---

170 Plath's beloved "Grammy" also died from cancer while Plath was at Cambridge.
171 Plath enjoyed incorporating details of Lepidoptera into her poems, as seen in *Fixed Stars Govern a Life*'s interpretations of poems such as "The Detective" and "Fever 103°." It should be noted that an archaic term for those who enjoy moths and butterflies is "aurelian," close to Plath's mother's name, Aurelia.

in 1848, and is considered the strongest persistent source of X-ray and gamma ray energies. Photographs of the Crab Nebula are as blue, red, and translucent as Plath's wording, and protruding from it are cord-like legs. The Crab Nebula corresponds to a bright supernova recorded by Chinese astronomers that occurred in 1054 A.D., creating lightning of blue (Hubblesite).

Astrologically, the moon represents feelings and the past. The moon and its corresponding sign of Cancer are symbols of protection, security and comfort. The moon also rules spontaneous reactions and feelings that do not make logical sense. It is a sign of intuitions, hunches, and instincts, and also of secrets, misunderstandings, and betrayal; all feelings expressed in Plath's "The Other."

Sixth Mirror: Humanities and the Arts

The flag of the city of Grabow, Germany, the country of Plath's father's, Otto Plath's, origin, bears a crescent moon with a face, and three stars. Its colors are blue, red, and what could be called a "lucent" yellow. The flag has a caricature of a moon's face with its sharp forehead and meat hook-like chin. The profile is turned to the right, visibly waning in what is considered to be the sinister direction. The three stars are the candies of fortune, honor, and fame. This flag was officially adopted as the coat of arms in 1991, long after Plath's death, but the design and description of it as a flag has been around since 1667, and Plath may well have had it on her wall, or at least known of it.

The mirror image associated with The Moon card leads us to Lewis Carroll's sequel to the famous 1865 children's story, *Alice's Adventures in Wonderland*: *Through the Looking-Glass, and What Alice Found There* (1871). Plath knew these books well; there are five references to characters from the books in her journals, as well as references to it in *Letters Home* (*LH*, 53). As *Alice's Adventures in Wonderland* draws on playing-card imagery, *Through the Looking-Glass* draws upon the game of chess, much of which "The Other" also reflects. The White King is one of the first chess pieces introduced to Alice in the story, as Plath introduces the second-person narrative "You" in the first line of "The Other" (LeRoy).

Alice is a pawn to the White King, the chess piece that may be left untouched on his marble doorstep of the back rank, or home line, of pieces. Certainly a "White Nike" such as the White Queen might stream through a wall of pawns or other pieces lined up like milk bottles. In her journals, Plath wrote, "The future is what matters—because one never reaches it, but always stays in the present—like the White Queen who had to run like the wind to remain in the same spot" (*UJ*, 24). This quotation reflects the twelfth-couplet interrogation about breathlessness once again.[172] Lewis Carroll's White Queen lives in a looking glass, seeing only the future and the past, but never the present. She confesses to crimes before they've happened, reminiscent of the fourth stanza. She turns into a sheep that slowly evolves into a porcupine and begins the busy job of knitting with her needles. Two of these needles turn into oars, taking Alice on a boat ride. "You'll be catching a crab directly," the sheep/porcupine says, beginning a conversation with Alice about finding a crab. Plath's poem, "The Other," has six questions in it, and they are all as weird and unclear as Carroll's strange characters might posit in *Through the Looking-Glass*.

The next character Alice meets is Humpty Dumpty, the egg-man who is just a head on a wall, fitting Plath's ninth couplet. This also hearkens back to the Queen of Hearts in Carroll's preced-

---

172 Plath also refers to the White Queen in a 1950 letter to her mother: "I have to keep on like the White Queen to stay in the same place" (*LH*, 53). Plath had gotten her Red and White Queens mixed up, however, as it was the Red Queen who said, "It takes all the running you can do, to keep in the same place" (Carroll, Chap. II).

ing book, *Alice in Wonderland*. The Queen of Hearts was the foul-tempered monarch who repeatedly shouted "Off with their heads!" This queen has been often confused with the Red Queen since the 1951 Disney movie *Alice in Wonderland*, released in Plath's time, which gave the Queen of Hearts some of the Red Queen's lines. At the end of *Through the Looking-Glass*, the White Queen transforms into one of Alice's white cats, matching Plath's cat image.

Returning to the theme of chess, there is a burden of parts in the game, and some chess pieces are as black as shoes and made of plastic, as in Plath's fourth couplet. There is much staring down at the board and trying to guess at what "The Other" is thinking, reflecting the fifth couplet. Looking upon the pieces from overhead, they might resemble little candies again, rallying defense around one's own pieces. It is another example of hooking to oneself. Horses stolen are when a knight is taken, and "fornication" in chess would be "check mate." Chess pieces and boards are sometimes made of marble, as the eleventh couplet refers. Stretching this further, when chess players ponder the next move, perhaps they suck in breath and scratch their heads. It has been speculated that author Lewis Carroll incorporated numerology and mysticism into a hidden code for readers. The code reveals Carroll's relationship with the girl for whom he modeled his Alice, and several references to Carroll's favorite number, 42. Carroll was known to have definite interests in esotericism and theosophy (Leach).

In a 1921 letter to his patron, the writer James Joyce used Lewis Carroll's "Tweedledum and Tweedledee" characters to mock Sigmund Freud and Carl Jung in their professional conflict. This is interesting, as Plath was a great reader of all three men, Joyce, Freud, and Jung. "The Other" is written in couplets, echoing the idea of two personalities, and the couplets are divided into two groups of eight, showing division. Like Freud and Jung, Plath documented her dreams, believing them to be powerfully symbolic and nurturing to her creativity. In 1959, Plath wrote of her dream:

> "to read in Jung case-history confirmations of certain images in my story. [...] The word 'chessboard' used in an identical situation: of a supposedly loving but ambitious mother who manipulated the child on the 'chessboard of her egotism': I had used 'chessboard of her desire'" (*UJ*, 514).

It might be said that Carl Jung was a moon-like student to Sigmund Freud, who first appeared in the Mythology mirror of this poem. Jung became an adversary to Freud in psychoanalytic theory, and Plath's poem from the first-published arrangement of *Ariel*, "The Munich Mannequins," explores this relationship.[173]

There are correlations with *Through the Looking-Glass* and "The Other" beyond chess: The character of Alice has hair bright and blonde, as well as black shoes. In this story, Alice walks through a wall-hung mirror to another world. The doorstep in "The Other" is a doorstep to another reality. The White Queen speaks seeming nonsense about crabs, relating to other mirrors of Plath's "The Other." The White Queen also has this conversation with Alice:

"The rule is, jam to-morrow and jam yesterday – but never jam to-day."

"It MUST come sometimes to 'jam to-day," Alice objected.

"No, it can't," said the Queen. "It's jam every OTHER day: to-day isn't any OTHER day, you know" (Carroll).

The language emphasizes Plath's title; the capitalization is Carroll's.

Alice encounters Humpty Dumpty, an egg sitting on his wall, who celebrates his "unbirthday," an interesting correlation with ideas of menstruation and fruitless eggs. Humpty Dumpty had a

---

173 Plath herself had not intended "The Munich Mannequins" to be in her *Ariel* collection. The addition was made to the first publication of *Ariel* by her husband, Ted Hughes.

contemptuous smile, fitting Plath's third and last couplets. He discussed semantics with Alice, explaining what Plath would do generations after Carroll with her own words:

> "When I use a word," Humpty Dumpty said, in rather a scornful tone, "it means just what I choose it to mean—neither more nor less."
>
> "The question is," said Alice, "whether you can make words mean so many different things."
>
> "The question is," said Humpty Dumpty, "which is to be master——that's all."
>
> Alice was too much puzzled to say anything, so after a minute Humpty Dumpty began again. "They've a temper, some of them—particularly verbs, they're the proudest—adjectives you can do anything with, but not verbs—however, I can manage the whole lot! Impenetrability! That's what I say!" (Carroll)

In *Through the Looking-Glass,* Lewis Carroll's March Hare character returns from the first Alice book, symbolizing the moon in time with his lateness, and with the picture of the "hare on the moon," because many discern a hare on the moon's face. Alice wakes at the end of the story holding her kitten, fitting Plath's cat scratches. And who can forget the smiling Cheshire Cat of the first story? Plath references smiling in two different places in "The Other."

In the first draft of "The Other," there are references to the old, elaborate needlework samplers with morals and sayings embroidered into them. Plath also mentioned Germanic print, sometimes a part of these samplers when stitched by the Pennsylvania Dutch, whose name comes from the German word, *Deutsch.* Also crossed out by Plath in this early draft are two references to lilies. Poet and mystic W.B. Yeats, whom Plath and Hughes both idolized, was close with his sister Lily, who was famous for her embroidered samplers. Lily had W.B. Yeats' wife Georgie working with her in a studio that sold embroideries and prints. Germanic prints often included Norse gods and goddesses such as *Bil,* one of two sisters representing lunar activity. Bil came from the well *Byrgir,* Old Norse for "hider of something."

As the moon has two sides, Plath spent much time focused on the idea of "the double." In a letter home from Smith College where she worked on her thesis based upon Dostoevsky's *The Double,* she wrote of identifying her own egotism: "Am I wrong when this image insinuates itself between me and the merciless mirror?" (*LH*, 40). Thirteen years later, this would sound like her thirteenth couplet in "The Other." Plath's "The Other" mirrors Dostoyevsky's *The Double* well: Golyadkin's double comes into his home late and is seen fleetingly with a mischievous smile, sometimes in a mirror. Golyadkin is responsible for a bill for eleven pies his double ate, fitting Plath's wiping of lips. He is constantly in pursuit of the Double, and the Double also follows and chases him, fitting Plath's question of where he is going so out of breath.

Dostoyevsky doubled scenes throughout *The Double*: two appearances by a doctor, two gate-crashing scenes, two scenes with Golyadkin is lurking in the shadows, and more. This further supports why Plath chose to write "The Other" in couplets. There is also the Dostoyevsky-like changing of narrative voices throughout Plath's "The Other," beginning with the second-person narrative "You" voice, to a first-person switch asking what she left. "The Double" next moves to an omniscient, objective third-person observer describing how he moves and smiles. Here, Plath uses Dostoyevsky's free indirect discourse, in which the narrative voice mimics the character's voice or reflects the character's point of view without use of actual quotation.

Plath's close friend, Ruth Fainlight, had a younger brother named Harry whom Plath and Hughes both knew well. Harry Fainlight went to grammar school and Cambridge University with Ted Hughes. A wild youth, Harry embraced the Beat poets' movement and Allen Ginsberg called him, "the most gifted English poet of his generation." Like Ginsberg, Harry Fainlight was homosexual, Jewish, and a heavy user of recreational drugs. The December 1959 issue of *Encounter*, a magazine Plath and Hughes both read and wrote for, published "Three Poems by Harry Fainlight," and the last, very short poem, "Claire de Suburbia," reads:

Earth sleeps; its dental plate
Taken out. O half-moon.
These whited sepulchres ....
On doorsteps bottles full of empty milk,
In rooms hallucinatory dust-sheets,
A blind man's walking-stick in every hall.

Fainlight's "O half-moon" is Plath's same beginning in "Thalidomide" without a hyphen. Yet "The Other" addresses the moon in its glow, and continues to play with Fainlight's images of untouched doorstep bottles; his dust-sheets in Plath's departing motes of air; and the hallucinatory dream-quality of both poems. It appears that Plath was influenced by Harry Fainlight, who here was making a statement about keeping sane as a suburban housewife.

As in *The Double*, Plath's "The Other" circles around and around, leaving the reader uncertain of who is who, if all persons are the speaker, or a terrible hallucination. Both Plath and Dostoyevsky weave these voices together so subtly that one hardly has time to register their differences in the flow of reading, creating a narrative illusion of distance. Nevertheless, neither writer distances enough to reveal what the reader anxiously wonders: is the ghostly, terrible, betraying double real, or not?

Chapter Twenty: Too Much In the Sun
Card #19   The Sun Card   Corresponding Poem: "Stopped Dead"

Another poem that Ted Hughes left out of the original manuscript of *Ariel*, "Stopped Dead" is best known as a meditation on a trip with Ted Hughes' portly, rich Uncle Walter, whom Plath once described as "amazing Dickensian-Falstaffian." Walter once generously gave the couple fifty British pounds, and until this poem, Plath had deemed him her favorite relative (*LH*, 318). Later on she wrote that she thought Walter should have helped them more, as he knew she and Hughes were struggling. It is evident that something changed in Plath's relationship to the uncle, possibly Walt's allegiance to his nephew during Plath and Hughes' marital stress. It is all a fine fit for The Sun card.

First Mirror: The Tarot/Qabalah

The meanings for The Sun tarot card are children, happiness, riches, attainment and vitality. Reversed, this card represents vanity, ego and arrogance, hatred, lies, relationship difficulties, and misbehaving children. The Golden Dawn assigns the Hebrew letter *Resh* to The Sun, meaning, "the head of the individual allowed to first understand and analyze the deeper aspect of his or her own Self through reflection." Resh is a glyph that is bent over, symbolizing that intellect must be bent for the young to understand, and riches should be bent to help the poor. God, like the Sun, bends over the earth (Trugman). To draw Resh looks like a horizontal line and then a steep drop, as Plath's third line of "Stopped Dead" suggests.

The physical and emotional issues of The Sun card reversed are clearly portrayed in the poem; "Stopped Dead" mirrors this card in both pictorial description and meaning. A naked child, evident in the crying, birth, and baby of the third stanza symbolizes the innocent soul, and of course, The Sun card's picture features a baby. The gender of the baby is ambiguous, and the child is possibly rich enough to have its own pony, as does the girl in Plath's fifth stanza.

The first two lines of "Stopped Dead" represent the approach to the end of the great Wheel of Life, when the old life becomes a new, pure one. As the sun hangs over the world, The Sun card, positioned as the nineteenth of twenty-two major arcana cards in the tarot, hangs over Judgement[174] and The World before the drop back to The Fool, number zero, to begin again. Plath's colors of red and yellow in the second stanza of the poem are predominant colors of this card.

Autobiographically, most interpret the line about Spain in the second stanza as a reference to Plath and Hughes' difficult honeymoon in sunny Benidorm, with its resultant quarrelling over rooms, illness and more; quarrelling reinforces the meaning of this tarot card in reverse.

The uncle is an example of wealth and attainment, also properties of The Sun card. These ideas disgust Plath, as she makes clear in her first and fourth stanzas, matching his great wealth with gluttony.

Hermeticists write of the "Pearl of Great Price," and Plath's pearl suggests the same, referencing the New Testament's Book of Matthew, 13: 45-46, "[45]Again, the kingdom of heaven is like a

---

174 The Rider-Waite Tarot deck uses the British spelling of the word "Judgement."

merchant seeking beautiful pearls, who, when he had found one pearl of great price, went and sold all that he had and bought it."

Hermeticists believe the basic principle is that man must use his forces and blessings to be in harmony with the world. This is the connecting link between earth and heaven, between moral law and material law, between the Microcosm and the Macrocosm. Plath took it upon herself to judge the uncle and how he was living. She saw his life as shallow and meaningless, explaining her fourth stanza question about where he might hide his life.

In earlier drafts of this poem, words were cut about the furled shape of a snail's body, as well as a twig strong enough to hold someone small, but not someone big. It is a play on the New Testament's verse Mark 10:25: "It is easier for a camel to go through the eye of a needle, than for a rich man to enter into the kingdom of God." This fits well with the success of The Sun card, bearing its unfurled flag like a big red slug, and the child experiencing the simple joy of riding on the back of a pony not large enough for a big, rich adult.

Second Mirror: Alchemy

Alchemists assign The Sun card to represent The Greater Conjunction, the fourth operation in alchemical transformation. It is the coming together of opposing archetypal forces of the Sun and Moon, the King and Queen. Alchemical terms abound in "Stopped Dead," beginning with the cold temperature in the first stanza, and the rubbery "grubs" stopping up test tubes. The image of the grubs biting their tails is the Ouroboros, the circular symbol of a snake or dragon devouring its own tail as a symbol of infinity or wholeness.

The colors of red and yellow in the poem represent mercury and gold in alchemy. When heated or melted, the elements are an apt metaphor for the marriage of these two passionate, bickering poets. As mercury and gold become molten, the metals could be said to writhe and sigh, as in Plath's second stanza; they violently explode as in Plath's third stanza, in line with the explosive properties of The Sun tarot card. Just as in creating fire, to write the word *fire* in Hebrew, one needs two letters together: Aleph (air) and Chin/Shin (fire).

In "Stopped Dead" however, Plath is after something bigger and angrier than her alchemist forefathers in England, France, and Ireland. Purity feels a long way off as she struggles with her hot temper and a few expletives around the idea of a baby. The word "bloody" is considered profane in Great Britain.

In alchemy, the philosophical child is the offspring of the King and Queen, the result of their marriage or union. A "bloody baby" reinforces this idea, as blood is the universal fluid, the materialized "vital light," or Sun (Hall, 173). Alchemists believe that blood, being fluid, carries properties of water, and the body represents earth. Plath adds *air* to bring the elements together with fire, her sunset image, creating gold. The golden child is the philosopher's stone.

The fourth stanza's number seven is the seven stages of alchemy. "Chin," a.k.a. "shin" is the Hebrew letter meaning "teeth," another correlation with gluttony. The word "still" is alchemical equipment for distillation, to separate pure essence from waste and unnecessary matter. "Ham" is Hebrew for "hot" or "burnt," good fits for The Sun card. Plath sees Uncle Walt's golden riches as waste.

"Uncle, uncle?" is some fun with the colloquialism to beg for mercy. It is the tearing down of the ego, part of the psychological transformative process to divine wholeness.

The soul in alchemy is the passive presence within everyone that survives through all eternity. It is part of the original substance, the First Matter, of the universe. Soul was considered beyond the four material elements and thus conceptualized as a fifth element, or Quintessence. In the last stanza, Plath questions whether the uncle values his soul as he values materials. Plath also suggests in that final stanza that in Gibraltar, she will live "on air." This is another triple meaning of the alchemical element of air; of living with no money; and that she will survive as the Rock of Gibraltar has, through her resolute, quintessential spirit.

Third Mirror: Mythology

In ancient times, the Romans considered the Rock of Gibraltar to be one of the Pillars of Hercules (the other one found in Africa) marking the distance Hercules traveled. Hercules was said to have straddled the strait, with a foot on each continent like a Colossus. The ancient Phoenicians believed the Rock of Gibraltar marked the limit to the known world, and going past it would be a "dead drop" into the abyss.

Plath's idea of "ham" and "Hamlet" may also reference Egypt, as the Bible refers to Egypt as "the land of Ham" in *Psalms* (Holy Bible). The "hot" and "burnt" meanings of the Hebrew seen in the last mirror also reflect Egypt's climate and people of dark skin. The Hebrew word for Egypt was *Mizraim*, meaning "the two lands," and the name of one of Ham's sons. In "Stopped Dead," Plath separates herself from the rich, wasteful life she deems sinful, and curses the wealthy as in Noah's Biblical *Curse of Ham*. In this mirror therefore, "Sad Hamlet, with a knife" references the Biblical Ham, who had Noah castrated while sleeping off drunkenness.

In Ancient Greek, Nordic, and other cultures, it was believed that the Sun was a golden chariot riding across the sky. When night occurred, its brakes were said to squeal. A new day might be compared to Plath's cry at birth. The Old Norse word for the Sun is Sól. In the 13th century Norse *Poetic Edda*, the verses from the poem Völuspá illustrate both Plath's steep cliff, as well as the idea of searching for a place to live. Plath's last line of "Stopped Dead" echoes the Völuspá:

> "The sun, the sister of the moon, from the south
> Her right hand cast over heaven's rim;
> No knowledge she had where her home should be" (Bellows, 4)

In the Old Norse poem, "Gylfaginning," the Sun and Moon are steered by the two beautiful children of Mundilfari, who chase each other in a wheel around the sky, reflecting Plath's second stanza. The Norse god Odin was said to refer to the Sun as *the bright bride* of the heavens and also as *shining*, suggesting money or dowry, fitting capitalistic and materialistic themes of "Stopped Dead" (Lindow, 198-199).

The Greek god Apollo was known as the Sun god, Helios, and Titan, god of the Sun, among other epithets. At the Oracle of Delphi, the Sibyl, a prophetess probably under the influence of hallucinogenic vapors rising from the earth, channeled the words of Apollo as she writhed and sighed in frenzy, suiting Plath's second stanza.

Apollo was the illegitimate son of Zeus and Leto. When Zeus' wife Hera learned of the pregnancy, she forbade Leto to give birth on land. Leto was hung out over this same geographical dead drop of Plath's poem. Leto found a way to create a floating land called Delos, which, like the Rock of Gibraltar with its sandy strip connecting to Spain, is neither mainland, nor is it a real island. Leto gave birth to Apollo, and Zeus secured the island to the bottom of the ocean. Zeus was forever unfaithful to Hera, always impregnating other goddesses and mortal women, reflecting Plath's third stanza frustrations over the babies.

The god Apollo is associated with the Ancient Greek's "Golden Mean," espousing moderation and virtue over gluttony and over-indulgence. The inscription over Apollo's Oracle at Delphi reads "Nothing in excess." Plath's "Stopped Dead" looks upon obesity and materialism with Apollo-like disdain.

Fourth Mirror: History and the World

Plath's poetic choice to live in sunny subtropical Gibraltar is relevant to her own autobiography, to history and geography at large, and as metaphor. Gibraltar is, of course, off the southwestern tip of Europe on the Iberian peninsula. This fits Plath's acknowledgment that she was not looking at England, France, or Ireland in the second stanza. The Rock of Gibraltar is right off the coast of Spain, a country also mentioned in the poem.

The rock is a monolithic promontory with a steep drop that would require "A squeal of brakes" to stop fast and turn around. As it declines toward sea level, its many layers of shale and limestone could be compared to many "chins." The rock has a "violent" past: it has been captured and recaptured by the Moors, by the Spaniards, and by the British. Despite many sieges over the centuries, nothing has been able to destroy the rock or its people.

The Rock of Gibraltar's Gorham's Cave is an ancient shrine full of several thousand personalized scarabs left by travelers passing through the straits from the Atlantic into the Mediterranean, or vice-versa. The Egyptian scarab is modeled after the

"Look round, my boys, and view how beautiful the Rock appears by the light of the glorious fire."

— George Augustus Eliott, 1st Baron Heathfield, at the end of the sortie, 27 November 1781

dung beetle, as a symbol of the sun and the sun god, Ra. Metallurgy was important in the ancient Mediterranean region of Gibraltar, where the Phoenicians had learned that combining the two metals of tin and copper produced the strong, sunny, hot metal, bronze. This echoes Plath's second stanza. During World War II the British used Gibraltar as a base, and its many deep caves were outfitted to hide soldiers and personnel in case of attack, a fit to Plath's line about where to stash life (Serfaty).

Gibraltar had meaning for Plath and Hughes. Hughes' Uncle Walter was born on Gibraltar and fought there in World War II (G. Hughes, 4). Plath's close friend, Ruth Fainlight, spent time in Gibraltar, along with her husband and the writer Paul Bowles (Fainlight). Gibraltar is a British territory, but under its own governance. That independence no doubt appealed to Plath.

Plath's "yowl" in the third stanza fits the huge population of tail-less Barbary macaques that live on the Rock of Gibraltar and attract many visitors each year to see them. It could be said that these monkeys' tails look bitten off, fitting Plath's second stanza. The Rock of Gibraltar is one of the last sites where Neanderthals were known to live, and Plath may have also been snidely calling Hughes' Uncle Walt "a Neanderthal" by setting him in the scene of this poem (Smithsonian). Plath was not always kind in how she talked about others, as unpublished excerpts of her *Letters Home*, as well as journal entries and her *Bell Jar* characterizations reveal.

In the 1600s, the time of Shakespeare, France's absolutist King Louis XIV was known as "the Sun King" for his great patronage to the arts. He created the dazzling Palace of Versailles, renovated and improved the Louvre, and much more. Louis XIV was both obese and a millionaire, fitting Plath's fourth line of "Stopped Dead."

Louis XIV was interested in the territorial expansion of France and married Maria Theresa of Spain to increase his empire. Maria Theresa was to renounce all claims to Spain and its territory, including the Rock of Gibraltar, and to provide a dowry. This did not happen, and became grounds for France's attack on the Spanish Netherlands. In the War of Spanish Succession, lands were divvied up, with Gibraltar remaining British territory. Louis XIV had an uncommonly close relationship with his mother, similar to the oedipal notes of Shakespeare's Prince Hamlet. Like Hamlet, Louis was ostentatious, vengeful, and egotistical, once declaring, "I am the state," and giving Plath's rhetorical "Who do you think I am" the meaning of the people asking about their own value. In royal portraiture such as Le Brun's *Le roi gouverne par lui-même, modello*, Louis was sometimes idealized as Apollo. In accord with The Sun tarot card, Louis XIV raised France to its preeminent position during the Enlightenment (Le Brun).

Fifth Mirror: Astrology and Astronomy

Astronomy asserts that the sun formed by gravitational collapse within a molecular cloud, illustrated in Plath's first line. Thermonuclear fusion formed within its core, birthing the sun from this initial collapse, and appropriate to the second line of "Stopped Dead." To us, this sun-star appears "Red and yellow," and there are two mentions of sunsets in the third stanza of "Stopped Dead." The sun's climate could be said to be "violent," and as we know no star lasts forever, "We're here on a visit." Through other destructions and gravitational collapses, new stars are born all the time, echoing Plath's entire third stanza. The sun is covered with a dense plasma layer like a boiling, gooey liquid and fitting Plath's image of liquefied metals. It rotates faster at its equator than at its poles, like Plath's tail-biting rubber in a wheel of rotation. It is believed that the sun has an abundance of heavy elements, particularly gold and uranium, yet two more heated metals.

The sun is disc-shaped, looking sometimes bronze, sometimes white, and fitting Plath's question of whether it is a penny or pearl. The Ancient Romans called it "Sol," a homophone for "soul," an important image in Plath's last stanza.

The sun dictates time. Original ancient calendars documented length of days, months, change of seasons, and length of the year based on sunlight. Twice a year, at the solstice, the sun reaches its highest or lowest point on the horizon. These two events are sometimes seen as a "wheel" of time. It is Plath's second stanza once again.

The word *solstice* comes from the Latin meaning for "sun," joined with *sistere,* meaning "to stand still," very much like "Stopped Dead." To ancient Romans such as Pliny, *solstice* was defined as "sun standing." At the solstice, from the earth's point of view, the sun stands still in a decline, very much hanging over a steep drop, before it reverses direction. In many cultures, the solstice marks the beginning of winter and summer, with the summer solstice marking the longest and the winter solstice marking the shortest days of the year before returning to the northern hemisphere. The maximum elevation, like the tip of the Rock of Gibraltar, occurs at the summer solstice; the minimum elevation, the unusual three days of mostly darkness, occurs in the winter solstice. This fits Plath's "out cold" and sunset imagery.

Astrologically, the sun and moon are considered the *luminaries* and some of the most important planets.[175] The sun is associated with the ego, self, expressions of power and authority, and good times and celebration. These are all characteristics of The Sun tarot card, of Hughes' Uncle Walt, and of the character of Uncle Claudius in *Hamlet*, to be examined shortly.

The Zodiac wheel of constellations is said to revolve around the sun. Where the sun aligns with the constellations when someone is born determines his or her sun sign, the most important influence on a personality in astrology.

Sixth Mirror: Humanities and the Arts

Plath mentions Shakespeare's *Hamlet* in the fourth stanza of "Stopped Dead." This violent tragedy, famous for its melancholy and insanity, contains many aspects of The Sun card in reverse. In one scene, Hamlet quips to his Uncle Claudius, a comparison to Hughes' uncle: "I am too much in the sun" (I.ii.67). Hamlet, Prince of Denmark, is of course the son/sun of the king.

Sigmund Freud analyzed *Hamlet* as a story of the Oedipus complex. To Freud, the knife was a phallic symbol. Hamlet's pain is therefore interpreted as sexual confusion and anger over his uncle taking his mother. Ultimately, Hamlet's vengeance destroys his love, Ophelia, and their unborn child. Hamlet has been seen as a mystical play since the 1800s, with Hermetic ideas in lines such as "There is nothing good or bad, but thinking makes it so," and the infamous and existential, "To be or not to be."

Lines from *Hamlet* echo Plath's "Stopped Dead" in word or meaning, most importantly in Act 3, Scene 2 when Hamlet says, 'do you think I am easier to be played on than a pipe?" This is very much the mindset of Plath's sarcastic "Who do you think I am."

In the play, Hamlet's Uncle Claudius murdered his own brother, the prince's father, to obtain the throne of Denmark and marry King Hamlet's widow. Prince Hamlet spends much of the play feigning madness, or else truly going mad, and seeking revenge. He kills his lover Ophelia's father with a knife by mistake, fitting the end lines of Plath's fourth stanza.

The pregnant Ophelia is consumed with grief and descends into madness herself. She consumes rue, a word to mean "regret," but also a plant known for its powerful abortive properties. It is another meaning for a bloodied baby. Ophelia then climbs into a willow tree, the branch breaks, and she drowns. This is considered one of the most poetic deaths in literature.

Plath surely also recognized in *Hamlet* a point that author Mary Pipher did almost forty years later in her 1994 book, *Reviving Ophelia*: Ophelia, like the modern American adolescent girl, had competing pressures from parents, peers, and the media to achieve an impossible ideal. Girls are expected to go through physical changes, continually meet their goals, be forever positive and remain emotionally well balanced. Plath knew the pain of this one personally.

In Plath's personal copy of Dante Alighieri's *The Divine Comedy*, she underlined and annotated many correspondences with The Sun tarot card, and all of the principle themes and images in "Stopped Dead" are present. In *Paradiso,* the last of the three books of the Comedy, *Canto VI*, Plath underlined that the sun represents of the supreme gift of free will, and that truth is seen clearly.

Paradiso Canto VI explains that Constantine had *wheel*ed back the host toward *Spain*,[176] counter to the course of heaven (Alighieri, 431, 433). Plath underlined "within the present pearl shineth the light of Romeo." Also of interest is that a character in this Canto has many chins (Alighieri, 434); on another page about the sun, Plath underlined "glorious wheel revolve and render" (466); and from

---

175 Astronomers now know that the sun is actually a star, and is the moon is not a planet. However, since ancient times, astrologers have tended to call the sun and moon both planets.
176 Italics mine.

Paradiso Canto XI, "From this slope, where most it breaks the steepness of decline, <u>was born into the world a sun</u>" (470). In the book, Plath also underlined the phrase, "<u>the greatest and most shining of these pearls</u>" (539). At Canto XXIX, Plath drew a star and wrote "ha!" in the margin, underlining this passage that seems to define her judgment on Uncle Walter and her beliefs of the higher road to take: "<u>It was not to acquire any good for himself, but that his reflected light might itself have *the joy of conscious existence*, that God, in his timeless eternity, uttered himself as love in created beings, themselves capable of loving</u>" (583).[177]

Also not lost on the Bloomsday bride Sylvia Plath was the fact that James Joyce's famous *Ulysses* character, the feisty Molly Bloom, was from Gibraltar. With a name as floral as the flowers in the background of this tarot card, Molly Bloom, ends the book with her famous soliloquy, in a tone very much of this card's happiest upright endowment:

> "...I was a Flower of the mountain yes when I put the rose in my hair like the Andalusian girls used or shall I wear a red yes and how he kissed me under the Moorish wall and I thought well as well him as another and then I asked him with my eyes to ask again yes and then he asked me would I yes to say yes my mountain flower and first I put my arms around him yes and drew him down to me so he could feel my breasts all perfume yes and his heart was going like mad and yes I said yes I will Yes" (Joyce).

Joyce's joyful, happy narrative for Molly Bloom, the Andalusia territory in Spain, and even the Moorish wall are a part of The Sun tarot card.

In contrast, Joyce's protagonist and alter-ego in *Ulysses*, Stephen Dedalus, embodies aspects of Hamlet. It is said, in fact, that James Joyce wanted his *Ulysses* to be a more upbeat version of *Hamlet*, while also being structured along with Homer's *Odyssey* (Thompson, 123–126). And like Shakespeare's Hamlet and Plath both asking in their ways, "Who do you think I am," Joyce's Dedalus asserts himself in reversal of God's "I Am that I Am" (Exodus 3:14)[178] saying, "As I am. As I am."

---

177 The phrase, "joy of conscious existence" was double-underlined, and not italicized as shown here.
178 "I Am That I Am" is sometimes translated to "I will be" or "I shall be" and is considered to be one of the most famous verses in the Torah. "I am I" is quoted on sixteen different occasions in Plath's journals. Plath played with this idea in other poems such as "Suicide off Egg Rock," and perhaps most famously, in chapter 20 of her novel *The Bell Jar*: "I took a deep breath and listened to the old brag of my heart: I am, I am, I am."

Chapter Twenty-One: Becoming Death
Card #20   The Judgement Card   Corresponding Poem: "Poppies In October"

In an unpublished excerpt of an October 1962 letter to her mother, Plath wrote of the late-blooming poppies and cornflowers on her desk at Court Green.[179] The poems "Poppies in October," along with "Ariel," were both written on her thirtieth birthday; they are some of the infamous October poems Plath blazed through in her first month of real abandonment by Hughes. The publication of this poem in *The Collected Poems* of Sylvia Plath does not include the dedication to her Portuguese poet friend Helder and his wife Suzette Macedo, nor does it include the final exclamation point Plath had intended. "Poppies in October" was a gift of love: from God to Plath, and from Plath to her readers.

First Mirror: The Tarot/Qabalah

The meaning of the Judgement[180] card is spiritual unfolding and realization. This card symbolizes resurrection or new birth, all limitations put away, and spiritual gifts and healing. The angel pictured is the True Self, veiled by clouds, made of water and symbolizing the mind. In accordance with Qabalah and tarot teaching, the mind often gets in the way of seeing the True Self. The Golden Dawn assigns the Hebrew letter *Shin* to the Judgement card, meaning: "the (wisdom) tooth which allows (mental) chewing of the spiritual dimensions of the (physical) aspects (four elements) of the manifestation." We were introduced to the Hebrew letter *Shin/Chin* in the last poem. With its several different pronunciations, Shin is also know as *Sin*. It is a letter meaning *almighty* and *fire*. The glyph represents three flames, fed by air. The letter Shin's design is a comprised of two other Hebrew letters written together: *Yud* and *Vav* (Trugman). Yud means "the infinite point" and Vav means "connection." Vav possesses the ability to invert the past to the future and the future to the past. It alludes to the power to connect and inter-relate all

JUDGEMENT.

twenty-two individual powers of Creation, the twenty-two letters of the Hebrew alphabet from *Alef* to *Tav*. The goal is to draw from the future into the past, to heal, repent, and return to God in love (Ginsburgh).

In tarot and Qabalah, this card's number 20 is comprised of two completed cycles of ten. The number two represents two ones, God and man united, therefore, twenty is the full physical and spiritual experience made complete. It is a rebirth, a resurrection, and renewal. In Gematria, the name of the letter Shin written out, ShYN, corresponds to 360, the number of degrees in a complete circular cycle. Likewise, the lines on Shin give the magical significance of spirit descending upon tongues of fire, like the bright red of poppies.

"Poppies in October" is one of Plath's best examples of her poem describing a tarot card's pictorial images: The Judgement card contains clouds around a bright day,

---

179 This letter from Sylvia Plath to Aurelia Plath, dated October 25, 1962, may be found at the Lilly Library, Indiana University-Bloomington.
180 British spelling.

corresponding to Plath's first line. Her second line's use of the word "nor" fits the sexual ambiguity of the angel. The poem and card picture are full of sky and paleness. Plath's ambulance and red heart symbols are apt for the red cross of medicine, seen on the flag of the trumpet. Plath's gift image fits well: October was Plath's birth month, she wrote this poem on the last birthday of her life, and this tarot card represents the gift of new life. The poem clearly presents the card's pictured frost on the mountains and the dominating color of cornflower blue.

"Poppies in October" suggests communication with the other side of this life, yet it is not by Ouija board or Plath and Hughes' other routes of spiritism.[181] The poem declares she received something without asking for it, perhaps an epiphany or vision from the sky: Plath's poetic mouths are late because the card's pictured dead bodies are rising from coffins. Earlier drafts of this poem had references to a hearse, being shut away forever, grey architecture and limbo. These all well-describe the burial vaults of the Judgement card's picture.

Second Mirror: Alchemy

Alchemists describe the Judgement card as Resurrection and Rejuvenation. "Poppies in October," from the alchemical perspective, is to become one with God by uniting the masculine consciousness with the feminine subconscious.

Through the alchemical lens, "Even the sun" could be taken as direction, to level this golden material; Plath did not start the sentence with the word "Not." In alchemy, the Sun is one of the major symbols representing gold, the philosopher's stone, and perfection. Clouds in alchemy symbolize the spirit rising to the top of the vessel (Abraham, 42). Plath's Sun appears to be a kind of cloud itself. This makes sense, as the alchemist believes this separation of body and spirit is "sun and shadow," shadows and clouds being an interchangeable alchemical metaphor. Alchemist Michael Maier wrote, "the Sun is the tongue, the Shadow is the language" (Abraham, 195).

In Shakespeare's Sonnet 33, he uses this alchemical imagery to explain an understanding of a love's infidelity. Shakespeare's Sun gilds "pale streames with heauenly alcumy," sounding very much like Plath's third tercet in "Poppies in October." The clouds eclipse Shakespeare's forlorn narrator as he accepts that he is wiser through love and forgiveness (Abraham, 195-196).

Plath's "skirts" reference the feminine White phase, often pictured in alchemical engravings as the appearance of a queen dressed in shining white robes within the alchemical flask, and looking very much like the angel on the Judgement card. This phase produces a white tincture that marks a process of inner change when the alchemist integrates with the purified feminine subconscious component of the soul.

Plath's third tercet of "Poppies in October" is alchemy in action, naming the gas on fire that brings about a successful transmutation of substance under the pale flame, with her eyes protected. From alchemy's physiological perspective, it is a successful suicide, transmuting to the spirit form. This may have been planning or prophecy for how Plath herself would leave the physical world to join God.

---

181 See footnote in the Humanities and the Arts mirror of *Fixed Stars Govern a Life*'s interpretation of "Lady Lazarus" for an explanation of the difference between spiritism and spiritualism.

190

Third Mirror: Mythology

Back in tarot card #1 of the major arcana, The Magician, we met Hermes. In the mythology behind the Judgement card, Hermes is revealed as the deity of the underworld, summoning the dying by laying his golden staff upon their eyes, fitting the last line of Plath's third tercet. Hermes wears a winged hat that could be called a "bowler," and as the trickster, manages to "skirt" around the law and avoid being caught. He represents humankind as both the judge and the accused who must look back on the past to decide the future direction.

Occasionally, Hermes summoned souls back to life, and he prepared them for a new life in the underworld of Hades. Hermes the Summoner and Psychopomp[182] represents summing up the critical moments of this life to reveal an intelligent pattern, the consequences of experience, varied actions and intuition, and allowing all dead beneath consciousness to speak, be understood, and accepted. It is Plath's "late mouths" crying open.

Hermes calls for the dead to rise. Whether an artist is blocked and struggling with random ideas before they come together in the creative work, or the psychology patient searching through disconnected memories and feelings of the past and present before clarity arises, Hermes is said to bring this cohesion together and make sense of the pieces. This is Hermes' greatest magic. It is the entirety of The Fool's journey and returns the person to a kind of second birth, a dawning that emerges out of the past.

The constellation of Pavo represents the male peacock that fans his tile out behind him as Hermes' wings are spread on the Judgement card. One of the mythical attributes given to the peacock is compassion. In an Indian story, a peacock took pity on Indra, the Hindu leader of the gods. When Indra's enemies were coming, the bird raised its tail to form a blind or screen behind which Indra could hide. The many eyes on his feathers, in pale blue and flaming copper, dulled the enemies' sight. It was Plath's gift of love imagery, because Indra was saved by a bird's feathery skirt. As a reward for this act of compassion, the bird was honored with the jewel-like blue-green plumage that it bears to this day.

Fourth Mirror: History and the World

In 1917, the country of Russia was in a political, economic, and social crisis. By fall, half of its industrial production had closed down, its national debt was high, the cost of living unmanageable, and there was mass unemployment and civil unrest. Workers and soldiers had been demonstrating and rising up throughout the year, and in some cases violence was used against them. The October Revolution, which took place in November by our Gregorian calendar but in October on the Julian calendar, was when Vladimir Lenin led the Red Army of Bolsheviks to storm the Winter Palace which the provisional government had taken over after imperialism had been overthrown.[183]

Plath had a keen interest in Russian history. One of her favorite writers and the subject of her undergraduate thesis, Dostoevsky, concentrated on his country's historical themes and settings. Plath dated a young Russian man in 1951 and 1952, and had two Russian history classes at Smith College. Dostoevsky was friendly with the Imperial Romanov family and rabidly defended both the Romanovs and the Russian Orthodox faith, believing and writing

182 A psychopomp guides souls to rest in the place of the dead.
183 Plath's "Poppies in July," as well as her poems "Candles" and "Tulips" all seem to address aspects of the murder of the Romanov imperial family that took place in July 1917. Note the similar imagery throughout these poems. Additionally, poppies, especially the larger blossoms, are sometimes likened to tulips.

prophetically that radicalism and godless ideals would be the downfall of Imperialist Russia (Volkov, 193-208).

The poppy flower blooms in late spring to early summer, and so the idea of "Poppies in October" is surprising, but not unheard of in unusually warm weather. The poppy is mainly grown in eastern and southern Asia, and southeastern Europe, including vast regions of Russia. Poppies are the principal source of opiate drugs such as morphine and codeine, pain-relievers often found in an ambulance. Plath's journals indicated that she used opiates on occasion: mainly doctor-prescribed codeine cough syrup (*UJ*, 31, 308,409). Because of its red color and opiate properties, the poppy is said to represent sleep, peace, and death. The ancient Greeks and Romans offered gifts of poppies to the dead, and ancient Egyptians had patients eat poppy seeds to relieve pain. The narcotic quality of the seeds disappears twenty days after the flower has opened, the number on the Judgement tarot card (Jonsson and Krzymanski, 1989). There is a correlation between the Greek root word *ops* and its possessive *opos*, meaning *eye*, *opsis*, meaning sight or appearance, and Greek *opos*, for *opium* (Wright).

The remembrance poppy, or the red-flowered corn poppy ("cornflowers") has been used since 1920 to commemorate soldiers who have died in wartime. John McCrae's "In Flanders Fields," one of the most popular and most quoted poems about World War I, made the poppy a symbol of remembrance. Plath wrote an article on wearing the remembrance poppy while at Cambridge (Peel, 254). The tradition began on Armistice Day, the end of World War I, and spread from the United States of America across the world. Pacifists sometimes choose to wear white poppies ("Palely") while the blood-red poppy is more traditional ("flamily"). In Persian literature, poppies represent love and those who die for love.

In the next mirror, the dwarf planet Pluto is matched to the month of October and its zodiac sign of Scorpio. From Pluto, one can make the leap to plutonium, the radioactive chemical element discovered soon after and named for it. Plutonium is at first silvery-gray in appearance, but dulls when oxidized. It is extremely powerful and may spontaneously ignite, making it dangerous to handle. These qualities all correspond with Plath's third tercet of "Poppies in October." The implosion assembly method for weapons-grade plutonium resembles a poppy in design. Likewise, the photograph published of the first nuclear explosion, the Trinity test,[184] taken on July 16, 1945 just sixteen minutes after the bomb's detonation, resembles a poppy seed pod. After this test, Dr. Robert Oppenheimer quoted the Hindu *Bhagavad Gita*: "Now I am become Death, the destroyer of worlds" (eyewitness).

This test bomb was developed for the "Fat Man" and "Trinity" weapons in 1945. The "Fat Man" atomic bomb was dropped on Nagasaki, Japan on August 9, 1945, killing 70,000 people and injuring 100,000 more. It was a terrible Judgement Day on Japan, and it soon repented, helping to bring about the end of World War II. Plutonium would go on to be stockpiled by the superpowers throughout the Cold War. Plath was very disturbed by the Cold War and the nuclear arms race, and wrote of it often.[185] As a pacifist, she no doubt had very mixed feelings, knowing that the Nazis had also been at work attempting to develop nuclear weapons. America did it first, and this terrible "gift" may have saved the free world.

---

184 The first nuclear explosion in the Trinity test was with a uranium-235 bomb, not plutonium. The devastation would have been all the same to Plath.

185 See *Fixed Stars Govern a Life's* interpretation of Sylvia Plath's poem, "Ariel," for more on nuclear weapons and the arms race.

Fifth Mirror: Astrology and Astronomy

In myths explaining the constellations, Hermes amputated the head of the many-eyed Argus, and his eyes were put on the tail of the peacock by Hera, or Juno in some versions, representing all the stars of the sky. This is the story attributed to the constellation of Pavo, the peacock, whose name in French derives from *Ponceau* for "corn poppy." According to Ovid, Mercury, a.k.a. Hermes, recounted a story that Argus tried to lull him to sleep, as an opiate might do, before he cut off Argus' head. "Poppies in October" contains Argus' eyes: the stars unseen when blocked by the "bowlers" of clouds.

In October of every year, the sun begins its month-long path through the zodiac sign of Scorpio whose ruling planet is Pluto, assigned to the Judgement card. In 2006, astronomers demoted it to a "dwarf planet," although astrologers still recognize Pluto as powerful. Pluto was discovered in 1930, so it does not have the ancient astrological history of other planets visible to the naked eye. From its discovery date until 2006, Pluto was classified as a planet, and this is what Plath understood it to be. Plath also did not know of any of Pluto's five moons, the first of which wasn't discovered until 1978.

In 1906, Bostonian Percival Lowell, founder of the Lowell Observatory and relative of Plath and Hughes' friend, poet Robert Lowell, suspected there was a ninth planet and called it "Planet X" as he searched the skies to prove its existence. Lowell did not prove this in his lifetime, but the Lowell Observatory did make its name with Pluto's discovery in 1930. Pluto's astrological symbol is the symbol for alchemy; it looks like Neptune's trident, as well as the Hebrew letter Shin, both with an added circle in the center resembling a poppy flower. This symbol means "spirit over mind" and is about transcending matter. Because Pluto is so hard to see, Plath's third-tercet images of the pale, the flame of a star, carbon monoxide, and dulled eyes all fit well.

"Though free to think and act, we are held together, like the stars in the firmament, with ties inseparable. These ties cannot be seen, but we can feel them."

--Nikola Tesla

Astrologers believe that Pluto is a kind of catalyst for change, as the Judgement card is a great awakening. Pluto is said to burn away what is unnecessary, either by our own initiations, or changes in external circumstances. It is sometimes about the agonizing process of letting go and trusting in faith. Pluto is death and rebirth, and resurrection for those who can abandon the baggage of their egos. Power and personal transformation are associated with Pluto's astrological influence. Plath's "Poppies in October" clearly mirrors Pluto's transformation (StarIQ).

On the negative side, Pluto's great power also can create corruption. Its discovery in 1930 coincided with the rise of fascism and Stalinism in Europe, bringing about World War II. Astrologers also associate Pluto with the Great Depression and the proliferation of organized crime in the United States.

Rather prophetically, and impossible for Plath to have known as it was classified information, at the end of 1962, just under two months after she wrote "Poppies in October," the United States Naval Research Laboratory launched the Poppy program, an electronic intelligence satellite system to monitor emissions from Soviet air and missile defense radar. The satellites looked like the opium seed pods of the poppy plant (NRO).

Sixth Mirror: Humanities and the Arts

In Frank L. Baum's classic children's story, *The Wonderful Wizard of Oz* (1900), red poppies are significant in the chapter, "The Deadly Poppy Field," threatening the characters made of flesh with the forever sleep of death. As the scene opens, the hint of cornflowers is there too:

"They walked along listening to the signing of the brightly colored birds and looking at the lovely flowers which now became so thick that the ground was carpeted with them. There were big yellow and white and blue and purple blossoms, besides great clusters of scarlet poppies, which were so brilliant in color that they dazzled Dorothy's eyes" (Baum).

The MGM movie adaptation of the novel, *The Wizard of Oz* (1939), was released when Plath as a girl, and it was one of the first movies in Technicolor. In the poppy field scene, Dorothy lies sleeping in the flowers in her cornflower blue gingham dress, matching the sky above her, streaked with clouds. Toto and the Lion are also drugged asleep. Glinda the Good Witch of the North has been called by the Scarecrow and Tin Man in this emergency, and she appears in the sky with her gift of love. In her sparkling frost skirts, the Good Witch waves her wand over the group tot make it snow. The frost wakes them, breaking the flesh's vulnerability to the drug. All four of Plath's stanzas are a perfect description of the movies scene.

Dostoevsky's 1866 novel, *Crime and Punishment*, contains all of the principles of the Judgement tarot card. An important book for Plath, it is one of Dostoevsky's major works, and she touched on themes of it in her own stories (*UJ*, 303). Dostoevsky's protagonist, Raskolnikov, sees himself as a Nietzschean Overman in society, a powerful person with the personal authority to commit murder under the rationale that it is better for society. Throughout the novel, Raskolnikov suffers more from a guilty conscience than from the law. In Russian, the name Raskolnikov means "to bring to light" or "to confess or acknowledge the truth."

Dostoevsky's manipulation of time in this novel became an influence for writers favored by Plath such as Henry James, Joseph Conrad, Virginia Woolf, and James Joyce. The original title of *Crime and Punishment* in Russian is literally translated as "a stepping across." The English meaning loses the physical idea of crossing over a barrier or a boundary, as well as Dostoevsky's religious implication of transgression, which in English refers to a sin rather than a crime (Morris, 28).

The question "What am I" is throughout *Crime and Punishment*, especially asked by Raskolnikov, who ponders every variation of the phrase: "Good Heavens! What am I to do?" (Pt. 1; Ch. V); "What am I glad of?" (Pt. 11; Ch. I) ;"But what am I to do with this now?" (Pt. II; Ch. I); "What am I to say to that?" (Pt. II; Ch. I); "But what am I to do with her?" (Pt. III; Ch. I); "What am I driving at?" (Pt. VI; Ch. II); "What am I?" (Pt. VI; Ch. III); "Ah! what am I coming to!" (Pt. VI; Ch. VIII); "What am I to her?" (Pt. VI; Ch. VIII); "What am I thinking about?" (Pt. VI; Ch. VIII).

Raskolnikov ultimately confesses his terrible murders to the courts in sorrow. He is sent to Siberia, Plath's "forest of frost," where he is at peace in his prison and finally understands who he truly is, and that true love is what he wants. *Crime and Punishment* has been seen as a prophetic warning about the Russian radicalism and communist ideas that would lead later to the Red October Bolshevik Revolution. The last lines of *Crime and Punishment*'s epilogue are a perfect summary of the Judgement card:

"But that is the beginning of a new story—the story of the gradual renewal of a man, the story of his gradual regeneration, of his passing from one world into another, of his initiation into a new unknown life. That might be the subject of a new story, but our present story is ended." -- Dostoevsky

Chapter Twenty-Two: Shattering the Room Full of Mirrors
Card #21   The World Card   Corresponding Poem: "The Courage of Shutting-Up"

When Sylvia Plath's marriage broke up, Ted Hughes openly socialized and was seen around town with his mistress, Assia Wevill. Plath felt humiliated, gossiped about, and alone. Most readers assume this challenging poem is solely about this time. References to Rangoon can be tied to Wevill, who had married her husband and lived there. But Plath, in her brilliance, tied her personal melodrama into something much larger and more sinister:

First Mirror: The Tarot/Qabalah

The World tarot card means that the cycle started by the Fool is complete. The World is success and self-actualization; reason over emotion; and the use of limitation in a mature way. It is also the fulfillment of desires, high and low. This last card in the tarot's major arcana is sometimes also referred to as "the Universal Dancer," as the figure in the center does the dance of life. The spiraling batons in the dancer's hands represent integration and disintegration. In many card designs, the ring around the figure is a snake eating its own tail: the Ouroboros. It is a symbol for the ancient world's inexhaustible life, forever devouring and recreating itself. While she is assumed to be a beautiful woman, the card's figure is considered by many tarot scholars to be the hermaphrodite: the perfect union of male and female within a single body. In schools of mysticism

such as alchemy, the feminine aspects in men and/or the masculine aspects in women are seen as a kind of self-actualization, rising beyond the limitations of the physical and uniting opposites. The Golden Dawn assigns the Hebrew letter *Tau* to The World, defining it as: "the cross upon which each of the four elements are pinned in order that, through their death and resurrection, their higher purposes and meaning be reflected." Tau represents a "seal or witness." God's sealing of creation is a fundamental idea in qabalistic literature.

Plath addresses the properties of this tarot card in many lines within the poem, "The Courage of Shutting-Up" (*ARE,* 45-46): Her opening line of courage and a shut mouth is The World card's self-discipline, as well as the Ouroboros snake with its tail in its mouth.

The outraged sky and lined brain in that same first stanza refer to the card's design of a lined and bumpy wreath against the blue. The clouds pictured in three of the four corners are gray storm clouds.

Plath's second stanza reflects on The World card's meaning in reverse. A first draft of this poem addressed the idea of dates and times, corresponding with the World's idea of completion.

The image of the needle in a groove is the cycle of life, turning around like a record on a phonograph. Plath's same grievances, tattooed over and over, are repeated errors from this life to the next one. These ideas work with the card's circular design on a blue background, and many tattoos are pictures of naked girls, as on this card. The third stanza images of snakes, babies, tits, and "two-legged dreamgirls" are a good fit too, as well as the fourth stanza's "antique billhook." An early draft mentioned tiger heads and American flags, corresponding to the lion and the eagle in the lower and upper right-hand corners. Notice that The World card illustration might also portray a mirror, and the wreath is a kind of a room for the woman pictured, as in Plath's sixth stanza. This illustration, if viewed on its side, resembles an eye, mentioned in that same stanza.

Second Mirror: Alchemy

There is a strong alchemical interpretation to the poem, "The Courage of Shutting-Up." The hermaphrodite represents sulfur and mercury after their conjunction in the alchemy of transformation. The earthly body is considered to be masculine. Therefore, this card is about reconnecting the masculine with the divine feminine through the sacred dance of sex, the alchemical wedding. The woman prepares her body to become the vessel, the primordial waters for birthing the masculine or manifested self.

Silver, named in Plath's second stanza, is one of the seven metals of alchemy and associated with the operation of Distillation. In the alchemical laboratory, the hooks and discs may be equipment. Through this interpretation, Plath is the surgeon and the tattooist, going over and over her work with little success, grieving over the same troubles. As she makes her adjustment, the tireless purple flame, seen in the poem's fourth stanza, grows toward its goal. As flames expand into a larger fire, they become "dangerous," with many tongues that flay the air, all fitting the fourth stanza.

Plath bitterly pictures her tongue hung as a trophy, representing meaningless words, gossip and spite. Alchemy strives to overcome the ego, as the British overcame and colonized Rangoon, referencing the fifth stanza engravings. Alchemical work and secrets were most often passed on through engravings, and Rangoon was a center of Burmese alchemy. [186]

Plath's exclamation over the things pierced speaks for more than a metaphorical penis or the sharp words of the tongue, but for the alchemist's knife, which also divides and breaks apart powders upon mirrored surfaces. Mirrors in alchemy represent the moon, a metaphor for the practice of alchemy itself, the Double, and more. The residue on a mirror from cut and measured powder might expose the secret alchemist's work, as in the sixth stanza.

Plath's sixth stanza's face of a dead man is also a statement about the alchemist's rebirth. The whiteness of the seventh stanza refers to the alchemist's White phase, the second stage of the Great Work that takes place during distillation.

A stool pigeon, seen in the last stanza, is a colloquialism for someone who gives away secrets or informs others, especially the police. Originally, stool pigeons were dead birds nailed to a tree stump as a lure for larger prey; it is a trick to distract attackers. For thousands of years, mystics and alchemists have written in code and metaphor, in part to hide from punishing religions and governments, and to guard their knowledge from getting into the wrong hands. As Christianity and the age of the Rationalists overtook pagan and alchemical ideas, Plath's forgotten country of the last stanza becomes that of the nomadic, hidden mystics who were unsafe everywhere. Might Plath have been referring to protecting the anonymity of mystics in the same way a homosexual, transgender, or hermaphrodite might keep in the metaphorical closet? Plath sees this secret endurance as "obstinate independency." Her resolve to be her elemental, true self will not be broken down and is "Insolvent" among her mountainous obstacles.

---

186 Burmese Alchemy, derived from India, was a central part of Theravāda Buddhism, the national religion of Burma, in the 11th century, with many elements of the practice still existing today.

Third Mirror: Mythology

The mythology associated with The World card is the story of Hermaphroditus, the child of Hermes and Aphrodite. The "Shutting-Up" and "shut mouth" in this poem imply secrecy, reflecting two lines in the first verse of Sir Samuel Garth's poetic translation of "The Story of Salamacis and Hermaphroditus" from Ovid's *Metamorphoses:*

"And what the secret cause, shall here be shown;

The cause is secret, but th' effect is known" (Ovid).

According to Ovid, fifteen-year-old Hermaphroditus, born fully male, was bathing in a pool of water when Salamacis, a river nymph fitting Plath's mermaid image, fell in love with him and wanted to possess him. Because Hermaphroditus was too young to understand love, he rejected her. Salamacis held naked Hermaphroditus in a violent embrace, coiled around the boy like a snake, reflecting the third stanza's second and third lines. She was lifted by an eagle into the air as she wrapped around him, Plath's billhook image, the two of them whirling about in the air. Their four legs, four arms, and Hermaphroditus' penis, a focus for Salamacis as she wanted to make love to him, create Plath's image of nine tails:

"And now she fastens on him as he swims,

And holds him close, and wraps about his limbs.

The more the boy resisted, and was coy,

The more she clipt, and kist the strugling boy.

So when the wrigling snake is snatcht on high

In Eagle's claws, and hisses in the sky,

Around the foe his twirling tail he flings,

And twists her legs, and wriths about her wings."

--Ovid. From *Metamorphoses*

Book IV The story of Salamacis and Hermaphroditus

Metamorphoses continues with Salamacis asking the gods to make her and Hermaphroditus one being, so she would never be apart from him. The gods granted her wish, making them one form: a weakened being of both sexes. After this, Hermaphroditus asked his parents to curse the waters where he swam, weakening everyone who entered them. In this way, Ovid's story casts women as cunning and suggests the weakening of one who is made feminine.

The animals Plath names throughout "The Courage of Shutting-Up" are all pagan symbols: witches were believed to shape-shift into foxes, and in the Middle Ages, foxes represented the devil. The fox is also a warning to hold silence, a key theme of this poem. The otter was considered to be very magical to the Celts. Otters were known as strong protectors, and able to recover from any crisis. Rabbits were symbols of fertility, intuition, rebirth and transformation, and their movements were watched to foretell the future.

Fourth Mirror: History and the World

Julia Ward Howe was an American abolitionist, an activist, and the author of the "Battle Hymn of the Republic." A transcendentalist after Emerson, both Howe and Emerson once lived in Plath's hometown area of Boston. Howe wrote an unpublished and incomplete novel called *Laurence,* a.k.a., *The Hermaphrodite*, the tale of a hermaphrodite poet who lives at different times as both man and woman. Several of the story's characters consider the fictional poet to be "unified" and "superhuman," both traits of The World tarot card (Williams). The text for this unpublished story is kept at the Houghton Library at Harvard where Plath may have read it or at least been told of it.[187]

Sigmund Freud believed that all humans begin as hermaphrodites in the embryonic stage of gestation. Hermaphroditus' brother was Priapus, the god best known for his giant penis. Plath speaks of the tongue as: "Indefatigable, purple. Must it be cut out?" There is a sexual suggestion about this indefatigable tongue that is set up in preceding stanzas full of tits, mermaids, and "two-legged dreamgirls," causing the reader to question just how many legs a dream-girl might have otherwise. After all, the colloquial third leg on a dream-girl might mean that she is a *he*. Plath alludes to the penis and its danger in her fourth stanza, but in Plath's poem, like the tongue being cut out, the penis is cut off and hung like a trophy with animal heads.

Freud might have accused Plath of penis envy, and her journals seem to back this idea up. Plath knew of Freud's penis envy ideas, and wrote about the subject after reading about the penis and anus-fetishes in Japanese aborigine Aino folktales (*UJ*, 457). Plath had, in fact, written of being jealous of men and wanting the man's life (*UJ*, 98), and was aware that Freud perpetuated Ovid's idea of femininity as Hermaphroditus' curse and weakness.

It is here where one can draw parallels between this poem and the Aino, or *Ainu*, meaning "human," aboriginal people of Japan. A favorite book of Plath's, *The Golden Bough*, explores this population in detail. As quiet hunter-gatherers who live on Japan's outlying islands, the Ainu have no written language and, like alchemists, believe everything in nature has a spirit. In 1868, the Japanese government, in a quest to modernize and unite, took over their land and forced them with arms ("in spite of artillery!") to assimilate into Japanese culture. At this time, the Ainu were no longer allowed to speak their indigenous language, another support of Plath's shut-mouth image. They were forbidden to continue religious practices such as animal sacrifice, or the ritual tattooing of the Ainu women's mouths, fitting the tattooing of the second and third stanzas. Consequently, their language has become nearly extinct, fitting Plath's image of the tongue cut out. The Ainu hunted fox, otter, and rabbits, all seen in the fifth stanza, as well as sea eagles fitting Plath's billhook image again. Their hunting was done with arrows and spears, the piercing that closes out that same fifth stanza.

Capital punishment did not exist among the peaceful Ainu people, despite the models of force and violence used upon them by their own government. Inter-racial marriage ultimately did them in, in the same way Salamacis took over Hermaphroditus. In addition to marrying with the Japanese, many World War II soldiers occupying Japan took Ainu brides. Through these intermarriages and destruction of the Ainu language, this culture has been mostly lost. Still, pockets of these people persevere, trying to keep their culture alive in remote mountainous villages. It is the perfect correspondence to the last stanza of "The Courage of Shutting-Up."

Plath's fifth stanza reference to Rangoon also has a link to the Japanese. In 1942 through 1945, Rangoon, in the country of Burma during Plath's time, was under Japanese occupation. Interestingly, in 1947, Burma was known to have one of the freest presses in Asia (Irrawaddy). There is much in "The Courage of Shutting-Up" to conjure the image of the printing press, with its revolving discs, repetitive grooves, the silver beast and tattoo imagery, as a printer makes its whoosh of noise, flaying air and paper.

Ted Hughes' mistress, Assia Wevill, had been married to David Wevill, who was born in Japan.

---

187 Plath also took a summer school course at Harvard in 1954. Howe's great-granddaughter, Frances Minturn Howard, was a friend of Plath and Hughes,' and Plath's journals note a supper at her home in 1958 (*UJ*, 489).

David Wevill went on to teach in Burma, where he and Assia married. While Plath was outwardly upset, David Wevill kept his mouth shut, somehow tolerating Assia's affair with Ted Hughes, and for a time after Plath's death, raising Ted and Assia's daughter, Shura, as his own.

In Plath's time and continuing to this day, Britain's scandalous *Daily Mirror* newspaper reported events ("Mirrors can kill and talk"), gossips and half-truths, fitting the poem's second stanza, "Loaded, as they are, with accounts of bastardies. / Bastardies, usages, desertions and doubleness." Some reports were taken out of context with surgeon-like excisions.

In "The Courage of Shutting-Up," the poet likens what homosexuals have endured to the Salem witch-hunts, trials and tortures. This was the Cold War era, and Plath's Smith College town of Northampton, Massachusetts had its officials rabidly seek out and remove those from society deemed undesirable, a form of sexual McCarthyism.

While Plath was heterosexual, she pondered in writing about lesbians and the lifestyle (*UJ*, 460, 528).[188] As an undergraduate at Smith College, she was close to her professor, the writer Mary Ellen Chase. Chase lived openly as a lesbian with her companion, Eleanor Shipley Duckett. At this time, lesbians could get away with their lifestyle more easily, viewed then as asexual spinsters rather than women declaring a nontraditional sexual orientation. For gay males, however, it was a different situation.

On September 2, 1960, local and state police and a postal inspector raided the homes of three male Smith College professors where they found publications featuring pictures of well-muscled, partially-dressed men that might be compared to Calvin Klein ads today. Personal diaries were also found revealing details of closeted gay life.

Plath's friend, professor, and colleague, Newton Arvin, was one of these homosexuals, along with another Smith instructor, Edward Spofford. An undisputed genius, Newton Arvin won the National Book Award for nonfiction in 1950 for his work on Herman Melville. Arvin had also had a two-year-long love affair with Truman Capote in the late 1940s. Of Arvin's brilliance and influence upon him, Capote wrote, "Newton was my Harvard" (Werth, 108-13).

In December 1958, Plath attended a Capote reading, and later noted in her journals her husband's disdain for the effeminate author, writing, "Ted & [other] men hated the homosexual part of him with more than usual fury. Something else: jealousy at his success? If he [Capote] weren't successful there would be nothing to anger at. I was very amused, very moved" (*UJ*, 442).

After the public revelation of their sexual orientation, Arvin and Spofford lost their jobs at Smith College, while being charged with lewd and lascivious behavior, fined, and publicly disgraced. Arvin also lost a position on the board at Yaddo. These events brought on a severe depression in Arvin, and he went on to suffer a mental breakdown before committing himself to a psychiatric hospital.[189] Plath, who had moved to England, could do nothing long-distance but watch this new form of a Massachusetts witch hunt with her own mouth shut.

Plath's "The Courage of Shutting-Up" reveals the writer's sympathies toward, and even admiration of homosexuals, hermaphrodites, and those who unite with and accept their own diverse natures as a whole and complete self while also daring to keep quiet.

The Daily Mirror scandal sheet was modeled after the New York City tabloids, fitting Plath's eagle bill imagery again. *The Daily Mirror* had emerged as Britain's dominant, if questionable, news source with a leftist, everyman slant. It was known for gossip and political criticism fitting the entire third stanza. *The Daily Mirror* was notorious for its excessive "purple prose," Plath's untiring color in

---

188 See the Humanities and Arts mirror of *Fixed Stars Govern a Life*'s interpretation of "Lesbos" for more on Plath's interest in lesbianism.

189 Newton Arvin died of pancreatic cancer one month after Plath committed suicide in 1963.

the fourth stanza; its coverage of war that fills the hands of the reader at the end of the third stanza; its short features, corresponding to Plath's question of cutting something out; and its multi-panel cartoons, little square "rooms." The cartoons included "Jane," a half-dressed pin-up girl, fitting Plath's tit and dream-girl imagery[190]; "Garth," the military adventurer fitting Plath's cannon muzzles; "Just Jake," which featured a squire with heads of animals on the walls, fitting the fifth stanza again; "Andy Capp," whose eyes never show beneath the brim of his hat, and bring the reader to ask Plath's sixth stanza question; and "The Perishers," a group of parentless children, fitting Plath's baby imagery (Gascoigne).

In 1949, the paper's editor was convicted for publishing sensationalist information that prejudiced the trial of a man convicted for murder. The left-wing journalist, William Connor, pretended to be a woman (a revealing psychological projection itself), who wrote under the pseudonym "Cassandra," and was famous for his controversy and bitter attacks that included the outing of Liberace as a homosexual in 1956. *The Daily Mirror* was sued for Connor's words about the performer: "…the summit of sex—the pinnacle of masculine, feminine, and neuter. Everything that he, she, and it can ever want… a deadly, winking, sniggering, snuggling, chromium-plated, scent-impregnated, luminous, quivering, giggling, fruit-flavoured, mincing, ice-covered heap of mother love"(*Times*, 16).

Meanwhile, in the United States, the McCarthyism of the 1950s brought the police and press to sometimes work together, setting up criminals and homosexuals. Lumped together as the same, criminals and homosexuals were considered pathological, and to be security risks as traitors and dissidents. Law enforcement installed one-way mirrors in men's restrooms and hotel rooms to catch these perpetrators in what was seen as their anti-American criminal sexual activities. It was another way Plath's mirrors could kill and talk, and what terrible rooms they were (JLaw).

Plath must have helplessly felt that she could only watch this torture, as her sixth stanza suggests. Anyone unlucky enough to get his picture on the cover had "the face of a dead man." Plath begins her last stanza addressing the papers' white quietness. Yet, there was nothing shy about them, which she likens to "death rays folded like flags."

Mirrors are a fascinating symbol used often in Plath's poetry. In ancient Egyptian, the word for *mirror* was the same for *life*. Buddhists claim all existence to be synonymous with a mirror's reflection. Witches have used mirrors for scrying, or gazing into an object to foretell the future, in the same way as crystal balls. And both the Roman god Vulcan, and Al-Asnam from *Arabian Nights* had magic mirrors capable of revealing the past, present, and future. Qabalah mirrors aspects of itself, as do all of Plath's poems, which can be interpreted in a variety of corresponding, related ways.

Returning to The World tarot card's hermaphrodite, in biology, a hermaphrodite[191] has both male and female sex organs. For many species, such as the worm of the first stanza, hermaphrodites are the norm. Being a bastard, deserting, and doubling are all apt descriptions of the hermaphroditic worm dividing itself into new and separate beings. In *The Other Sylvia Plath*, author Tracy Brain astutely noted that Plath had ability to create voices that "might be described as hermaphrodite in their ability to slip between masculinity and femininity" (Brain, 4).

"The Courage of Shutting-Up" is also a poem about the torture of witches in history, beyond witch burning. In Great Britain, judicial corporal punishment for witchcraft had only been removed from the statute book in 1948, and punishment was still used in Australia until 1957. Plath and Hughes actively engaged in occult activities such as astrology, Ouija, and tarot that in past history sometimes had their users meet terrible ends. Thus, this was obviously a concern. In "The Courage

---

190 The "Jane" cartoon was considered too racy for the United States.
191 Today, the preferred term is "intersex.".

of Shutting-Up," Plath must hold her tongue, like her homosexual friends in public, and like the witches of Salem. In this interpretive view, she compares her unspeaking mouth to a wound. Plath keeps her eyes shut and prefers not to witness the torture and attacks.

"The Courage of Shutting-Up" is loaded with methods of torture for witches and homosexuals: the red-hot poker, the executioner's sword, the guillotine, the iron maiden, chair of spikes, and hooks for hanging (Buckland, 472-475). Plath's black and outraged discs are the Wheel, a cruel torture device on which a naked body was slowly smashed, but not killed, and another visual match to the World tarot card. Plath's surgeon/tattooist is the executioner or torturer, repeating the floggings, scarring the skin over and over. The cannon muzzles mean the end of a cannon or gun, but it may also refer to the Gossip's Bridle or 'Brank', an iron muzzle to prevent speaking, which angry husbands sometimes used on uncooperative wives. This *cannon* may also be a play on *Canon Episcopi*— the 10th century ecclesiastical rule that belief in witchcraft was heretical. In the 12th century, the heresy of witchcraft became part of Canon Law (Buckland, 76-77). Plath also may have felt, as she wrote in her *Ariel* poems, that her own tongue went too far. She may have expected persecution as a witch, if not by title, then by poetic deed. Tearing or cutting out the tongue was common torture for witches to prevent them from further incantations.

The Cat-O-Nines is a whipping device, also known as the "Scourge." It has a baton, similar to the ones the figure in the picture of The World card holds. The device has nine tails attached to one end, fitting Plath's "nine tails" in the fourth stanza. It works and sounds like a whip, with much more physical damage.

In Plath's journals, she juxtaposes many of these interpretations in a single entry recounting a dream, revealing another possible source for the "The Courage of Shutting-Up":

> "I had seen suffering Christs & corrupt judges & lawyers by Rouault[192] (who died this last Wednesday night) & under these pictures a title or blurb written in French explaining the theme; then a black & white valentine from Elly with a photo-montage of lovers, of three men behind barbwire at a Concentration Camp clipped from the Times from a review which I read about tortures & black trains bearing victims to the furnace – all this I traced into my terrible primitive-drawing dream, a series, like flipped pictures in a book, of black-line drawings (almost like cartoon stick figures) on a white ground of all varieties of tortures – hangings, flaying, eye-gouging, and in a bright crude blood red, lines & spots indicating the flow of blood – all stick figures having red-hands to the wrist & being depicted in crude animation with "La torture" written in bastard dream-French under the drawings" (UJ, 330).

Fifth Mirror: Astrology and Astronomy

The World card most obviously points to the planet Earth, our world. The World card shows four beings in its corners to represent the astrological elements: the lion is Leo, for fire; the bull is Taurus, for earth; the man is Aquarius, for air; and the eagle is Scorpio, for water (DeVore, 355). These symbols also express the Earth's four elements, the four suits of the tarot, the four compass points, four seasons, and the four corners of the universe.

"Discoveries of any great moment in mathematics and other disciplines, once they are discovered, are seen to be extremely simple and obvious, and make everybody including the discoverer, appear foolish for not having discovered them before."

– G. Spencer Brown,
"Law of Form"

---

192 Georges Henri Rouault (1871-1958) was a French Fauvist and Expressionist painter. His dark paintings, such as *Jeu de massacre* (Slaughter), were known to be interpreted as social and moral criticism.

The World is one of Plath's revolving planetary discs in the sky, seen in the first stanza. Our globe is lined with measurements for latitude and longitude, with the two darkened canyons of the Atlantic and Pacific oceans separating the great masses of land loaded with all sorts of terrible grievances and history, as in Plath's second stanza. The moon is earth's mirror, reflecting light as the earth turns to look upon it at night. Plath's sixth stanza shows that the moon has a dark side, and its eyes watch the terrible happenings on the earth without intervening. This man on the moon is dead to us.

The World card is cyclical, symbolizing completion. Therefore its planetary ruler is not earth, but Saturn, the symbol of time. This explains the black, outraged disc behind the world, as Plath sees it in the first stanza of "The Courage of Shutting-Up." In this stanza, Plath presents a sky that is lined, diagramming revolving discs as an astrological chart. An individual's natal chart is "loaded" with his or her potential, terrible and otherwise. The surgeon is the astrologer, plotting and deliberating whether a person should be cut out of his life for having negative traits. According to his poem "St. Botolph's," Hughes, a noted astrologer, claimed to have foreseen a doomed relationship with Plath early on, based on her natal chart (Hughes, 14).

The constellation of Virgo symbolizes a dream-girl virgin, as in Plath's third stanza. The word "virgin" comes from *vir-* (Latin for *man*) and *-gyne* (Greek for *woman*), a man-woman or androgyne. The Greek word for virgin is *parthenos*, meaning to self-fertilize, thus including the hermaphrodite in its definition. She is considered to be a heroic maiden, acting like a man. The spinster is sometimes also considered to be the virgin; she is named "spinster" because she is a spinning woman, at her wheel, or else she is like the old mythological Salamacis whirling in the air. Keats' poem "Lines on the Mermaid Tavern" refers to the constellation Virgo as "The mermaid in the zodiac," reflecting Plath's third stanza.

The ancient astronomer Manilius portrayed Virgo, as Justice a.k.a. Dike, holding the scales of Libra. Manilius' description is full of Plath's judgment of double-talk and actions, the complaining that needs to be heard, and most especially, the shut mouth. About Virgo, he wrote:

> "She will give not so much abundance of wealth as the impulse to investigate the causes and effects of things. On them she will confer a tongue which charms, the mastery of words, and that mental vision which can discern all things, however concealed they be by the mysterious workings of nature. From the Virgin will also come the stenographer [*scriptor crit velox*]: his letter represents a word, and by means of his symbols he can keep ahead of utterance and record in novel notation the long speech of a rapid speaker. But with the good there comes a flaw: bashfulness handicaps the early years of such persons, for the Maid, by holding back their great natural gifts, puts a bridle on their lips and restrains them by the curb of authority. And (small wonder in a virgin) her offspring is not fruitful." [*Astronomica*, Manilius, first century AD, p.237 and 239]

Sixth Mirror: Humanities and the Arts

Hermaphrodites have been a part of the arts since the beginnings of time. Ancient Greece depicted Hermaphroditus in lekythos pottery, circa 4 B.C. Lekythos is red clay with high-contrast black markings, or vice-versa. The subject of Hermaphrodites seems to disappear from post-classical art history until the Renaissance, when writers of alchemical treatises rediscovered them as non-erotic symbols for the union of opposites (a potent image for later Jungian psychology), and emblem books portrayed them as symbols of marriage. At this time when Plath's marriage was coming apart, these emblems were likely difficult to keep quiet over.

Many masters have portrayed the tale of Hermaphroditus and Salmacis in Renaissance and Neoclassical art. A famous second century Roman marble sculpture, the *Sleeping Hermaphrodite*, was found in Rome near the ancient baths of Diocletian in 1608. Lady Dorothy Walpole Townshend famously proclaimed the sculpture was the only happy couple she had ever seen (Ajootian, 220). In 1854, Napoleon brought the Sleeping Hermaphrodite to Paris where it has remained. Plath vacationed in Paris a few times and being no stranger to the museums there was likely to have seen this statue.

In 19th century Paris, Félix Tournachon, known as Nadar, was one of the most sought-after photographers of his time. In 1861, the Parisian medical community asked Nadar to photograph a hermaphrodite for medical and scientific research. Two of these images are still held at the Musée d'Orsay. In the pictures, the doctor carefully reveals the male and female genitalia of the reclining patient. The patient places a hand over the breasts and uses the other to obscure the face. Unlike Nadar's other famous portraitures, these are only of the body, revealing no personality. Nadar took nine photographs—nine tales, or Plath's homophone, "nine tails." In 1860s France, when Nadar's photographs were taken, it was illegal to remain an adult hermaphrodite. A 2007 article in *LTTR* states, "A specialist, such as the surgeon Jules-Germain Maisonneuve, whose hand we see revealing the sex organs of the reclining figure in the Nadar images, would determine the "true" sex and operate accordingly, since dual sexuality was not recognized or tolerated as a possibility. The pretext for these nine images may have been the beginning of such an inquiry and subsequent surgery" (Blume). This of course fits Plath's fourth stanza question, "Must it be cut out?"

Since ancient times, societies have been fascinated by, uncomfortable with, and sometimes envious or even worshipful of hermaphrodites. Metaphorically, the lesbians-gays-transgenders and hermaphrodites have been victims of witch hunts across the centuries. It is a life of wholeness and independence that stirs up confusion in the majority of society. The World tarot card celebrates this wholeness and completion as a new life. At the time Sylvia Plath wrote "The Courage of Shutting-Up," her marriage was asunder, her health was poor, a serious depression had taken hold, and her mother had been encouraging her to come back home to America. Plath wrote to her mother, "I cannot face you again until I have a new life" (*LH*, 465).

WORKS CITED
Abbreviations
Ariel- Plath, Sylvia. *Ariel.* New York: Harper & Row Publishers, 1965. Print.

ARE – Plath, Sylvia. *Ariel, the Restored Edition.* New York: HarperCollins Publishers, 2004. Print.

CP – Plath, Sylvia, and Ted Hughes. *The Collected Poems.* New York: HarperPerennial, 1992. Print.

LTH- Plath, Sylvia, and Christopher Reid. *Letters of Ted Hughes.* New York: Farrar, Straus and Giroux, 2008. Print.

LH— Plath, Sylvia, and Aurelia S. Plath. *Letters Home: Correspondence, 1950-1963.* New York: Harper & Row, 1975. Print.

UJ- Plath, Sylvia, and Karen V. Kukil. *The Unabridged Journals of Sylvia Plath, 1950-1962.* New York: Anchor Books, 2000. Print.

WP- Hughes, Ted, and William Scammell. *Winter Pollen: Occasional Prose.* London: Faber and Faber, 1994. Print.

Introduction Works Cited:
Bloom, Harold. *Kabbalah and Criticism.* New York: Seabury Press, 1975. Print.

Hughes, Ted, and Christopher Reid. *Letters of Ted Hughes.* New York: Farrar, Straus and Giroux, 2008. Print.

Joyce, James, and Harry Levin. *The Portable James Joyce.* New York: Viking Press, 1947. Print.

Myers, Lucas. *Crows Steered Bergs Appeared: A Memoir of Ted Hughes and Sylvia Plath.* Sewanee, Tenn: Proctor's Hall Press, 2001. Print.

Plath, Sylvia, and Aurelia S. Plath. *Letters Home: Correspondence, 1950-1963.* New York: Harper & Row, 1975. Print.

Plath, Sylvia, and Karen V. Kukil. *The Unabridged Journals of Sylvia Plath, 1950-1962.* New York: Anchor Books, 2000. Print.

Rákóczi, Basil Ivan. *The Painted Caravan: a Penetration into the Secrets of the Tarot Cards. [with Illustrations].* The Hague: L.J.C. Boucher, 1954. Print.

Sonnenberg, Ben. "Ted's Spell". Counterpunch.org 22 JUN. 2002. 24 OCT. 2013. Web. http://www.counterpunch.org/2002/06/22/ted-s-spell/

"Morning Song" Works Cited:
Alexander, Paul. *Rough Magic: A Biography of Sylvia Plath.* New York: Da Capo Press, 1999. Print.

Allen, Richard H., and Richard H. Allen. *Star Names: Their Lore and Meaning.* New York: Dover Publications, 1963. Print.

Aniane, Maurice. "Alchemy: the Cosmological Yoga." *Alchemy Journal* Vol.1 No.1. 24 Oct. 2013. <http://www.alchemylab.com/AJl-l.htm>

Cashford, Jules. *The Moon: Myth and Image.* New York: Four Walls Eight Windows, 2003. Print.

Graves, Robert. *The White Goddess: a historical grammar of poetic myth.* Farrar, Straus and Giroux, 1948 and renewed 1975. Print.

Heinrich, Clark. *Magic Mushrooms in Religion and Alchemy* (formerly called *Strange Fruit*). Park Street Press, 2002. Print.

Huxley, Aldous. *Brave New World.* New York: Harper Perennial Modern Classics, 2006. Print.

Lindgren, Carl Edwin. *The way of the Rose Cross; A Historical Perception,* 1614–1620. Journal of Religion and Psychical Research, Volume 18, Number 3:141–48. 1995. Web. 24 Oct. 2013. <http://users.panola.com/lindgren/rosecross.html>

Maier, Michael. *Atalanta fugiens* Commentary by John Eberley. Web. 24 Oct. 2013 <http://www.esoteric.msu.edu/Eberly/AtalantaCommentary.html>

Pearce, David. "Brave New World? A Defence of Paradise-Engineering" *Aldous Huxley : Brave New World*. Web. 24 October 2013. <http://www.huxley.net>

Plath, Sylvia. *Ariel: The Restored Edition*. New York: HarperCollins Publishers, 2004. Print.

Plath, Sylvia, and Ted Hughes. *The Collected Poems*. New York: HarperPerennial, 1992. Print.

Plath, Sylvia, and Karen V. Kukil. *The Unabridged Journals of Sylvia Plath, 1950-1962*. New York: Anchor Books, 2000. Print.

Rákóczi, Basil Ivan. *The Painted Caravan: a Penetration into the Secrets of the Tarot Cards. [with Illustrations]*. The Hague: L.J.C. Boucher, 1954. Print.

Ridpath, Ian. "Canus Major The greater dog." *Star Tales*. 24 Oct. 2013. <http://www.ianridpath.com/star-tales/canismajor.htm>

Wilson, Andrew. *Mad Girl's Love Song: Sylvia Plath and Life Before Ted*. New York: Scribner, 2013. Print.

"The Couriers" Works Cited:

Allen, Richard H., and Richard H. Allen. *Star Names: Their Lore and Meaning*. New York: Dover Publications, 1963. Print.

The Bible. Old Testament, "The Book of Amos." NetBible.com. 24 Oct. 2013. <http://classic.net.bible.org/dictionary.php?word=Tin>

Bergman, Ingmar. "'The Magician' reviews." *The Magic Works of Ingmar Bergman*. 28 Jan. 2014. <http://bergmanorama.webs.com/films/magician_reviews.htm>

Borrow, George. *The Zincali: An Account of the Gypsies of Spain, with an Original Collection of Their Songs and Poetry*. London: Constable, 1923. Print.

Brontë, Emily. "Wuthering Heights." *The Project Gutenberg ebooks*. 24 Oct. 2012. Web. <http://www.gutenberg.org/files/768/768-h/768-h.htm>

Carlson, W. Bernard. *Tesla: Inventor of the Electrical Age*. Princeton: Princeton UP, 2013. Print.

Cavendish, Richard. *The Black Arts*. New York: Putnam, 1967. Print.

Doyle, Sir Arthur Conan. "Sir Arthur Conan Doyle: Complete Works." *The Conan Doyle Encyclopedia*. New York: Berkley Pub., 1968 15 Jan. 2012. <http://www.sshf.com/encyclopedia/index.php/Main_Page>

The Daily Illustrated Mirror, March 18, 1904, Page 3. "Houdini and the Mirror Handcuff Challenge." Web. 24 Oct. 2013. <http://www.handcuffs.org/mirror/>

Hughes, Ted and Christopher Reid. *Letters of Ted Hughes*. New York: Farrar, Straus and Giroux, 2008. Print.

Tesla, Nikola. "How To Signal Mars - Wireless the Only Way Now, Says Nikola Tesla – Mirror Plans Not Practicable." *Tesla Universe*. First published in The New York Times. 23 May 1909. 24 Oct. 2013. <www.teslauniverse.com/nikola-tesla-article-how-to-signal-to-mars>

Plath, Sylvia. *Ariel:The Restored Edition*. New York: HarperCollins, 2004. "The Couriers," p 6. Print.

Plath, Sylvia, and Karen V. Kukil. *The Unabridged Journals of Sylvia Plath, 1950-1962*. New York: Anchor Books, 2000. Print.

TTBOOK. "Paranormal Pop Culture: Gary Spencer Millidge on Alan Moore." *To the Best of Our Knowledge*. National Public Radio. KWMU, 11 Dec. 2011. 24 Oct. 2013. <http://ttbook.org/book/paranormal-pop-culture>

Wilson, Andrew. *Mad Girl's Love Song: Sylvia Plath and Life before Ted*. New York: Scribner, 2013. Print.

"The Rabbit Catcher" Works Cited:

Allen, Richard H., and Richard H. Allen. *Star Names: Their Lore and Meaning*. New York: Dover Publications, 1963. Print.

The Bookman (London), October 1928, pp 27-28. As cited in *"A Whiff of Collaboration: The Tracy-Shiel Connection"* by John D. Squires, 2006. 29 August 2010. http://www.alangullette.com/lit/shiel/essays/shiel_tracy.htm.

Brasch, Walter M. *Brer Rabbit, Uncle Remus, and the 'cornfield Journalist': The Tale of Joel Chandler Harris.* Macon, GA: Mercer University Press, 2000. Print.

Carrol, Lewis, John Tenniel. *The Annotated Alice: Alice's Adventures in Wonderland & Through the Looking-Glass.* New York: Bramhall House, 1970. Print.

Chesnutt, Charles W. *The Conjure Woman.* Boston: Houghton, Mifflin and Company, 1899. Print. Book cover picture: 29 Aug. 2010. <http://en.wikisource.org/wiki/The_Conjure_Woman>

Chesnutt, Charles W. *The House Behind the Cedars.* Champaign, IL: Project Gutenberg, 1996. Internet resource. 29 Aug. 2010 <http://www.gutenburg.org/ebooks/472>

The Charles Chesnutt Digital Archive. 29 Aug. 2010 <http://www.chesnuttarchive.org/siteinfo.html>

Cochran, Robert. "Black father: the subversive achievement of Joel Chandler Harris."*African American Review* 38.1 p. 21. 2004.

Espinosa, A. "A new classification of the fundamental elements of the tar-baby story on the basis of two hundred and sixty-seven versions," *Journal of American Folklore* 56 (1943): 31–37.

Feinstein, Elaine. *Ted Hughes: The Life of a Poet.* New York: Norton, 2001. Print.

"Short Biography of Joel Chandler Harris." *Georgia State University.* 29 Aug. 2010. <http://www2.gsu.edu/~wwwelf/elfjch.html>

Graves, Robert. *The White Goddess: a historical grammar of poetic myth.* Farrar, Straus and Giroux. 1948 and renewed 1975. Print.

Hardy, Thomas. *Tess of the D'Urbervilles: A Pure Woman Faithfully Presented.* London: James R. Osgood, McIlvaine, 1893. Volume 3. Print.

Hughes, Ted. *Birthday Letters.* New York: Farrar, Straus and Giroux. 1998. Print.

Hughes, Ted. and Christopher Reid. *Letters of Ted Hughes.* New York: Farrar, Straus and Giroux, 2008. Print.

Hughes, Ted and William Scammel. *Winter Pollen: Occasional Prose.* London: Faber and Faber, 1994. Print.

Jung, C. G, and Marie-Luise. Franz. *Man and His Symbols.* Garden City, N.Y: Doubleday, 1964. Print.

Lear, Linda. *Beatrix Potter: A Life in Nature.* New York: Macmillan, 2008. Print.

"Poisonous Silence: the dumb cane" *Living Rainforest.* 23 Oct. 2013. <http://www.livingrainforest.org/about-rainforests/poisonous-silence-the-dumb-cane/>

Dobbs, B.J. and A.G. Debus. "Newton's Commentary on the Emerald Tablet of Hermes Trismegistus." *Sacred Texts.* 1988. 29 Aug. 2010. http://www.sacred-texts.com/alc/emerald.htm

Plath, Sylvia. *Ariel: the Restored Edition.* New York: HarperCollins, 2004. "The Rabbit Catcher" pp 7-8. Print.

Plath, Sylvia, and Karen V. Kukil. *The Unabridged Journals of Sylvia Plath, 1950-1962.* New York: Anchor Books, 2000. Print.

Ridpath, Ian. "Lepus The Hare" *Star Tales.* 24 Oct. 2014. 14 Nov. 2010. <http://www.ianridpath.com/startales/lepus.htm>

Robson, B.Sc., Vivien E. *Fixed Stars and Constellations in Astrology,* Whitefish, MT: Kessinger Legacy Reprints. 2010. Print.

Steele and Singer. "Twelfth Century Latin Translation of *The Emerald Tablet* From Latin." *Sacred Texts.* 1928. <http://www.sacred-texts.com/alc/emerald.htm>

Stewart, R.J. *The Miracle Tree: Demystifying the Qabalah.* New Jersey: New Page Books, 2003. Print. 30 Aug. 2010. As cited on http://shadowlight.gydja.com/iormungand.html

Tour Egypt. "Egypt Magic-Magical Names." 29 Aug. 2010. http://www.touregypt.net/egyptmagic6.htm.

Villanova, Arnald of (pseudonym of unknown 14th Century alchemist). "De Secretis naturae." European Association for Chemical and Molecular Sciences. 29 Aug. 2010. <http://www.euchems.org/binaries/29_Rampling_tcm23-139374.pdf.>

"Thalidomide" Works Cited:

Alexander, Paul. *Rough Magic: A Biography of Sylvia Plath.* New York: Da Capo Press, New York, 1999. Print.

Allen, Richard H., and Richard H. Allen. *Star Names: Their Lore and Meaning.* New York: Dover Publications, 1963. 7 Nov. 2010. <http://constellationsofwords.com/Constellations/Corvus.html>

Artephius. *The Secret Book of Artephius.* First published 1612. Facsimile reprint, Largs: Banton, 1991. Print.

Bedford, Sybille. *Aldous Huxley: A Biography, Volume Two: 1939–1963,* Chatto & Windus, UK. 1974. Print.

Blake, William. *The Marriage of Heaven and Hell.* 1790. 8 Nov. 2010. <http://www.gailgastfield.com/mhh/mhh.html>

BBC "On This Day August 26, 2012" 30 Jul. 2012. <http://news.bbc.co.uk/onthisday/hi/dates/stories/august/26/newsid_3039000/3039322.stm>

Cornell Lab of Ornithology. *All About Birds,* "Great Cormorant." 8 Nov. 2010. <http://www.birds.cornell.edu/AllAboutBirds/BirdGuide/Great_Cormorant.html>

Cronquist, Arthur. *The Evolution and Classification of Flowering Plants.* New York Botanical Garden Press; New York. 2nd edition. 1988. Print.

Denman, Leslie Van Ness. *The Peyote Ritual; Visions and Descriptions of Monroe Tsa Toke.* Grabhorn Press, San Francisco. 1957. 7 Nov. 2010. <http://nac-art.com/Tsatoke_mini.htm>

Hughes, Ted, and Christopher Reid. *Letters of Ted Hughes.* New York: Farrar, Straus and Giroux, 2008. Print.

Huxley, Aldous. *Brave New World.* Chatto and Windus, UK. 1932. Print.

Huxley, Aldous. *The Doors of Perception.* Harper & Row, U.S. 1954. Print.

Linden, Stanton J. (ed.) *The Booke of the Secrets of Alchimie, composed by Galid the sonne of Jazich,* (also known as Calid and Khalid) in Roger Bacon's *The Mirror of Alchimy,* p. 126. First published: London. 1597. New York: Garland Publishing [English Renaissance Hermeticism 4]. 1992. Print.

Plath, Sylvia. *Ariel: The Restored Edition.* New York: HarperCollins Publishers, 2004. "Thalidomide." pp 9-10. Print.

Plath, Sylvia, and Karen V. Kukil. *The Unabridged Journals of Sylvia Plath, 1950-1962.* Journal entry from June 20, 1959. New York: Anchor Books, 2000. Print.

Roob, Alexander. *The Hermetic Cabinet: Alchemy & Mysticism.* Köln; New York: Taschen. 2009. Print.

Sargent, William "Chemical Mysticism," *British Medical Journal,* Vol. 1, No. 4869 (May 1, 1954). Print.

"The Applicant" Works Cited:

Abraham, Lyndy. *A Dictionary of Alchemical Imagery.* Cambridge, UK: Cambridge University Press, 1998. Print.

Aeschylus. *The Oresteian Triology: Agamemnon, the Choephori, the Eumenides.* Translated by Philip Vellacott. USA: Penguin Classics. 1960. Print.

Ammer, Christine. *The American Heritage ® Dictionary of Idioms.* New York: Houghton Mifflin Harcourt. 1997. Print.

Alexander, Paul. *Rough Magic: A Biography of Sylvia Plath.* New York: Da Capo Press, New York. 1999. Print.

Carrol, Robert P. *The Bible: Authorized King James Version; Ed. with an Introd. and Notes by Robert Carrol and Stephen Prickett.* Book of Genesis, Chapter 35, verse 4; Book of Joshua, Chapter 24, verses 25-27; Book of Isaiah, Chapter 61, verse 3. Oxford, UK: Oxford University Press, 1997. Print.

Dee, Arthur, Elias Ashmole, Thomas Cross, and Jean Espangnet. *Fasciculus Chemicus, Or, Chymical Collections: Expressing the Ingress, Progress, and Egress of the Secret Hermetick Science, Out of the Choisest and Most Famous*

Authors....Whereunto Is Added, the Arcanum, Or, Grand Street of Hermetick Philosophy. London: Printed by J. Flesher for Richard Mynne, 1650. Internet source.

Dobbs, Betty Jo Teeter, *The Janus Faces of Genius: The Role of Alchemy in Newton's Thought*, Cambridge: Cambridge University Press, 1975. Print.

Gleason, John. "Centaurus OB1" Hydrogen Alpha Emission Line Imaging. Southern Hemisphere Hydrogen Alpha Objects23 September, 2007. 9 Dec. 2010. <http://jpgleason.zenfolio.com/p803558559/hD80856E#hd80856e>

Graves, Robert. *The White Goddess: a historical grammar of poetic myth*. New York: Farrar, Straus and Giroux. 1948 and renewed 1975. Print.

Icons: a portrait of England. "Oak Tree: Tree of the Thunder God." Icons Online Limited, 2006. 9 Dec. 2010. <http://www.icons.org.uk/theicons/collection/oak-tree/features/the-sacred-history-of-oak-trees>

Irish Astrology. "Celtic Tree Astrology: Duir/Oak June 10 – July 7." 9 Dec. 2010. <http://www.irishastrology.com/celtic-astrology/Oak/celtic-tree-sign-astrology-oak.html>

Panther Observatory. "Nebulosity Around NGC6231" 9 Dec. 2010 <http://panther-observatory.com/gallery/deepsky/doc/NGC6231_wide.htm>

Plath, Sylvia. *Ariel: The Restored Edition*. New York: HarperCollins Publishers, 2004. "The Applicant" pp 11-12. Print.

Plath, Sylvia, and Aurelia S. Plath. *Letters Home: Correspondence, 1950-1963*. New York: Harper & Row, 1975. Print.

SSRO Star Shadows Remote Observatory "RCW 75" 9 Dec. 2010. <http://www.starshadows.com/gallery/display.cfm?imgID=141>

University of Michigan-Dearborn. :Quereus kelloggii Newberry. California Black Oak; Fagaeeae." *Native American Ethnobotany*. A Database of Foods, Drugs, Dyes and Fibers of Native American Peoples, Derived from Plants. 9 Dec. 2010. <http://herb.umd.umich.edu/herb/search.pl?searchstring=Quercus+kelloggii>

University of Michigan-Dearborn. "Penstemon ambiguus Torr. Gilia Beardtongue; Scrophulariaceae" *Native American Ethnobotany*. A Database of Foods, Drugs, Dyes and Fibters of Native American Peoples, Derived from Plants. 2003. 9 Dec. 2010. <http://herb.umd.umich.edu/herb/search.pl?searchstring=Penstemon+ambiguus>

"Barren Woman" Works Cited:

Abraham, Lyndy. *A Dictionary of Alchemical Imagery*. Cambridge, UK: Cambridge University Press, 1998. Print.

Allen, Richard H, and Richard H. Allen. *Star Names: Their Lore and Meaning*. New York: Dover Publications, 1963. Print.

Carmer, Carl L. *Stars Fell on Alabama*. Illustrated by LeRoy Baldridge. Farrar and Rinehart, 1934. 14 Dec. 2010. http://www.dauphinislandhistory.org/stars_fell/stars_menu.htm

Graves, Robert. *The White Goddess: a historical grammar of poetic myth*. Farrar, Straus and Giroux. 1948 and renewed 1975. Print.

Hearin, Emily S. *Mobile Press Register*. "Island Has A Rich History." 13 Feb. 1995. 14 Dec. 2010. http://www.dauphinislandhistory.org/n_hearin_history.htm

Hesiod. "*Theogony* Greek epic C8th or C7th B.C." trans. Evelyn-White. 775 ff. Theoi Greek Mythology. 14 Dec. 2010. <http://www.theoi.com/Khthonios/PotamosStyx.html>

Homer, *Iliad* 15. 35. Perseus.Tufts.Edu. 13 Dec. 2010. http://www.perseus.tufts.edu/hopper/text?doc=hom.+il.+15.605 Last accessed 13 December, 2010

Koren, Yehuda and Eilat Negev. *Lover of Unreason: Assia Wevill, Sylvia Plath's Rival and Ted Hughes' Doomed Love.* New York: Carroll & Graf Publishers, 2007. Print.

Leadbetter, Ron. "Delphi." Encyclopedia Mythica. 1999. 13 Dec. 2010.
http://www.pantheon.org/articles/d/delphi.html Web. Last accessed 13 December, 2010

McCann, Maurice. "William Lilly's Prediction of The Fire of London." The Astrological Journal. XXXII: 1, Jan/Feb 1990. Reprinted for Skyscript. 16 Dec. 2010.
http://www.skyscript.co.uk/fire.html Web. Last accessed 16 December, 2010

McWilliams, Richebourg Gaillard. "Dramatic History of Dauphin Island" DI Park & Beach Board. 14 Dec. 2010.
http://www.dauphinislandhistory.org/index.html Web. Last accessed 14 December, 2010

Moore, Sir Thomas, Esq., *The works of Lord Byron complete in one volume.* John Murray: London. 1842. 20 Jan. 2011.
http://books.google.com/books?id=TWxAAAAAYAAJ&pg=RA1-PA473&dq=Lord+Byron+Diary+1821&hl=en&ei=dNk4TeKnCJD3gAfshKTyCA&sa=X&oi=book_result&ct=result&resnum=4&ved=0CDIQ6AEwAw#v=onepage&q=twenty%20to%20thirty&f=false Web. Last accessed 20 January, 2011

Morden, Margaret E. *Delphi: The Oracle of Apollo.* Odyssey, Adventures in Archaeology, 2001. 13 Dec. 2010.
http://www.odysseyadventures.ca/articles/delphi/articledelphi.htm

Ovid. *Metamorphoses* 4. 433: Virginia.edu 13 Dec. 2010.
http://ovid.lib.virginia.edu/trans/Metamorph4.htm Last accessed 13 December, 2010

Plant, David. "The Life & Work of William Lilly" Skyscript. 16 Dec. 2010.
http://www.skyscript.co.uk/lilly.html

Plath, Sylvia. *Ariel:* The Restored Edition. New York: HarperCollins Publishers, 2004. "Barren Woman." p 13. Print.

Plath, Sylvia, and Karen V. Kukil. *The Unabridged Journals of Sylvia Plath, 1950-1962.* New York: Anchor Books, 2000. Print.

Regardie, Israel. *The Golden Dawn.* Sixth edition. Llewellyn Publications, 1989. Print.

Robson, B.Sc., Vivien E.. *Fixed Stars and Constellations in Astrology,* Whitefish, MT: Kessinger Legacy Reprints. 2010. Print.

Rolleston, Frances. *Mazzaroth.* "Sualocin and Rotanev." First published in London in 1862. Reprinted by Kessinger Publishing, LLC. 2003

"Lady Lazarus" Works Cited:

Abraham, Lyndy. *A Dictionary of Alchemical Imagery.* Cambridge, UK: Cambridge University Press, 1998. Print.

Alexander, Paul. *Ariel Ascending: Writings About Sylvia Plath.* New York: Harper & Row, 1985. Includes "Sylvia Plath: A Memoir" by A. Alvarez.; and "Enlargement or Derangement?" by Barbara Hardy. Print.

Baender, Paul (editor) *Twain, Mark,* "What is man?: and other philosophical writings." 1973. University of California Press. Print.

Bang, Mary Jo. "The Mythic Love Poem: Where white-hot sexuality and white-hot hatred meet." Slate.com. Tuesday, September 25, 2012. 02 Oct. 2012.
http://www.slate.com/articles/arts/classic_poems/2012/09/the_mythic_love_poem_where_white_hot_sexuality_and_white_hot_hatred_meet_.html

Blanchard, Paula. *Margaret Fuller: From Transcendentalism to Revolution.* 1987. Reading, Massachusetts: Addison-Wesley. Print.

Carroll, Robert P. *The Bible: Authorized King James Version ; Ed. with an Introd. and Notes by Robert Carroll and*

Stephen Prickett. The The Book of John, Chapter 11, v. 44. Oxford, UK: Oxford UP, 1997. Print.

Claerr, David. "Statue of Liberty Modeled on a Pagan Goddess" May 9, 2009. 02 Oct. 2011. www.associatedcontent.com

Connors, Kathleen and Sally Bayley (editors). *Eye Rhymes: Sylvia Plath's Art of the Visual.* 2007. Oxford: Oxford UP. Print.

Darwin, Charles. *Insectivorous plants.* New York: D. Appleton and Company, 1875. 23 Feb. 2011. http://darwin-online.org.uk/EditorialIntroductions/Freeman_InsectivorousPlants.html

Decoded. "Statue of Liberty." 2011. *The History Channel website.* Episode 3, Season One. First aired December 10, 2010. Jan. 22, 2011.
<http://www.history.com/shows/brad-meltzers-decoded/episodes/episodes-guide>
Available to view on YouTube.com: http://www.youtube.com watch?v=scmF84XdZu8

Mark Twain Speaks for Himself. Ed. Paul Fatout. West Lafayette, IN: Purdue UP, 1997. pp 135-136.

Graves, Robert. *The White Goddess: a historical grammar of poetic myth.* Farrar, Straus and Giroux. 1948 and renewed 1975. Print.

Gray, Eden. *The Complete Guide to the Tarot.* Toronto: Bantam Books, 1982. Print. The Independent. "The GreatGloucestershire glow-worm" by Cole Moreton. 11 Aug. 1996. 25 Jun. 2012. http://www.independent.co.uk/news/uk/home-news/the-great-gloucestershire-glowworm-hunt-1309177.html Last accessed 25 June, 2012

Jewish Virtual Library. "Frank, Eva". 27 Apr. 2012.
http://www.jewishvirtuallibrary.org/jsource/judaica/ejud_0002_0007_0_06690.html

Khan, Yasmin Sabina. Enlightening the World: The Creation of the Statue of Liberty. 2010. Ithaca, New York: Cornell UP. Print.

Milbrath, Susan. "Star gods of the Maya: astronomy in art, folklore, and calendars." University of Texas Press, 1999. Print.

Moore, Virginia. *The Unicorn: William Butler Yeats' Search for Reality.* New York: The Macmillan Company. 1954. Print.

PBS NewsHour. "Mark Twain's Autobiography Set for Unveiling, a Century After His Death". 7 Jul. 2010. 25 Jun. 2012. Nine Network, St. Louis, MO. 23 Jul. 2014.
<http://www.pbs.org/newshour/bb/entertainment-july-dec10-twain_07-07/>

Plath, Sylvia. *Ariel: The Restored Edition.* New York: HarperCollins Publishers, 2004. "Lady Lazarus." pp 14-17. Print.

Plath, Sylvia, and Karen V. Kukil. *The Unabridged Journals of Sylvia Plath, 1950-1962.* New York: Anchor Books, 2000. Print.

Rosicrucian text: *The Chymical Wedding of Christian Rosenkreutz.* 1459. 26 Jan. 2011.
<http://zebratta.com/cwcr.htm>

Slater, Abby. *In Search of Margaret Fuller.* New York: Delacorte Press, 1978. Print.

Twain, Mark. "That Awful German Language." Appendix D from Twain's 1880 book, *A Tramp Abroad.* 24 Jan. 2011. <http://www.cs.utah.edu/~gback/awfgrmlg.html>

Wilson, Andrew. *Mad Girl's Love Song: Sylvia Plath and Life before Ted.* New York: Scribner, 2013. Print.

"Tulips" Works Cited:

Abraham, Lyndy. *A Dictionary of Alchemical Imagery.* Cambridge, UK: Cambridge UP, 1998. Print.

Alexander, Paul. *Rough Magic: A Biography of Sylvia Plath.* New York: Da Capo Press. 1999. Print.

Canaday, Marquis. "Operation Black Tulip; Germans Kicked out of Netherlands." Associated Content. 12 Mar. 2009. 5 Mar. 2012.

http://www.associatedcontent.com/arti le/1530749/operation_black_tulip_pg2.html?cat=37

Crowley, Alistair. *Orpheus: A Lyrical Legend*. Vol. Two. Poem: "Dionysus" Boleskine Foyers Inverness, 1905. 5 Mar. 2012. <http://books.google.com/> and "The Rite of Jupiter, Part III." 13 Jun. 2010. <http://hermetic.com/crowley/the-rites-of-eleusis/jupiter.html>

Crowther, Gail and Peter K. Steinberg. "These Ghostly Archives 4: Looking for New England" *Plath Profiles*, 5. Indiana University Northwest. 2012. 1 Jul. 2012. <http://www.iun.edu/~nwadmin/plath/vol5/Crowther_Steinberg.pdf>

Fülöp-Miller, René. *Rasputin. The Holy Devil*. 1962. New York: The Viking Press. Print.

Gäckler, Christine. "Wild Tulips in the Steppes", *The Epoch Times*. Germany. 3 May 2007. 1 Jul. 2012. <http://www.theepochtimes.com/news/7-5-3/54831.html>

Graves, Robert. *The White Goddess, a historical grammar of poetic myth*. Farrar, Straus and Giroux. 1948 and renewed 1975. Print.

Greer, Germaine, Susan Hastings, Jeslyn Medoff, Melinda Sansone (eds.) *Kissing the Rod: An Anthology of Seventeenth-Century Women's Verse*, London, Virago, 1988. Lines 7-16. Print.

Grimal, Pierre. *The Dictionary of Classical Mythology*. Oxford: Blackwell Publishing, 1986. Print.

Heine, Heinrich. *A Winter's Tale*. 1844. Germany. 2 Feb. 2013. <http://www.heinrich-heine.net/winter/winteregoodb.htm>

Idel, Moshe. *Kabbalah and Eros*. New Haven, CT: Yale UP. 2005. p. 92. Print.

Idel, Moshe. "Metamorphoses of a Platonic Theme in Jewish Mysticism." 2 Feb. 2012. <http://web.ceu.hu/jewishstudies/yb03/08idel.pdf>

Pasternak, Boris. *Dr. Zhivago*. 1997. New York: Pantheon Books. Print.

Plath, Sylvia. *Ariel: The Restored Edition*. New York: HarperCollins Publishers, 2004. "Tulips," pp 18-20. Print.

Plath, Sylvia, and Aurelia Schober. Plath. *Letters Home: Correspondence, 1950-1963*. New York: Harper & Row, 1975. Print.

Plath, Sylvia, and Karen V. Kukil. *The Unabridged Journals of Sylvia Plath*. New York: Anchor Books, 2000. Print.

Plato. *Symposium*. MIT Classics. 13 Jun. 2010. <http://classics.mit.edu/Plato/symposium.html>

Pollan, Michael. *The Botany of Desire*. New York: Random House. 2002. Print.

Romanov Memorial. "The Heines Poem" and "The Mystic Signs." 13 Jun. 2010. <http://www.romanov-memorial.com/HeinesPoem.htm#Top>

Roob, Alexander. *The Hermetic Cabinet: Alchemy & Mysticism*. Illustration: Abraham von Franckenberg, Raphael oder Arzt-Engel, 1639. Kolu; New York: Taschen. 2009. Print.

Salinger, J.D., *Franny and Zooey*. Boston: Little, Brown and Company. 1955. Print.

Salinger, J.D. *Nine Stories*. Boston: Little, Brown and Company, 1948. Print.

Steiner, Rudolf. *Cosmic Memory (Prehistory of Earth and Man)*. Germany. 1904. 13 Jun. 2010. <http://www.golden-dawn.com/eu/UserFiles/en/File/pdf/Rudolf_Steiner_-_Cosmic_Memory.pdf.> p.48

Updike, John. "Anxious Days for the Glass Family." *The New York Times* Books Review. 17 Sept. 1961. 13 Jun. 2010. <http://www.nytimes.com/books/98/09/13/specials/salinger-franny01.html>

Whitlock, Dr. Luder. *TULIP the five points of Calvinism in the Light of Scripture*. Grand Rapids, MI: Baker Books, 1979. Print.

"A Secret" Works Cited:

Abraham, Lyndy. *A Dictionary of Alchemical Imagery*. Cambridge, UK: Cambridge UP, 1998. Print.

Alexander, Paul. *Rough Magic: A Biography of Sylvia Plath*. New York: Da Capo Press, 1999. Print.

Alvarez, A. *Where Did It All Go Right? A Memoir*. London: Richard Cohen Books. 1999. Print.

Andewski, Gene and Julian Mitchell. "Lawrence Durrell: The Art of Fiction No. 23" *The Paris Review*. 23 Apr. 1959. 23 Sept. 2010. <http://www.theparisreview.org/interviews/4720/the-art-of-fiction-no-23-lawrence-durrell>

Crowley, Aleister. *Liber Aleph*, Part 5. {Delta}{sigma} DE LIBIDINE SECRETA. 23 Sept. 2010. <http://www.bibliotecapleyades.net/crowley/aleph_5.htm>

Crowley, Aleister. "Liber Samekh." *Thelemapedia*. 21 Jun. 2010. <http://www.thelemapedia.org/index.php/Liber_Samekh>

Diboll, Mike. "Lawrence Durrell's Alexandria Quartet in its Egyptian Contexts" 21 Jun. 2010. <www.mellenpress.com/mellenpress.cfm?bookid=6100&pc=9>

Durrell, Lawrence. *The Alexandria Quartet*. London: Faber & Faber. 1962. The first of *The Alexandria Quartet* novels, *Justine*, was published in London: Faber & Faber. 1957. It was followed by *Balthazar*. London: Faber & Faber. 1958; *Mountolive*. London: Faber & Faber. 1958; and *Clea*. London: Faber & Faber. 1960. All books published individually and collectively with London: Faber & Faber. Print.

Fraser, Antonia. *The Wives of Henry VIII*. New York: Vintage, 1993. Print.

Frye, Northrop. "Anatomy of Criticism," referred to in G.S. Fraser's biography, *Lawrence Durrell* "6. Tunc And Nunquam". 21 Jun. 2010. <www.ourcivilisation.com/smartboard/shop/frasergs/durrell/chap6.htm. >

Graves, Robert. *The White Goddess, a historical grammar of poetic myth*. Farrar, Straus and Giroux. 1948 and renewed 1975. Print.

Koren, Yehuda and Eilat Negev. *Lover of Unreason: Assia Wevill, Sylvia Plath's Rival and Ted Hughes's Doomed Love*. New York: Carroll and Graf Publishers, 2007. Print.

Lillios, Anna. "A Brief Analysis of Lawrence Durrell's Fiction." Reproduced with permission for the International Lawrence Durrell Society from *Magill's Survey of World Literature*, volume 7, pages 2334-2342. Hackensack, NJ: Salem Press. 1995. 21 Jun. 2010. <www.lawrencedurrell.org/analysis.htm>

Liukkonen, Petri and Ari Pesonen. Biography and Works of Lawrence Durrell. 2008. 21 Jun. 2010. www.kirjasto.sci.fi/durrell.htm

Millais, John Guille. *Newfoundland and its Untrodden Ways*. London: Longmans, Green & Co., 1907. Print.

NASA/Goddard Flight Center. "Six Millennium Catalog of Venus Transits: 2000 BCE to 4000 CE." NASA Elipse Web Site. 22 Jun. 2010. <http://eclipse.gsfc.nasa.gov/transit/catalog/VenusCatalog.html >

Plath, Sylvia. *Ariel: The Restored Edition*. New York: HarperCollins Publishers, 2004. "A Secret" pp 21-22. Print.

Tarotpedia. "Justice." 5 Mar. 2012. <http://www.tarotpedia.com/wiki/Golden_Dawn>

Temple, Robert. *The Genius of China: 3000 Years of Science, Discoveries and Inventions*. pp. 135-137 New York: Simon and Schuster. 1986. Print.

"Venus in Transit histories". Bemyastrologer.com 21 Jun. 2010. <http://bemyastrologer.com/venustransit.html>

Webster, Nester. *Louis XVI and Marie-Antoinette Before the Revolution*. New York: G.P. Putnam's sons. 1938

White, Gavin. *Babylonian Star-lore*. London: Solaria Publications. 2008. Print.

"The Jailor" Works Cited:

Abraham, Lyndy. *A Dictionary of Alchemical Imagery*. Cambridge UP, 1998. pp. 137 – 138. Print.

Allen, Richard Hinckley. *Star Names: Their Lore and Meaning*. 1889. 7 Nov. 2010. <http://constellationsofwords.com/Constellations/Corvus.html>

Barker, Juliet. *Wordsworth: A Life*. New York: Harper Perennial. Abridged edition. 2006. Print.

Benjamin, David. "Joseph Jacobs" in The Journal of the Australian Jewish Historical Society, Vol.111, Part 11, 1949. pp.72-91. Print.

Childs, Jessie. *Henry VIII's Last Victim: the Life and Times of Henry Howard, Earl of Surrey*. New York: Macmillan, 2007. p. 98. Print.

De Quincey, Thomas. *Confessions of an English Opium-Eater*. New York: Penguin Classics. 2003. Print.

Easton's 1897 Bible Dictionary. "jailer. (n.d.)." 2 Dec. 2011. Dictionary.com
<http://dictionary.reference.com/browse/jailer>

Eliot, T.S. *Four Quartets*. New York: Mariner Books. 1968. Print.

Eliot, T.S. *Little Gidding*, lines 241-42. Columbia.edu. 7 Nov. 2010.
<http://www.columbia.edu/itc/history/winter/w3206/edit/tseliotlittlegidding.html>

Grimal, Pierre. *The Dictionary of Classical Mythology*. Oxford: Blackwell Publishing. 1986. Print.

Hughes, Ted. *Birthday Letters*, "The Blackbird," p. 162. New York: Farrar, Straus and Giroux. 1998. Print.

Jung, Carl Gustav. *Man and His Symbols*. New York: Dell. 1964. Print.

Jung, Carl Gustav. *Symbols of Transformation: An Analysis of the Prelude to a Case of Schizophrenia*. Second Edition Translated by R.F.C. Hull. Princeton, NJ: Princeton UP. 1990. Print.

le Fèvre, Nicolas. *A Discourse upon Sr. Walter Rawleigh's Great Cordial*. trans. Peter Belon, London: Octavian Pulleyn, 1664. Quoted from Abraham's *A Dictionary of Alchemical Imagery*. Cambridge: Cambridge UP, 1998. Print.

Meyer, G.J. *The Tudors: The Complete Story of England's Most Notorious Dynasty*. New York: Bantam Books. 2011. Print.

Motz, Anna (ed.) *Managing Self-Harm: Psychological Perspectives*. New York: Routledge. 2009. p. 207. Print.

Steven Naifeh and Gregory White Smith. *Van Gogh: The Life*. New York: Random House Trade Paperbacks; Reprint edition. 2012. Print.

Nicholls, Mark and Penry Williams. *Sir Walter Raleigh: In Life and Legend*. Continuum; 1 edition. 2011. Print.

Plath, Sylvia. *Ariel: the Restored Edition*. New York: HarperCollins Publishers. 2004. "The Jailor," p. 23. Print.

Plath, Sylvia, and Ted Hughes. *The Collected Poems*. New York: Harper & Row, 1992. Print.

Plath, Sylvia, and Karen V. Kukil. *The Unabridged Journals of Sylvia Plath, 1950-1962*. New York: Anchor, 2000. Print.

Rákóczi, Basil I. *The Painted Caravan: a Penetration into the Secrets of the Tarot Cards. [with illustrations.]* The Hague: L.J.C. Boucher, 1954. Print.

Sharman-Burke, Juliet. *The Mythic Tarot*. Stamford, CT: United States Game Systems. 1986. Deck and Book Set. Print.

Stratford, Stephen. "British Military & Criminal History in the period 1900 to 1999." Stephen's Study Room. 30 Nov. 2012. <http://www.stephen-stratford.co.uk/josef_jakobs.htm.>

Svoboda, Dr. Robert E., Robert Edwin Svoboda. *The Greatness of Saturn: A Therapeutic Myth*. Twin Lakes, WI: Lotus Press. 1997. Print.

"Cut" Works Cited:

Abraham, Lyndy. *A Dictionary of Alchemical Imagery*. Cambridge UP, 1998. Print.

Allen, Abigail Ann Maxon. *Life and Sermons of Jonathan Allen*. From "Thanksgiving Sermon,'

Delivered before the students, and others, of Alfred, November 24, 1881." Oakland, CA: Pacific Press Publishing Co. 1894. Archive.org. 21 Dec. 2011.
<http://www.archive.org/stream/lifesermonsofjon01alle_dju.txt>

DiBenedette, Ken. Moonchalice.com. "Sylvia Plath: Ego, Blood and Spirit: The Violent Atavism of 'Cut'" and "Dark and Terrible 'Apprehensions" 18 Jul. 2010.
http://moonchalice.com/2index.html. Last accessed July 18, 2010

EyeWitness to History, "The Ku Klux Klan, 1868." 2006. 21 Dec. 2011.
> <http://www.eyewitnesstohistory.com/kkk.htm>

EyeWitness to History, "Napoleon Exiled to St. Helena, 1815." 2004. 21 Dec. 2011.
> <http://www.eyewitnesstohistory.com/napoleon.htm>

EyeWitness to History, "P.T. Barnum Discovers 'Tom Thumb', 1842." 2011. 21 Dec. 2011.
> <http://www.eyewitnesstohistory.com/tomthumbbarnum.htm >

"The Ku Klux Klan." Fort Lewis College Foundation, Center of Southwest Studies. 21 Dec. 2011.
> <http://swcenter.fortlewis.edu/inventory/kkk.htm>

Frazer, Sir James George. *The Golden Bough: A Study in Magic and Religion.* Oxford: Oxford UP. 1890. A New Abridgement from the Second and Third Editions. Edited with an Introduction and Notes by Robert Fraser. 1994. Oxford: Oxford UP. Print.

George, Christopher T. "The Eroica Riddle: Did Napoleon Remain Beethoven's 'Hero'?" The International Napoleonic Society. 5 Dec. 2011.
> <http://www.napoleon-series.org/ins/scholarship98/c_eroica.html#1>

Grand Lodge of British Columbia and Yukon A.F. & A.M. "Napoleon I. And Freemasonry" ARS QUATUORCORONATORUM Transactions of the Quatuor Coronati Lodge No. 2076 LONDON. Original translation of the French by P. MORAND 33; 8 October, 1843. Updated: 16 Mar. 2001. 02 Feb. 2013. <http://freemasonry.bcy.ca/aqc/napoleon.html>

Graves, Robert. *The White Goddess: a historical grammar of poetic myth.* Farrar, Straus and Giroux. 1948 and renewed 1975. Print.

Halliburton, Richard. *The Flying Carpet.* New York: Grosset and Dunlap. 1932. Print.

Halliburton, Richard. *Richard Halliburton's Complete Book of Marvels.* Indianapolis, IN: Bobbs-Merrill. 1941. Print.

Halliburton, Richard. *The Glorious Adventure.* New York: Garden City. 1927. Print.

Hersholt, Jean. (Trans.) "Thumbelina." English translation. The Hans Christian Andersen Center. 4 Dec. 2011.
> <http://webcache.googleusercontent.com/search?q=cache:http://www.andersen.sdu.dk/vaerk/hersholt/Thumbelina_e.html>

Hughes, Ted, and Christopher Reid. *Letters of Ted Hughes.* New York: Farar, Straus and Giroux, 2008. Print.

Novalis. *Philosophical Writings.* "Teplitz Fragment." Translated and edited by Margaret Mahoney Stoljar. Albany, NY: State UP of New York. 1977. Print.

Plath, Sylvia. *Ariel: The Restored Edition.* New York: HarperCollins Publishers, 2004. "Cut" pp 25-26. Print.

Plath, Sylvia. *The Bell Jar.* New York: Harper Perennial Modern Classics; 1 edition 2005. Print.

Plath, Sylvia, and Aurelia S. Plath. *Letters Home: Correspondence, 1950-1963.* New York: Harper & Row, 1975. Print.

Plath, Sylvia, and Karen V. Kukil. *The Unabridged Journals of Sylvia Plath, 1950-1962.* New York: Anchor Books. 2000. Print.

Plath, Sylvia. *Winter Trees.* ed. by Ted Hughes. New York: Harper and Row. 1972. Print.

Rákóczi, Basil Ivan. *The Painted Caravan: a Penetration into the Secrets of the Tarot Cards. [with illustrations.]* The Hague: L.J.C. Boucher, 1954. Print.

Sawyer, Joseph Dillaway. *History of the Pilgrims and Puritans, Their Ancestry and Descendents. Volume II.* 1922. New York: The Century History Company. p. 192. Print.

Sharman-Burke, Juliet. *The Mythic Tarot.* Stamford, CT: United States Game Systems. 1986. Deck and Book Set. Print.

Siegel, Elaine V. *Psychoanalytic Perspectives on Women.* Psychology Press. 1992. Press.

Steiner, Rudolf. *The Occult Significance of Blood: an esoteric study.* A lecture by Rudolf Steiner, Berlin, October 25, 1906.

GA 55. Rudolph Steiner Archive. "Lectures." 19 Dec. 2011.

    <http://wn.rsarchive.org/Lectures/19061025p01.html>

Temple, Robert. "Dogon Nommos, Sirius Amphibious Gods." 19 Dec. 2011.

    <http://www.bibliotecapleyades.net/esp_dogon03.htm>

TWA. "Moye W. Stephens, Richard Halliburton and the Flying Carpet" Reprinted in part from *Tarpa Topics*, April 1996. The Retired Trans World Airline Pilot's Magazine.22 Aug. 2012.

    <http://www.opencockpit.net/moye.html>

Weider, Ben. CM, PhD. "Napoleon: Man of Peace" The International Napoleonic Society. 21 Dec. 2011.

    <http://www.napoleon-series.org/ins/weider/c_peace.html>

Wine. "Champagne Wine Quotes." WineIntro.com. 02 Feb. 2013.

    <http://wineintro.com/champagne/quotes.html>

"Elm" Works Cited:

Abraham, Lyndy. *A Dictionary of Alchemical Imagery*. Cambridge, UK: Cambridge UP, 1998. Print.

Alleby, Michael. "Finding Gold in Fault Zones". Oxford Dictionary of Earth Sciences. Oxford, UK: Oxford UP. 2003. 02 Jan. 2012.

    <http://factoidz.com/finding-gold-in-fault-zones-1/>

Barton, Bernard. *The Death of Robin Hood*. 1828. The Robin Hood Project. A Robbins Library Digital Project. University of Rochester. 18 Jul. 2010.

    <http://d.lib.rochester.edu/robin-hood/text/barton-death-of-robin-hood>

Böhme, Jakob Translated by William Law. *The Works of Jacob Behmen, The Teutonic Theosopher. Volume the Fourth.* (From Figures) Printed for G. Robinson, London. 1776. PassTheWord.org. "Jacob Boehme 1575-1624" 18 Jul. 2010. <http://www.passtheword.org/Jacob-Boehme/>

Britannia Tours. "Robin Hood's Well". 18 Jul. 2010.

    <www.britannia.com/tours/rhood/rhwella1.htm/>

Bundtzen, Lynda K. *Plath's Incarnations: Woman and the Creative Process*. "The Female Body of Imagination." 1989. Ann Arbor, MI: University of Michigan Press. 1989. Print.

Cashford, Jules. *The Moon: Myth and Image*. New York: Basic Books, 2003. pp 32-33. Print.

Contemporary Poetry Review. "The Poet Realized: An Interview with Ruth Fainlight." Interviewed by Katy Evans-Bush. 2008. 21 Dec. 2011. <http://www.cprw.com/Bush/fainlight.htm>

Crowther, Gail and Peter K Steinberg. "These Ghostly Archives 4: Looking for New England." *Plath Profiles, 5.* Indiana University Northwest. 2012. 1 Jul. 2012.

    <http://www.iun.edu/~nwadmin/plath/vol5/Crowther_Steinberg.pdf>

Dee, Lawrence. "Snake River Gold." 2 Jan. 2012.

    <http://imnh.isu.edu/digitalatlas/geog/historic/histtxt/Gold.pdf>

Evelyn, John. *Sylva*, or A Discourse of Forest-Trees and the Propagation of Timber in His Majesty's Dominions." First Edition, 1664. London: John Martyn for the Royal Society. Project Gutenberg. Gutenberg.org. 21 Dec. 2011. <http://www.gutenberg.org/ebooks/20778>

Fainlight, Ruth. Poetry Society of America. "Jane Bowles and Sylvia Plath, a memoir by Ruth Fainlight". First published in the United States in Crossroads, Spring 2004. 21 Dec. 2011.

    <http://www.poetrysociety.org/psa/poetry/crossroads/tributes/jane_bowles_and_sylvia_plath_a_m/attachment.pdf>

Finn, Elizabeth Anne. *Home in the Holyland*. James Nisbet and Co., London. 1866. New York: Elibron Classics. 2011. Print.

Graves, Robert. *The White Goddess: a historical grammar of poetic myth*. Farrar, Straus and Giroux. 1948 and renewed 1975. Print.

Haughton, Brian. "Bella in the Wych Elm. A Midlands Murder Mystery." BrianHaughton.com. 23 Dec. 2011. <http://brian-haughton.com/articles/bella_in_the_wych-elm/>

Hughes, Gerald. *Ted and I.* The Robson Press. 2012. p. 114. Print.

Mystical World Wide Web. "Trees." 19 Jul. 2010. <http://www.mystical-www.co.uk/trees/speak.htm.>

Mystical World Wide Web. "Trees: World Tree." 19 Jul. 2010. <http://www.mystical-www.co.uk/trees/worldtree.html>

Mystical World Wide Web. "Trees: Mystery Tree." 19 Jul. 2010. <http://www.mystical-www.co.uk/trees/mystree.htm>

Neihardt, John G. *Black Elk Speaks.* New York: William Morrow & Company. 1932. Print.

Plath, Sylvia. *Ariel: The Restored Edition.* New York: HarperCollins Publishers, 2004. "Elm" pp 27-28. Print.

Plath, Sylvia. *The Bell Jar.* With biographical note by Lois Ames. New York: Harper & Row. 1971. Print.

Plath, Sylvia. *The Colossus and other poems.* "Snakecharmer." 1998. New York: First Vintage International Edition. pp 54-55. Print.

Plath, Sylvia. *Crossing the Water.* ed. by Ted Hughes. New York: Harper and Row. 1971. Print.

Plath, Sylvia, and Karen V. Kukil. *The Unabridged Journals of Sylvia Plath, 1950-1962.* New York: Anchor Books. 2000. Print.

Ridpath, Ian. "Star Tales: Leo". 27 Dec. 2011. <http://www.ianridpath.com/startales/leo.htm.>

Ridpath, Ian. "Star Tales: Hydra". 27 Dec. 2011. <http://www.ianridpath.com/startales/hydra.htm>

Ridpath, Ian. "Star Tales: Ophiuchus". 27 Dec. 2011. <http://www.ianridpath.com/startales/ophiuchus.htm>

Transpersonal Lifestreams, "Kundalini: a transpersonal perspective." 1997-2011. 3 Jan 2012. <http://www.transpersonal.com.au/kundalini/index.htm>

"The Night Dances" Works Cited:

Abraham, Lyndy. *A Dictionary of Alchemical Imagery.* Cambridge UP, 1998. Print.

Brivic, Sheldon. "The Mind Factory: Kabbalah in Finnegans Wake." James Joyce Quarterly. Vol. 21, No. 1, Fall. Philadelphia: Temple UP. 1983 Print.

"dissolute." Dictionary.com Unabridged. Random House, Inc. 09 Jan. 2012. <Dictionary.com http://dictionary.reference.com/browse/dissolute>

Dossier Journal. "David Malek". Interview with artist David Malek by Timothée Chaillou. 13 October, 2011. Brooklyn, New York. 09 Jan. 2012. <http://dossierjournal.com/blog/art/david-malek/>

Gabler-Hover, Janet, Kathleen Plate. "The House of Mirth' and Edith Wharton's 'Beyond!" Philological Quarterly, Summer 1993. 07 Jan. 2012. <http://findarticles.com/p/articles/mi_hb3362/is_n3_v72/ai_n28633514/>

Graves, Robert. *The White Goddess: a historical grammar of poetic myth.* Farrar, Straus and Giroux. 1948 and renewed 1975. Print.

Hirsch, Emil G., Immanuel Löw. "Lily" Jewish Encyclopedia. 1906. 07 Jan. 2012. <http://www.jewishencyclopedia.com/articles/9987-lily>

Iqbal, Muzaffar. *Dawn in Madinah: A Pilgrim's Progress.* New York: The Other Press. 2007. Print.

Jewels For Me, Inc. 2002-2011. New York. 24 Jul. 2010. <www.jewelsforme.com/Smoky-Quartz-History.asp>

Johnston, Ian. "There's Nothing Nietzsche Couldn't Teach Ya About the Raising of the Wrist" Monty Python. A Lecture in Liberal Studies. 1996. 06 Jan. 2012. <http://records.viu.ca/~johnstoi/introser/nietzs.htm>

Levine, Rick. "The Star of Bethlehem". StarIQ. 09 Jan. 2012. <http://www.stariq.com/main/articles/p0000443.htm>

Liddell, Henry George, Robert Scott. "Comet". *A Greek–English Lexicon*. Revised and augmented throughout by Sir Henry Stuart Jones, with the assistance of Roderick McKenzie. Oxford: Clarendon Press. 1940. 09 Jan. 2012. <http://www.perseus.tufts.edu/hopper/text?doc=Perseus%3Atext%3A1999.04.0057%3Aentry%3Dkomh%2Fths>

Marillier, H. C. *Dante Gabriel Rossetti, An Illustrated Memorial of His Art and Life*. London: George Bell and Sons, Chiswick Press, Charles Whittingham and Co. 1899. 24 Jul. 2010. <http://www.rossettiarchive.org/docs/nd497.r8.m33.rad.html>

Moakley, Gertrude Charlotte. *The Tarot Cards Painted by Bonifacio Bembo for the Visconti-Sforza Family; An Iconographic and Historical Study*. 1966. New York Public Library, New York. Print.

NASA Solar System Exploration. "Titan: Overview." 07 Jan. 2012. <http://solarsystem.nasa.gov/planets/profile.cfm?Object=Titan>

NASA. Casini "Unlocking Saturn's Secrets; Saturn's Strange Hexagon". 27 March, 2007. 09 Jan. 2012. <http://www.nasa.gov/mission_pages/cassini/multimedia/pia09188.html>

Nietzsche, Friedrich. *The Genealogy of Morals*. Preface, Section 1. (1887; tr. 1956) Preface: 1. Stanford Encyclopedia of Philosophy. "Friedrich Nietzche." 06 Jan. 2012. <http://stanford.library.usyd.edu.au/archives/spr2004/entries/nietzche/>

Nietzsche, Friedrich. *Thus Spake Zarathustra. A Book for All and None*. Translated by Thomas Common. 06 Jan. 2012. <http://4umi.com/nietzsche/zarathustra/0>

Nietzsche, Friedrich. *The Use and Abuse of History for Life*. 1874. classicauthors.net. <http://www.classicauthors.net/Nietzsche/abuse/>

Nine Planets. "Titan". 07 Jan. 2012. <http://nineplanets.org/titan.html>

Palomar College. "Soap Lilies in California". San Marcos, CA. 23 Jul. 2010. <http://waynesword.palomar.edu/pldec198.htm>

Plath, Sylvia. *Ariel: The Restored Edition*. New York: HarperCollins, 2004. "The Night Dances" pp 29-30. Print.

Rákóczi, Basil Ivan. *The Painted Caravan: a Penetration into the Secrets of the Tarot Cards. [with Illustrations.]* The Hague: L.J.C. Boucher, 1954. Print.

Stewart, Lyle. *The History and Practice of Magic*. Secancus: NJ: University Books. Published by arrangement with Lyle Stewart, 1979, Vol. II. Print.

Tirmizi, *Saying of the Prophet*, Collection of *The Virtues and Noble Character of the Prophet Muhammad*. Classic Book of Hadeeth. 207-279. A.H. Inter-Islam.org. Tirmizi, VII, 49.23 Jul. 2010. <http://www.inter-islam.org/hadeeth/stmenu.htm>

Wharton, Edith. *The House of Mirth*. New York: Charles Scribner's Sons, USA. 1905. Books One and Two Images of blood and bleeding appear in *The House of Mirth* on pages 92, 103, 141, 168, 177, 216, 264, 288, 307, 363, 410, 433, 455, 491, 499, 513, 516, and 517. Images of lamps and lampposts appear on pages 10, 39, 227, 261, 262, 311, 352, 494, and 502.

"The Detective" Works Cited:

Abraham, Lyndy. *A Dictionary of Alchemical Imagery*. Cambridge: Cambridge University Press, 1998. Print.

Alchemy-Works. "Asclepias Incarnata". 6 Jun. 2010. <http://www.alchemy-works.com/asclepias-incarnata.html>

Alderson, Lawrence. "Foot-and-Mouth Disease in the United Kingdom 2001; its cause, course, control and consequences." Rare Breeds International. 6 Jun. 2010. <www.warmwell.com/Aldersonsept3.html>

Allen, Richard Hinckley. *Star-Names. Their Lore and Meaning*. G.E. Stechert, New York. 1889. 11 Jan. 2012. <http://books.google.com/ebooks/reader?id=5xQuAAAAIAAJ&printsec=frontcover&output=reader

&pg=GBS.PR3 Last accessed 11 January, 2012

BBC News. Interview with Agatha Christie. This interview was reproduced as the "Introduction" to *Hercule Poirot: The Complete Short Stories* by Agatha Christie. Harper Collins, 1999. p. viii. Web. http://news.bbc.co.uk/today/hi/today/newsid_7612000/7612534.stm Last accessed July 25, 2010

Bulows, Ernest. "Traditional Navajo Taboos". navajocentral.org. Web. http://navajocentral.org/navajotaboos/taboos_nature.html Last accessed 13 January, 2012

Chisholm, Hugh, ed (1911). "Aconitum" *Encyclopedia Britannica* (11th ed.). Cambridge University Press.

Christie, Agatha. "The Murder at Hazelmoor" (US title) and as "The Sittaford Mystery" (UK Title). Published by Dodd, Mead & Company, 1931. Published in the UK by Collins Crime Club, 1931

Doyle, A. Conan. *The Hound of the Baskervilles.* Grosset & Dunlap, 1901. New York.

Flower Society. "Milkweed Plant". http://www.flowersociety.org/Milkweed-Plant-Study.htm Web. Last accessed 6 June, 2010

"Mount Hesperus" Web. http://thssite.tripod.com/shel2/hesp.html Last accessed 13 January, 2012

I.H.W., "*The Dartmoor Massacre* by I.H.W." 1815. Library of the University of California. Class i

Lapahie, Jr., Harrison. Lapahie.com http://www.lapahie.com/Sacred_Mts.cfm

Legendary Dartmoor. "Beatrice Chase". http://www.legendarydartmoor.co.uk/beat_chase.htm Web. Last accessed 25 July, 2010

Legendary Dartmoor. "Buckfastleigh Church" Web. http://www.legendarydartmoor.co.uk/buckfastleigh_church.htm Last accessed 25 July, 2010

Milligan, Spike. "Tales of Old Dartmoor" for *The Goon Show*, produced by Peter Eaton. Series 6, Episode 21. Performed with Peter Sellers, Harry Secombe and Michael Bentine. Web. http://goonshowscripts.afraid.org/raw/series06/s06e21.html and http://www.thegoonshow.net/shows_list.asp?series=06 Last accessed 6 June, 2010

"The Navajo Language: A Blessing in Disguise." Web. http://www.bpcomp.com/history/long_walk.html Last accessed 6 June, 2010

Peel, Robin. *Writing Back: Sylvia Plath and Cold War Politics.* 2002 Rosemont Publishing & Printing Corp.

Plath, Sylvia. *Ariel: The Restored Edition.* HarperPerennial 2004. "The Detective" pp 31-32

Plath, Sylvia, and Aurelia Schober. Plath. *Letters Home: Correspondence, 1950-1963.* New York: Harper & Row, 1975

Plath, Sylvia. *The Unabridged Journals of Sylvia Plath.* 2000. Anchor Books, New York

Regardie, Israel. *The Golden Dawn.* Llwellyn Publications. Sixth Corrected Edition, 1989. Fifteenth Printing, 2008

Royal Commission. "*Minerological Collections – Phosphate of Lime-Clays. By Great Britain Royal Commission for the Exhibition of 1851 Exhibition of the Works of Industry of All Nations.*" Printed for the Royal Commission by William Clowes & Sons, Stamford Street and Charing Cross. London 1851

Scudamore, Paula. *Dear Robert, Dear Spike, The Graves-Milligan Correspondence* ed. by Pauline Scudamore. Sutton Publishing Ltd. England. 1991

Sheep Veterinary Society. Division of the British Veterinary Association. "Foot and Mouth Disease". Updated 7th March, 2001. http://svs.mri.sari.ac.ok/NewsFM.htm Web. Last accessed 6 June, 2010

Sowerby, James, and John Thomas Boswell, Phebe Lankester, J. W. Salter, John Edward Sowerby. *English Botany, Or, Coloured Figures of British Plants.* Third Edition Published by Robert Hardwicke, London,1866. Web. http://books.google.com/books?id=V0cAAAAAQAAJ&printsec=frontcover&source=gbs_ge_summary_r&cad=0#v=onepage&q&f=false

Steiner, Rudolf and A.H. Parker. *The Effects of Spiritual Development.* Rudolf Steiner Press; 3rd Revised Edition. London. 1978

Wells, H.G. *The War of the Worlds.* http://wells.thefreelibrary.com/War-Of-The-Worlds/1-4#lipless

Sowerby, James, and John Thomas Boswell, Phebe Lankester, J.W. Salrer, John Edward Sowerby. *English Botany, Or, Coloured Figures of British Plants*. Third Edition. Published by Robert Hardwicke, London, 1866. 6 Jun. 2010. <http://books.google.com/books?id=V0cAAAAAQAAJ&printsec=frontcover&source=gbs_ge_summary_r&cad=0#v=onepage&q&f=false>

Steiner, Rudolf and A.H. Parker. *The Effects of Spiritual Development*. London: Rudolf Steiner Press; 3rd Edition. 1978. Print.

Wells, H.G. *The War of the Worlds*. Online excerpt from TheFreeLibrary.com. 13 Jan. 2012. <http://wells.thefreelibrary.com/War-Of-The-Worlds/1-4#lipless>

"Ariel" Works Cited:

Abraham, Lyndy. *A Dictionary of Alchemical Imagery*. Cambridge: Cambridge University Press, 1998. Print.

Alexander, Paul. *Rough Magic, a Biography of Sylvia Plath*. Plath's written response to "Juggernaut, The Warfare State," by Fredrick J. Cook, published in *The Nation*. New York: Da Capo Press. 1999. Print.

Ashmole, Elias. "The Hunting of the Greene Lyon" in *Theatrum chemicum Britannicum*, 1652. facsimile reprint, Johnson Reprint Corporation, New York and London. 1967. 14 Sept. 2010. <http://www.theatra.de/repertorium/ed000100.pdf>

Brain, Tracy. *The Other Sylvia Plath*. Essex, England: Pearson Education Limited. 2001. Print.

Buckland, Raymond. *The Witch Book: The Encyclopedia of Witchcraft, Wicca, and Neo-paganism*. Detroit: Visible Ink Press. 2002. Print.

Chun, Clayton K.S. *The Doolittle Raid 1942: America's First Strike Back at Japan*. Oxford, UK: Osprey, 2006. Print.

Crowley, Aleister. *Liber Samekh,* Being the Ritual employed by the BEAST 666 for the Attainment of the Knowledge and Conversation of his Holy Guardian Angel during the Semester of His performance of the Operation of the Sacred Magick of ABRAMELIN THE MAGE. THE INVOCATION. Sections F and ff. 14. Hermetic.com. Sept. 2010. <http://hermetic.com/crowley/libers/liber800a.pdf>

Graves, Robert. *The White Goddess, a historical grammar of poetic myth*. New York: Farrar, Straus and Giroux. 1948. Print.

Hughes, Ted, and Christopher Reid. *Letters of Ted Hughes*. London: Faber and Faber, 2007. Print.

Hughes, Ted and William Scammell. *Winter Pollen: Occasional Prose*. London: Faber and Faber. 1994. Print.

Kroll, Judith. *Sylvia Plath: Chapters in a Mythology*. New York: Harper Colophon Books, 1976. Print.

Malory, Sir Thomas. *Le Morte d'Arthur*. Ed. Matthews, John. Illustrated by Ferguson, Anna-Marie. London: Cassell. 2000. Print.

Passic, Frank. "Around the World with Gwen Dew." Historical Albion Michigan. Albion History/Genealogy Resources. 1999. 19 Aug. 2010. <http://www.albionmich.com/history/histor_notebook/S_Dew.shtml>

Plath, Sylvia. *Ariel: The Restored Edition*. New York: HarperCollins Publishers, 2004. "Ariel" pp 33-34. Print.

Plath, Sylvia, and Aurelia Plath. *Letters Home*. New York: Harper & Row. 1975. Letter to her mother, dated 21 April, 1960. Print.

Plath, Sylvia, and Karen V. Kukil. *The Unabridged Journals of Sylvia Plath, 1950-1962*. New York: Anchor Books. 2000. Print.

Regardie, Israel. *The Golden Dawn, Sixth Edition Revised and Enlarged*. Woodbury, MN: Llewellyn Publications, MN. 2008. Print.

Ridpath, Ian. *Star Tales*. "Sagittarius." 14 Sept. 2010. <http://www.ianridpath.com/startales/sagittarius.htm Last accessed>

Rollyson, Carl. *American Isis: The Life and Art of Sylvia Plath*. New York: St. Martin's Press. 2013. Print.

White Moon Gallery. "Cerridwen." 14 Sept. 2010.. <http://www.orderwhitemoon.org/goddess/Cerridwen.html.>

"Death & Co." Works Cited:

Abraham, Lyndy. *A Dictionary of Alchemical Imagery*. Cambridge: Cambridge UP. 1998. Print.

Alexander, Paul. *Rough Magic: A Biography of Sylvia Plath*. New York: Da Capo Press, 1999. Print.

Alvarez, A. *Where Did It All Go Right?* London: Richard Cohen Books, 1999. Print.

Blake, William, David V. Erdman, and Harold Bloom. *The Complete Poetry & Prose of William Blake*. Berkeley, CA.: University of California Press, 2008. Print.

Eous, Peri. *Dawn, De Aurora Libellus Apollonii*. Biblioteca Arcana. 10 May 2010.
<http://www.cs.utk.edu/~Mclennan/BA/JO-DAL.html>

Graves, Robert. *The White Goddess: a historical grammar of poetic myth*. Farrar, Straus and Giroux. 1948 and renewed 1975. Print.

Greer, Mary K. "History of Tarot." 10 May 2010.
<http://marygreer.wordpress.com/2008/05/20/1969-the-tarot->

Hebrew for Christians. 10 May 2010. <www.hebrew4christians.com>

Krummenacher, Beat. "Verdigris, Green Lion and Vitriol: The Basis of the Philosopher's Stone." *The Stone* 20. May-June 1997. 10 May 2010. <http://www.triad-publishing.com/stone20e.html>

Kurtzman, Mary. "Plath's 'Ariel' and Tarot." *The Centennial Review*. Summer 1988: pp 290-295. Print.

Little, Tom Tadfor. "The Hermitage: A Tarot History Site." 10 May 2010.
<http://www.tarothermit.com/>

Plath, Sylvia. *Ariel: The Restored Edition*. New York: HarperCollins Publishers, 2004. "Death & Co." pp 35-36. Print.

Plath, Sylvia, and Karen V. Kukil. *The Unabridged Journals of Sylvia Plath, 1950 – 1962*. New York: Anchor Books, 2000. Print.

Plath, Sylvia, and Ted Hughes. *The Collected Poems*. New York: Harper & Row, 1981. Print.

Rákóczi, Basil Ivan. *The Painted Caravan: a Penetration into the Secrets of the Tarot Cards. [with Illustrations]*. The Hague: L.J.C. Boucher, 1954. Print.

Rituals of the Societas Rosicrucianis in Anglia. 10 May 2010.
<http://www.scribd.com/doc/6836084/Rituals-of-the-Societas-Rosicrucianis-in-Anglia>

Skea, Dr. Ann. *Ted Hughes: Alternative Horizons*. ed. Joanny Moulin. London: Routledge, 2004. Reprinted on AnnSkea.com. 10 May 2010. <http://ann.skea.com/PoetMag.htm>

Steiner, Rudolf and A.H. Parker. *The Effects of Spiritual Development*. 3rd Revised Edition. London: Steiner, Rudolf Steiner Press. 1978. Print.

Valentinus, Basilius. *The Seventh Key in The Track of Basilius Valentinus: The Benedictine, Concerning The Great Stone of the Ancient Sages*, commentary by Theodorus Kerckringius. Amsterdam, 1671. Scribd.com. 10 May 2010. <http://www.scribd.com/doc/30452581/Basilius-Twelve-Keys>

"Magi" Works Cited:

Abraham, Lyndy. *A Dictionary of Alchemical Imagery*. Cambridge: Cambridge UP. 1998. Print.

Borges, Jorge Luis. "The Library of Babel". Translated by James Irby. 1941. 03 Feb. 2012.
<http://jubal.westnet.com/hyperdiscordia/library_of_babel.html>

The Free Dictionary. "Bossing." 03 Feb. 2012. <a href="http://www.thefreedictionary.com/bossing">bossing</a>

Boyce, Mary. *A History of Zoroastrianism: The Early Period*. 2nd ed. vol. 1. Netherlands: E.J. Brill. 1989. Print.

Brown, Terence. *The life of W.B. Yeats: a critical biography*. Oxford, UK: Blackwell Publishers. 1999. Print.

Burkert, Walter. *Greek Religion*. Cambridge, MA: Harvard UP. 1985 . Print.

Burton, Robert. *The Anatomy of Melancholy*. 1621 Project Gutenberg- Public Domain. 03 Feb. 2012.
    <http://www.gutenberg.org/files/10800/10800-h/10800-h.htm>

Coetzee, J.M. "Holderlin, 'The Poet in the Tower." Akhenaten's Dream In Plato's Mind. October 19. 2006.
    The New York Review of Books. 03 Feb. 2012.
    <http://www.nybooks.com/articles/archives/2006/oct/19/the-poet-in-the-tower>

Collodi, C. "The Adventures of Pinocchio." PublicLiterature.org. 13 Feb. 2012.
    <http://publicliterature.org/books/adventures_of_pinocchio/1>

Grubber, Hudson. The Vaults of Erowid. "Mandragore; Mandrake." 13 Feb. 2012.
    <http://www.erowid.org/psychoactives/cultivation/cultivation_growing-the-hallucinogens
    shtml#MANDRAKE>

Grieve, Mrs. M. Botanical.com. "A Modern Herbal: Mandrake". 13 Feb. 2012.
    <http://www.botanical.com/botanical/mgmh/m/mandra10.html>

Grimm's Saga No. 84 "Der Alraun / The Mandrake." 13 Feb. 2012.
    <http://www.fairytalechannel.org/2008_07_17_archive.html>

Groom, Nigel. *Frankincense & Myrrh: A Study of the Arabian Incense Trade*. London and New York: Longman,
    1981. Print.

Imagi-Nation.com. "Samuel Beckett." 12 Feb. 2012. <http://www.imagi-nation.com/moonstruck/clsc7.htm>

Jung, C.G. *Alchemical Studies*, Collected Works of C.G. Jung, Volume 13, Princeton, N.J.: Princeton UP. 1968.
    Print.

Merriam-Webster. "Simulacrum." 12 Feb. 2012.<http://www.merriam-webster.com/dictionary/simulacrum>

Plath, Sylvia. *Ariel: The Restored Edition*. New York: HarperCollins Publishers, 2004. "Magi" p 37. Print.

Rich, Nathaniel. "Bad Things Happen to Bad Children: The real *Pinocchio* is nothing like you remember."
    24 Oct. 2011. Slate.com. 13 Feb. 2012. <http://www.slate.com/articles/arts/books/2011/10/carlo_
    collodi_s_pinocchio_why_is_the_original_pinocchio_subjecte.html>

Segelberg, Eric. "The Benedictio Olei in the Apostolic Tradition of Hippolytus," *Oriens Christianus*. Wiesbaden,
    Germany: Otto Harrassowitz Verlag. 1964. Print.

Spark, Muriel. *Mary Shelley*. London: Cardinal. 1987. Print.

Yeats, William Butler. "The Tower." The Literature Network. 03 Feb. 2012.
    <http://www.online-literature.com/yeats/782/>

Yeats, William Butler. *The Collected Works of W.B. Yeats. Volume XIII* "A Vision" The Original 1925 Version.
    Edited by Catherine E. Paul and Margaret Mills Harper. New York: Scribner. 2008. Print.

"Lesbos" Works Cited:

Abraham, Lyndy. *A Dictionary of Alchemical Imagery*. Cambridge: Cambridge UP. 1998. Print.

Alexander, Paul. *Rough Magic* Da Capo Press, New York. 1999. Print.

All Things Considered, National Public Radio. "Flannery O'Connor's Private Life Revealed in Letters." 12
    May 2007. 16 Feb. 2012. <http://www.npr.org/templates/story/story.php?storyId=10154699>

Allen, Richard Hinckley, and Richard H. Allen. *Star Names: Their Lore and Meaning*. New York: Dover, 1963.
    Print.

Aniane, Maurice. *Alchemy: the Cosmological Yoga Part 2: Phases of the Work*, 12 Feb. 2012.
    <www.alchemylab.com/AJ2-1.htm.>

Gordon, Sarah. "Flannery O'Connor (1925-1964)" 3 Mar. 2009.

Arts and Culture: Literature. Georgia College State University. 15 Feb. 2012. <http://www.georgiaencyclope-
    dia.org/nge/Article.jsp?id=h-498>

Graves, Robert. *The White Goddess: a historical grammar of poetic myth*. Farrar, Straus and Giroux. 1948 and renewed 1975. Print.

Kazan, Elia. *Elia Kazan: A Life*. New York: Da Capo Press, 1997. Print.

Matteson, John. *Eden's Outcasts: The Story of Louisa May Alcott and Her Father*. New York: W. W. Norton, 2007. Print.

O'Connor, Flannery. *The Habit of Being*. Ed. Sally Fitzgerald. New York: Farrar, 1979: p. 90. Print.

Place, Robert M. From accompanying booklet for *The Alchemical Tarot: Renewed, designed and illustrated by Robert M. Place*. New York: Hermes Publications 1994 - 2007. Print.

Plath, Sylvia. *Ariel: The Restored Edition*. New York: HarperCollins, 2004. "Lesbos" p 38-40. Print.

Plath, Sylvia, and Aurelia Schober. Plath. *Letters Home: Correspondence, 1950-1963*. New York: Harper & Row, 1975. Print.

Plath, Sylvia, and Karen V. Kukil. *The Unabridged Journals of Sylvia Plath, 1950-1962*. New York: Anchor Books. 2000. Print.

Ridpath, Ian. *Star Tales*. 17 Feb. 2012. <http://www.ianridpath.com/startales/aquarius.htm>

Riley, James Whitcomb. "Little Orphant Annie" From *James Whitcomb Riley: The Complete Works*. Indianapolis: Bobbs-Merrill, 1916. 16 Feb. 2012. <http://www.poetry-archive.com/r/little_orphant_annie.html>

Sappho. *English Translations*. 14 Feb. 2012. <http://www.thehypertexts.com/Sappho%20Translations.htm>

Smith, Bruce. *The History of Little Orphan Annie*. Ballantine Books. 1982 pp. 43–63. Print.

Summers, Anthony. *Goddess, The Secret Lives of Marilyn Monroe*. London: Guild Publishing, 1985. Print.

Waite, Arthur Edward. *The Secret Tradition in Alchemy*. 2nd ed. Whitefish, MI: Kessinger Publishing, 1992. Print.

"The Other" Works Cited:

Abraham, Lyndy. *A Dictionary of Alchemical Imagery*. Cambridge: Cambridge UP. 1998. Print.

Cashford, Jules. *The Moon: Myth and Image*. New York: Four Walls Eight Windows, 2002. Print.

Cicero, Chic and Sandra Tabatha Cicero. *Self-Initiation Into the Golden Dawn Tradition*. First edition, fifth printing. Woodbury, MN: Llewellyn, 2007. Print.

Ebers Papyrus 821. "Honey" by Christian Ratsch. Excerpted from *Encyclopedia of Psychoactive Plants*. South Paris, ME: Park Street Press. 2005. 23 Feb. 2012. <http://www.erowid.org/animals/bee/bee_info1.shtml>

Freud, S. *Sexuality and the Psychology of Love*. New York: Collier. 1963. pp. 212-213. Print.

Finishing.com. "Liver of Sulfur for 'antique' mirror manufacturing." 23 Feb. 2012.
        <http://www.finishing.com/299/54.shtml>

Eirenaeus Philalethes and Carl Jung.
        http://www.persee.fr/web/revues/home/prescript/article/rhs_0151-4105_1996_num_49_2_1254

Hubblesite.org. "Space Movie Reveals Shocking Secrets of the Crab Nebula" 19 September 2002.
        http://hubblesite.org/newscenter/archive/releases/2002/24/ Web. Last accessed 14 March, 2012

Leach, Karoline. *In the Shadow of the Dreamchild: A New Understanding of Lewis Carroll*. London: Peter Owen. 1999. Print.

LeRoy, Christophe and Sylvain Ravot. "Lewis Carroll and Chess." 24 Feb. 2012.
        <http://www.echecs-histoire-litterature.com/index_english.html>

Plath, Sylvia. *Ariel: The Restored Edition*. New York: HarperCollins, 2004. "The Other." p 41-42. Print.

Plath, Sylvia. *The Collected Poems of Sylvia Plath*, 1981 ed. by Ted Hughes. New York: HarperPerrenial Modern Classics. 1981. Print.

Plath, Sylvia, and Aurelia Schober. Plath. *Letters Home: Correspondence, 1950-1963*. New York: Harper & Row, 1975. Print.

Sunan Abu-Dawud . *Book 32, Number 4050* Hasan, Ahmad, translator. Muslim Access. 15 Mar. 2012.
        <http://www.muslimaccess.com/sunnah/hadeeth/abudawud/032.html>

Hubblesite.org. "Space Movie Reveals Shocking Secrets of the Crab Nebula." 19 Sept. 2002.
    <http://hubblesite.org/newscenter/archive/releases/2002/24/>

Murien, Petri. "Antimony Oil" Society of Alchemical Mercury. Oils of Metals by A.M. W. House, C.H.. 15
    Mar. 2012. <http://icanseefar.tripod.com/oilsofmetals.htm>

Eirenaeus Philalethes and Carl Jung. "Decknamen or pseudochemical language? Eirenaeus Philalethes and
    Carl Jung." by William R. Newman. *Persee Scientific Journals.* 1996. vol. 49; 49-2-3. 15 Mar. 2012. <http://
    www.persee.fr/web/revues/home/prescript/article/rhs_0151-4105_1996_num_49_2_1254.

NASA Science News. "Radioactive Moon." Sept. 8, 2005. 15 Mar. 2012.
    <http://science.nasa.gov/science-news/science-at-nasa-2005/08sep_radioactivemoon/>

Venefica, Avia. "Elemental Alchemy Symbols: Antimony". Whats-Your-Sign.com. 15 Mar. 2012.
    <http://www.whats-your-sign.com/elemental-alchemy-symbols.html>

Venefica, Avia. "Animal Symbolism of the Moth" Whats-Your-Sign.com. 16 Jan. 2012.
    <http://www.whats-your-sign.com/animal-symbolism-moth.html>

"Stopped Dead" Works Cited:

Abraham, Lyndy. *A Dictionary of Alchemical Imagery.* Cambridge: Cambridge UP. 1998. Print.

Holy Bible. The Old Testament Book of Psalms, 78:51; 105:23,27; 106:22; 1 Ch 4:40. Authorised King James
    Version. London and New York. 1948. Collins' Clear-Type Press. 1948. Print.

Abarim Publications. "Meaning and Etymology of the Hebrew word Ham": 15 Jan. 2013.
    http://www.abarim-publications.com/Meaning/Ham.html#.UPbWj288B8E

Bellows, Henry Adams (trans.) *The Poetic Edda.* American-Scandinavian Foundation. 1923. 15 Jan. 2013.
    <http://www.norron-mytologi.info/diverse/BellowsThePoeticEdda.pdf>

Fainlight, Ruth. "A Memoir of Tangier and Paul Bowles." 1992. The Authorized Paul Bowles
    Web Site. 20 Jan. 2013. <http://www.paulbowles.org/fainlight.html>

Hall, Manly P. *Man: The Grand Symbol of the Mysteries, Essays in Occult Anatomy.* Original copyright 1932 by the
    Philosophical Research Society. Whitefish, MT: Kessinger Legacy Reprints. 2004. Print.

Hughes, Gerald. *Ted & I.* 2012. London: The Robson Press. Print.

Le Brun, Charles. *Le Roi gouverne par lui-même.* Oil painting. Circa 1680. Palace of Versailles, Paris, France.
    Modello for the central panel of the ceiling of the Hall of Mirrors. Accession number : MV 8975

Lindow, John. *Norse Mythology: A Guide to the Gods, Heroes, Rituals, and Beliefs.* Oxford: Oxford UP. 2001. Print.

Plath, Sylvia. *Ariel: The Restored Edition.* New York: HarperCollins, 2004. "Stopped Dead." p 43. Print.

Serfaty, William, dip. Arch. (Leics.). "Gibraltar, The Pillars of the Phoenicians" 1997. The Home of
    Phoenician Study. 21 Jan. 2013. <http://phoenicia.org/gibraltar.html>

Smithsonian.com "Hominid Hunting. Rock of Gibraltar: Neanderthals' Last Refuge" by Erin Wayman.
    19 Sept. 2012. 15 Jan. 2013. <http://blogs.smithsonianmag.com/hominids/2012/09/the-rock-of-gibral-
    tar-neanderthals-last-refuge/>

Strong's Hebrew Concordance. "Chin." 15 Jan. 2013 <http://biblesuite.com/hebrew/2433.htm>

Thompson, Ann and Neil Taylor, eds. 2006a. *Hamlet.* The Arden Shakespeare, third ser. Vol. one. London:
    Arden. Print.

Trugman, Rabbi Avraham Arieh. "Secrets of the Hebrew Letters: Reish" 20 Jan. 2013. Based on
    the book "The Hebrew Letters" by Rabbi Yitzchak Ginsburgh. <http://www.youtube.com/
    watch?v=9d6M8Latfp4>

Wood, David "A Comprehensive History of Gibraltar" Andalucia.com. 14 Jan. 2013.
    <http://www.andalucia.com/gibraltar/comprehensive-history.htm>

"Poppies in October" Works Cited:

Abraham, Lyndy. *A Dictionary of Alchemical Imagery*. Cambridge University Press, 1998. Print.

Eyewitness to History. "The First Atomic Bomb Blast, 1945." 20 Feb. 2013. <http://www.eyewitnesstohistory.com/atomictest.htm>

Metro-Goldwyn-Meyer. *The Wizard of Oz*, film adaptation of the novel. 1939.

Morris, Virginia B. *Fyodor M. Dostoevsky's Crime and Punishment*. Barron's Educational Series.

National Reconnaissance Office to the Director, "The History of the Poppy Satellite System." 1984. 23 Jun. 2013. <http://www.nro.gov/foia/docs/History%20of%20Poppy.PDF>

Peel, Robin. *Writing Back: Sylvia Plath and Cold War Politics*. Cranbury, NJ: Rosemont Publishing & Printing Corp. 2002. Print.

Plath, Sylvia. *Ariel: The Restored Edition*. New York: HarperCollins 2004. "Poppies in October" p 44. Print.

StarIQ. "Tarot and the Sign Scorpio." 21 Feb. 2013. <http://www.stariq.com/Main/Articles/P0001657.htm>

Trugman, Rabbi Avraham Arieh. "Secrets of the Hebrew Letters: Shin" Based on the book, "The Hebrew Letters" by Rabbi Yitzchak Ginsburgh. YouTube. 20 Jan. 2013. <http://www.youtube.com/watch?NR=1&v=ie9LqKeEQbk>

Volkov, Solomon. *Romanov Riches: Russian Writers and Artists Under the Tsars*. Chapter 12: "Dostoevsky and the Romanovs" New York: Alfred A. Knopf. 2011. Print.

Wright, Anne. Constellations of Words: "Pavo the Peacock" 2008. 21 Feb. 2013. <http://www.constellationsofwords.com/Constellations/Pavo.html>

YouTube. "The Red Poppy." 1955. 21 Feb. 2013. <http://www.youtube.com/watch?v=DkTm5OVKyKc>

"The Courage of Shutting-Up" Works Cited:

Abraham, Lyndy. *A Dictionary of Alchemical Imagery*. Cambridge University Press, 1998. Print.

Ajootian, Aileen *Naked Truths: Women, Sexuality and Gender in Classical Art and Archaeology* Chapter 11. "The Only Happy Couple: Hermaphrodites and gender" 2003. London: Routledge. p. 220. Print.

Blume, Anna. "Mesh: The Tale of the Hermaphrodite." LTTR. 22 Sept. 2010. <http://www.lttr.org/journal/4/mesh-the-tale-of-the-hermaphrodite>

Brain, Tracy. *The Other Sylvia Plath*. Essex, England: Pearson Education Limited, 2001. Print.

Buckland, Raymond. *The Witch Book: The Encyclopedia of Witchcraft, Wicca, and Neo-paganism*. Detroit: Visible Ink Press. 2002. Print.

DeVore, Nicholas. *Encyclopedia of Astrology*. 1947. Philosophical Library. 22 Sept. 2010. <www.astrologiahumana.com.>

Gascoigne, Bamber. *Encyclopedia of Britain. The A-Z of Britain's Past and Present*. New York: Macmillan. 1993. Print.

Hughes, Ted. *Birthday Letters*. New York: Farrar, Straus, Giroux, 1998. "St. Botolph's" pp. 14-15. Print.

The Irrawaddy. Covering Burma and Southeast Asia. 22 Sept. 2010. < http://www.irrawaddy.org/research_show.php?art_id=3533>

Manilius: *Astronomica* Loeb Classical Library No. 469 English and Latin Edition. 1977. Cambridge, MA: Harvard UP.

Ovid, translated by Sir Samuel Garth, John Dryden, et. al. Metamorphoses, Book IV. "The story of Salamacis and Hermaphroditus." <http://en.wikisource.org/wiki/Metamorphoses/Book_IV#The_story_of_Salamacis_and_Hermaphroditus>

Plath, Sylvia. *Ariel: The Restored Edition*. New York: HarperPerennial, 2004. "The Courage of Shutting-Up" pp 45-46. Print.

Plath, Sylvia, and Aurelia Schober. Plath. *Letters Home. Correspondences 1950-1963*. New York: Harper & Row. 1975. Print.

Plath, Sylvia, and Karen V. Kukil. *The Unabridged Journals of Sylvia Plath, 1950-1962*. New York: Anchor Books. 2000. Print.

J Rank.org. "Homosexuality and Crime--Modernity." 22 Sept. 2010.
    <http://law.jrank.org/pages/1336/Homosexuality-Crime-Modernity.html>

The Times. High Court Of Justice; Queen's Bench Division, "I Don't Care What My Readers Think", Liberace V. Daily Mirror Newspapers Ltd" p. 16. June 12, 1959. *The Times* archives. 22 Sept. 2010.
    <http://www.thetimes.co.uk/tto/news/>

Williams, Gary. "Hermaphroditism, Androgyny, and the Swedenborgian Integral Soul: Functions of the Man-Woman Protagonist in Julia Ward Howe's "Laurence" Manuscript" University of Idaho. Society for the Study of American Women Writers International Conference, San Antonio, Texas. February 2001. San Antonio, TX. 22 Sept. 2010. <http://www.class.uidaho.edu/jgw/SanAntonio2001.htm>

Wright, Anne. Constellations of Words. "Virgo the Virgin." 2008. 15 Feb. 2013.
    <http://www.constellationsofwords.com/Constellations/Virgo.html>

CPSIA information can be obtained at www.ICGtesting.com
Printed in the USA
BVOW11s2246240215

389166BV00004B/8/P